# THE BUDGET'S NEW CLOTHES

## A Critique of Planning-Programming-Budgeting and Benefit-Cost Analysis

**LEONARD MEREWITZ**

*University of California at Berkeley*

and

**STEPHEN H. SOSNICK**

*University of California at Davis*

Markham Series in Public Policy Analysis

MARKHAM PUBLISHING COMPANY/Chicago

# MARKHAM
# SERIES IN PUBLIC POLICY ANALYSIS
Julius Margolis and Aaron Wildavsky, editors

Copyright © 1971 by Markham Publishing Company
Second Printing August 1972
All rights reserved
Printed in the United States of America
Library of Congress Catalog Card Number: 72-146018
Hardcover Standard Book Number 8410-0913-9
Paperback Standard Book Number: 8410-0920-1

*To Harriet and Max and Natalie and Ben,*
*with gratitude and love*

# PREFACE

In places we have been very negative in this book. Lest the reader think we are suggesting that governments or business firms eschew Planning-Programming-Budgeting (PPB), we want to make it clear that we feel many large organizations will continue to use PPB and benefit-cost analysis and, frankly, we hope to take part in this activity. We would hardly lay to rest systematic analysis. We are, rather, reacting against what seems to us to be an overabundance of laudatory and superficial discussions of PPB. Exposition as well as critique of these techniques has been our intention. Instead of condemning PPB, we are suggesting that some attention be given the negative side before expensive decisions to proceed are made. It may have been *The New Yorker* which proclaimed: we need balanced libraries, not balanced books. This does not pretend to be a balanced book, but its authors are not unbalanced either.

We wish to thank the following organizations for permission to reprint: University of California Press; Royal Economic Society; the RAND Corporation; Goodyear Publishing Company; John Wiley and Sons; McGraw-Hill Book Company; Vanderbilt University Press; Praeger Publishing Company; *Inquiry,* a publication of the Blue Cross Association; the Shell Briefing Service of the Asiatic Petroleum Corporation; The Brookings Institution; The American Society for Public Administration; Harvard University Press; the Committee for San Francisco; and *Administrative Science Quarterly.*

The following individuals were kind enough to let us reproduce some of their words: Harry Hatry, Aaron Wildavsky, Robert N. Grosse, Verne B. Lewis, Roland N. McKean, Melvin Anshen, Roy Radner, Gloria Grizzle, Thomas Schelling, Arthur Hammann, Gene Fisher, A. R. Prest, Ralph Turvey, Emil Mrak, Maynard Amerine, Paul J. Feldstein, Robert H. Haveman, W. John Carr, Roger Bolton, and Alvin Duskin.

We wish to thank David E. Keefe for assistance which approached co-authorship. Ang Kiat-Poon and Craig Blake were also very helpful.

Robin Gurse, Linda Gakel, Kay Long, Ellen McGibbon, Betty Kendall, Helen Way, Jan Siebert, Kathy Roud, Judi Traynham, Kiyo Noji, and Dorothy Ter Avest; the Institutes of Business and Economic Research, and of Urban and Regional Development; and the Schools of Business Administration at Berkeley helped us at various stages of work on the manuscript.

Jonathan Weiner and William Vatter came to our aid with budget material. Bill F. Roberts helped with his time and resources. Christopher D. Foster, Paul Distenfeld, and C. Bart McGuire gave generously of their valuable critical counsel.

Special thanks should go to Aaron Wildavsky, the intellectual leader of those who have taken a careful, critical approach to PPB, and to Julius Margolis, who first proposed that we collaborate on this book and who reviewed the manuscript at an advanced stage.

Finally, our wives, Sheila and Gale, are the sine qua non of this effort. They nurtured both the men and the ideas.

January, 1971    Leonard Merewitz, Berkeley, California
                 Stephen H. Sosnick, Badhoevedorp, The Netherlands

# CONTENTS

# One

# THE PPB JUGGERNAUT

PPB stands for planning, programming, and budgeting—a budgetary process that is supposed to make government operations more efficient and more effective. It is intended both to reform the assignment of funds within the public sector and to improve the allocation of funds between the private and public sectors.

In this chapter we intend to show how PPB differs from methods that preceded it, to describe the current rush to adopt it, to trace the sources of this movement, and to preview the conclusions of subsequent chapters.

## THE CONTENT OF PPB

How PPB differs from what preceded it depends on which of the many versions of the process you have in mind. The meaning of PPB has not become standardized; it means different things to different people. Some emphasize its restructuring budgets by accumulating expenditures under output categories that are more meaningful than the object categories which have become standard. Others stress its long time horizon: five years in the future and two previous years rather than the single budget year with two retrospective years for comparison. Other people associate PPB with benefit-cost, cost-utility, or systems analysis. "Finally, [some] understand the term to imply all the foregoing plus one significant addition—arrangements for enforcing the allocative decisions through . . . for example . . . institutional reorganization. . . . [Our] concept . . . embraces all four of the items listed above."[1]

[1] Roland N. McKean and Melvin Anshen, "Limitations, Risks, and Problems," in Fremont J. Lyden and Ernest G. Miller, eds., *Planning Programming Budgeting: A Systems Approach to Management* (Chicago: Markham, 1968), p. 338.

1

In our view, PPB has five distinguishing features: program account-ing, multi-year costing, detailed description of activities, zero-base bud-geting, and quantitative evaluation of alternatives or benefit-cost analysis. The instructions of the U.S. Bureau of the Budget, as revised in 1967, demand each of these features, which have rarely been used in other budget systems.

> The PPB system is built upon three types of documents: (a) *Program Memoranda* (PM) which [are drafted each year for each program category and] present . . . recommendations . . . within a framework of agency objectives, identify the alter-natives considered, and support the decisions taken; . . . (b) A comprehensive multi-year *Program and Financial Plan* (PFP) which [annually] presents in tabular form a complete . . . summary of agency programs . . . in terms of their outputs and costs; and (c) *Special Studies* (SS) which [are started and finished as appropriate and] provide the analytic ground-work reported in the Program Memoranda. [C]osts in the PFP are defined in a more limited sense than the costs which may— and usually should—be utilized in the Program Memoranda or in Special Studies. [T]he analysis of a problem should include economic opportunity costs, marginal costs, and sys-tems costs. . . . Special Studies will . . . review in terms of costs and benefits . . . prior efforts, compare alternative mixes of programs, balance increments in costs against increments in effectiveness, . . . and assess the incidence of benefits as well as their totals.[2]

The three documents embody the five features that we have men-tioned. The PFPs embody program accounting and multi-year costing. The PFPs, together with the PMs, provide detailed description. The PMs represent zero-base budgeting. The SSs are supposed to provide quantitative evaluation, that is, benefit-cost or cost-effectiveness analysis.

In subsequent chapters we will discuss the five features in detail. First, however, let us review some recent history—some incredible re-cent history. During the 1960s, PPB became an irresistible force.

## THE PPB EPIDEMIC

Procedures labeled *program budgeting* were first introduced in 1961. In that year Charles J. Hitch, who had been Chief Economist at the RAND Corporation and would later become President of the University of

---

[2]U.S. Bureau of the Budget, "Bulletin No. 68-2, July 18, 1967," in Lyden and Miller, *Planning Programming Budgeting*, pp. 431-38.

California, took office as Assistant Secretary of Defense (Comptroller). Hitch, with Secretary McNamara's encouragement, decided to prepare the Defense Department budget for fiscal 1963 in program terms.

In 1962 the U.S. Department of Agriculture climbed on the bandwagon. In April of that year, the USDA's Office of Budget and Finance issued its *Instructions for 1964 Agency Estimates*. These instructions declared:

> A new concept has been adopted for the 1964 agency estimates; namely, that of zero-base budgeting. This means that all programs will be reviewed from the ground up and not merely in terms of changes proposed for the budget year. . . . Consideration must be given to the basic need for the work contemplated, the level at which the work should be carried out, the benefits to be received, and the costs to be incurred. [T]he fact that programs are prescribed by statutory law [will not] be a controlling consideration.[3]

Six weeks later "25 sets of binders representing agency estimates, most taking up three feet of shelf space, appeared in the Office of Budget and Finance."[4]

On August 25, 1965, President Johnson announced at a news conference that he was instructing all agencies of the federal government to introduce PPB. Seventeen months later, in his budget message to Congress of January 24, 1967, the President reaffirmed his directive. He stated:

> Our most comprehensive effort to improve the effectiveness of Government programs is . . . the Planning-Programming-Budgeting System. This system, which was initiated throughout the executive branch a little over a year ago, requires all agencies to: Make explicit the objectives of their programs; . . . Set out specific proposed plans of work to attain those objectives; and Analyze and compare the probable costs and benefits of these plans against those of alternative methods. . . . This system is primarily a means of encouraging careful and explicit analysis of Federal programs. It will substantially improve our ability to decide among competing proposals for funds and to evaluate actual performance.[5]

---

[3]U.S. Department of Agriculture, Office of Budget and Finance, "Instructions for 1964 Agency Estimates" (April 1962), mimeographed.

[4]Aaron Wildavsky and Arthur Hammann, "Comprehensive Versus Incremental Budgeting in the Department of Agriculture," in Lyden and Miller, *Planning Programming Budgeting*, p. 147.

[5]John Fedkiw and Howard W. Hjort, "The PPB Approach to Research Evaluation," *Journal of Farm Economics* 49 (December 1967): 1426.

Meanwhile, state and local governments were joining the movement. For example, on May 17, 1966, Edmund G. Brown, Governor of California, directed that the entire state government adopt PPB—or rather PAB (Programming and Budgeting) as Californians renamed it.[6] A change of administration and political party a few months later made no difference. Brown's successor, Ronald Reagan, enthusiastically endorsed PAB in his inaugural address. With the presentation of the fiscal 1969 California budget, Caspar Weinberger, Director of Finance, congratulated his office on achieving PAB two years ahead of schedule. Other jurisdictions followed the example.[7] They too were encouraged to be comprehensive.[8] There was pressure to adopt similar techniques in education. By October 1968 the superintendent of the Davis (California) Unified School District had a PPB manual.

In June 1970 the Office of Management and Budget was created in the Executive Office of the President. It is too early to evaluate this office, or to decide whether the move represents further centralization of budget authority in the Chief Executive. It may be difficult to see how a move to take the Bureau of the Budget, already in the Executive Office, and incorporate it into the Office of Management and Budget in the Executive Office further centralizes authority. In the past the Bureau of the Budget has had few political appointees, and cabinet members often found their programs stymied by career civil servants in that bureau. Now, however, power seems to be lodged in the Domestic Council appointed by the

[6]California Department of Finance, *Programming and Budgeting System,* Sacramento (1967), looseleaf.

[7]Gloria Grizzle tells what was expected in Dade County, Florida:

> For the first time, departments were asked to make the objectives of new programs explicit, to construct measures for the attainment of objectives, to indicate which alternatives were considered and why the one included in the budget request was better than the others considered. They were also asked to estimate the cost and effect of the alternative recommended and to make a five-year projection of total program costs. This . . . asks for an evaluation of the cost and effect of only one alternative. Nevertheless, it was a substantial departure from the type of information required for previous budget justifications and was considered to be an important first step toward the provision of more useful information for decision making.

See Gloria Grizzle, "Systems Analysis in Dade County," paper presented at the ORSA/TIMS joint meeting in San Francisco (May 1–3, 1968), p. 5.

[8]Harry Hatry stated: "An initial trial to enable the staff to gain experience . . . is one approach. But since PPBS gains one of its major advantages by attempting to consider and balance program interrelations, it seems highly desirable that as soon as possible the system should be implemented across the board." Because Hatry regards program analyses as "the real payoff to PPBS," he adds that, "in-depth cost-benefit analyses on selected issues might be started in the early months." See Harry P. Hatry, "Considerations in Instituting a Planning-Programming-Budgeting System (PPBS) in State or Local Government," The George Washington University State and Local Finances Project, Washington, D.C. (October 7, 1966), pp. 21–22.

President. Some say that the planning and evaluation function will be taken out of the agencies and centralized in the President's office. This is consonant with PPB's demonstrated tendency to centralize authority. It is interesting to note that the Deputy Director of the Office of Management and Budget is Caspar Weinberger.

Given the wide and rapid spread of PPB, one might suppose that an overwhelming case for its adoption had been made. In fact, the opposite is true. The advocates of benefit-cost analysis and other parts of PPB have never shown—or even tried to show—that its own benefits outweigh its own costs.[9]

Few protests have been heard. In fact, the only loud voice has been Wildavsky's. He wrote, among other things, "We would be in a much stronger position to predict the consequences of program budgeting if we knew (a) how far toward a genuine program budget the Defense Department has gone and (b) whether the program budget has fulfilled its promise. To the best of our knowledge, not a single study of this important experiment was undertaken (or at least published) before the decision was made to spread it around the land."[10]

The chapters that follow represent our protest.

## THE SOURCES OF PPB

PPB did not arise from nothing. For a long time the idea or similar ideas have had their adherents—for example, Arthur Smithies, David Novick, and Frederick Mosher. The Committee for Economic Development

[9]It is true that McKean and Anshen "called attention to some costs or disadvantages that may be attributable, at least in part, to program budgeting." However, they promptly added, "Similarly, it is appropriate to call attention to the unpleasant side effects of penicillin, but it would be foolish to allow this to obscure its benefits or the limitations of alternative medical treatment." McKean and Anshen, "Limitations, Risks, and Problems," p. 352.

In subsequent writing, such as his recent textbook, McKean has been much less optimistic about PPB. Nevertheless he adds, "I am merely indicating some costs that should be weighted against the gains. . . . I am not condemning these devices, and I cannot indicate the extent to which they should be employed." Roland N. McKean, *Public Spending* (New York: McGraw-Hill, 1968), p. 154.

[10]Aaron Wildavsky, "The Political Economy of Efficiency: Cost-Benefit Analysis, Systems Analysis, and Program Budgeting," in Lyden and Miller, *Planning Programming Budgeting*, p. 391.

While such a study would be valuable, it would not be conclusive. As Schelling has pointed out, "The success of PPBS in the Department of Defense—and I think there can be no doubt that the system has been a great success—may be due as much to the quality of the people engaged, and their confidence in each other, as to the logic of the system." See Thomas C. Schelling, "PPBS and Foreign Affairs," Committee Print, Subcommittee on National Security and International Operations of the Committee on Government Operations, United States Senate, 90th Congress, 1st Session (Washington, D.C.: U.S. Government Printing Office, 1968).

(CED) and the Chamber of Commerce of the United States have advocated it vigorously. There is debate over whether this powerful movement has its sources in business or in the public sector. One aspect of PPB, benefit-cost analysis, has a history which can be documented back to 1844.

David Novick claims that the first program budget was the Controlled Materials Plan of 1942, which sought to allocate scarce real resources to essential programs of the war effort.[11] During the war economists flowed into Washington to consider management problems on a scale the nation had not faced before. World War II was as much a shock in the field of planning as it was in many other fields. Planning, both in the large business firm and in western governments, is a post-World War II phenomenon.[12]

In 1949 the Hoover Commission on Organization of the Executive Branch of Government endorsed "performance budgeting"—a budget organized in terms of functions. These recommendations were enacted in the Budget and Accounting Procedures Act of 1950. Economists were still dissatisfied with the budget, however. Novick urged more attention to outputs and Mosher described program budgeting as it was done in the Army in 1954.[13] In 1955 Arthur Smithies published a study of the American budgetary process in which he said "the appropriation process serves the dual purpose of reviewing the past and of programming for the future, and is satisfactory in neither respect."[14] The CED, which had sponsored Smithies' work, urged an analysis of the entire federal budget according to programs.[15] Finally, the movement toward unified commands in the Defense Department encouraged PPB, which many see as a centralization of authority. The Administration and Reorganization Act of 1958 made the Secretary of Defense more important vis-a-vis the military heads of the services.

Let us pause at the end of the 1950s and seek the origin of the several strains of PPB. Techniques of budgeting had been devised in business to control large organizations and budget scarce capital. Ideas from capi-

[11] David Novick, "The Origin and History of Program Budgeting," *California Management Review* (Fall 1968), p. 9.

[12] Neil Chamberlain, *Private and Public Planning* (New York: McGraw-Hill, 1967).

[13] David Novick, *Efficiency and Economy in Government Through New Budgetary and Accounting Procedures,* R-254 (Santa Monica: The RAND Corporation, 1 February 1954); and Frederick Mosher, *Program Budgeting: Theory and Practice with Particular Reference to the U.S. Department of the Army* (New York: American Book-Stratford Press, 1954).

[14] Arthur Smithies, *The Budgetary Process in the U.S.,* Committee for Economic Development Research Study (New York: McGraw-Hill, 1955), p. 171.

[15] Committee for Economic Development, *Control of Federal Government Expenditures* (New York: Committee for Economic Development, 1955).

tal budgeting began to enter government through benefit-cost analysis in the late 1950s.

### In Business

Much of business budgeting is in terms of *objects* of expenditure: labor, materials and supplies, and travel; or in terms of *functions:* production, marketing, and administration. Some business budgeting, especially at the highest levels, is in terms of *programs* or *outputs*. Some authorities claim that PPB was a contribution of *business* to government management.[16]

In the 1920s, many of the ultimate precursors of PPB arose. James McKinsey wrote a widely influential book on business budgeting.[17] A young assistant treasurer at DuPont, Donaldson Brown, began to use rational return-on-investment analyses for corporate planning. The technique of "systems analysis" was being developed by engineers at Bell Laboratories. During these years General Motors faced several crises. One involved cash flow and its regulation. Another stemmed from the practice of giving each division manager whatever appropriation he requested.[18] When DuPont contributed capital to General Motors in 1924, Donaldson Brown went with it. Brown claimed that the 1924 budget procedures were similar to program budgets: they identified major objectives and identified resources with the objectives they served.[19]

Some years later, Ford Motor Company entered the picture. Henry Ford, it is said, was opposed to quantitative analysis. Henry Ford II was not. He brought to the Ford Motor Company a management team, sometimes called "the whiz kids," who had worked together in the Air Force Statistical Control Program. Among these people were Robert McNamara and Charles "Tex" Thornton. Automobile companies, constantly planning several years' models at one time, are ideally suited for PPB. Their endeavors are amenable to organizing budgets by outputs: makes and models.

The problems of large business organizations and government organizations are similar. Planning for both consists of strategic or long-range planning with long horizons, programming of activities in the near future,

---

[16]George A. Steiner, "Program Budgeting: Business Contribution to Government Management," *Business Horizons* (Spring 1965), pp. 43–52.

[17]James O. McKinsey, *Budgetary Control* (New York: Ronald Press, 1922).

[18]Alfred P. Sloane, *My Years with General Motors* (Garden City, N.Y.: Doubleday, 1964), pp. 116–48.

[19]Novick, "The Origin and History of Program Budgeting," pp. 10ff.

and budgeting for the coming year. This "period planning concept" is recognized by the leading texts in the field of business budgeting.[20]

Donald Smalter describes a planning and budgeting procedure for the International Minerals and Chemicals Corporation that is very similar to the procedure used in the Department of Defense. "IMC has operated on this basis for two consecutive years [1963 and 1964]. We pioneered this approach without the benefit of observing DOD."[21] The analogs of program elements in IMC are its outputs: plant nutrition, plant health, animal feed and health, foundry supply, and flavor enhancers.

The question of where PPB originated is moot. It is less important to agree with either Steiner (private sector) or Novick (public sector) than it is to recognize the similarity of the management problems both face. Clearly, there has been symbiosis. McKinsey published *Budgetary Control* in 1922, but Congress passed the Budgeting and Accounting Act a year earlier. Automobile companies spawned PPB, but they also benefited from techniques developed for the Air Force. Smalter shows the irresolvability of the debate. He claims to have "pioneered" these budgetary techniques, yet the title of his article is "The Influence of DOD Practices on Corporate Planning." Charles Christenson is similarly ambivalent.[22]

Businesses have long faced the problem of choosing among possible investment schemes. This has been known as the capital budgeting problem. An early definition of a criterion for ranking investments was given by Irving Fisher.[23] In 1930, he defined the rate of return over cost as that rate that makes the present value of two investments equal. In 1935 Kenneth Boulding developed the concept of internal rate of return, or marginal efficiency of capital—the rate which makes present value zero.[24] This concept is often attributed to John Maynard Keynes, who used it only a year later.[25] George Terborgh discussed routine equipment replacement policies in 1949.[26] Joel Dean[27] published the work that has long been standard in the field, *Capital Budgeting*, in 1951.

[20] Glenn A. Welsch, *Budgeting: Profit Planning and Control* 2d ed. (Edgewood Cliffs, N.J.: Prentice-Hall, 1964), p. 44; and Robert Anthony, *Management Accounting* 3d ed. (Homewood, Ill.: Irwin, 1964), p. 392.

[21] Donald J. Smalter, "The Influence of DOD Practices on Corporate Planning," *Management Technology* 4, no. 2 (December 1964): 37–61.

[22] Charles Christenson, "Some Lessons in Business from PPBS," in Mark Alfandary-Alexander, *Analysis for Planning Programming Budgeting* (Potomac, Md.: Washington Operations Research Council, 1968).

[23] Irving Fisher, *The Theory of Interest* (New York: Macmillan, 1930).

[24] Kenneth Boulding "The Theory of a Single Investment," *Quarterly Journal of Economics* 49, no. 2 (May 1935): 475–94.

[25] John Maynard Keynes, *The General Theory of Employment, Interest and Money* (London: Macmillan, 1936), pp. 135–46.

[26] George Terborgh, *Dynamic Equipment Policy* (New York: McGraw-Hill, 1949).

[27] Joel Dean, *Capital Budgeting* (New York: Columbia University Press, 1951).

A series of articles in the mid-1950s analyzed the criteria by which investments should be chosen. Lorie and Savage noted the possibility of multiple internal rates of return for the same investment in 1955.[28] Ezra Solomon discussed present value, the internal rate of return, and assumptions contained in both in 1956.[29] Jack Hirshleifer contributed an enlightening exegesis of Irving Fisher's theory of capital and interest in 1958.[30]

Organized business groups championed PPB mainly for its promise to limit government expenditures. CED, in addition to sponsoring Smithies' early work, urged refashioning the entire federal budget along "program" lines in 1955. CED was not satisfied with PPB in the federal and state government levels only. In 1968, it declared

> Techniques of cost-effectiveness . . . and systems analysis . . . can now be employed in assessing the efficiency of school management. . . . We urge immediate exploration by school administrators of the application of program accounting techniques in order to identify costs in school systems and to take advantage of cost comparisons.[31]

The Chamber of Commerce of the United States championed "functional budgeting" in 1962, lauding the "revolutionary experiment" in the Defense Department.[32]

### History of Benefit-Cost Analysis

Benefit-cost analysis, which has been incorporated into PPB, actually has a longer history than PPB. In 1844 a French engineer, Jules Dupuit, discussed the measurements of benefits of public works.[33] At the turn of the century, many American cities used a crude form of benefit-cost analysis to sell to their citizens investment schemes for domestic water supplies. The Tennessee Valley Authority employed benefit-cost analysis

[28]J. Lorie and L. J. Savage, "Three Problems in Rationing Capital," *Journal of Business* (October 1955).

[29]Ezra Solomon, "The Arithmetic of Capital Budgeting Decisions," *Journal of Business* (April 1956).

[30]Jack Hirshleifer, "Theory of Optimal Investment Decision," *Journal of Political Economy* (August 1958).

[31]Committee for Economic Development, *Innovation in Education: New Directions for the American School* (New York: Committee for Economic Development, 1968).

[32]Chamber of Commerce of the United States, *Criteria for Government Spending* (Washington, D.C.: U.S. Chamber of Commerce, 1962), pp. 17ff.

[33]Jules Dupuit, "On the Measurement of the Utility of Public Works," *International Economic Papers* 2 (1952): 83–110 (translated from the French *Annales des Ponts et Chaussées* 2d Series, vol. 8 [1844]).

in the 1930s, providing momentum for much work in water resources. Less well known is its application to the evaluation of highway projects in Oregon starting in 1937.[34] During World War II techniques of quantitative analysis were extensively applied to national problems. Applied probability, statistical inference, linear programming, and other techniques were used and improved during the war on problems such as antisubmarine warfare.

After World War II several federal agencies had accumulated experience in flood control, rivers and harbors, navigation, and hydroelectric power projects. A need had arisen to clarify some of the rules of the game largely because of the competition which had developed between the Army Corps of Engineers, the Bureau of Reclamation, the Soil Conservation Service, and the Tennessee Valley Authority. The "Green Book,"[35] a product of a federal interagency committee, answered this need in 1950. This statement of rules (revised in 1958) never attained official standing.

The Bureau of the Budget, for its part, responded in 1952 with Circular A-47.[36] This document was criticized for its exclusive attention to national income or the efficiency objective, but was the basis for project appraisal by the bureau from 1952 through 1960.

By now enough data had accumulated so that Arthur Smithies could set his student Otto Eckstein to work on an important area of federal spending, water resources. Eckstein descended into the agencies in Washington and surfaced in 1955, seminal thesis in hand.[37]

Meanwhile, on the West Coast, the technology of systems analysis was transferred in the interdisciplinary corridors of RAND from one giant of government spending, the military, to another, public investment; especially in water resources. In 1958, two books appeared on that subject, Eckstein's and Roland McKean's.[38] In addition, Eckstein and John Krutilla had compiled a book of case studies of river basin systems.[39] Problems common to both applications were: statement of objectives,

---

[34]C. B. McCullough and John Beakey, *The Economics of Highway Planning,* Oregon State Highway Department Technical Bulletin No. 7 (Salem, Ore.: Oregon State Highway Commission, 1937).

[35]Inter-Agency Committee on Water Resources, *Proposed Practices for Economic Analysis of River Basin Projects* (Washington, D.C.: U.S. Government Printing Office, 1950).

[36]U.S. Bureau of the Budget, "Reports and Budget Estimates Relating to Federal Programs and Projects for Conservation, Development or Use of Water and Related Land Resources," Circular A-47, Washington (1952), hectographed.

[37]Eckstein's thesis, *Benefits and Costs,* was published as *Water Resources Development* (Cambridge, Mass.: Harvard University Press, 1958), Harvard Economic Studies.

[38]Roland N. McKean, *Efficiency in Government Through Systems Analysis* (New York: Wiley, 1958).

[39]*Multiple Purpose River Development* (Baltimore: John Hopkins Press, 1958).

planning future implications of present commitments and discounting future benefits, and uncertainty of both military developments and future hydrologic and demographic conditions.

The military applications were at first secret reports to RAND's client, the Air Force. This work had grown from early operations research studies during World War II, for example, one on antisubmarine warfare. RAND's intention was to maintain the critical mass of scientific personnel that had congregated in Washington during the war. To enable these men to think about long-range problems (more than a week away) RAND domiciled them 3,000 miles from Washington in the back rooms of the Douglas Aircraft Company in Santa Monica, California. By 1960, their work had been sufficiently abridged, disguised, emasculated, disinfected, or made obsolete that it could be published as an anthology under the names of Charles J. Hitch and Roland McKean.[40] In the same year other work at RAND, a large public policy issue in California, and another in New York motivated another RAND study on *Water Supply*.[41]

Thus the field of benefit-cost analysis was firmly implanted as a tool for public expenditure analysis. After 1960 many studies appeared in other fields seeking to apply the systems analysis or cost-effectiveness technique as exemplified by *The Economics of Defense in the Nuclear Age*, and the benefit-cost technique as used in *Water Resource Development*. In 1962 two studies were published at the University of California at Berkeley in the fields of transportation and urban renewal.[42] The next year the Brookings Institution held a conference, chaired by Robert Dorfman, in which papers on research and development, transportation, health, outdoor recreation, dropout prevention, and urban renewal were presented. Military and water resources problems were temporarily shelved to see how the technique could be applied elsewhere.[43]

In May 1962 a new interagency committee developed a set of standards that did receive Presidential imprimatur.[44] Senate Document 97 was approved for application by line agencies and the Bureau of the Budget. In June 1969 the Water Resources Council published its recom-

[40]*The Economics of Defense in the Nuclear Age* (Cambridge, Mass.: Harvard University Press, 1960).

[41]Jack Hirshleifer, J. C. DeHaven, and Jerome W. Milliman, *Water Supply: Economics, Technology and Policy* (Chicago: University of Chicago Press, 1960).

[42]Tillo E. Kuhn, *Public Enterprise Economics and Transport Problems* (Berkeley: University of California Press, 1962), and Nathaniel Lichfield, *Cost-Benefit Analysis in Urban Redevelopment*, Report No. 20 (Berkeley: University of California Real Estate Research Program, 1962).

[43]Robert Dorfman, *Measuring Benefits of Government Investments* (Washington, D. C.: The Brookings Institution, 1965).

[44]Water Resources Council, *Policies, Standards and Criteria for Formulation, Evaluation and Review of Plans for Use and Development of Water and Related Land Resources*, Senate Document 97, 87th Congress (Washington, D.C.: U.S. Government Printing Office, 1962).

mendations for replacing that document.[45] Policies the council proposes are much more permissive to goals other than efficiency. Hearings were held throughout the country in the summer of 1969 on the proposals and groups at four universities began to evaluate four river basins according to these proposed criteria to see how they would work in practice.

## PLAN OF THE BOOK

In the following chapters we will discuss the five elements of PPB. We will explain each element and describe the procedure, usually according to U.S. Bureau of the Budget guidelines. Then we will consider the benefits of this effort and its costs.

We will contend that it is unwise to impose program accounting, to tabulate future expenditures for established programs, to prepare statements of purposes, to defend budget requests without referring to the size of previous appropriations, or to undertake quantitative evaluation of alternatives wherever possible. These are the negative conclusions.

We will also try to be constructive: regrouping agencies according to function is an alternative way of obtaining output-oriented cost information; tabulating future expenditures is useful when a commitment is being created or a multi-year investment undertaken; preparing alternative budget requests would combine the best features of detailed description and zero-base budgeting; and it is reasonable to use quantitative evaluation to prescreen subsidized regional investment projects and in other cases when the decision-makers have sought this additional information.

Our comments on benefit-cost analysis start in Chapter 6. There we consider who should best do quantitative analyses, the criteria by which alternatives ought to be judged, constraints, and externalities.

Chapter 7 explores ways of making benefits and costs commensurable over time. It includes examples of discount rates actually in agency use and suggestions for dealing with uncertainty.

Chapter 8 surveys the methods that have been suggested for calculating benefits of particular types of expenditures: navigation, irrigation, flood control, water supply, hydroelectric power, recreation, highways, mass transit, civil aviation, academic and vocational education, health, and urban-renewal expenditures. After these particulars, we mention the general principles and techniques of benefit estimation that have emerged that can be used in other fields.

[45]Water Resources Council, *Procedures for Evaluation of Water and Related Land Resource Projects* (Washington, D.C.: Water Resources Council, June 1969).

Chapter 9 examines objectives of public spending other than efficiency. We discuss ways to deal with multiple objectives, paying attention to the equity objective and the question of merit wants.

Chapter 10, on cost analysis, catalogs several types of costs and then discusses factors controlling costs: rate of output, physical and performance characteristics of the output, cumulative output, and type of contract. How costs behave over the life of a project is discussed as well as how well costs can be predicted at various stages.

The next section supplements the survey of benefit calculation technique in Chapter 8 with two case studies of large public investment projects: the U.S. Supersonic Transport and the California Water Plan. These case studies lead us to a pessimistic view of the usefulness of benefit-cost analysis for projects as large as these.

Finally, we give a summary judgment of benefit-cost analysis. Can benefits or costs be evaluated objectively? What difference does benefit-cost analysis make depending on who consumes it and its quality? If benefits and costs cannot be evaluated objectively, what is the value of unreliable rankings of public expenditure schemes? Under what conditions is benefit-cost analysis useful?

An appendix details program budget categories for several federal agencies, for the State of California, and for New York City.

# Two

# PROGRAM ACCOUNTING

Program accounting is a way of organizing information with the objective of revealing how much is being spent for each purpose. This objective is to be attained by classifying expenditures in terms of programs regardless of which agencies spend the money or what kinds of things the agencies buy.

Four kinds of expenditures may be classified by program—past, permitted, proposed, and predicted. Past expenditures are outlays that already have been made, permitted expenditures are outlays that have been authorized, proposed outlays are those for which authorization is being sought, and predicted outlays are those for one or more years in the future. The official federal instructions require the Program and Financial Plan (PFP) to show all four kinds; that is, costs for "the fiscal year just past, the current year, and the budget year, plus at least four future years."[1]

In this chapter we will discuss the merits of classifying only three of the four kinds of expenditures by program: past, permitted, and proposed. Recording predicted expenditures, by program or otherwise, involves additional problems, and will be discussed in the following chapter under its own name—multi-year costing.[2] This chapter has four sections. In the first we try to explain what classifying expenditures by program involves. In the second, we discuss the benefits of classifying by program. In the third, we discuss the costs. Finally, we draw some conclusions.

[1] U.S. Bureau of the Budget, "Bulletin No. 68-2, July 18, 1967," in Fremont J. Lyden and Ernest G. Miller, eds., *Planning Programming Budgeting: A Systems Approach to Management* (Chicago: Markham, 1968), p. 434.

[2] Accordingly, this chapter relates to only part of program budgeting as that phrase usually is defined. As McKean says, "Program budgeting may mean different things to different persons [but its hallmarks] are (1) the restructuring of the budget in terms of intermediate outputs or missions and (2) the presentation of proposed costs for several years ahead." See Roland N. McKean, *Public Spending* (New York: McGraw-Hill, 1968), p. 132.

## THE NATURE OF PROGRAM ACCOUNTING

In this section we (1) examine what must be done in order to classify expenditures by program, (2) see how classifying in this way relates to the recommendations of the Hoover Commission, and (3) show how this method differs from conventional government accounting.

### How to Classify by Program

The two steps in classifying expenditures by program are: define a number of programs and list and aggregate expenditures according to the programs they serve.

First, programs must be defined. A program is a collection of activities that have the same purpose or that function together to produce the same outputs. McKean and Anshen state that a program budget is "organized in terms of categories that are closer to being true outputs than the older categories, which . . . are generally inputs with some mixture of ill-related outputs, all heavily influenced by administrative . . . history."[3] McKean adds, "The categories are inevitably intermediate rather than ultimate or even penultimate outputs. It is not helpful to think in terms of such final products as national security, or good health, or satisfaction. . . ."[4] These concepts lack units of measurement.

The programs are not to be coordinate and mutually exclusive. Advocates of PPB want a hierarchy of programs to be defined. A hierarchy can be constructed by delineating a number of elemental programs, by gathering them into a smaller number of more broadly conceived programs, and by further gathering *them* into an even smaller number of even more broadly conceived programs. This process of aggregation is supposed to continue until a small number of very broad programs have been identified. In aggregating, one may combine either close substitutes or close complements, since both relations imply similarity of purpose.

The broadest programs for Defense are illustrated in Table 2.1, which shows the categories as of 1965. The first category encompasses the long-range strategic mission including long-range bombers, air-to-ground and decoy missiles, and refueling tankers; land-based and submarine-based strategic missiles; and the systems for command and control of both. In the Fiscal 1970 Program Budget the categories had changed. Continental Air and Missile Defense Forces and Civil Defense had disappeared. New categories were intelligence and communications;

---

[3] Roland N. McKean and Melvin Anshen, "Limitations, Risks, and Problems," in Lyden and Miller, *Planning Programming Budgeting,* p. 338.

[4] McKean, *Public Spending,* p. 132.

TABLE 2.1. DEPARTMENT OF DEFENSE PROGRAM
CATEGORIES, 1965

|  |  |
|---|---|
| I. | Strategic retaliatory forces |
| II. | Continental air and missile defense forces |
| III. | General purpose forces |
| IV. | Airlift and sealift forces |
| V. | Reserve and National Guard forces |
| VI. | Research and development |
| VII. | General support |
| VIII. | Military assistance |
| IX. | Civil defense |

Source: David Novick, *Program Budgeting: Program Analysis and the Federal Budget*. 2d ed. (Cambridge, Mass.: Harvard University Press, 1967), pp. 92–93.

central supply and maintenance; Training, medical and other general personnel activities; and Retired pay. Military Assistance changed to the more euphemistic Support to other nations.

Program Categories as of 1970, with budget authority for three fiscal years, are shown in Table 2.2.

Commonly, three levels of aggregation are proposed. In the federal

TABLE 2.2. PROGRAM DISTRIBUTION OF BUDGET AUTHORITY
(in millions of dollars)

| PROGRAM CATEGORY | 1968 ACTUAL | 1969 ESTIMATE | 1970 ESTIMATE |
|---|---|---|---|
| Strategic forces | 7,364.5 | 8,309.6 | 9,087.4 |
| General purpose forces | 31,124.3 | 29,606.0 | 29,856.3 |
| Intelligence and communications | 5,492.4 | 5,697.2 | 5,832.4 |
| Airlift and sealift | 1,813.0 | 1,402.0 | 1,889.2 |
| Guard and reserve forces | 3,166.0 | 2,565.5 | 2,848.6 |
| Research and development | 4,395.4 | 4,598.0 | 5,500.3 |
| Central supply and maintenance | 8,175.4 | 8,662.8 | 8,848.8 |
| Training, medical, and other general personnel activities | 9,358.3 | 9,481.7 | 9,967.8 |
| Administration and associated activities | 1,292.1 | 1,404.3 | 1,407.3 |
| Support to other nations | 1,736.8 | 2,450.7 | 2,408.8 |
| Retired pay | 2,095.0 | 2,450.0 | 2,735.0 |
| Total distributed to programs above | 76,013.0 | 76,627.8 | 80,381.8 |
| Undistributed nonprogram financing adjustments | 415.5 | −132.9 | −144.3 |
| Total budget authority, Department of Defense | 76,428.5 | 76,494.9 | 80,237.5 |

Source: United States Congress, Joint Economic Committee, *The Analysis and Evaluation of Public Expenditures: The PPB System*, vol. 2 (Washington, D.C.: U.S. Government Printing Office, 1969), p. 745.

TABLE 2.3. PROGRAM CATEGORIES IN THE DEPARTMENT OF HEALTH, EDUCATION AND WELFARE

---

I.    Education
     Programs aimed at assisting in the development of individual skills and knowledge by formal training and education.
II.   Health
     Programs concerned with promoting normal physical and mental development and well-being and with repairing or containing the effects of injuries and disease.
III.  Social and rehabilitation services
     Integrated programs with both health and training components aimed at helping those who suffer from handicapping conditions to return to productive and gainful employment, and programs aimed at assisting individuals and families in social or economic difficulties to function more successfully in our society.
IV.   Income maintenance
     Public assistance and insurance programs designed to replace, in part, income which cannot be earned because of age, disabling conditions, or unfortunate family circumstances.

---

Source: United States Department of Health, Education and Welfare, Office of the Assistant Secretary (Planning and Evaluation), *Planning-Programming-Budgeting: Guidance for Program and Financial Plan.* Rev. April 17, 1968 (Washington, D.C.: U.S. Government Printing Office, 1968), p. 2.

instructions[5] the smallest programs are called *program elements*. Some program elements within the strategic forces category are B-52 forces, Titan missile forces, and the Polaris system. The intermediate aggregations are called *program subcategories* (they have also been called *program packages*). Within strategic forces program elements are grouped under the following program packages:

A.  Aircraft forces
B.  Missile forces
   1.  Land-based
   2.  Sea-based
C.  Command control, communications, and support.

The largest aggregations are called *program categories*. An illustration from the Department of Labor is Manpower Development Assistance, with Manpower Training constituting one subcategory in the category. Table 2.3 explains the program categories in the Department of Health, Education and Welfare.

A rule of thumb has emerged for an appropriate number of program categories. According to the Bureau of the Budget, "To facilitate top

[5]"Bulletin No. 68-2," pp. 430-43.

level review, the number of program categories should be limited. For example, a Cabinet Department should have as many as fifteen program categories in only a rare and exceptional case. Normally, an agency will have between five or ten major program categories."[6]

Some ideas have also emerged concerning an appropriate size of program elements, but the ideas are less specific. McKean and Anshen view program elements as: "The [smallest] compartments among which resource shifts require special permission."[7] The size of the compartments, they continue, "should vary according to the situation. The intention would be partly to keep top levels from being overburdened with minor decisions . . . partly to [have] it simpler to reach certain decisions, make substitutions, and implement resource shifts [and partly] to maintain lower level incentives to seek alternatives, to worry about uncertainties, and to criticize competing proposals. . . . To be sure, branches and agencies would have more leeway to make mistakes . . . but this would be worthwhile in the long run."[8]

A program element to HEW is represented by a six-digit code. Under Development of Health Resources (210000), we must proceed down through Increasing Knowledge (211000) to Cancer (211100) versus Heart Disease (211200) and Allergic and Infectious Diseases (211300). Under Heart Disease we finally arrive at the program elements.

| | |
|---|---|
| 211211 | Atherosclerosis |
| 211212 | Heart Drug Study |
| 211215 | Cardiovascular Research Centers |

Under the Income Maintenance Category, some subcategories are Aged Assistance, Disability Assistance, and Other Individual and Family Support. Under the last we have Aid to Families with Dependent Children (AFDC)-Basic and AFDC-Unemployed Father. Under AFDC-Unemployed Father we have 432100—Payments to Families with Persons in Employment and Training.

After defining a number of programs, the second step in classifying expenditures by program is to list expenditures according to the programs they serve and to calculate the total expenditures for each program. Because several levels of aggregation are to exist in defining programs, several degrees of summation are involved in calculating total expenditures. Total expenditures for a program element will be the sum of the

[6]"Bulletin No. 68-2," p. 432.
[7]McKean and Anshen, "Limitations, Risks, and Problems," p. 349.
[8]McKean and Anshen, "Limitations, Risks, and Problems," p. 354.

expenditures assigned to the program element; total expenditures for a program subcategory will be the sum of the expenditures for all the program elements assigned to the subcategory; total expenditures for a program category will be the sum of the expenditures for the various subcategories in the category. At each level in the hierarchy, the total expenditures shown for a program will represent the amount of money being spent for the purposes associated with the program.

All kinds of expenditures are to be included. According to the federal instructions: "The financial data presented in the PFP . . . should reflect total program costs inclusive of the program-oriented research and development, investment, and operating costs. . . ."[9] Accordingly, the distinction between capital outlays and operating expenses that is common in business accounting is not made.[10]

In sum, program accounting involves, first, defining a hierarchy of programs, each program representing activities that have a common purpose, and second, ascertaining the sum of all current expenses and current capital outlays that are chargeable to each program.

Examples of program structures for several federal agencies are given in the appendix, along with program structures for the State of California and the City of New York.

### Comparison with Performance Budgeting

The Hoover Commission recommended program or performance budgeting, a budget based on functions, activities, and projects, in order to increase responsibility and accountability in management. There are differences between these two approaches to budgeting. Performance budgeting is retrospective, while program budgeting is prospective. Per-

---

[9]"Bulletin No. 68-2," p. 437.

[10]Lazarus cites the example of the Department of Defense, which attempted to assess an agency for all measurable costs that it incurred. This had many benefits. It showed Congress what its appropriations were buying. To the agency head, it indicated the full cost of his activity. For the higher officials, it provided a way of comparing actual performance with planned performance and resources consumed with work done, and of determining the actual costs of specific missions.

The process of determining the full costs for which an organization was to be charged required four basic steps: "(1) Revise the accounts structure [to supplement categorizing by object of expenditure with categorizing by functions that aggregate program elements]. (2) Charge military personnel costs to organization units [to cost at the user level the largest single category of operating resources not now so charged]. (3) Purify the appropriation definitions [so that all capital items, such as inventory additions, appear in the continuing appropriation and all consumables appear in the operating appropriation]. (4) Extend the use of working capital mechanism [so as to charge the ultimate user, at the time of issue for consumption, for centrally procured items such as fuel]." See Steven Lazarus, "Planning-Programming-Budgeting Systems and Project PRIME," in Lyden and Miller, *Planning Programming Budgeting*, p. 365.

formance budgeting is concerned with the process of work whereas program budgeting is concerned with the purpose of work.

Performance budgeting gave rise to work measurement systems in the tradition of Frederick W. Taylor. It was retrospective or evaluative in the sense of measuring what was done. Program budgeting is prospective and connotes planning.

Allen Schick provides an example for comparison of the Coast Guard's performance budgeting categories with its program structure.[11]

| *Performance categories* | *Program categories* |
|---|---|
| Vessel operations | Search and rescue |
| Aviation operations | Aids to navigation |
| Repair and supply facilities | Law enforcement |

Here, performance categories were concerned with the mode of transportation used, while program categories relate more to the objectives of the Coast Guard. This difference is very much like budgeting for individual armed services versus budgeting for program categories. Performance budgeting is oriented towards the methods to be used; program budgeting is concerned with the objective.

Performance budgeting is chiefly relevant to the problems of the lower and middle echelons of an administrative hierarchy. Although it facilitates and encourages the application of techniques like cost accounting and scientific management, it was of little use to top-level officials. In some cases it even became an obstacle. Thus, the National Security Act of 1949 called for the segregation of *capital* and *operating* costs. This showed the influence of the Hoover Commission and should be contrasted to the PPB orientation that would lump the two types of cost together in any year to display *total system* costs.

Implementation of performance budgeting was, according to Weidenbaum, "slow and only partial."[12] What program accounting really supplants, therefore, is conventional government accounting. Let us see how the two differ.

### Comparison with Conventional Accounting

Proponents of PPB speak ill of the conventional method of government accounting. McKean, for example, characterizes conventional accounting as follows:

[11] Allen Schick, "The Road to PPB: The Stages of Budget Reform," in Lyden and Miller, *Planning Programming Budgeting,* pp. 39–41.

[12] Murray L. Weidenbaum, "Program Budgeting—Applying Economic Analysis to Government Expenditure Decisions," in Lyden and Miller, *Planning Programming Budgeting,* p. 168.

Often the budget categories that officials must consider increasing or decreasing (for example, general government; commerce, housing, and space technology; labor and welfare) are too broad for good judgments to be made about their relative size. Sometimes the categories are account titles or organization units, such as the Public Health Service or the Bureau of Land Management that include conglomerations of activities more closely related to the work of other agencies than to each other. Often the categories are across-the-board inputs, such as "salaries and expenses," "travel," or "printing," that help produce a variety of outputs but are not linked in a discernible way with any particular output.[13]

The contrast that McKean and others draw between program accounting and conventional accounting emphasizes the effect rather than the cause. The effect is a failure to classify outlays according to purpose. The *cause* is a failure to organize government agencies according to function; that is, a failure to have an administrative unit for each program element and to assemble these administrative units into a hierarchy according to similarity of purpose. If agencies were organized functionally, conventional accounting would produce the output-oriented cost information the advocates of PPB desire.

Conventional government accounting involves a two-way classification of outlays. First, as the advocates of PPB stress, outlays are classified by object of expenditure; that is, by kind of input. For example, they are totaled for salaries, for fringe benefits, for travel, for supplies, and so forth. Second, as advocates of PPB mention only in passing, outlays are classified by agency. For example, they are—or should be—totaled for each group, for all groups in a section, for all sections in a branch, for all branches in a division, for all divisions in a service, and for all services in the department.

An important conclusion follows: If government agencies were organized according to function, conventional accounting would be program accounting (and would simultaneously be object-of-expenditure accounting). Classification of outlays by agency would be the same as classification by program or purpose. The total outlays of an agency would represent the amount of money being spent for the program element, program subcategory, or program category administered by that agency. For example, if there were an agency (perhaps named the Farm Income Division) in the U.S. Department of Agriculture that contained every activity designed to raise incomes of farmers, and only such activities, then the budget of this division would represent the amount being spent for the purpose of raising farm income.

[13]McKean, *Public Spending*, p. 129.

The advocates of PPB do not, however, advocate that government agencies be reorganized according to function. Indeed, they are pleased to note that programs consist of activities selected from a number of agencies. Thus, in the U.S. Department of Agriculture, according to Fedkiw and Hjort, "there are 154 different program elements. . . . Most involve the work of more than one agency."[14]

Neither do the advocates of PPB recommend—or at least expect— that conventional accounting will be abandoned. McKean and Anshen, for example, predict:

> [T]he old budget structure will . . . exist side by side. . . .
> Congress would in all likelihood wish to use the input cate-
> gories to which it is accustomed. In addition, for some time
> agency officials would need the old structure. . . . The reason
> is that program-element costs . . . although they would serve
> for broad allocative decisions . . . would not serve for pro-
> gram management of "frying the fat" out of programs. For
> some inputs it may [be] desirable to constrain the total amount
> permitted. Cutting and managing such inputs may need to be
> done in terms of the old appropriations structure.[15]

With this background, we can see what it is that the advocates of program accounting really are recommending. We have seen that, if agencies were organized according to function, conventional government accounting would be program accounting (and object-of-expenditure accounting). We have also seen that the advocates of program account- ing do not recommend that agencies be reorganized according to function or expect that conventional accounting will be abandoned. Accordingly, the demand for program accounting really is a demand that government accounting move from a two-way classification of expenditures (by ob- ject of expenditure and by agency) to a three-way classification (by object, by agency, and by program). This is the essence of the proposal.

## THE BENEFITS OF PROGRAM ACCOUNTING

The benefits of cross-classifying expenditures by program supposedly are better decisions—choices that are different and that improve the allocation of resources either *within* the government or *between* it and the rest of the economy. As Schick says, "The case for PPB rests on the assumption that the form in which information is classified and used governs the actions of budget-makers. . . . Take away the assumption

[14]John Fedkiw and Howard W. Hjort, "The PPB Approach to Research Evaluation," *Journal of Farm Economics* 49 (December 1967): 1427.
[15]McKean and Anshen, "Limitations, Risks, and Problems," p. 344.

. . . and the movement for PPB is reduced to a trivial manipulation of techniques."[16]

To our knowledge, no empirical evidence has been offered to support the proposition that more desirable decisions—or even different decisions —will emerge. Indeed, it is not even evident that one could test whether the proposition is true or false. (In positivist circles, this is a serious consideration; positivists regard a proposition as meaningful if, and only if, it is verifiable, at least in principle.)

The case is wholly a priori. Better decisions supposedly will result for two reasons: first, because classifying outlays by program will supposedly enable decision-makers to see how much money is being spent for each purpose, and second, because high-level decision-makers will supposedly exercise greater control over budgets. Let us examine these contentions in turn.

### Enlightenment

The first way in which cross-classifying expenditures by program supposedly will foster better decisions is by enabling decision-makers to see how much money is being spent for each purpose. As a result, they supposedly will be less likely to allocate too little money to some purposes and too much money to other purposes; also, they will be more likely to reject or terminate programs whose benefits are not worth what they cost.

The program budget is supposed to make the decision process more effective "by clearly defining the alternatives among which choices must be made,"[17] and by generating the information which allows the comparison of anticipated costs and benefits.[18]

There is, however, reason to doubt that the information produced

---

[16]Schick, "The Road to PPB," p. 48.

[17]McKean and Anshen, "Limitations, Risks, and Problems," p. 340.

[18]McKean elaborates on this to show how the process of budget formation used prior to PPB failed to provide top-level officials with needed information in cases where outputs were substitutes or inputs, complements. Where specifications were made prior to the estimation of costs, as was often the case, "choices [became] embedded in the budget without conscious . . . comparison of benefits with costs," so that officials could easily make decisions about these expenditure categories without ever having taken the possibility of substitutes or other key interrelationships into account. "The value of the missile Thor depended on whether or not another agency was developing Jupiter. . . ." Also, this emphasis upon input categories made it hard to make judgments about prospective purchases in the face of complementarities. "[I]f a bakery manager tried to decide how much flour, sugar and butter to buy without linking these items to the amounts of bread and pastries to be produced, he would be handicapped in reaching good decisions." See McKean, *Public Spending,* p. 129.

by program accounting actually will foster better decisions. McKean's own conclusion is noteworthy:

> [T]he value of the information . . . is rather limited. First . . . many or even most activities relate to more than one intermediate output, and the best way to classify them to aid decision-makers is not easy to perceive. As you make one choice easier, you make another more difficult. . . . Second, cost estimates for program elements are less meaningful than many people imagine. . . . The costs of administrative staffs that serve a whole agency, or repair shops . . . that serve numerous program elements, are likely to be allocated on an almost arbitrary basis. Third . . . it is incremental cost that is relevant to specific choices. Incremental costs depend upon the particular circumstances: Do administrative or servicing facilities really have to be expanded proportionately? Fourth, the program budget . . . provides no clues as to the effectiveness or benefits from increments to program elements. . . . A final limitation [is that it] may have little or no impact on decisions. For a number of years, the U.S. Budget Bureau had something like a program budget . . . called "Civil Works Proposals." It was organized in meaningful functions or outputs, it crossed department lines, it showed costs for six or so years ahead—and it apparently had no effect on choices! Had the new Defense Department budget been merely an information system without increased centralization of authority, it might have had virtually no impact. . . .[19]

These limitations on the value of the information to be generated are serious if, as McKean and Anshen stated, "the major gains to be derived from the . . . program budget . . . depend in large part on the quality of the data presented in the budget operation."[20]

### Coordination

The other way in which cross-classifying outlays by program supposedly will foster better decisions is by enabling high-level decision-makers to exercise greater control over budgets. Greater control arises because, as Wildavsky puts it: "Cutting across the subunits of the organization, . . . the program budget could only be put together by the top executive. A more useful tool for increasing his power to control decisions vis-a-vis his subordinates would be hard to find."[21]

[19]McKean, *Public Spending*, pp. 132–35.
[20]McKean and Anshen, "Limitations, Risks, and Problems," p. 355.
[21]Aaron Wildavsky, "The Political Economy of Efficiency: Cost-Benefit Analysis, Systems Analysis, and Program Budgeting," in Lyden and Miller, *Planning Programming Budgeting*, p. 390.

Schelling regards the greater control as revolutionary:

> The most crucial thing that Secretary Hitch ever did was to identify his basic "program packages." [I]n a foreign-affairs budget [the least unsatisfactory] basic package is not the program—Peace Corps, intelligence, AID, agricultural surpluses, technical assistance, Ex-Im bank credits—but the country. . . . Just getting recognition that the country, rather than the agency or program is the basic unit of analysis would be a heroic step. . . . This is revolutionary not just because somebody would be looking at the totality of U.S. programs with respect to a particular country . . . relating them to the same set of objectives, comparing them with respect to their effectiveness, demanding that the objectives be acknowledged . . . eliminating inconsistency and reducing duplication. Nor is it that . . . countries would be compared with each other as claimants for U.S. resources. . . . No, what would be revolutionary is that somebody . . . has to do this. [T]o put this responsibility on the Secretary of State is to give him . . . the kind of authority that has never . . . been wholly acceptable. . . . But this is where we are led by the philosophy of PPB. . . .[22]

It is interesting to note that the State Department is the only Cabinet-level department which has not yet come forth with a program budget. Only the cultural affairs segment has a program budget, and this is not even the tip of the iceberg.

There is, however, reason to question whether greater centralization will foster better decisions. No one knows how much central control is desirable, and even the advocates of PPB are concerned that it may produce excessive centralization. Determining the appropriate degree of central control is a difficult task. McKean explains:

> In a world of vast uncertainties . . . increased centralization will, beyond some point, bring increasing costs, especially in the long run. [R]ivalry among agencies—the threat of one agency's introducing an innovation that would encroach on another agency's activity—is more effective than good intentions in preventing alternatives from being overlooked. The Navy's Polaris probably played a larger role than good analysis and a broad viewpoint in arousing Air Force interest in reducing the vulnerability of Minuteman. Rivalry among . . . Interior . . . Agriculture, and the Corps of Engineers has helped direct . . . attention to unconventional sources of

[22] Thomas C. Schelling, "PPBS and Foreign Affairs," Committee Print, Subcommittee on National Security and International Operations of the Committee on Government Operations, United States Senate, 90th Congress, 1st Session (Washington, D.C.: U.S. Government Printing Office, 1968), p. 7.

water, such as the reclaiming of sewage. . . . Where there
are fewer uncertainties or more crucial interdependencies,
as in the actual conduct of military or postal operations with
a given technology, a high degree of centralization may bring
fewer costs and more gains.[23]

In short, "There are certainly ways to use program budgeting without excessive centralization . . . but the problems . . . deserve careful
thought."[24]

## THE COSTS OF PROGRAM ACCOUNTING

### Set-up Costs

The costs of setting up the system are not trivial. Three kinds of set-
up costs can be anticipated—struggles with program delineation, confusion over cost allocation, and difficulties in educating personnel.

*Struggles with program delineation* will occur because *how* programs
are defined will affect *who* has budgetary control. Program delineations
are arbitrary definitions and arbitrary allocations of budget power. Program elements can be delineated and aggregated in many different ways.
"The Defense Department budget," Virginia Held observes, "has . . .
been divided into . . . nine major programs . . . and over 800 'program
elements. . . .' But the possibilities for regrouping are almost endless."[25]
"There are as many ways to conceive of programs as there are of organizing activity," Wildavsky comments. "In the case of foreign affairs," he
continues, "it is not at all clear whether it would be preferable to emphasize country teams, with the budget made by the State Department to
encompass activities of the other Federal agencies abroad, or to let Commerce, Agriculture, Defense, and other agencies include their foreign
activities in their own budgets. Program budgeting will unleash great
struggles of this kind in Washington."[26]

*Confusion over cost allocation* is bound to occur. Costs were formerly displayed according to organizational divisions. Functions, of
course, cut across jurisdictional units and so some means must be found

[23]McKean, *Public Spending,* pp. 148–49, 152.
[24]McKean and Anshen, "Limitations, Risks, and Problems," p. 346.
[25]Virginia Held, "PPBS Comes to Washington," in Lyden and Miller, *Planning
Programming Budgeting,* p. 14.
[26]Concerning the Defense categories, incidentally, Wildavsky has observed "[O]nly
two of the nine program categories used in the Defense Department appear to be genuine
programs in the sense of pointing to end purposes or objectives." Wildavsky, "The Political
Economy of Efficiency," p. 391.

to allocate costs of the divisions among functions. Allocation aids must be found to apportion an administrator's time over the several program elements he affects. It is not surprising that Attorney General Mitchell initially asked all attorneys in the Department of Justice to report their activities over each working day in 12-minute intervals.

*Difficulties in educating personnel* will probably be encountered. McKean and Anshen report:

> Public administrators have little experience in developing, evaluating, or using . . . cost estimates. . . . Extensive educational efforts and strengthening of staff capabilities for cost estimating and analysis will be required in the Executive departments, the Bureau of the Budget, and, probably, the staffs of at least some congressional committees.[27]

Lazarus provides an illustration of how much effort is involved. He reports (apparently with pride): "DOD Instruction 7040.5, 'Definition of Expenses and Investment Costs,' dated September 1, 1966 . . . consumed five months of steady effort, went through 13 separate revisions, and was analyzed in three separate DOD-wide reviews."[28]

### Operating Costs

Superimposing program accounting on conventional accounting will entail an additional set of ledgers, as well as an additional process of reconciliation ("crosswalks" in PPB jargon). McKean and Anshen describe the result: "With the two structures . . . will develop large amounts of paperwork, conflicts between program decisions and decisions about input categories, and difficulty in gearing the new system to an annual budget cycle."[29]

Will there be offsetting savings, so that the total payroll ends up smaller? According to Hatry, a PPB advocate, the answer is no: "[F]ederal experience indicates that establishment of . . . central analysis staffs has not led to staff reductions. If anything, the increased need for information seems more often to cause increases in the government's total staffs."[30] Table 2.4 shows that 1,145 positions were added between 1966 and 1969 in twenty-one agencies of the federal government in pursuance of PPB. Operating costs, too, are not trivial.

[27]McKean and Anshen, "Limitations, Risks, and Problems," p. 355.
[28]Lazarus, "Planning-Programming-Budgeting Systems and Project PRIME," p. 367.
[29]McKean and Anshen, "Limitations, Risks, and Problems," p. 355.
[30]Harry P. Hatry, "Considerations in Instituting a Planning-Programming-Budgeting System (PPBS) in State or Local Government," The George Washington University State and Local Finances Project, Washington, D.C. (October 7, 1966), p. 20.

TABLE 2.4. NUMBER OF PPB POSITIONS SHOWN IN
THE FISCAL YEAR 1969 BUDGET[a]

| | ADDED 1966–68 | ADDED 1968–69 | TOTAL 1969 |
|---|---|---|---|
| Central staff; analytic: | | | |
| Professional | 177 | 21 | 198 |
| Support | 82 | 6 | 88 |
| Program monitoring and data handling: | | | |
| Professional | 105 | 9 | 114 |
| Support | 46 | 5 | 51 |
| Other (including subordinate agencies): | | | |
| Professional | 428 | 85 | 513 |
| Support | 159 | 22 | 181 |
| Recapitulation: | | | |
| Total professional | 710 | 115 | 825 |
| Total support | 287 | 33 | 320 |
| TOTAL | 997 | 148 | 1,145 |

[a] Represents only 21 agencies. Department of Defense (military), Central Intelligence Agency, Small Business Administration, Civil Service Commission, and Tennessee Valley Authority are excluded.

Source: U.S. Congress, Joint Economic Committee, *Analysis and Evaluation of Public Expenditures: The PPB System,* vol. 2 (Washington, D.C.: U.S. Government Printing Office, 1969), p. 636.

### Revision Costs

McKean and Anshen anticipate "substantial change" over the years.

[T]he initial program budget will need . . . amendment and modification . . . as a result of experience. [B]usiness organizations which have installed information-decision systems that resemble the program budget concept . . . discovered a need to revise their systems in the light of practice and to accord, as well, with the changing nature of their own dynamic decision processes. . . . Unfortunately . . . it is impossible to devise program elements (or even broad programs) that are not . . . interdependent. This means that there should and will be considerable groping at first for an improved program-element structure.[31]

This groping, moreover, is not likely ever to terminate. What is involved is not a process of successive approximation to a demonstrably

[31] McKean and Anshen, "Limitations, Risks, and Problems," p. 343.

correct solution. It is not even a matter of finding an answer that will be approximately correct for a period of time. Because program delineation is arbitrary, there is no correct answer, and selection is a matter of taste. Accordingly, program delineation will be determined by the preferences of the highest authority who regards the matter as important.[32] One should wish him a long life. If his successor's preferences are different, the whole supplementary accounting system may be changed.

## CONCLUSION

The advocates of program accounting have been wise to avoid (or at least to obscure) a recommendation that the conventional method of government accounting be abandoned. Whether or not agencies are organized along functional lines, there is reason to retain both conventional ways of classifying government outlays.

Classifying outlays by object of expenditure is useful. To budget and record outlays in this way helps administrators schedule procurement and utilization of each of their inputs over a year, helps auditors see whether funds have been spent in unauthorized ways, helps purchasing departments control inventories and obtain quantity discounts, helps planners predict the effect of changing prices for supplies, and helps legislators forecast the costs of changing salary scales. These are important benefits.

Classifying outlays by agency is also useful. Budgeting and recording outlays by agency lets the head of the agency know how much money he is currently authorized to spend. Administrators need to know this in order to abide by their constraints, to schedule utilization of funds over the year, and to allocate funds within the several input categories. Classifying by agency is the financial aspect of a chain of command.

Program accounting adds a third way of classifying expenditures— by purpose. The advantages of classifying by purpose are supposed to be production of output-oriented cost information and greater centralization. Both of these effects, however, have questionable value, while the costs of a third classification—set-up costs, operating costs, and revision costs—would clearly be substantial. The proponents of program

---

[32] This is reasonable. It is sensible to classify the activities that an administrator supervises in the way that he finds best. Categories should be named in a way that he finds meaningful and should be so structured that he can understand how they differ, can choose among them in allocating funds, and can trust allocations of joint costs. The point is not that revision is unreasonable, but that it is expensive.

accounting have not assumed the burden of proof, and there is good reason to doubt that the benefits would outweigh the costs.

There is, furthermore, an alternative way to obtain both output-oriented cost information and greater centralization while avoiding at least the operating costs associated with a third classification. The alternative is to reorganize agencies along functional lines. This kind of reorganization, it is true, is not always appealing. The Attorney General's National Committee to Study the Antitrust Laws, for example, concluded that both the Antitrust Division of the Department of Justice and the Federal Trade Commission should continue to enforce the antitrust laws, and that the FTC should continue to police both the "level of competition" and the "plane of competition." Evidently the members of the committee felt that output-oriented cost information and greater centralization were less important than were recognition "of past experience, present manpower, and [the different] remedies available to each agency.[33] Similarly, there seem to be good reasons for leaving Polaris submarines and Minuteman missiles in different services even though both provide capability for homeland destruction. Clearly, more is at stake than having a pleasing organization chart or having expenditures grouped by purpose.    Whether, or rather where, reorganization along functional lines would be wise is debatable. Among other considerations, account should be taken of personnel problems, of maintaining continuity, and of fostering rivalry among agencies. The only generalization that seems appropriate here is that reorganization (and its costs) should at least be considered before turning to program accounting.

We conclude that both of the conventional ways of classifying government expenditures should be maintained, that classifying expenditures by purpose should be introduced only if reorganization along functional lines has been considered and rejected, that the case for introducing program accounting even then is not persuasive, and, finally, that the people who expect program accounting to reduce government spending are in for a big surprise.

[33] U.S. Attorney General's National Committee to Study the Antitrust Laws, *Report* (Washington, D.C.: U.S. Government Printing Office, 1955), p. 377.

# Three

# MULTI-YEAR COSTING

In Chapter 2 we discussed program accounting, the first distinguishing feature of PPB. In this chapter we discuss the second, tabulation of predicted expenditures. Advocates of PPB argue that budget requests should contain not only expenditures for which approval is being sought but also expenditures that are predicted for a number of years in the future. The federal Bureau of the Budget instructions specify; "The PFP should show . . . costs . . . for each program element, grouped . . . by category and subcategory, for . . . at least four future years."[1]

In this chapter we discuss what multi-year costing involves, its asserted benefits, and its apparent costs. Finally, we offer an alternative to undertaking multi-year costing for every program or agency.

## THE NATURE OF MULTI-YEAR COSTING

Multi-year costing has not yet been clearly defined. The federal instructions, devoting a section to the subject, state:

> PPB applies not only to current programs, but to proposals for new legislation. . . . The years beyond the budget year are included primarily to show the future implications of current (past and present) decisions. [W]here a program is undertaken as an experiment or demonstration to provide a basis for future program decisions [and] the current decision does not provide for full-scale operation, . . . costs should not be projected beyond the next decision point [in the PFP. Instead,] the expected cost . . . of the full-scale program . . . should . . . be discussed in the PM. . . . Where an existing

[1]U.S. Bureau of the Budget, "Bulletin No. 68-2, July 18, 1967," in Fremont J. Lyden and Ernest G. Miller, eds., *Planning Programming Budgeting: A Systems Approach to Management* (Chicago: Markham, 1968), p. 434.

program is expected to continue throughout the planning period but no decision has been made as to its future level, it should be shown at its current level unless (a) . . . changes are required under existing law, by uncontrollable workload, or by demographic or other factors, or (b) explicit justification . . . is provided. . . . The PFP . . . will not necessarily reflect [program or] agency budget totals for the years beyond the budget year, because it omits new programs not yet recommended and fails to reflect program level changes, including termination. . . .[2]

Table 3.1 gives the Program and Financial Plan (PFP) for part of the Vocational Rehabilitation category of the Department of Health, Education and Welfare.

These instructions are much more specific than those they replaced. The initial version simply stated: "The Program and Financial Plan will [s]how the program levels which the agency head thinks will be appropriate over the entire period [and] the cost of carrying out the activity described."[3] Nevertheless, the revised version, too, leaves considerable room for interpretation in preparing the PFP. In particular, four points are judgmental.

First, to decide which rules apply to a program occasionally will be a matter of judgment. The instructions refer to "an experiment . . . not . . . full-scale" and to "an existing program . . . expected to continue." Choosing between these categories could be difficult for, say, space probes, foreign aid, and urban renewal. Moreover, the instructions do not say how to proceed in the case of new programs of full scale, such as proposals to build a dam, pay family allowances, inspect vehicles, forbid discrimination, or enforce antifraud laws. Presumably any figures may be inserted, provided an agency head gives them "explicit justification."

Second, for a program classified as "an experiment . . . not full-scale," it is a matter of judgment to decide what "full-scale operation" would involve. For example, if direct payments, or price supports in general, are (or, turning back the clock, were) so classified, what commodities, support levels, and so forth, would full-scale operation involve? When unemployment insurance was being considered, should full-scale operation have included coverage for farm and domestic workers? What is full scale for space probes, foreign aid, urban renewal, Medicare, F-111's, and antiballistic missiles? It is true that multi-year costing for an experimental program is to be presented, not in the PFP, but in a PM, so there will be room for alternative assumptions to be discussed. This presentation, however, does not make instructions unnecessary.

[2]"Bulletin No. 68-2," pp. 430, 434, 435.
[3]U.S. Bureau of the Budget, "Bulletin No. 66-3, October 12, 1965," in Lyden and Miller, *Planning Programming Budgeting*, p. 411.

## TABLE 3.1. PROGRAM AND FINANCIAL PLAN, DEPARTMENT OF HEALTH, EDUCATION AND WELFARE

| | EXISTING, NEW, AND FUTURE LEGISLATION GENERAL FUNDS, TRANSFERS, TRUST FUNDS, AND OTHER | | | | | | | |
| --- | --- | --- | --- | --- | --- | --- | --- | --- |
| | 1967 | 1968 | 1969 | 1970 | 1971 | 1972 | 1973 | TOTAL |
| **3 VOCATIONAL REHABILITATION** | | | | | | | | |
| TOT RSA | 335749 | 410987 | 497776 | 627370 | 758450 | 889540 | 1020620 | 4540492 |
| TOT RSA | 328898 | 395631 | 481396 | 610060 | 740060 | 870060 | 1000060 | 4426165 |
| | 6851 | 15356 | 16380 | 17310 | 18390 | 19480 | 20560 | 114327 |
| **31 REHABILITATION FOR DISABLING CONDITION** | | | | | | | | |
| TOT RSA | 233261 | 280870 | 333273 | 395947 | 483686 | 573152 | 682790 | 2982979 |
| TOT RSA | 233261 | 280870 | 333273 | 395947 | 483686 | 573152 | 682790 | 2982979 |
| **311 SPECIFIC DISABILITIES** | | | | | | | | |
| TOT RSA | 233261 | 280870 | 333273 | 395947 | 483686 | 573152 | 682790 | 2982979 |
| | 233261 | 280870 | 333273 | 395947 | 483686 | 573152 | 682790 | 2982979 |
| **3111 TUBERCULOSIS** | | | | | | | | |
| TOT RSA | 4303 | 3643 | 700 | 775 | 950 | 1125 | 1200 | 12696 |
| TOT RSA | 4303 | 3643 | 700 | 775 | 950 | 1125 | 1200 | 12696 |
| 130310 VOC REHAB SERVICES RSA | 4248 | 3443 | 300 | 275 | 250 | 225 | 200 | 8941 |
| 130510 RSA RES+TNG FOR CURR RSA | 55 | 200 | 400 | 500 | 700 | 900 | 1000 | 3755 |
| **3112 NEOPLASMS** | | | | | | | | |
| TOT RSA | 1417 | 2008 | 4018 | 4261 | 6027 | 7032 | 8036 | 33159 |
| TOT RSA | 1417 | 2008 | 4018 | 4261 | 6027 | 7032 | 8036 | 33159 |
| 130310 VOC REHAB SERVICES RSA | 1417 | 2008 | 4018 | 4261 | 6027 | 7032 | 8036 | 33159 |
| **3113 MENTAL HEALTH + ILLNESS** | | | | | | | | |
| TOT RSA | 38660 | 50977 | 61886 | 79279 | 104356 | 132211 | 167526 | 634895 |
| TOT RSA | 38660 | 50977 | 61886 | 79279 | 104356 | 132211 | 167526 | 634895 |
| 130310 VOC REHAB SERVICES RSA | 36346 | 48503 | 58926 | 76062 | 100571 | 127856 | 162519 | 610783 |
| 130410 VOC REHAB RES+DEMO RSA | 1542 | 1604 | 1796 | 1840 | 2080 | 2305 | 2542 | 13709 |
| 130420 VOC REHAB TRAINING RSA | 365 | 370 | 564 | 677 | 805 | 950 | 1165 | 4896 |
| 130510 RSA RES+TNG FOR CURR RSA | 407 | 500 | 600 | 700 | 900 | 1100 | 1300 | 5507 |
| **3114 NERVOUS SYSTEM + SENSE ORGANS** | | | | | | | | |
| TOT RSA | 63672 | 75277 | 91002 | 105887 | 125673 | 144367 | 167294 | 773172 |
| TOT RSA | 63672 | 75277 | 91002 | 105887 | 125673 | 144367 | 167294 | 773172 |
| 130310 VOC REHAB SERVICES RSA | 53337 | 64005 | 78242 | 92272 | 110623 | 127607 | 148744 | 674830 |
| 130410 VOC REHAB RES+DEMO RSA | 4279 | 4448 | 4850 | 4990 | 5620 | 6260 | 6900 | 37347 |
| 130420 VOC REHAB TRAINING RSA | 4828 | 4874 | 5560 | 5675 | 5780 | 5900 | 6050 | 38667 |
| 130430 VOC REHAB SP CEN PRO RSA | 100 | 250 | 350 | 950 | 1350 | 2000 | 2600 | 7600 |
| 130460 CENTER DEAF-BLIND RSA | 0 | 400 | 600 | 500 | 500 | 500 | 500 | 3000 |

Source: Department of Health, Education and Welfare, Office of the Assistant Secretary (Planning and Evaluation), *Planning-Programming-Budgeting: Guidance for Program and Financial Plan*, rev. April 17, 1968 (Washington, D.C.: U.S. Government Printing Office, 1968), p. 5.

Third, for an activity classified as an "existing program . . . expected to continue," it is a matter of judgment to decide what it means to show "the current level," to decide what "uncontrollable workload" requires, and to decide what changes in the current level should be introduced and given "explicit justification." With respect to the Federal Trade Commission, for example, does showing the "current level" mean holding constant the number of complaints per year, the amount of delay in adjudication, the percentage of violations caught, the number of advertisements and mergers examined, the current budget, the number of professional employees and their support, or what? Does an uncontrollable increase in the number of companies, or in the number of ads or mergers, require a change in expenditures? Should mislabeling be added to coverage or interlocking directorates subtracted? The "current level," "uncontrollable" changes, and "explicit justification" are not simple concepts.

Fourth, how uncertainty is to be recognized is a matter of judgment. Should inflation be anticipated? If so, how much? Should the funding levels be given in current or constant dollars? Should the uptrend in construction costs relative to other costs be incorporated? Which population forecast should be used? What level of unemployment should be assumed? How do you decide how many changes will be made in designing a supersonic transport? Should you enter an optimistic guess, a best guess, a pessimistic guess?

Perhaps new instructions will be issued to clarify these ambiguities. Meanwhile, all we know is that we do not know what the figures shown for future expenditures really mean. What is more important, neither do the decision-makers.

## THE BENEFITS OF MULTI-YEAR COSTING

Here, too, the benefits supposedly are better decisions, in particular, more frequent rejection of programs whose costs would outweigh their benefits. Again the case is supported by explanation as distinct from evidence.

In the absence of multi-year costing, proponents of major new activities need not analyze future requirements carefully. They can "sell" their programs more effectively if initial expenditures are deceptively small.

> The program budget [promises] to provide better information that is better organized for better decision making. . . .
> One of the characteristics of better decisions will be . . .

illumination of the long-range cost implications of proposals with relatively painless initial expenses, and consequent harder screening with [a] higher rejection rate.[4]

This explanation of why multi-year costing will increase the rate of rejection for programs not worth their cost, along with every other explanation that we have seen, is incomplete. Let us try to fill out the argument.

There seem to be five steps. (1) Some programs not worth their cost will receive multi-year costing. (2) Decision-makers will see the expenditures predicted for some or all of these programs. (3) Otherwise, they would not have known as much about future expenditures. (4) Learning more about future expenditures will lead the decision-makers to reject a larger number of the programs not worth their cost. (5) Other things will be equal, that is, the same programs and current expenditures will be proposed, the same ones will not be worth their cost, and the ones that are worthwhile will have the same rate of acceptance.

These statements are not verifiable. Since whether a program is worth its cost is a matter of judgment, there is no objective way to identify programs that are not. Accordingly, there is no way to test whether the rejection rate of such programs increases. One can, however, say something—two things, in fact.

First, it is unlikely that the rejection rate will increase for the whole set of programs for which predicted expenditures are to be shown in the PFP. These are not programs likely to be rejected because of their future costs; they are existing programs "expected to continue." There is no reason to believe that any more would be rejected because of multi-year costing. For example, might the FTC, the Judiciary, or the Bureau of the Budget be rejected when their predicted expenditures are shown? Funds for these agencies either are required because of previous commitments or are justified by benefits that will accrue whether or not the programs are continued beyond the budget year.

Second, it would be foolish to reject such programs now because of their future costs. Where no new commitment is involved and where the

---

[1]Roland N. McKean and Melvin Anshen, "Limitations, Risks, and Problems," in Lyden and Miller, *Planning Programming Budgeting,* pp. 355–57. Hitch indicates that the short view formerly prevailed in the Defense Department. He explains. "Because attention was focused on only the next fiscal year, the services had every incentive to propose large numbers of 'new starts,' the full cost dimensions of which would only become apparent in subsequent years. [I]t is essential that the decision-makers have before them the total cost implications of alternatives—not only total in the sense of cutting across appropriation categories, but also in the sense of being projected forward over a five-year period." See Charles J. Hitch, *Decision Making for Defense* (Berkeley: University of California Press, 1965), pp. 24ff.

benefits are not a product of current and future expenditures, the appropriate question is not whether the expenditures predicted for the next five years are worthwhile, but whether the expenditures proposed for the budget year are worthwhile. If the budget-year expenditures are worthwhile, they should be approved regardless of what is predicted for the following years. If the future expenditures are not worthwhile, they can be canceled in the future. They are not "future implications of current decisions." Multi-year costing where no new commitment is involved, and where the benefits from current expenditures are not conditional on future expenditures, simply diverts attention from where it belongs.

## THE COSTS OF MULTI-YEAR COSTING

Multi-year costing entails preparation costs—the time and paper that will be consumed in making and tabulating predictions of future expenditures —and rigidification costs, the consequences of reducing flexibility.

As far as we know, no estimates are available of the magnitude of preparation costs, but it is obvious that they are not negligible. Rigidification costs involve estimates previously made. Appropriations may be held to earlier estimates, forcing the elimination of part of the program if the original cost estimates prove to be too low. Or, the choices recorded in the original program may be narrowly adhered to despite newer evidence favoring some of the alternatives. As McKean puts it: "There is a sort of Gresham's law of programming: whatever is recorded . . . tends to drive out the other options, and the longer the period covered, the greater the extent to which decisions based on little information drive out decisions based on more information."[5]

To incur these costs with respect to ongoing programs is a strange decision when multi-year costing is not likely to increase the rate of rejection for such activities and will divert attention from whether their budget-year expenditures are worthwhile.

## AN ALTERNATIVE TO UBIQUITY

Multi-year costing could be done, not for all programs, but for selected programs—or rather for selected decisions. In particular, multi-year costing might be used only for discussions for which it seems helpful to know what expenditures are being implied for the future.

[5] Roland N. McKean, *Public Spending* (New York: McGraw-Hill, 1968), p. 153.

There seem to be two types of present decisions for which it would be helpful to know future expenditures, namely, decisions that create a commitment and decisions that find justification in benefits that are a joint product of current and future expenditures. We will discuss the two types in turn.

First, knowing future expenditures would be helpful if the present decision would create a commitment to make expenditures in the future (or would give up the opportunity to rescind a commitment made earlier). For example, if the present decision relates to introducing, continuing, or expanding a subsidy such as price supports, depletion allowances, or family allowances, a commitment is involved to provide for every person who is eligible. Similarly, if the decision relates to introducing, continuing, or expanding supervisory activities such as prohibition, meat inspection, or trust funds, a commitment is being made for enforcement or administration. In these cases, future expenditures indeed are "implications of current decisions," and knowing the future expenditures implied by the commitment could be helpful in deciding whether or not to undertake it. In principle, the commitment involved might be a moral or psychological obligation as well as a legal one, but to simplify identification and reduce costs, multi-year costing might be undertaken only where legal commitments are being created.

In such cases the appropriate form for multi-year costing seems fairly clear. The objective would be to estimate the savings that rejection of the commitment would produce. In the case of subsidies (as with price supports), the savings will consist of payments the commitment would require; therefore, a prediction must be made as to how many people would be eligible. In the case of enforcement or administration (as with meat inspection), since workload can be varied the savings will depend on the level or intensity chosen, and the appropriation proposed for a representative year can be used. Fixed or joint costs (such as the salary of the Attorney General) that are likely to be incurred whether or not the commitment is undertaken should be omitted. If the commitment would extend indefinitely into the future, the focus might well be not on the next five years, but on the year in which set-up costs will be incurred, on the nearest year after that in which all provisions of the commitment would become effective, and on the rate of growth in expenditures thereafter. For each of these amounts, uncertainty can be acknowledged by presenting, not a single figure, but an optimistically low figure, a best guess, and a pessimistically high figure.

Second, knowing future expenditures appears to be helpful in reaching a present decision if the expenditures that the decision would authorize would not be justified unless it were possible to continue expenditures for the project in the future. For example, getting started on a dam or an antiballistic missile would not be worthwhile unless the work could be completed in the future. In these cases, future expenditures are not "implications of current decisions," because the future expenditures may never be authorized. Nevertheless, virtually no benefits will emerge unless the project becomes operational, and knowing the total expenditures required—to make the project operational and to operate it—could help people to decide whether or not to initiate it.[6]

The class of decisions at issue in this second case is not easy to define operationally. In principle, any current expenditure whose benefits can be enlarged by future expenditures might be one that would not be justified unless the future expenditures were possible. However, the class clearly does include multi-year investments. For such projects, virtually no benefits would emerge unless expenditures were continued in future years. To simplify identification and reduce costs, multi-year costing might be made routine for multi-year investments, and be made discretionary for the remainder of the class.

Here, too, the appropriate form for multi-year costing seems clear intuitively. The most helpful figures to produce would seem to be the annual expenditures needed to complete the project as currently designed, together with representative annual operating expenses. And here, too, three kinds of estimates might well be presented—optimistically low estimates, best guesses, and pessimistically high estimates. Anticipated changes in relative prices, but not inflation, should be incorporated in order to maintain comparability with current expenditures.

The alternative of selective multi-year costing just outlined appears to dominate the version required by the federal instructions. To predict

---

[6]McKean reaches the same conclusion by a different route: "[F]uture costs are not always inevitable once the activity has been started for they may still be avoided by cancellation of the activity. Nonetheless, the future costs are often implied." Once a sizable sum has been invested, the likelihood that the additional benefits of the program will compare favorably with the additional costs is usually much increased. Therefore, an estimate of the total and not just the initial costs should be made before any funds are committed, "just as the probable full costs should be recognized . . . when . . . making decisions about building a house. . . ."

Earlier, McKean and Anshen reached a different conclusion, namely, that predicted expenditures should not be shown for activities which are not permanent. Their reasoning was as follows: The desire to avoid having to reopen an issue may lead to one-shot decisions being made in situations that call for a sequence of decisions and this should be avoided. "Whenever commitments should be postponed, it would be better not to record tentative decisions in the official programs." As an example of a case where commitments should be postponed, they cite the development of facilities for the conversion of salt water into fresh. "Choices about research, . . . the advanced development of facilities and investment in specific operational installations ought to be a sequence of decisions." See McKean, *Public Spending*, p. 131, and McKean and Anshen. "Limitations, Risks, and Problems," pp. 349, 354.

future expenditures for only the two kinds of decisions mentioned above would be much less burdensome than to predict them for all decisions or programs. There would be preparation costs or a reduction in flexibility for many fewer decisions. The benefits to be obtained, on the other hand, would seem to be as large; this will be true if we are right in saying that multi-year costing is helpful only when a commitment is being created or when current expenditures find justification in benefits that are products of both current and future expenditures, since these are the two kinds of decisions for which future expenditures would be predicted under our selective approach.

Whether even selective multi-year costing is worth its cost, however, must be regarded as an open question until more evidence becomes available.

# Four

# DETAILED DESCRIPTION AND MEASUREMENT OF ACTIVITIES

The third distinguishing feature of PPB is provision of a detailed description of each program. In this chapter we discuss what detailed description involves, what its asserted benefits are, and what its apparent costs are.

## THE NATURE OF DETAILED DESCRIPTION

Under the federal rules, six aspects of a program are supposed to be described in addition to its expenditures—objectives, targets, choices made, alternatives considered, outputs, and effectiveness.

Conceptually, the six features are distinct. *Objectives* are long-range goals. They identify the benefits being sought. For example, one objective of a program might be to increase poor people's earning capacity. Some objectives of the Department of Transportation are given in Table 4.1. *Targets* are quantified goals to be aimed at in the short run; for example, to increase the incomes of 100 ghetto dwellers next year. One expects targets to be selected in the light of the obstacles or costs that prevent instant or total attainment of objectives. *Choices made* are courses of action that have been selected; for example, to train 100 Los Angeles dropouts to be practical nurses. *Alternatives considered* are courses of action that were recognized but rejected; for example, to train 100 Sacramento tomato pickers to operate tractors. *Outputs* are immediate results; for example, preparing 50 people to do the work of practical nurses. Some examples of output measures used in the Department of Health, Education and Welfare are given in Table 4.2. *Effectiveness* is the degree to which objectives or targets are attained. For ex-

TABLE 4.1. "GOALS AND OBJECTIVES" IN THE U.S.
DEPARTMENT OF TRANSPORTATION

A.  Economic efficiency in transportation
B.  Optimal use of environmental resources
C.  Safety
D.  Support of other national interests
    1.  National defense
    2.  Economic growth
    3.  Social development
    4.  Advancement of scientific research

Source: U.S. Department of Transportation, *Goals and Objectives,* May 19, 1968 (Washington, D.C.: U.S. Government Printing Office, 1968), pp. 1, 7.

ample, effectiveness might consist of increased incomes for 25 of 100 trainees. Effectiveness reflects the worth of output. As the Bureau of the Budget states, "[A] program which showed 'low output'—in terms of the numbers of workers trained—might be more effective . . . because it was better taught, or focused on skills in shorter supply, than a program that showed a higher 'output'"[1] Further output measures in HEW are displayed in Table 4.3.

The Bureau clearly distinguishes among choices made, alternatives considered, output, and effectiveness, and it requires that agencies describe all four; it does not so clearly distinguish between objectives and targets, but it does seem to indicate that both of them also should be described. The instructions declare:

> The Program Memoranda should outline the broad program strategy . . . for the future years . . . They define long-range goals and objectives and anticipated program accomplishments. With respect to the *annual* budget . . . the Program Memoranda [should show] *what* choices have been made [and] make clear *why* particular choices have been made, by identifying agency objectives in a measurable way, and comparing alternative programs in terms of their costs and their achievement of the objectives. [T]he PFP will display outputs—that is, a quantitative measure of end products or services produced by a program element. Where it is meaningful to do so, outputs should be aggregated by subcategory and category. [W]herever meaningful measures of achievement and effectiveness are available . . . the PFP should display them [too]. In certain cases, such as research programs,

[1] U.S. Bureau of the Budget, "Bulletin No. 68-2, July 18, 1967," in Freemont J. Lyden and Ernest G. Miller, eds., *Planning Programming Budgeting: A Systems Approach to Management* (Chicago: Markham, 1968), p. 436.

# TABLE 4.2. OUTPUTS, DEPARTMENT OF HEALTH, EDUCATION AND WELFARE

| CATEGORY BUDGET CODE | ACT CODE | UNIT OF MEASURE | 1967 | 1968 | 1969 | 1970 | 1971 | 1972 | 1973 |
|---|---|---|---|---|---|---|---|---|---|
| 028210 | | HANDI PRESCHOOL+SCH | | | | | | | |
| | | CHILDREN SERVED | 0 | 33330 | 83330 | 163934 | 233333 | 288000 | 331928 |
| | | ADDITIONAL EXPENDITURE PER CHILD | 0 | 600 | 600 | 610 | 610 | 625 | 625 |
| | | PERCENT OF CURRENTLY UNSERVED HANDICAPPED CHILDREN SERVED | | 1.1 | 2.6 | 5.2 | 7.4 | 9.2 | 10.5 |
| 028220 | | HANDI TEACHER EDUCA | | | | | | | |
| | | PROGRAM DEVELOP. GRANTS FOR PROFESSIONAL TRAINING | 65 | 65 | 98 | 145 | 159 | 159 | 159 |
| | | NEW PERSONNEL TRAINED | 3760 | 3760 | 5692 | 8300 | 8880 | 8727 | 8570 |
| | | PERCENT OF TEACHER SHORTAGE MET | 2.2 | 2.5 | 3.7 | 5.6 | 6.3 | 6.6 | 6.9 |
| | | TEACHERS RECEIVING INSERVICE TRAINING | 7800 | 7800 | 12487 | 18562 | 20249 | 20249 | 20249 |
| | | PERCENT OF INSERVICE TRAINING NEED MET | 53 | 50 | 73.0 | 91.0 | 84.0 | 74.6 | 66.0 |
| | | PROG. DEVELOP. GRANTS FOR SUBPROFESSIONAL TRAINING | 0 | 0 | 8 | 14 | 16 | 16 | 16 |
| | | SUBPROFESSIONALS TRAINED | 0 | 0 | 3960 | 7720 | 15638 | 27100 | 30500 |
| | | PERCENT OF SUBPROFESSIONAL NEED | 0 | 0 | 9.3 | 19.1 | 36.0 | 60.0 | 75.0 |
| 028230 | | HANDI RESEARCH + DEMO | | | | | | | |
| | 1 | RESEARCHERS SUPPORTED PERCENT MAN YEARS | 314 | 433 | 546 | 708 | 810 | 891 | 1013 |
| | 2 | R + D CENTERS SUPPORTED | 16 | 17 | 17 | 20 | 23 | 23 | 23 |
| 028250 | | HANDI INSTRUC MATER | | | | | | | |
| | 1 | R+D CONTRACTS | 6 | 6 | 16 | 26 | 28 | 30 | 30 |
| | 3 | TEACHERS TRAINED | 85 | 90 | 170 | 266 | 285 | 304 | 304 |
| | 4 | UNITS OF MATERIAL DISTRIBUTED | 43000 | 45500 | 86112 | 134000 | 144000 | 153600 | 153600 |
| 028260 | 4 | HANDI REG RESOUR CEN / SCHOOL CHILDREN SERVED | 30000 | 35000 | 71311 | 111300 | 119250 | 127200 | 127200 |
| | | CENTERS ESTABLISHED | | | 4 | 4 | 2 | 0 | 0 |
| | | CENTERS SUPPORTED | | | 0 | 4 | 8 | 10 | 10 |
| 028270 | | HANDI PERSONNEL+INFO | | | | | | | |
| | | CONTRACTS AWARDED | | | 16 | 16 | 16 | 16 | 16 |
| L26100 | 7 | HANDIC-INNOVA PROG / PLANNING GRANTS | | | 5 | 5 | 10 | 15 | 20 |

Source: Department of Health, Education and Welfare, Office of the Assistant Secretary (Planning and Evaluation), *Planning-Programming-Budgeting: Guidance for Program and Financial Plan*, Rev. April 17, 1968 (Washington, D.C.: U.S. Government Printing Office, 1968), p. 9.

## TABLE 4.3. OUTPUT AND EFFECTIVENESS INDICATORS

| PROGRAM | OPERATIONS INDICATOR | PROGRAM IMPACT INDICATOR |
|---|---|---|
| Construction of public libraries | number of libraries built<br>number of libraries remodeled or expanded<br>square feet constructed (in thousands)<br>as a percent of needed construction | population using libraries once or more per year (millions) |
| Adult basic education | number of participants<br>number completing courses<br><br>number of teachers trained<br>percent of target population enrolled | employment rate of students completing courses<br><br>illiteracy by (adult) age group, ethnic group |
| Educationally deprived children (ESEA I) | number of school districts receiving aid, by median family income<br>number of pupils participating in Title I projects (in millions)<br><br>number of special teachers enrolled in training<br>number of teachers added through Title I project funds<br>number of teacher-aides added thru Title I project funds | increase over previous year in per pupil expenditure of aided schools<br>dropout rates of school districts receiving aid compared to average drop-out rates of all school districts<br><br>average increases in achievement test results in school districts receiving aid |
| Manpower resources | students supported (by profession)<br><br>percent of program output (by profession) to national output<br>first year places provided (by profession) by construction grants | population-physician ratio<br>physician-nurse-aid ratio<br>population-dentist ratio<br>dentist-technician ratio |
| Disease prevention and control (by specific disease factors) | number of persons covered by program<br><br>number of persons covered<br>diagnosed<br>treated<br>cured | morbidity and mortality for each factor (national)<br><br>number of productive years added to population served (for each factor) |

TABLE 4.3. *(Continued)*

| PROGRAM | OPERATIONS INDICATOR | PROGRAM IMPACT INDICATOR |
|---|---|---|
| | percent of persons covered diagnosed treated cured | disease incidence disease prevalence |
| Health services crippled child maternity and infant care school and pre-school maternal and child health family planning migrant health | number of assisted or receiving services percent of total eligible (or in need) | morbidity and mortality diseases for beneficiary groups: (plus) infant mortality birth defects-(major) change in average family size group aided unwanted children avoided |
| Old age assistance | aged recipients average monthly assistance payment average caseload per case-worker aged recipients with no other income | percent of recipients to poverty-level aged population |
| Old age insurance | retired workers receiving payments at mid-FY average monthly benefit payment (retired worker) total recipients of OAI average monthly benefit payment (All OAI recipients) | recipients below the poverty line recipients kept above the poverty line by benefit payments |
| Aid to families with dependent children (basic program) | children aided adults aided average monthly payments per family (by HEW region) average caseload per case-worker (by HEW region) average length of time on assistance (by HEW region) | percent of recipients to poverty level family population percent of family cases closed 25 self-sufficient percent of monthly assistance payments to poverty income level |

TABLE 4.3. *(Continued)*

| PROGRAM | OPERATIONS INDICATOR | PROGRAM IMPACT INDICATOR |
|---|---|---|
| Aid to families with dependent children (unemployed father) | same as basic program plus:<br><br>number of states with AFDC-UF plans<br><br>number of recipient parents in work training | percent of recipient parents to total unemployed poverty level parent population |

Source: Department of Health, Education and Welfare, Office of the Assistant Secretary (Planning and Evaluation), *Planning-Programming-Budgeting: Guidance for Program and Financial Plan,* Rev. April 17, 1968 (Washington, D.C.: U.S. Government Printing Office, 1968), pp. 135–42.

where meaningful measures of output cannot be defined, the best available quantitative nonfinancial description of the program should be used (e.g., the number of projects . . .).[2]

The six features have different reference periods. Output and effectiveness refer to the fiscal year just past. Choices made and alternatives considered refer to the budget year. Targets and objectives refer to the current year, the budget year, and at least four future years.[3]

To understand the application of these detailed description categories, it would be useful to refer to the program package and elements of an agency. The Department of Agriculture's Program Categories, perhaps the most flamboyant, are shown in Table 4.4. The objective of Program Category I, "Income and Abundance," is "to improve the performance of the American agricultural industry to assure that consumers have adequate supplies of food and fiber at reasonable prices, while farmers receive a fair return on their capital and labor." Its first subcategory consists of activities aimed at maintaining or increasing farmers' income; the second has the objective of "improving the productivity of agriculture and the conservation and maintenance of the resource base." The third, "agricultural marketing and distribution system," includes programs designed to improve "the efficiency and performance of all phases of marketing and distributing agricultural products." "Growing Nations—New Markets" is the second category and other imaginative titles are "Dimensions for Living," and "Communities of Tomorrow."

Tables 4.5, 4.6, and 4.7 show an actual PFP for seven years in the urban transportation category of the Department of Transportation.

[2] "Bulletin No. 68-2," pp. 432–36.
[3] Actually, it is outputs, not targets and objectives, that the federal instructions say should be specified for the current year, the budget year, and at least four future years. Outputs not yet produced, however, are equivalent to targets. See "Bulletin No. 68-2," p. 434.

## TABLE 4.4. USDA PROGRAM CATEGORIES

I.  Income and abundance
    A.  Farm income
        1.  Price support activities
        2.  Crop land diversion programs
        3.  Farm ownership loans and farm operating loans
        4.  Crop insurance
        5.  Related research and extension
    B.  Agricultural production capacity
        1.  Plant and animal disease and pest control programs
        2.  Soil and water conservation programs
        3.  Production efficiency research
        4.  Cost-sharing for land development
        5.  Federal range land maintenance activities of the Forest Service
        6.  Related research and technical assistance
    C.  Agricultural marketing and distribution system
II.  Growing nations—new markets
    A.  Food for Freedom—sales and donations of American agricultural products to lesser developed countries
    B.  Export market development—the foreign trade fairs and other market promotion activities carried out to expand foreign markets for U.S. agricultural products
    C.  Agricultural development—the technical assistance work done in cooperation with the Agency for International Development
    D.  International agricultural services—the agricultural attache service
    E.  Imports—the inspection services operated at posts-of-entry to assure that imports of foreign animals and agricultural products are not introducing diseases or pests detrimental to domestic varieties
III.  Dimensions for living
    A.  Diets and nutrition
        1.  Food Stamp Program
        2.  School Lunch Program
        3.  Direct distribution of commodities through local welfare agencies
    B.  Health
        1.  Meat and poultry inspection
        2.  Pesticide research and regulation
        3.  Defense mobilization
        4.  Civil defense
    C.  Education and training
        1.  The Job Corps Centers—Forest Service
        2.  The 4-H Clubs—Extension Service
    D.  Service for living
        1.  Clothing and textiles
        2.  Improved food products
IV.  Communities of tomorrow
    A.  Community development services—loan and grant programs to help local communities to plan and install water and sewer systems
    B.  Housing—loans and grants for housing
    C.  Public facility and business expansion—loans for electric and telephone systems

TABLE 4.4. *(Continued)*

---

   D.  Resource protection and environmental improvement
     1.  Multi-purpose land management
     2.  Other natural resource conservation and development
   E.  Recreation, wildlife and natural beauty—Forest Service recreation and wildlife programs
   F.  Timber
V.  General support—those expenses which cannot be realistically allocated to other programs
   A.  Office of the Secretary
   B.  Department Staff Offices
   C.  General Counsel's Office
   D.  Inspector General's Office
   E.  National Agricultural Library
   F.  Some central service operations

---

Source: William A. Carlson, *The Planning-Programming-Budgeting System* (Washington, D.C.: U.S. Department of Agriculture, 1968).

Table 4.5 gives expected outputs and benefits of subcategories and program elements. Table 4.6 shows budget authority by program element. Finally, Table 4.7 gives planned funding by commitment class such as statutory formula, and new programs requiring legislation.

There is an important difference between an activity, operations, or output indicator and a program impact, effectiveness, or success indicator. The first gives an indication of the level of effort at which a program is being run. The second is more interesting, but unfortunately more difficult to define and measure. In adult basic education, the second program element in the education section of Table 4.3, we find a good example of the difference between an activity indicator and an effectiveness indicator. Having participants in classes is the activity. The number in classes is a quantitative measure of the level of effort of that activity. Being in class is not valued for itself, however. It is valuable only if it leads to literacy or employment, the true objectives of the program. Thus the employment rates of students completing the courses and literacy rates are measures of output. It is possible to have many students in classes of poor quality which do not result in effects desired by program formulators. Then we would have a situation of a high activity level with low effectiveness.

## THE BENEFITS OF DETAILED DESCRIPTION

The benefits description yields are, again, supposedly better decisions. And again the case is wholly a priori. It relates to high-level adminis-

# TABLE 4.5. OUTPUTS AND BENEFITS

FISCAL YEAR 1970 PROGRAM AND FINANCIAL PLAN
PROGRAM CATEGORY 1—URBAN TRANSPORTATION

| | FISCAL YEAR— | | | | | | |
|---|---|---|---|---|---|---|---|
| | 1968 | 1969 | 1970 | 1971 | 1972 | 1973 | 1974 |
| **A. Highways:** | | | | | | | |
| 1. Interstate system: | | | | | | | |
| Outputs: Lane miles | 1,550 | 1,550 | 1,550 | 1,550 | 1,550 | 1,550 | 1,550 |
| Benefits: | | | | | | | |
| Added daily VMT carried (1,000's) | 16,840 | 17,260 | 17,690 | 18,135 | 18,590 | 19,050 | 17,640 |
| Range of fatalities prevented | 50–86 | 51–88 | 52–90 | 53–92 | 54–95 | 57–95 | 52–90 |
| Accidents prevented | 14,945 | 15,315 | 51,700 | 16,085 | 16,475 | 16,890 | 15,650 |
| 2. Other primary: | | | | | | | |
| Outputs: Lane miles | 360 | 365 | 370 | | | | |
| Benefits: | | | | | | | |
| Added daily VMT carried (1,000's) | 5,170 | 5,320 | 5,385 | | | | |
| Fatalities prevented | 35 | 35 | 40 | | | | |
| Accidents prevented | 3,799 | 4,145 | 4,190 | | | | |
| 3. Secondary system: | | | | | | | |
| Outputs: Lane miles | 350 | 375 | 375 | | | | |
| Benefits: | | | | | | | |
| Added daily VMT carried (1,000's) | 1,805 | 1,920 | 1,920 | | | | |
| Fatalities prevented | 13 | 14 | 14 | | | | |
| Accidents prevented | 1,440 | 1,525 | 1,525 | | | | |
| 4. Urban extensions: | | | | | | | |
| Outputs: Lane miles | 1,085 | 1,225 | 1,225 | | | | |
| Benefits: | | | | | | | |
| Added daily VMT carried (1,000's) | 8,245 | 8,900 | 8,900 | | | | |
| Fatalities prevented | 60 | 65 | 65 | | | | |
| Accidents prevented | 6,495 | 6,950 | 6,950 | | | | |
| 5. TOPICS | | | | | | | |
| 6. Railway-highway grade crossing elimination: | | | | | | | |
| Outputs: Crossings improved | 237 | 214 | 292 | | | | |
| Benefits: Estimated fatalities prevented | 45 | 50 | 60 | | | | |
| 7. Roadside hazard reduction; spot improvement: | | | | | | | |
| Outputs: | | | | | | | |
| Miles of highway reconstruction to acceptable standards | 995 | 1,037 | 1,037 | | | | |
| Projects completed | 45 | 104 | 104 | | | | |
| Benefits: Range of accident reductions (thousands) | 5–15 | 5–15 | 5–15 | | | | |
| 8. Roadside beautification; billboard and junkyard removal: | | | | | | | |
| Outputs: | | | | | | | |
| Number of billboards removed | 70 | | 920 | | | | |
| Number of junkyards screened or removed | 195 | | 300 | | | | |
| 9. Relocation assistance: | | | | | | | |
| Outputs: Number of displacements | | 43,045 | 43,045 | | | | |
| 10. Metropolitan area planning: | | | | | | | |
| Outputs: Number of studies | 205 | 210 | 215 | | | | |
| 11. Advance acquisition of rights-of-way: | | | | | | | |
| Outputs: Number of States using advanced funds | | 17 | 32 | | | | |

## TABLE 4.6. BUDGET AUTHORITY

### (in thousands of dollars)

| | FISCAL YEAR— | | | | | | |
|---|---|---|---|---|---|---|---|
| | 1968 | 1969 | 1970 | 1971 | 1972 | 1973 | 1974 |
| A. Highways: | | | | | | | |
| 1. Insterstate system | 1,428,300 | 1,460,500 | 1,460,500 | 1,600,000 | 1,600,000 | 900,000 | |
| 2. Other primary | 56,900 | 58,500 | 58,500 | | | | |
| 3. Secondary system | 57,300 | 60,400 | 60,400 | | | | |
| 4. Urban extension | 182,000 | 194,200 | 194,200 | | | | |
| 5. TOPICS | | 180,000 | 180,000 | | | | |
| 5. Railway-highway grade crossings | 25,900 | 19,800 | 19,800 | | | | |
| 7. Roadside hazard reduction and spot improvement | 77,800 | 81,900 | 81,900 | | | | |
| 8. Roadside beautification, and billboard and junkyard regulation | 400 | 9,500 | 25,900 | | | | |
| 9. Relocation assistance | | 35,900 | 35,900 | | | | |
| 10. Metropolitan area planning | 21,900 | 18,800 | 18,800 | | | | |
| 11. Advance acquistion of rights-of-way | | 40,000 | 40,000 | | | | |
| Subtotal subcategory A | (1,850,500) | (2,159,500) | (2,175,900) | (1,600,000) | (1,600,000) | (900,000) | ( ) |
| B. Urban mass transit: | | | | | | | |
| 1. Present program | | 168,484 | 252,898 | 303,000 | 3,000 | 3,000 | 3,000 |
| 2. Legislation | | | | | 400,000 | 500,000 | 600,000 |
| Subtotal, subcategory B | ( ) | (168,484) | (252,898) | (303,000) | (403,000) | (503,000) | (603,000) |
| Total, category | 1,850,500 | 2,327,984 | 2,428,798 | 1,903,000 | 2,003,000 | 1,403,000 | 603,000 |

TABLE 4.7. PROGRAM LEVEL BY COMMITMENT CLASS, BUDGET AUTHORITY

(in millions of dollars)

| | FISCAL YEAR— | | | | | | |
|---|---|---|---|---|---|---|---|
| | 1968 | 1969 | 1970 | 1971 | 1972 | 1973 | 1974 |
| 1. Statutory formula: Coast Guard retired pay | 48.2 | 52.4 | 55.7 | 58.5 | 61.4 | 64.4 | 67.4 |
| 2. Workload level | | | | | | | |
| 3. Market-oriented programs | | | | | | | |
| 4. New programs requiring legislation: | | | | | | | |
| Mass transit | | | 5.0 | 300.0 | 400.0 | 500.0 | 600.0 |
| Boating safety | | | 5.0 | | | | |
| SLS lock repair | | 13.1 | | | | | |
| Airport development | | | 95.0 | | | | |
| Air revenue program | | | 170.0 | | | | |
| Subtotal, line 4 | (—) | (13.1) | (275.0) | (300.0) | (400.0) | (500.0) | (600.0) |
| 5. Administration commitments: | | | | | | | |
| Interstate highway grants | 3,526.6 | 3,691.8 | 3,680.2 | 4,000.0 | 4,000.0 | 2,225.0 | |
| Other highway grants | 1,335.4 | 1,883.0 | 2,003.5 | | | | |
| Highway safety grants | 100.0 | 75.0 | 100.0 | | | | |
| Mass transit | | 168.5 | 175.0 | | | | |
| Airports grants (current program) | 66.0 | 70.0 | 30.0 | | | | |
| Subtotal, line 5 | (5,028.0) | (5,888.3) | (5,988.7) | (4,000.0) | (4,000.0) | (2,225.0) | (—) |
| 6. Level of appropriations: | | | | | | | |
| (a) Capital acquisitions | 161.2 | 210.7 | 266.1 | 157.7 | 7.0 | 7.0 | 6.0 |
| (b) Operating programs | 1,109.2 | 1,245.8 | 1,490.3 | 1,414.8 | 1,418.2 | 1,414.0 | 1,408.2 |
| (c) Research and development | 187.3 | 51.2 | 478.8 | 264.4 | 142.8 | 34.0 | 12.0 |
| Subtotal, line 6 | (1,457.7) | (1,507.7) | (2,235.2) | (1,836.9) | (1,568.0) | (1,455.0) | (1,426.2) |
| Total, budget authority | 6,533.5 | 7,461.6 | 8,554.6 | 6,195.4 | 6,029.4 | 4,244.4 | 2,093.4 |

Source: U.S. Congress, Joint Economic Committee, *Analysis and Evaluation of Public Expenditures: The PPB System*, vol. 2 (Washington, D.C.: U.S. Government Printing Office, 1969), pp. 734–737.

trators, to low-level administrators, and to nonadministrative employees.

The decisions of high-level administrators might improve in several ways. According to McKean and Anshen, "One of the characteristics of better decisions will be identification and possible removal of overlapping and redundant activities. Another will be exposure of ineffective or inefficient employment of resources."[4] They do not go into detail, but we can guess the rest. Removal of redundant activities might follow from revealing that some programs have no output or no effectiveness. Removal of overlapping activities might follow from revealing that certain pairs of programs have purposes or objectives that are either identical or antagonistic. Exposure of ineffectiveness might follow from rating effectiveness or from comparing outputs with targets. Exposure of inefficiency might follow from disclosing what choices were made and what alternatives were available but rejected. For all of these reasons, operating decisions might receive better review.

Low-level administrators might be helped too. Discussing targets and costs in the same memorandum is conducive to recognizing that, as Enthoven put it: ". . . costs must be considered in choosing strategies and objectives. [T]he advantages of a somewhat more ambitious strategy [may or may not be] worth its somewhat greater cost."[5] "Precise specification of objectives," Chase adds, "is necessary if alternative methods of attaining the same goals are to be considered."[6] Procurement might be improved also. To specify targets in a measurable way could enable branch chiefs or section heads to, as McKean says,

> relate . . . ingredients to the desired outputs and therefore to make sound judgments about the amounts to buy. [I]f a bakery manager tried to decide how much flour, sugar, and butter to buy without linking these items to the amounts of bread and pastries to be produced, he would be handicapped in reaching good decisions.[7]

At the lowest level, the decisions that supposedly will be improved are more personal. A list of objectives is alleged to remind employees of what they are supposed to be after, and a list of purposes supposedly leads employees to work harder.

[4] Roland N. McKean and Melvin Anshen, "Limitations, Risks, and Problems," in Lyden and Miller, *Planning Programming Budgeting* p. 356.

[5] Alain Enthoven, "Systems Analysis and the Navy," in Lyden and Miller, *Planning Programming Budgeting*, p. 277.

[6] Samuel B. Chase, Jr., "Introduction and Summary," in Samuel B. Chase, Jr., ed., *Problems in Public Expenditure Analysis* (Washington, D.C.: The Brookings Institution, 1968), p. 1.

[7] Roland N. McKean, *Public Spending* (New York: McGraw Hill, 1968), p. 130.

The foregoing arguments strike us as imaginative—and improbable. Nevertheless, we find it plausible that some benefits occasionally will emerge as a consequence of describing five of the six features—targets, outputs, effectiveness, choices made, and alternatives considered.

Description of targets, outputs, and choices made seems to us likely to change, somewhat, that which emerges from the decision process. To describe targets for the current year, the budget year, and for several future years seems likely to clarify for high-level officials what it really is that their subordinates are trying to accomplish and what the average cost will be; doing so may lead the high-level officials more often to declare that what is being sought is not worth the cost. To describe output for the fiscal year just past—when this can be done meaningfully—will enable reviewers to compare previous targets with actual outputs and may help them to judge their subordinates' reliability and performance. To describe choices made for the budget year will help reviewers to know where and why subordinates exercised discretion; knowing this may help them to evaluate their subordinates' judgment and may encourage them to substitute their own choices. In each case, the tendency will be to make the decisions that emerge after review more like those that would have emerged if each reviewer could have made his subordinates' decisions in addition to his own. High-level officials presumably will view this result as an improvement. On balance we agree.

Similarly, description of last year's effectiveness and of alternatives considered for the budget year may produce occasional changes in decisions and proposals. Knowing that effectiveness will be described seems likely to encourage some operating officials to be more concerned about improving effectiveness—or the appearance of effectiveness. Description of alternatives considered may encourage people to give more attention to new ideas and occasionally to rock the boat. In the net, we like these tendencies.

On the other hand, the information about targets and outputs that is required by the federal instructions is not the kind that will facilitate choosing an appropriate scale for a program. Targets and outputs are to be shown for only one scale. Ths procedure may help reviewers to decide whether or not the scale selected is worth its cost, but it does not help them to decide whether they would prefer a somewhat larger or smaller scale. In the next chapter we describe a way of stating targets, outputs, and choices made that will also facilitate choice among alternative scales, and therefore will further help high-level officials to allocate funds among programs.

We should add that none of the benefits of detailed description mentioned above depends on the introduction of program accounting. For agencies as well as programs, personnel can undertake to describe targets, outputs, effectiveness, choices made, and alternatives considered.

We react quite differently to the idea of describing objectives. We find it implausible that anything beneficial will emerge. Agreement on a list of objectives is not necessary for agreement on targets or funding, and having a list of objectives is not likely to be helpful in conducting the program. The remainder of this discussion of the benefits of detailed description will explain this assertion.

Agreement on a statement of objectives is unnecessary because people can agree as to whether and how a program should be conducted even if they cannot agree as to why. For example, every legislator might agree that brush should be cleared in some area and that the work should be done at least cost; but one-third of the legislators might feel that the objective is to prevent wildfires, while two-thirds do not; another third might feel that the objective is to provide additional job opportunities for seasonal farm workers, while two-thirds do not; and the remaining third might feel that the objective is to make government an employer of last resort while two-thirds do not. The disagreement as to objectives is not critical. What matters is whether the legislators decide to appropriate funds for the program.

Furthermore, a statement of objectives is not likely to be helpful in deciding how to conduct a program. The statement is likely to be too vague to provide any guidance. For example, the first item in the list of objectives of the California Department of Agriculture is "To efficiently, economically, and faithfully fulfill the public trust."[8] Big help.

Vagueness seems likely to occur for two reasons. First, as in the brush-clearing example, supporters may not agree among themselves as to objectives. Second, being candid about objectives may be embarrassing or offensive, and it may also alert opponents and give them something specific to attack. Think, for example, of legislation concerning espionage, oil "conservation," civil rights, birth control, and aid to private schools.[9] For both of the above reasons, a statement of objectives is likely to consist of useless platitudes. Even a precise statement of objectives, however, would settle nothing. Decisions still would hinge on subjective judgments.

[8] California Director of Finance, *Sample Program Budgets for the Fiscal Year July 1, 1967 to June 30, 1968,* Sacramento (May 1, 1967), p. 7.

[9] Virginia Held puts it this way: "How honest can an agency be in declaring its intentions without getting into difficulties, how open about its criteria of evaluation? If the Department of Agriculture, for instance, is trying to shift a lot of people out of farming, would it be wise to advertise this objective?" See Virginia Held, "PPBS Comes to Washington," in Lyden and Miller, *Planning Programming Budgeting,* p. 15.

A precise statement would not settle how much money should be allocated to the program nor how ambitious should be its targets. How much money should be allocated to the program depends on what outputs and effectiveness would emerge if various amounts were to be spent—a question of fact—and on which increments in output and effectiveness the decision-makers feel are worth the extra money—a question of taste. How much output or effectiveness should be sought depends on how expenditures would change if various levels of output or effectiveness were to be sought—a matter of fact—and on which increments in expenditures the decision-maker feels are justified by the extra output of effectiveness—a matter of taste. Having a precise statement of objectives would not determine the appropriate scale.

Neither would having a precise statement of objectives settle how any given amount of money that might be allocated to the program should be spent. The various objectives will make conflicting demands. In other words, more than one spending pattern will exist that is efficient—efficient in the sense that there is no alternative pattern that would serve at least one objective better and serve no objective worse. Such conflicts can only be resolved arbitrarily. To demonstrate that one of the efficient patterns is best, one would need to quantify and weigh the extent to which an objective is served, and there is no "right" way to do this.[10]

In short, describing objectives has no effects that we regard as beneficial. In contrast, we anticipate that decisions preferred by high-level officials occasionally will emerge from describing targets, choices made, alternatives considered, outputs, and effectiveness, but we do not think that the format that has been adopted for these features is as beneficial as one to be proposed in Chapter 5.


## THE COSTS OF DETAILED DESCRIPTION

To provide a detailed description of activities consumes considerable time and effort—and paper. Unfortunately, no estimate of the magnitude of preparation costs seems to be available. With respect to describing objectives, however, even a qualitative indication may be helpful. If we are right in our view that having a statement of objectives yields no benefits, then the existence of any costs suffices to condemn it. Having a statement of objectives does entail costs, of two kinds.

[10] To conclude that a decision-maker should choose that one of the efficient patterns that has the greatest utility would add nothing. The pattern with the greatest utility means nothing more than the most preferred pattern. Such circularity does, however, make a pretty picture. The picture shows an isocost kissing an indifference curve.

First, a statement of objectives, even though it has no factual input and need not be prepared annually, does have periodic preparation and revision costs. Something that recently occurred in a particular school district will illustrate. The superintendent of schools, PPB manual in hand, succeeded in allocating the time of the Educational Objectives subcommittee of the district's Curriculum Council for the whole of the 1968-69 academic year to amplifying the district's brief statement of objectives. The subcommittee consisted of himself, two teachers, three parents, and a pupil. The time they spent this way could have been devoted instead, and we believe would have been had it not been for the directive of the PPB manual, to a project with some payoff, namely, to examining the variety, content, and sequencing of courses.[11]

Second, a statement of objectives may impair flexibility. For instance, the purposes of the Federal Reserve System, as stated in the preamble of the Federal Reserve Act of 1913, are "to furnish an elastic currency, to afford a means of rediscounting commercial paper, [and] to establish a more effective supervision of banking." Contracyclical monetary policy is conspicuously absent here. Few of us would want the system to be so limited today. But neither does it seem worthwhile to hold costly conferences and hearings in order to obtain a restatement. In this case, fortunately, everyone ignores the initial statement. Think, however, of trying to extend 4-H clubs into the ghettos in the face of a rural-oriented statement of objectives. A statement of objectives may become a nuisance later on.

We conclude that describing objectives is not worth the cost. We also conclude that describing targets, choices made, alternatives considered, output, and effectiveness may or may not be worth the cost; evidence is not in yet, and the current format is not necessarily the best one available.

[11] Perhaps occupying the subcommittee with this task "keeps them out of trouble" from the superintendent's point of view.

# Five

# ZERO-BASE BUDGETING

The fourth distinguishing feature of PPB is defense and review of the *total* expenditure proposed for a program, instead of the *changes* from its previous appropriation. As Hatry puts it: "PPBS will . . . tend to lessen the use of the current widespread practice . . . of giving excessive attention to the *changes* from the preceding year's budget with too little attention to a review of an agency's budget as a whole in the sense of reconsidering the value of existing programs."[1]

In this chapter we shall discuss the nature, benefits, and costs of zero-base budgeting and then present an alternative procedure that is more likely to facilitate choice among alternative scales for a program.

## THE NATURE OF ZERO-BASE BUDGETING

It is not really clear what quality or quantity of defense and review of a budget request is required in order to have zero-base budgeting. We have two authoritative sets of instructions, but neither one—we hope—was intended to be taken literally.

One set of instructions was issued by the Office of Budget and Finance of the U.S. Department of Agriculture. These instructions apparently grew out of a suggestion made to the Secretary of Agriculture by the Director of the Bureau of the Budget. Director Bell, in a letter dated August, 1961, said: "I think we should in a real sense reconsider the basic funding for each program—justify from zero in the budgetary

---

[1] Harry P. Hatry, "Considerations in Instituting a Planning-Programming-Budgeting System (PPBS) in State or Local Government," The George Washington University State and Local Finances Project, Washington, D.C. (October 7, 1966), p. 21.

phrase."[2] The USDA's instructions, which were issued in April 1962 and applied only to the budget then being prepared, state:

> All programs will be reviewed from the ground up and not merely in terms of changes proposed for the budget year. . . . Consideration must be given to the basic need for the work contemplated, the level at which the work should be carried out, the benefits to be received, and the costs to be incurred. . . . Program goals based on statutes enacted to meet problems or needs that today are of lesser priority must be re-evaluated. . . . The justifications should be prepared on the assumption that all information needed for making budget decisions should be included.[3]

The other relevant set of instructions was issued by the Bureau of the Budget and applied indefinitely and to various agencies. In the initial (1965) version, the Bureau declared: "The overall system is designed to enable each agency to [evaluate] thoroughly and compare the benefits and costs of programs.[4] A 1966 supplement explained: "It is important that the . . . Program Memoranda be prepared with as much attention paid to reducing and modifying obsolete and low priority programs as expanding others and introducing new ones."[5]

In the 1967 version, however, the Bureau recognized that "in some cases" agencies will not be able to provide a thorough defense of their requests. Nevertheless, it asked such agencies to do the best they could. The 1967 version states:

> The principal objective of PPB is to improve the basis for major program decisions. . . . The program categories used in each agency should provide a suitable framework for considering and resolving the major questions of mission and scale of operations. . . . The limits imposed by the availability of analytic staff resources or other circumstances may in some cases make it impossible to provide full treatment of alternatives and their analysis in each Program Memoranda. Such instances will diminish as the PPB system is developed. Nevertheless, since the Program Memoranda are to constitute the principal basis for major program decisions in the budget

[2] Aaron Wildavsky and Arthur Hammann, "Comprehensive Versus Incremental Budgeting in the Department of Agriculture," in Fremont J. Lyden and Ernest G. Miller, eds., *Planning Programming Budgeting: A Systems Approach to Management* (Chicago: Markham, 1968), p. 143.

[3] U.S. Department of Agriculture, Office of Budget and Finance, "Instructions for 1964 Agency Estimates" (April 1962), processed.

[4] U.S. Bureau of the Budget, "Bulletin No. 66-3, October 12, 1965," in Lyden and Miller, *Planning Programming Budgeting*, p. 407.

[5] U.S. Bureau of the Budget, "Supplement to Bulletin No. 66-3, February 21, 1966," in Lyden and Miller, *Planning Programming Budgeting*, p. 422.

review process, it is essential that such decisions . . . be recorded in the PM and that the reason . . . be stated.[6]

Perhaps the essence of zero-base budgeting is simply that an agency
provides a defense of its budget request that makes no reference to the
level of previous appropriations. If this is the nature of zero-base budgeting, it is not a new idea. Wildavsky and Hammann quote a proponent
of "justify from zero," E. Hilton Young, who wrote in 1924.[7] Of course,
some good ideas must wait their time. Let us see whether zero-base
budgeting is a good idea.

## THE BENEFITS OF ZERO-BASE BUDGETING

Here, too, the benefits are supposed to be better decisions. The working assumption of PPB is, as Schick says, "that all claims must be pitted
against one another."[8] The anticipated result, according to Fedkiw and
Hjort is "the determination of the proper balance of program effort."[9]

This time we have some evidence as to whether better—or rather
different—decisions do in fact emerge. In 1963 Wildavsky and Hammann
interviewed 57 "budget officers, directors or assistant directors, and
staff people in nearly every agency in the Department of Agriculture,
as well as department level officials . . . every person at a high level who
was intimately involved in the zero-base budget experiment." Few decisions could be attributed to the zero-base budget. An excess expenditure
for files was identified and a $100,000 reduction in an obsolete research
program was attributed to the zero-base budget, but in general very few
changes were due to its use.[10]

However, some unexpected byproducts turned up. The investiga-
tors report:

> [N]early half of those interviewed commented quite favorably
> on the experience after it was over. . . . For the large minority
> who expressed positive feelings about zero-base budgeting,
> the experience appears to have satisfied a longing to believe

[6]U.S. Bureau of the Budget, "Bulletin No. 68-2, July 18, 1967," in Lyden and Miller,
*Planning Programming Budgeting,* pp. 430, 431, 433.

[7]Quoted with evident approval by A. E. Buck in *The Budget in Governments of
Today* (New York: Macmillan, 1934), p. 172.

[8]Allen Schick, "The Road to PPB: The Stages of Budget Reform," in Lyden and
Miller, *Planning Programming Budgeting,* p. 42.

[9]John Fedkiw and Howard W. Hjort, "The PPB Approach to Research Evaluation,"
*Journal of Farm Economics* 49 (December 1967): 1428.

[10]Wildavsky and Hammann, "Comprehensive Versus Incremental Budgeting,"
pp. 142, 151, 161.

that they were proceeding according to the canons of rational methods of calculation.[11]

Those who felt they learned something new were likely to be new at their jobs. None had been in his position over three years. Looking at the budgetary data was for them a learning experience, but did not impart information appropriate to the decisions they were required to make. Perhaps those who felt the zero-base exercise was worthwhile were displaying the "Hawthorne effect" in which one's ego is enhanced when one is engaged in an experiment. Wildavsky and Hammann add "zero-base budgeting helped those who previously decided they wanted to review a program by providing them with [a] reason for not delaying, . . . with weapons which forced the disgorging of . . . information, [and with] the belief that the zero-base approach was more rational."[12]

In short, the side effects zero-base budgeting in the USDA gave to a substantial minority of officials were *feelings* that they were proceeding rationally, that others were interested in their opinions, that they were entitled to rock the boat, and (for new staff members) some background information. Whether even the side effects would exist if zero-base budgeting became an annual event, however, is doubtful. The authors further report, "No one suggested that the zero-base approach be followed every year."[13] The general conclusion of the Department was that it might be useful every five years.[14]

The central finding of Wildavsky and Hammann's study is that "there was widespread agreement that the zero-base budget did not significantly affect outcomes."[15] Any other finding would have been surprising. The purpose of zero-base budgeting is to discourage agency heads from taking program perpetuation for granted and to encourage them to reallocate funds as they think appropriate. However, we will show that zero-base

[11]Wildavsky and Hammann, "Comprehensive Versus Incremental Budgeting," p. 153.

[12]Wildavsky and Hammann, "Comprehensive Versus Incremental Budgeting," p. 156.

[13]Wildavsky and Hammann, "Comprehensive Versus Incremental Budgeting," p. 156.

[14]This was also Wildavsky and Hammann's conclusion. They state, "[A]ctivities which do not change much from year to year . . . are the ones that may escape periodic review. Since they do not alter radically, a thorough review every four or five years ought to be sufficient. . . . Department budget offices, the bureaus themselves, the Bureau of the Budget, and the House and Senate appropriations subcommittees and their investigating staffs, might . . . review a few programs . . . every year. . . . More active participation by high-level officials is encouraged because the material to be considered at a given time is not overwhelming." Wildavsky and Hammann, "Comprehensive Versus Incremental Budgeting," p. 158.

[15]Wildavsky and Hammann, "Comprehensive Versus Incremental Budgeting," p. 153.

budgeting makes an impossible demand of these men, provides no help in deciding whether the allocation of funds could be improved, and tells them to discard some information that might help.

First, it is not possible to justify a program's appropriation. To be sure, every activity has effects that can be called *outputs* or *benefits*. A case can be made even for aiding dictators, destroying farm products, and publishing a revised directory one week before a new Administration takes office. Furthermore, the asserted outputs or benefits ordinarily will increase with the size of the appropriation. To *justify* an appropriation, however, it is necessary to show that the benefits to be obtained outweigh the benefits that could be obtained by spending the same amount of money for other purposes or by cutting taxes. And this cannot be shown. No procedure is available that will show whether expenditures are or are not justified. The answer is a matter of subjective judgment. Appropriations cannot be justified; zero-base budgeting is wrong to presuppose that they can be.

Second, zero-base budgeting provides no help for agency heads in deciding whether the allocation of funds could be improved. A rational man does not decide that funds should be shifted from one program to another by noting the purposes and existing appropriations of the various programs.[16] The relevant question is whether the benefits to be lost where funds would be decreased outweigh the benefits to be gained where funds would be increased. The answer depends in part on what outputs would be lost and gained, and in part on the allocator's subjective judgment as to which outputs are more valuable. Ideally, funds should be allocated among program elements—therefore among program categories—in such a way that $1,000 could not be transferred from one element to another without losing something more valuable than would be gained. Since the outputs that would be lost and gained by reallocating funds are matters of fact, an information system can help budget-makers to choose among allocations. It can help them by telling them what changes in the quantity or quality of each program's output would occur if its funds were decreased or increased by specified amounts. Zero-base budgeting, however, does not produce this information.

Third, to exclude reference to previous years' appropriations is self-defeating. A request for funds whose relation to the current appropria-

---

[16] Referring to the broad purposes and existing appropriations of various programs seems to be what some advocates of PPB have in mind. Thus Lazarus states, "[T]here should be a tendency on the part of top management to move in the direction of control of aggregates and away from control by bits and pieces." See Steven Lazarus, "Planning-Programming-Budgeting Systems and Project PRIME," in Lyden and Miller, *Planning Programming Budgeting,* p. 368.

tion is unclear is needlessly hard to evaluate. The way a program operates currently is observable and is the subject of comment from various sources. Superior officials have an opportunity to judge the efficiency, effectiveness, and value of the program as presently conducted. Occasionally, they also find time to consider whether the quantity and quality of program output should be maintained at the current level or should be expanded or contracted.[17] If a request for funds is not expressed as a change from the current appropriation, reviewers cannot relate the request to their impressions of the program's current operations and cannot compare the request with their earlier conclusions as to an appropriate scale for the program. Furthermore, they cannot tell whether the request violates current imperatives as to increases in total spending, and they cannot decide for themselves whether the amount requested is more than enough to maintain program output and therefore involve new policy. Zero-base budgeting, however, rejects reference to previous appropriations.

For these reasons, the USDA experience can be extrapolated. Zero-base budgeting is not likely to produce a better allocation of funds.


## THE COSTS OF ZERO-BASE BUDGETING

An annual in-depth defense and review of every existing program would be very costly, in terms of both time and political effects. Zero-base budgeting takes time. Wildavsky and Hammann give us an idea of how much time the USDA effort consumed. It is, they say, a "conservative estimate that at least 1,000 administrators spent an average of thirty hours a week for six weeks.[18] The time involved presumably would have been less if zero-base budgeting had been a regular annual chore. Nevertheless, it seems clear that to demand more in the way of preparing and presenting reports and testimony can effect programs only adversely. It will increase staffs, and it will decrease the time that administrators devote to making programs more efficient and more effective. If the legislature, too, is involved, legislators will be spread thin over many programs and, as a result, will have less time to devote to programs that have received serious challenge and to new legislation. "Attempts to do

---

[17]The occasion usually arises when a relatively large increase in funds is requested. Wildavsky and Hammann tell us: "New programs and substantial increases in old programs . . . receive close attention." See Wildavsky and Hammann, "Comprehensive Versus Incremental Budgeting," p. 157.

[18]Wildavsky and Hammann, "Comprehensive Versus Incremental Budgeting," p. 161.

everything are not only self-defeating, they are inefficient in diverting resources from tasks which can be managed and give promise of some results."[19]

Political costs, too, will enter if zero-base budgeting annually re-opens policy questions, that is, if, as the USDA instructions indicate, statutes must be re-evaluated. If nothing is regarded as settled, attention will focus, not on progressing, but on not regressing. Interested parties and their lobbyists will feel obliged to demonstrate that "the public" still supports various programs. The executive branch will use up its energy and political capital defending old programs. Every year the same fights will be fought, the same wounds reopened, the current alliances disrupted, and a huge amount of energy wasted. These are ugly prospects.

The defects of seeking a thorough annual review have been recognized for many years. In a 1952 article, Verne Lewis defended budget reviewers.[20] That they concentrate on increases and do not appear to ask if the base amount is justified is understandable given the volume of work they face. Even if time were available it would be wasteful to re-view every request each year. A periodic review would suffice to respond to the changing environment.

In sum, the idea of zero-base budgeting stems from a commendable desire to curtail or terminate ineffective or obsolete programs—and from a deplorable neglect of the costs of thorough annual review and a serious misconception of how to achieve reallocation.

## AN ALTERNATIVE

The purpose of zero-base budgeting is to encourage officials to reallocate funds as they think appropriate. However, zero-base budgeting does not provide any basis for judging what is appropriate nor any impetus to reallocation. A procedure that Verne Lewis has proposed (citing Herbert A. Simon as a predecessor) would provide both. The idea is that each official in the budget-making hierarchy would inform his superior as to what would be gained or lost if his agency's appropriation were expanded or contracted by selected amounts.

> Budget estimates and justifications are rarely prepared
> in a manner . . . which makes it easy to compare relative

[19]Wildavsky and Hammann, "Comprehensive Versus Incremental Budgeting," p. 157.
[20]Verne B. Lewis, "Toward a Theory of Budgeting," in Lyden and Miller, *Planning Programming Budgeting,* p. 134.

merits. We shall . . . outline a budget system designed to facilitate such comparisons. . . . The system . . . will be called the alternative budget system. Under this procedure, each administrative official who prepares a budget . . . would . . . prepare a basic budget estimate supplemented by skeleton plans for [e.g.] . . . 80, 90, 110, and 120 percent of that amount. [He] would indicate the recommended revisions for each of the alternatives and the benefits or sacrifices. . . . At each superior level the responsible official would review the alternative proposals submitted by his several subordinates and select from them the features that would be . . . the most advantageous to the taxpayers for each alternative amount set for him by the next highest . . . level. Finally, the President would submit alternative budgets to the Congress.[21]

Although the basic idea of Lewis' proposal is very appealing, we have two reservations about its design. First, to develop plans for five levels of expenditure (80, 90, 100, 110, and 120 percent) seems excessive. Three levels would suffice to represent contraction, stability, and expansion, and using three would be less costly. Second, to work with fixed percentages seems inflexible. There are indivisibilities that can make 90 or 110 percent unsuitable levels. Accordingly, we shall present a version of our own, recognizing that trial and error may uncover shortcomings and indicate improvements.

We indicated a preference for considering three levels of expenditure. Which three levels should be considered? For a jurisdiction with a growing population or rising prices, the best three levels are figures that we shall call the *same-dollar amount,* the *same-performance amount,* and the *recommended amount.* The same-dollar amount is the sum last appropriated for the agency at issue. The same-performance amount is the sum that the agency head predicts will be needed in order to produce the same quantity and quality of output that the last appropriation produced. Output might increase while performance remained the same in the sense that the same formula for eligibility was maintained, for example. The recommended amount is the sum that the agency head believes would be most appropriate for his agency.[22] Relative to each of these three amounts, an agency head would be expected to provide his

---

[21] Lewis, "Toward a Theory of Budgeting," pp. 128ff.

[22] The same-performance amount and the recommended amount have counterparts in the federal instructions for multi-year costing. Recall that the instructions state, "Where an existing program is expected to continue . . . it should be shown at its current levels unless (a) . . . changes are required under existing law, by uncontrollable workload, or by demographic or other factors, or (b) explicit justification . . . is provided. . . ." The same-performance amount corresponds to (a) here, and the recommended amount corresponds to (b). Accordingly, there will often be room for judgment in ascertaining the same-performance amount (recall the FTC example in Chapter 3). See "Bulletin No. 68-2," p. 435.

superior with both numerical and supplementary information. Let us explain.

An agency head at the lowest level of the administrative hierarchy would be expected to provide his superior with three kinds of numerical information: (1) the same-performance amount for his agency, (2) the difference between the same-performance amount and the same-dollar amount for his agency, and (3) the difference between the recommended amount and the same-performance amount for his agency. In other words, a lowest-level administrator would specify the appropriation that he thinks he needs in order to maintain his level of output, together with the amount of money that would be saved if his agency's expenditures were held constant and the amount that would be added if expenditures were enlarged as he recommends.

The lowest-level administrator also would provide five kinds of supplementary information: (1) an explanation of the difference between the same-performance amount and the same-dollar amount, in terms of changes in input prices, changes in population served, and changes in output per dollar of expenditure; (2) a description and explanation of the changes, if any, that he plans to make in inputs or outputs even if the same-performance amount is appropriated; (3) a description of the quantity and quality of output that he predicts will result if the same-performance amount is appropriated; (4) a description of the reduction in quantity or quality of output that he predicts would occur if his agency were to receive the same-dollar amount instead of the same-performance amount, together with his rating of the reduction (say, on a scale ranging from "worthless" to "vital");[23] and (5) a description of the increase in quantity or quality of output that he predicts would occur if his agency were to receive the recommended amount instead of the same-performance amount, together with his rating of the increase. In other words, the lowest-level administrator would explain why he needs more money in order to maintain his level of output, what revision in activities he plans to make even if he receives the same-performance appropriation, what results that appropriation would produce, what would be sacrificed if his agency's expenditures were held at this year's level, and what would be gained if his agency's expenditures were enlarged as he recommends.

The process would be repeated at higher administrative levels. After receiving the figures and supplementary information from his various

---

[23]The value of an activity is a matter of judgment. To compare activities, a superior official can rely on his subordinates' ratings, on his own judgment, or on some combination that he thinks is appropriate. Presumably, administrators will choose a combination, and the exact mix will vary according to how busy they are, how much self-assurance they have, and how trustworthy they think their subordinates' ratings are.

subordinates, an official at the second level up in the administrative hierarchy would prepare similar information for his own superiors. He, like his subordinates, would prepare three kinds of figures and five kinds of supplementary information. There would, however, be some differences, reflecting the fact that subagency allocations are involved.

At the second level up, and at every higher level, the three kinds of figures would be these: (1) the same-performance amount for the agency, together with the agency head's recommendation as to the division of that amount among the agencies within his agency; (2) the difference between the same-performance amount and the same-dollar amount for his agency, together with the agency head's recommendation as to the corresponding differences for each of the subagencies; and (3) the difference between the recommended amount and the same-performance amount for the agency, together with the agency head's recommendation as to the corresponding differences for each of the subagencies. In other words, an official above the lowest level would specify how much money he would assign to each of his subagencies if his appropriation were large enough to maintain each subagency's level of output, together with how much money he would withhold from, or add to, each subagency's budget if, instead, he received his same-dollar appropriation or his recommended appropriation.

This supplementary information should be transmitted by officials at the second and higher levels: (1) an explanation of the difference between the same-performance amount and the same-dollar amount for the agency, in terms of changes in input prices, changes in the population served, and changes in output per unit of input (the production function); (2) a description and explanation of the differences, if any exist, between the subagencies' same-performance amounts and the amounts that the agency head recommends for the subagencies in his same-performance allocation; (3) a description of the quantity and quality of the subagencies' outputs that he predicts will result if his same-performance amount is appropriated; (4) a description of the reduction in the quantity or quality of his subagencies' outputs that he predicts would occur if his agency were to receive the same-dollar amount instead of the same-performance amount together with his rating of the reduction (say, on a scale ranging from "worthless" to "vital"); and (5) a description of the increase in the quantity or quality of the subagencies' outputs that he predicts would occur if his agency were to receive the recommended amount instead of the same-performance amount, together with his rating of the increase. In other words, an official above the lowest level would explain why he needs more money in order to maintain his subagencies' levels of outputs, what revision in the subagencies' activities and appropriations he plans to make even if he receives the same-performance appropriation, what results the same-performance appropriation would produce, what would be sacrificed if his agency's expenditures were held at this year's level, and what would be gained if his agency's expenditures were enlarged as he recommends.

In deciding how best to allocate any one of his three amounts among his subordinate agencies, a superior official may want to consider assigning some of the agencies less than their same-dollar amounts. (Indeed, if he assigns any subagency more than its same-dollar amount when he chooses his same-dollar allocation, he will be forced to assign other subagencies less than their same-dollar amounts.) If he does assign some agencies less than their same-dollar amounts, he will need to mention the effect of such reductions in the supplementary information that he transmits to his superior. The effect of a zero appropriation has been covered in the third kind of supplementary information that his subordinates will provide—expected output. To clarify the effect of allocating an amount between zero and the same-dollar amount, a preliminary step can be introduced. It involves what we will call *specified levels*.

Specified levels would be handled as follows. If an official decides to consider an amount between zero and the same-dollar amount for an agency in his domain, he would (presumably after appropriate consultation) specify one or more such amounts. The head of the subagency would be expected to predict the quantity or quality of output that would be sacrificed at each of the specified amounts compared to the same-performance level. The superior official then would choose one of the specified amounts. The sacrifices associated with the level that the superior official chooses would be described in part two of the supplementary that he transmits to his own superiors. In this way, his own superiors would be notified of his intention to reallocate among his subagencies.

Let us summarize the procedure. Each administrator would make conditional plans for his domain and submit them to his superiors for ratification. Each would determine the size and best utilization of his same-performance appropriation, the best way to adjust to constancy in the dollar amount of his appropriation, and the best size and utilization of an increase. Each would then tell his superiors what would be lost if either zero or the same-dollar amount were appropriated instead of the same-performance amount, and also what would be gained if the amount he recommends were appropriated. It would be up to the superiors to decide which of these (or other) amounts is appropriate and whether the plan for utilizing the chosen amount is acceptable. Each administrator can be viewed as maximizing the value of his agency's output subject to several alternative budget constraints, and as providing his superiors with information they need in order to confirm maximization and to choose the appropriate constraint.

One should not overlook the possibility of biased reporting. Two ways to discourage deliberate exaggeration come to mind. First, it can be announced that the numerical and supplementary information received from each subordinate will be circulated to other subordinates for review and that confidential comments will be invited. Second, each subordinate can be required to submit, both for himself and for his subagency, a comparison between predicted performance and actual performance in the past, together with an explanation of the differences. Both measures would help superior officials to judge the reliability of the information they receive, and also would discourage subordinates from submitting exaggerated descriptions of what would be lost if their appropriations were cut and of what would be gained if their appropriations were enlarged. Other safeguards may come to mind as the procedure is implemented.

The alternative budget approach outlined above has important advantages over zero-base budgeting. Both procedures seek to encourage officials to consider curtailing or terminating ineffective or obsolete programs. The alternative budget approach, however, does not throw away information about last year's appropriation and does not demand justifications that cannot be given. It recognizes that what is the best allocation of funds is a matter of judgment, and it seeks to provide decisionmakers with the information needed to pass judgment. This information consists of a description of what would be gained in one program and lost in another if funds were reallocated. The alternative budget approach would, as Key has said, "place alternatives in juxtaposition."[24] It may not, as Key added, "compel consideration of relative value," but it will surely encourage it. Whether even the alternative budget approach would be worth its cost, however, is uncertain. We suggest that the USDA give it, too, a trial.

In *The Politics of the Budgetary Process* Wildavsky observed that budgeting tends to be incremental. Rarely are gross changes made. The vocabulary of the cognizant Congressional committees is preoccupied with percentage changes from previous years. What Wildavsky was saying was that budgeting was not comprehensive as zero-base budgeting counsels.

In subsequent systematic empirical studies with Dempster and Davis, he identified the phenomena of a budget *base* on which an agency

---

[24]V. O. Key, Jr., "The Lack of a Budgetary Theory," *American Political Science Review* 34 (December 1940): 1142.

could count, and a "fair share" or fraction which a division within an agency regarded as its rightful due was identified.[25]

PPB came after these studies. Thus the question arises: Is budgeting any less incremental and more comprehensive since the advent of PPB? If Davis, Dempster, and Wildavsky's theory is a good one, it should allow the hypothesis of incrementalism to be rejected by the proper data. By now, some of that data has accumulated and such a study is appropriate.

[25]Otto A. Davis, M. A. H. Dempster, and Aaron Wildavksy, "On the Process of Budgeting: An Empirical Study of Congressional Appropriation," in Gordon Tullock, ed., *Papers on Nonmarket Decision Making* (Charlottesville: University of Virginia, 1966), p. 66; and Davis, Dempster, and Wildavsky, "A Theory of the Budgetary Process." *American Political Science Review* 60 (September 1966): 529–47.

# Six

# QUANTITATIVE EVALUATION OF ALTERNATIVES

The fifth and last distinguishing feature of PPB is the quantitative evaluation of alternatives or benefit-cost analysis. Benefit-cost analysis is required by the federal instructions for PPB:

> Special Studies are a vital element of PPB. They will review in terms of costs and benefits the effectiveness of prior efforts, compare alternative mixes of programs, balance increments in costs against increments in effectiveness at various program levels . . . and assess the incidence of benefits and costs as well as their totals. . . . In every case a Special Study will contain specific recommendations for future action.[1]

Special Studies may also be called *cost-effectiveness, cost-utility,* or *systems analysis.* The word effectiveness is often used when benefits cannot be measured in units commensurable with costs. In a cost-effectiveness analysis the output or level of effectiveness is usually taken as given and several methods of achieving it are examined in the hope that one will probably have lower costs than the others. A typical cost-effectiveness problem might be this: In order to achieve capability to transport one infantry division and one fighter-bomber wing from Travis Air Force Base in California and two fighter-bomber wings from Tokyo to a hypothetical city in the Middle East, in the event of a peripheral war, while continuing routine worldwide resupply of military bases, consider several means of achieving that capability and choose the one hav-

---

[1] U.S. Bureau of the Budget, "Bulletin No. 68-2, July 18, 1967," in Fremont J. Lyden and Ernest G. Miller, eds., *Planning Programming Budgeting: A Systems Approach to Management* (Chicago: Markham 1968), p. 438.

ing minimum cost.[2] It is impossible and unnecessary to quantify the worth of this capability in dollar terms, so it is left in physical terms.

The question of which individual actually performs this analysis can be answered by cataloging some of the work that has been done in the past. Further, we will make some normative statements about who *ought* to perform such analysis to get the best results. In analyzing benefits and costs one must compare one social state against another— that is, the world with the project versus the world without it. Although some criteria have already been defined, we find practitioners preoccupied with economic efficiency to the exclusion of other considerations.

We will consider the traditional measures of desirability of investments: net benefits, benefit-cost ratios, internal rate of return, and the like. Although others have been dogmatic on which measure is preferable, we will only report the advantages and disadvantages of each and suggest that the practitioner use more than one measure if that perspective will illuminate the situation. Constraints and externalities are also discussed.

## WHO PERFORMS BENEFIT-COST ANALYSIS?

Benefit-cost analysis arose in the 1930s, and can be dated from the Flood Control Act of 1936. It was first applied to water resources projects, then to transportation and to defense expenditures. Lately, all other public expenditures have become fair game. The method seems to have become ubiquitous. Transportation projects, income maintenance programs, retraining programs, proposed research and development projects, health programs, and law enforcement are all likely candidates. The following list of some recent studies indicates the current scope of benefit-cost analysis.

U.S. Office of Economic Opportunity. *Evaluating the War on Poverty,* by Robert A. Levine.
U.S. Office of Economic Opportunity. *Benefit/Cost Estimates for Job Corps,* by Glen Cain. Madison, Institute for Research on Poverty, University of Wisconsin, 1967.
U.S. Department of Agriculture. *Benefit/Cost Analysis of Research on Live Poultry Handling.*
U.S. Department of Defense. *Recommended FY 67-71 Airlift and Sea-*

---

[2]C. B. McGuire, "An Illustrative Application of Economic Analysis," in Charles J. Hitch and Roland N. McKean, *The Economics of Defense in the Nuclear Age* (Cambridge, Mass.: Harvard University Press, 1960), p. 133.

*lift Forces Attachment to Supplement to Bureau of the Budget Bulletin No. 66-3.* 1965.

U.S. Department of Defense. *Army Corps of Engineers. Salem Church Reservoir, Rappahannock River, Va.* Washington, D.C., Government Printing Office, 1967. (S. Doc. No. 37, 90th Cong., 1st Sess.)

U.S. Department of Health, Education, and Welfare. Office of Program Coordination. *Motor Vehicle Injury Prevention Program.* August 1966. 183 pp. (Program Analysis 1966-1; Disease Control Programs)

U.S. Department of Health, Education, and Welfare. Office of Program Coordination. *Adult Basic Education; Work Experience and Training.* September 1966. (Program Analysis 1966-7: Human Investment Programs)

U.S. Department of Health, Education, and Welfare. Office of Program Coordination. *Selected Disease Control Programs.* September 1966. (Program Analysis 1966-5: Disease Control Programs)

U.S. Department of Health, Education, and Welfare. Vocational Rehabilitation Administration. Division of Statistics and Studies. *An Exploratory Cost-Benefit Analysis of Vocational Rehabilitation,* 1967.

U.S. Department of Housing and Urban Development. *An Evaluation of the Open Space Land Program—1961-67.*

U.S. Post Office Department. Office of Planning and Systems Analysis. *Five Methods of Delivery; A Study and Cost Estimate.* October 14, 1966. 76 pp.

U.S. Department of Transportation. Federal Aviation Administration. *Staff Study of Costs Versus Benefits of Airport Approach Aids,* 1967.

U.S. Bureau of the Budget. Program Evaluation Staff. *A Primer on the Analysis of Air Pollution Control.* 1967.

U.S. Bureau of the Budget. Program Evaluation Staff. *Chemical Escapes From Reality: What Is the Public Interest?* 1967.

U.S. Bureau of the Budget. Program Evaluation Staff. *Criteria for Evaluating Urban Renewal Projects.* 1967.

In most cases, agencies analyze their own programs. This is convenient because detailed knowledge of operating data is required to do a good analysis. In some cases, such as the paper for the Office of Economic Opportunity by Glen Cain, a consultant or contract institute will perform an independent appraisal. The consultant or contractor is usually working for the agency and is likely to adopt its values. Although candid analyses are sometimes commissioned by enlightened administrators, critical ones are rarely publicized.

The California Water Project was evaluated from several different points of view.[3] Initial studies were made by the California Division (later Department) of Water Resources. An early study was made by an engineering firm that could expect large contracts for earthmoving and dam and aqueduct construction if the project were authorized. Later, three studies were made by independent economists and engineers who had no bureaucratic or financial interests in the project except as taxpayers.

Initial studies by the division were sanguine about the economic prospects of the plan. The Bechtel (engineering) report was also optimistic, although more guarded in its praise. The independent studies, however, were more critical. One indicated that revenues forthcoming would not cover costs. Another by a group of engineering students explored the alternative of reclaiming water from sewage. A third urged the use of pricing to induce water-saving behavior, by adducing instances where high prices caused firms to recycle water.

There is certainly danger of overoptimism when the institution that will execute the project is asked to evaluate it, for it has an interest in the outcome of the analysis.[4] The history of benefit-cost analysis of water resource projects especially shows many instances of distinterested analysts—usually from universities or the RAND Corporation— finding that agencies have exaggerated the benefits or understated the costs of their own projects. The SST at first offered a new possibility for an agency to evaluate its own work. This dangerous situation, wherein the FAA would certify the safety of its own creation, was averted, as we shall see in Chapter 11.

This problem still arises frequently with the Corps of Engineers, the Bureau of Reclamation, and the Soil Conservation Service. These agencies, which perform benefit-cost analysis and oversee engineering and construction of water resources projects, have a tendency to be biased in favor of project justification.

Another source of bias is perhaps more subtle. States, localities, and irrigation districts often allow private engineering firms to do initial studies of "feasibility," that is, initial comparisons of benefits and costs. A project is economically feasible if estimated benefits exceed estimated costs. Frequently, however, it happens an engineering firm will bid below cost on a feasibility study because once it has done the feasibility study, it knows the plans and objectives. It has an advantage over other engi-

---

[3]For a detailed study of planning for this investment see Chapter 11.

[4]Irving K. Fox and Orris C. Herfindahl, "Attainment of Efficiency in Satisfying Demands for Water Resources," *American Economic Review* 54, no. 3 (1964): 201ff.; L. B. Leopold and T. Maddock, Jr., *The Flood Control Controversy* (New York: Ronald Press, 1954), p. 137; and O. Eckstein, *Water Resource Development* (Cambridge, Mass.: Harvard University Press, 1958), p. 126.

neering firms that might bid on the engineering work. Losses sustained on the feasibility study are justified by the hope of winning an engineering contract whose potential profits dwarf those losses. Obviously, the feasibility study is not objective or unbiased.

One alternative is to have the analysis done by an agency that will not engineer or administer the project. Such a group could be created as an independent economic evaluation agency for water resources, or for natural resources in general. The Federal Contract Research Centers such as RAND, Institute for Defense Analyses, and Research Analyses Corporation may serve as models of dispassionate analytical agencies.

Another alternative is to increase the staff of the Bureau of the Budget for independent evaluation of projects. Charles Schultze, a former director of that bureau, has suggested a staff of "partisan rationalizers" who would become experts in their respective fields. Their mission would be to state the case *against* expenditures and counter the opinions of agency bureaucrats who usually want to expand their agency's budget. This is healthy. Bureaucrats should be dedicated to the field in which they work and convinced of its important. We probably would not want any other type of people running our programs. Nevertheless, even if they are very competent and dedicated, their judgment is not reliable when it comes to allocating scarce public funds between their program and others. Hence, the need for partisan rationalizers.

Of course, Congress has final control over appropriations and expenditures. Both the Senate and the House have committees on appropriations and subcommittees on particular areas of spending. One might expect expertise and partisan rationalizers to have developed in these committees. But a reading of the hearings of these committees makes it clear that the committees themselves do very little analysis. They rely on the testimony of expert witnesses, frequently drawn from the operating agencies. Sometimes a legislator will enter into the record a critical newspaper article or letter from a constituent and ask the agency to respond. That Congress has no analytical staff for itself indicates that as a whole it is more concerned with the political impact of its decisions than with economic efficiency.

Senator William Proxmire says that the chairmen of the appropriations subcommittees want their part of the budget to grow, and asserts that little analysis is undertaken by the legislature. According to Proxmire, Chairman of the Senate Subcommittee on Economy in Government, "the powerful people on the appropriations subcommittees—the Chairmen—. . . are not interested in careful scrutiny and evaluation of their own budgets."[5] This point too indicates a use for an office of bud-

[5] U.S. Congress Joint Economic Committee, *The Analysis and Evaluation of Public Expenditures: The PPB System*, vol. 1, p. vii.

getary analysis for Congress, or increased PPB capability for the General Accounting Office. Some independent source of information is needed to counteract the partisan position of the committees.

Perhaps there is something to be learned at the federal level from the Legislature's Joint Budget Committee Analyst in California. This office acts as a sort of bureau of the budget in that it is a clearinghouse for all spending and revenue programs. It compares one with another and judges whether partisans' projections of a bill are realistic and consistent with the legislative program. The office is responsible only to the legislature. It has a career civil service staff that is nonpartisan in the sense that personnel do not change with a change in the party in control of the legislature. The Governor of California also has an analogue to the Bureau of the Budget in the Department of Finance.

## PHILOSOPHICAL CRITERIA

Welfare economists have proposed several criteria for evaluating alternative social states. One of these is almost the same as the criterion used in benefit-cost analysis. We should understand what the welfare theorists have suggested and what other theorists have said in criticism.

### The Pareto Criterion

Near the turn of the century Vilfredo Pareto proposed this measure of desirability: A change is desirable, he said, if it would make some persons better off (in their own judgment) and would make no one worse off (in his own judgment). Thus a change is good if it would move some persons to positions they prefer and move no one to a position he prefers less than his present one. Conversely, a change is undesirable if it would make some persons feel worse off and no one feel better off. A change that would make some better off and some worse off is not evaluated by the Pareto criterion.

The Pareto criterion takes no account of the *reasons* why persons feel that they would be better off or worse off. In particular, the criterion does not distinguish between cases in which the losers would suffer an absolute deterioration in their positions (such as reduced incomes) and cases in which they would suffer only from envy, prejudice, or ideology (such as the Jones' new car, a disliked minority making progress, or creeping socialism). In practice, many people do make this distinction. Most of us seem to feel that only persons who suffer an absolute deterioration in their positions are "entitled" to object to others' gains. The Pareto criterion, in contrast, approves an alternative only if no one objects to it for any reason.[6]

The Pareto criterion has been widely accepted by economists since the early 1930s. Indeed, it is from the Pareto criterion that contemporary welfare theorists deduce all their normative conclusions.[7] The analysis these theorists have produced even has its own name: "new welfare economics."

The economists who belong to this school have made two points in defense of the Pareto criterion: it is ethically appropriate and the answers obtained by using it are potentially verifiable.

The criterion is ethically appropriate, that is, it is morally right to make a change if it would move some persons to more preferred positions and no one to a less preferred position, and it is morally wrong to make a change if it would move no one to a more preferred position but would move some persons to less preferred positions.[8]

Changes which would move some persons to more preferred positions and no one to a less preferred position are verifiable. How the persons affected would evaluate the effects is in principle a resolvable question of fact.

The new welfare economics is an application of logical positivism. This is a philosophical school or outlook expounded early in the nine-

---

[6]It is sometimes said that the Pareto criterion is biased toward the status quo. This is true only if one interprets nonevaluation of a change from the status quo as equivalent to approving perpetuation of the status quo. If the alternative would make some persons better off and some worse off, then the alternative simply is not ranked relative to the status quo by the Pareto criterion. It does not follow that the status quo should be perpetuated. We concede, however, that some proponents of the Pareto criterion decline to pass judgment except where the criterion can be invoked. By their inaction, they help to perpetuate the status quo.

[7]For example, the conclusion that the price of every homogeneous product should be the same for all consumers, that the marginal cost of producing the product should be the same for all producers, and that price should equal marginal cost.

[8]Although the Pareto criterion may, at first glance, seem unexceptionable, there are respectable grounds for challenging it. The criterion presupposes that the person passing judgment on some alternatives agrees that it is desirable to give people whatever they want, that it is undesirable to impose anything that the affected people do not want, and that nothing matters except what the affected people want or do not want. If the person passing judgment finds any of these principles unacceptable in the case under consideration, he may well reach a different conclusion than the Pareto criterion would produce. In fact, there are good reasons why someone might find the principles unacceptable in particular cases. Giving people what they want, or not imposing on them what they do not want, may have doubtful merit. This is clearly so if the people involved are ill-informed (as with hazardous products or complicated medical care), if the people are incompetent (as with youngsters, oldsters, and morons), or if they have lost self-control (as with addicts, drunks, and the bereaved). Moreover, what the affected persons want may not be everything that matters to the person passing judgment. He may be concerned about national interests, about accurate reporting, about due process of law, about making prison unpleasant, and so on. Even a humanitarian, then, and certainly a dictator, may find the Pareto criterion unacceptable at times.

teenth century by the French philosopher August Comte. The only statements a positivist considers scientifically meaningful are those that can
be shown to be true or false by empirical evidence, at least in principle.
Let us see how this attitude relates to the Pareto criterion.

If one adopts the Pareto criterion and then states that a change is
desirable, the statement becomes equivalent to two other statements:
first, the change would move some persons to more preferred positions
and no one to a less preferred position; second, the person making the
statement approves of the change. If, as the new welfare economists believe, people's preferences can be ascertained in principle, then these
two derived statements can be shown to be true or false by empirical
evidence. Accordingly, if one adopts the Pareto criterion, the statement
that a change is desirable becomes scientifically meaningful.

Unfortunately, opportunities to use the Pareto criterion are likely
to be rare. A change would rarely move no one to a less preferred position. This is particularly true of changes imposed by government. Urban
renewal has been renamed "Negro removal"; construction projects, such
as roads or dams, involve use of the government's power of eminent
domain to force people in the way to sell their property. Public spending decisions, in short, can rarely be evaluated using the Pareto criterion.
For most practical purposes, its domain is too small.[9]

Proponents of the Pareto criterion are well aware of its narrow domain. They respond that it is intrinsically judgmental to evaluate changes
that lie outside the domain. In other words, it is inherently subjective
to evaluate changes that would make some persons better off and some
worse off. To do so in an acceptable way, one must compare the gainers'
gains with the losers' losses, and it is not possible to demonstrate that
the gains exceed the losses. Why is it not possible? The reason is that the
gainers' gains are not comparable with the losers' losses because no
meaning can be attached to the relative magnitudes of different peoples'
feelings. Verifiable interpersonal comparisons are not possible.

### The Kaldor-Hicks Criterion

In 1939, a suggestion was made that seemed to provide a way to
evaluate changes that are outside the domain of the Pareto criterion
without comparing the gainers' gains to the losers' losses.

[9]Another reason that the Pareto criterion is of little use for public decisions is that
it ranks alternatives only if the affected persons and their reactions are known with certainty. In practice, it is seldom—perhaps never—known for sure who would be affected
and how they would evaluate the effects. This problem is especially serious if some of
the persons who will be affected are not yet born, or if "tendencies" are involved, such
as a tendency to weaken incentives.

Using repeal of Britain's Corn Laws (restrictions on grain importation) in 1846 as an illustration, Roy Harrod had asserted that the gain to the whole society could be considered larger than the loss to the landlords only if all individuals were considered to be alike. In response, Nicholas Kaldor denied the need for such interpersonal comparison:

> Where a certain policy leads to an increase in physical productivity, and thus of aggregate real income . . . it is *possible* to make everybody better off than before. . . . There is no need [that] nobody in the community is going to suffer. [It] is quite sufficient . . . to show that even if all those who suffer . . . are fully compensated for their loss, the rest of the community will still be better off than before. Whether the landlord in the free-trade case should in fact be given compensation or not, is a political question. . . .[10]

J. R. Hicks promptly supported Kaldor's proposition,[11] and in a subsequent paper, Hicks gave his own statement of what is now generally called the Kaldor-Hicks criterion:

> If A made so much better off by a change that he could compensate B for his loss and still have something left over, then the change is an unequivocal improvement.[12]

Thus, the Kaldor-Hicks criterion says that a change is desirable if it is desirable according to the Pareto criterion, or (b) a position that is Pareto-better than the initial position could be attained by making the change and then having the persons who gained give or trade something to the persons who lost. We may infer that a change is undesirable if the opposite change is desirable.

The Kaldor-Hicks criterion is important to us because it is almost the same as the criterion used in benefit-cost analysis. If the benefits exceed the costs of a project,[13] a position that is Pareto-better than the initial position could be attained by proceeding with the project and then having the gainers compensate the losers. This change would be desirable according to the Kaldor-Hicks criterion.

[10]N. Kaldor, "Welfare Propositions of Economics and Interpersonal Comparisons of Utility," *Economic Journal* 49 (1939): 350.

[11]J. R. Hicks, "The Foundations of Welfare Economics," *Economic Journal* 49 (1939) 696–712.

[12]J. R. Hicks, "The Rehabilitation of Consumer Surplus," *Review of Economic Studies* 8 (1940–1941): 108.

[13]And, if they are both instantaneous, properly valued and certain.

### The Little Criterion

We can learn more about the Kaldor-Hicks criterion by contrasting it with a criterion proposed by I. M. D. Little. According to Little, "an economic change is desirable (and increases welfare) if it causes a good redistribution of wealth, and if the potential losers could not profitably bribe the potential gainers to oppose it."[14] And, we may infer, a change is undesirable if the opposite change is desirable.

Thus, the Little criterion says that a change is desirable if (1) the person passing judgment on the change approves of the gains and losses that people would receive *and* either (2a) the change is desirable according to the Pareto criterion *or* (2b) we cannot effect a position Pareto-superior to that caused by the change by having the losers (from the change) give something to the gainers.

Part 2b of the Little criterion (let us call this part the *Little efficiency criterion*) resembles part b of the Kaldor-Hicks criterion. The two criteria, however, are not the same. They require different information to evaluate a given change. And even with full information, they may produce different answers, as we shall soon see. An illustration will show how it is possible for the Kaldor-Hicks and the Little efficiency criteria to generate contradictory evaluations.

The illustration involves three assumptions. Assume, first that a publisher is indifferent between two financial arrangements that it might make with two co-authors; for example, Merewitz and Sosnick. One arrangement (call it alternative A) would provide Merewitz and Sosnick with royalties of 9 percent each, together with a prepayment of $1,000 each. The other arrangement (alternative B) would provide Merewitz and Sosnick with royalties of 6 percent each, together with a prepayment of $1,500 each. Assume, second, that Merewitz and Sosnick are free to trade their shares between themselves. They could, for example, modify alternative A so that Merewitz receives 12 percent and no prepayment, while Sosnick receives the remaining 6 percent and the entire $2,000 (call this modification alternative A'). Similarly, they could modify alternative B so that Merewitz receives, say, 12 percent and $750, while Sosnick receives the remaining zero percent and $2,250. Assume, finally, that (because Merewitz feels that any additional 3 percent is worth about $800, while Sosnick feels that it is worth about $400), Merewitz ranks the alternatives B' over A over A' over B, while Sosnick ranks them A' over B over B' over A. If so, the alternatives have positions in utility

[14] I. M. D. Little, *A Critique of Welfare Economics* 2d ed. (Oxford: Clarendon Press, 1957), p. 109. Little added, "always assuming that no still better change is therefore prejudiced."

space as shown in Figure 6.1.[15] The Scitovsky Paradox is so called because Scitovsky discovered that both a change from B to A and the reverse change from A to B can be called good.

Note that in Figure 6.1 B' lies east of A while A' lies north of B. As a result, the two utility possibility curves[16] will cross, provided they both have negative slopes. If the curves do have negative slopes, they must cross somewhere east of A', west of A, south of B, and north of B', that is, somewhere within the rectangle shown in the center of Figure 6.1.

Thus, the Kaldor-Hicks criterion can produce contradictory evaluations. If A' is Pareto-better than B, a change from B to A is desirable according to the Kaldor-Hicks criterion. And because B' is Pareto-better than A, a change from A to B also is desirable. Hence, the criterion can be useless.[17]

There is no sound basis for choosing between the Kaldor-Hicks criterion and the Little efficiency criterion. Either they give the same answer or one gives contradictory answers while the other does not

[15]The notation in Figure 6.1 needs explanation. $U_s(6\%, \$2,000)$ represents the value that the index of Sosnick's utility would have if Sosnick received 6 percent and $2,000. This value is a number, say, 17.03, but it is given only ordinal meaning, that is, it shows only how Sosnick ranks the combination (6%, $2,000) relative to other combinations. For example, if $U_s(6\%, \$1,500)$ equals, say, 12.97, we know only that Sosnick prefers (6%, $2,000) to (6%, $1,500). The difference between 17.03 and 12.97 is not, in general, comparable to the difference between, say, $U_s(6\%, \$1,500)$ and $U_s(0\%, \$2,250)$, and never are any comparisons made to values of Merewitz's utility index. The latter, of course, is indicated by $U_m( \ , \ )$.

[16]Utility possibility curves represent possibilities that exist for efficient compensation (redistribution). $UPC_B$ is an abbreviation meaning utility possibility curve given B. A point on $UPC_B$ such as B' represents the position that would be reached if B were chosen and then the gainer from having B instead of A (Sosnick) made the loser (Merewitz) a gift with the following property: of all the possible gifts that would make Merewitz as well off as he is at B', the one selected leaves Sosnick as well off as possible. Similarly, any other point on $UPC_B$ shows the highest value that Sosnick's utility index could reach if B were to be chosen and then a gift made that puts Merewitz's utility index at the level shown by that other point.

[17]The contradictions that arise in ranking two alternatives with the Kaldor-Hicks criterion can be avoided by adding a qualification. In particular, part b of the criterion can be altered to the following: A change is desirable if, first, the gainers can compensate the losers and still be in a more preferred position and, second, the gainers from the opposite change cannot do the same. Unfortunately, this version can also produce contradictions. It can produce intransitive (inconsistent) rankings when three or more alternatives are being compared. See, for example, James Quirk and Rubin Saposnik, *Introduction to General Equilibrium Theory and Welfare Economics* (New York: McGraw-Hill, 1968), p. 128.

That the Kaldor-Hicks criterion can produce contradictory evaluations was discovered shortly after the criterion was proposed. Tibor Scitovsky pointed out in "A Note on Welfare Propositions in Economics," *Review of Economic Studies* (1942); 98-110, that cases can arise in which the gainers from a change are able to compensate the losers and still be better off, and yet the losers also could profitably bribe the gainers into returning to the initial position. In other words, cases like the one shown in Figure 6.1 can exist.

FIGURE 6.1. THE SCITOVSKY PARADOX

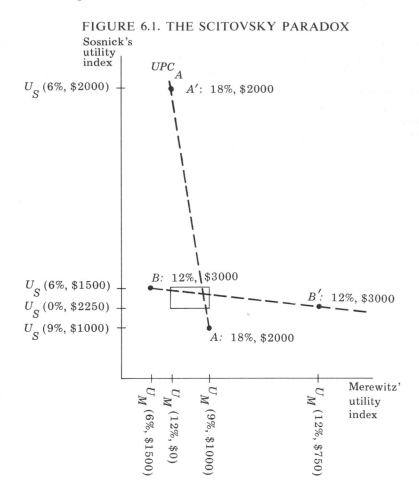

evaluate. The Little efficiency criterion, however, is only part of the Little criterion.

Part 1 of the Little criterion relates to whether the person who is passing judgment approves of the gains and losses that people would receive. A change is desirable according to the Little criterion only if the person passing judgment regards the gains and losses as fair. Because of this part, the Little criterion is qualitatively different from the Kaldor-Hicks criterion. The Kaldor-Hicks criterion does not even raise the question of fairness. It asks only whether the gainers are *able* to compensate the losers. Herein lies a crucial defect.

The mere possibility of compensation is hardly enough to assuage the losers, and therefore is hardly enough to make a person who is passing judgment on a possible change approve. For example, it would hardly be enough to know that the persons who move into a renewed urban area would be in more preferred positions even if they had to pay enough extra rent to compensate the former residents. Eviction may still seem unfair. Furthermore, if the new residents are prosperous and the former residents are poor, the sum of money that would be transferred if compensation were paid probably is, in some relevant sense, worth less to the new residents than it is to the former residents; hence, no inference is warranted that the change is worth more to the new residents.

Part 1 of the Little criterion is, therefore, a very important addition. It appears that all welfare theorists now agree to this. The consensus seems to be that, even if the Kaldor-Hicks criterion (like the Pareto criterion) produces answers that in principle are verifiable, the criterion itself (unlike the Pareto criterion) is not ethically appropriate. It is unacceptable to ignore the question of fairness.

## ANALYTICAL CRITERIA

Benefit-cost analysis seeks to rank alternative uses of public funds. In the usual situation, several projects are competing for scarce funds. Each one can be pursued at one or more scales. The problem may be to choose which of several projects to engage in and then to choose its optimal scale from the several which may be available. Another way to see the problem is: choose the best scale for each project and then choose the best alternative among several projects, each at its optimal scale. For either formulation, we seek a ranking function with which to compare alternatives. More frequently, the real world presents us with particular predesigned projects. The only decision to make is: "Yes" or "no." This is inadequate because too little freedom is allowed to choose an optimum. Nevertheless, our ranking function may enable us to make this decision.

The first step in a benefit-cost analysis is to select an indicator of success, a numerical index with a larger value for a more desirable alternative and a smaller value for a less desirable one. Conceptually, an indicator of success is something to maximize. For example, businessmen are sometimes reputed to maximize profits. One maximizes that indicator indirectly by adopting the alternative for which the indicator has the highest value.

Public servants often are instructed to minimize costs in carrying out their statutory responsibilities. What should public planners maximize or minimize? What success indicator should they use for ranking projects—or for needling their civil service board for a higher GS rating, a general pay raise, or at least a bigger budget to spend next year?

One sometimes hears it said that the goal is to maximize benefits and minimize costs. Both cannot be done simultaneously. One can minimize costs by spending nothing and doing nothing, but in that case no benefits result. One can maximize benefits within a particular project by spending until marginal benefits are zero, but that action may require much more money than is available. Accordingly, some composite criterion is needed. Three obvious ones are:

(1)  maximize benefits for given costs,
(2)  minimize costs while achieving a fixed level of benefits, or
(3)  maximize net benefits (benefits minus costs).

Other criteria are used from time to time, so we should become familiar with them.

Probably the first criteria to be used were the *benefit-cost ratio* and the *internal rate of return*. The former was implied by the Flood Control Act of 1936. The latter was both a legacy of prominent economists, such as Kenneth Boulding and John Maynard Keynes, and a concept well established in the business world. To this day, students of finance are the sharpest in discussing the criterion problem, a question of public finance.[18]

The next indicator to be introduced is the one which will win out in the end: benefits minus costs or *net benefits*. Since this success indicator purports to summarize all relevant factors, it is intuitively appealing. However, first we should talk about the present value of benefits and the present value of costs.

## Present Values

Benefit-cost analysis usually is done on long-lived investment projects. Such projects typically have sizable planning costs, followed by larger construction or procurement costs and by a stream of relatively small costs of operation and maintenance. A major feature is the occurrence of costs and benefits in widely separated years. It will not do to ignore timing and simply add the benefits and subtract the costs. This would be analogous to saying that a house costs the sum of the payments on a mortgage. At some mortgage interest rates, the payments amount

---

[18]See, for example, David Quirin, *The Capital Expenditure Decision* (Homewood, Ill.: Irwin, 1967), Chapter 3. However, we do not agree with his preference for the benefit-cost ratio. At a more advanced level see Ezra Solomon, *The Management of Corporate Capital* (Glencoe, Ill.: The Free Press, 1959).

to twice the cash purchase price.[19] Calculating a present value involves multiplying each cost and benefit that occurs in the future by a *discount factor*. This factor gets smaller as the cost or benefit gets farther in the future. To be concrete, the discount factor equals

$$\frac{1}{(1 + i)^n}$$

where $i$ is the relevant interest rate per period (for example, per year) and n is the number of periods into the future the benefit or cost will accrue.[20] If, as is usual, $i$ is positive, the farther an event is in the future, the smaller is its present value. A high discount rate means the present is valued considerably over the future; that is, there is considerable *time preference*.[21] Time preference means a higher regard for present benefits than for equal future benefits or a willingness to trade amount of benefits for promptness. We will postpone discussion of the discounting method until the next chapter.

### Net Benefits

The formula for the present value of net benefits then is[22]

$$N = -C_0 + \frac{(B_1 - C_1)}{(1 + i)} + \frac{(B_2 - C_2)}{(1 + i)^2} + \cdots \tag{1}$$

The subscripts identify the periods in which the benefits and costs occur.

Net benefits is the criterion recommended, if not used, most frequently. Two projects of equal net benefits might not be regarded indifferently. Suppose both offered net benefits of $1,000, but one involved a present value of benefits of $2 million and a present value of costs of $1.999 million while the other had a present value of benefits of $10,000 and a present value of costs of $9,000. Suppose that something went

[19] If a $40,000 house is bought with a $6,000 downpayment and a $34,000 loan at 9 percent interest, a total of $79,420 is paid over a twenty-year mortgage, with monthly payments.

[20] The formula applies to the present value of flows at discrete points of time. If time is treated as continuous with an infinite number of periods, and we wish to know a present value at any point in time, the factor which will yield that quantity is $e^{-it}$, where $t$ represents the amount of time into the future.

[21] The classic reference on this is A. C. Pigou, *The Economics of Welfare* 4th ed. (London: Macmillan, 1932). Pigou argued that most people have a "defective telescopic faculty;" that is, they prefer the present over the future more than they should. This leads to too much consumption and not enough investment (and, therefore, saving) for the future.

[22] In continuous time, we use (the elongated S or) integral notion:

$$\int_0^\infty (B_t - C_t)e^{-it}dt.$$

wrong—perhaps the calculation of costs or benefits was off by 10 percent. The first project might have negative net benefits of about $200,000. The second would do no more than break even. The criterion of net benefits does not take into account the size of the commitment, while the benefit-cost ratio does. The net benefit criterion has been criticized because it favors large projects over small. If used with budget constraints this bias can be avoided.

### Internal Rate of Return

In similar notation, the internal rate of return (call it $r$) is defined by the following equation:

$$r: \sum_{t=0}^{T} \frac{B_t}{(1 + r)^t} = \sum_{t=0}^{T} \frac{C_t}{(1 + r)^t} . \tag{2}$$

Notice that in the above equation, we do not say the internal rate of return equals something. The right-hand side of the equation is the present value of costs and left-hand side is the present value of benefits. The internal rate of return, $r$, is the rate of return that makes the two sides equal. Why should we want the two sides to be equal? We do not. We simply want to learn at what interest rate they would be equal. Then we can compare this interest rate with the cost of capital.

Usually, for favorable projects, the undiscounted sum of benefits exceeds that of costs. Because costs usually accrue first, the sum of benefits has to be considerably larger to equalize the present values. A high $r$ means that even if the future benefits are discounted harshly, the two sides of equation (2) are equal. A lower $r$ would mean that the undiscounted benefits exceed costs by less. A low discount rate must be used in order that the early costs do not exceed the later benefits in present value. Several problems are encountered in trying to rank alternatives according to their internal rates of return.

One problem is that $r$ is not necessarily unique. More than one value of $r$ may satisfy equation (2). Equation (2) becomes a polynomial equation as soon as $t$ is greater than or equal to two; that is, as soon as the project has more than two years of economic life. One example will show the difficulty. Suppose the benefits and costs of a three-year project are as follows:

| Year | Benefits | Costs |
|------|----------|-------|
| 0 | 0 | $ 1,600 |
| 1 | $10,000 | 0 |
| 2 | 0 | 10,000 |

FIGURE 6.2. NET PRESENT VALUE AND RATE OF RETURN

Net present value
(in dollars)

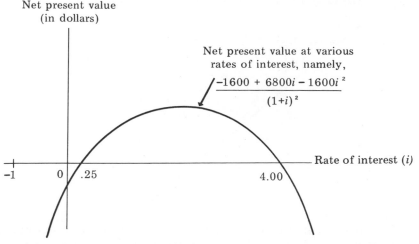

Net present value at various
rates of interest, namely,

$$\frac{-1600 + 6800i - 1600i^2}{(1+i)^2}$$

Rate of interest ($i$)

-1    0   .25                    4.00

Perhaps the project is a farm labor camp or a mining enterprise which has low set-up costs, is used for one year, and is levelled after a year. To find $r$, we proceed as follows:

$$0 + \frac{10,000}{(1 + r)} + \frac{0}{(1 + r)^2} = 1600 + \frac{0}{(1 + r)} + \frac{10,000}{(1 + r)^2} .$$

Multiplying through by $(1 + r)^2$ gives a quadratic equation. When solved, the equation yields two values for $r$: .25 and 4.00; that is, 25 percent and 400 percent. The reason for finding two answers is that, in general, a quadratic equation has two roots. A higher-degree equation, of course, would have still more. Figure 6.2 may help you visualize the situation.

The sum of undiscounted benefits is $10,000 and that of costs is $11,600. If, as presumably is more usual, undiscounted benefits exceed undiscounted costs, there will be a single internal rate of return.[23]

The usual case of a profitable investment is shown in Figure 6.3. The project has positive present value of net benefits at discount rates below $r$, and a negative present value of net benefits at discount rates above $r$. The rate that makes present value zero is the internal rate of return $r$.

[23]Jack Hirshleifer, "On the Theory of Optimal Investment Decision," in Ezra Solomon, *The Management of Corporate Capital* (New York: The Free Press, 1959) pp. 224ff. An excess of undiscounted benefits over costs is a necessary and sufficient condition for the existence of a single positive internal rate of return. See Quirin, *The Capital Expenditure Decision*, pp. 56ff.

FIGURE 6.3. SOLVING FOR $r$ WHEN BENEFITS EXCEED COSTS

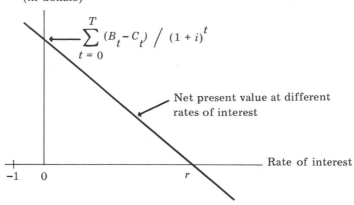

The internal rate of return makes a good measure of desirability when all the alternative investment possibilities are of the same *order of magnitude,* but when the alternatives are of different scales, it is not so useful. If we can invest a dime and make a dime in a year, that has a 100 percent rate of return; but we can invest $10,000 at only a seven percent rate of return. If we could duplicate the first investment *ad infinitum,* we should do that; but, alas, of course we cannot. The internal rate of return tells us nothing about the absolute size of the net benefits.

**Annual Net Benefits**

One can think of how much a house will cost in several terms: total absolute payments, the present value of costs, or the equal monthly payments required. A criterion for public investment projects has been suggested which uses the concept of annualized benefits and costs.

Suppose we forecast a benefit stream: $B_0, B_1, B_2, \ldots B_n$. Given an interest rate, the present value of this stream can be calculated and an annual amount over the same period that has the same present value can be calculated. Call this equivalent annual amount $b$. Similarly, the set of costs accruing in the several years can be annualized into a figure which will be equal every year over the same period, $c$.

These annual benefits and costs can be combined into a criterion of annual net benefits, the difference between $b$ and $c$, which will be perfectly equivalent in ranking to (total) net benefits, $N$.

To find the equivalent annual cost or benefit, find the present value of the stream. Determine the time horizon for the project and the discount rate. Then consult a table that gives the size of an annuity whose present value is one.[24] The entry in the table for the discount rate and the time horizon should be multiplied by the present value to obtain equivalent annual benefits or costs. A table such as "Present Value of Annuities: $1 per year"[25] will give a figure by which to divide the present value in order to get the equivalent annual payment.

Equivalent annual benefits and costs can be used exactly as we use present values of benefits and costs; we can subtract to get a net benefit or divide to get a benefit-cost ratio. Since using these annual equivalents involves first obtaining present values, there is no advantage over present value methods. This criterion is often used, however, when the present value of costs (investment plus operation) is to be compared to the benefits in a "typical" year. It is biased in favor of the project because the "typical" year is usually one of capacity operation and ignores the early years of "startup."

### Benefit-Cost Ratio

The gross *benefit-cost ratio* is:

$$R \equiv \frac{\sum_{t=0}^{T} B_t(1 + i)^{-t}}{\sum_{t=0}^{T} C_t(1 + i)^{-t}} \equiv \frac{b}{c} \tag{3}$$

which is the present value of the benefits over the present value of the costs or annual benefits divided by annual costs. Benefit-cost ratios net of operating or associated costs have been suggested also.[26]

$$R_N \equiv \frac{B - P}{K}$$

Where all quantities are in present values, $P$ represents operating costs and $K$ represents capital costs. Netting emphasizes return on invested capital with comparatively little attention to operating costs. The gross benefit-cost ratio, $R = \dfrac{B}{K + P}$, usually will lead to more capital-intensive

[24]Chemical Rubber Co., *Standard Mathematical Tables* 15th ed. (Cleveland: Chemical Rubber Co., 1964), pp. 603–10.

[25]Quirin, *The Capital Expenditure Decision,* Appendix B, p. 250.

[26]Bernhard Schwab and Peter Lusztig, "A Comparative Analysis of the Net Present Value and the Benefit-cost Ratio As Measures of the Economic Desirability of Investments," *Journal of Finance* 24, no. 3 (June 1969): 507–16.

projects because it emphasizes economizing on both capital and operating costs whereas $R_N$ emphasizes economizing on capital costs.[27]

Bain has argued for the use of $R$ rather than $R_N$ because he believes legislatures should consider $P$ as well as $K$ and give agencies credit for savings on $P$ by allowing them to spend more on $K$.[28] Net benefit-cost ratios may be preferable for private enterprises whose capital is more constraining than operating expenses, especially when taxes are considered.

### The Criteria Compared

That the net present value of project 1 is greater than the $N$ of project 2 does not imply that the benefit-cost ratio of project 1 is greater than the $R$ of project 2. A simple example will illustrate this point. In project 1, suppose benefits have a present value of $1,500 and costs have a present value of $500. This makes $N$ $1,000 and $R$ 3.0. In Project 2, let the present value of benefits be $1,000 and that of costs $200. Project 2 has a smaller $N$—$800—but a higher $R$—5.0. Why is $N$ higher in project 1, but $R$ higher in project 2? Because the former is a difference while the latter is a ratio. If we know the benefit-cost ratio, we must also know the size of the project before we have as much information as is given in the present value of net benefits, $N$.

The benefit-cost ratio is inferior to net benefits when it is not clear whether an item should be considered a benefit or a cost saving. For example, suppose a project cost $1,000, had benefits of $1,200, increased some land values by $400, but decreased other land values by $200.[29] Land value increases could be included in benefits. Land value decreases could be included in costs: $R_1 = \dfrac{1200 + 400}{1000 + 200} = 1.33$. All land value changes could be included either in benefits or costs:
$$R_2 = \frac{1200 + 400 - 200}{1000} = 1.4, \text{ or } R_3 = \frac{1200}{1000 - 400 + 200} = 1.5.$$

[27]The Corps of Engineers, which builds capital-intensive projects like dams, uses $R$. The Soil Conservation Service of the USDA has preferred the internal rate of return for its watershed improvement projects which have a higher ratio of operating to capital costs. See Arthur Maass, "Protecting Nature's Reservoir," in C. J. Friedrich and J. Kenneth Galbraith, eds., *Public Policy* 3 (1954): 71–106 and Eckstein, *Water Resource Development* (Cambridge, Mass.: Harvard University Press, 1958), pp. 59ff.

[28]Joe S. Bain, "Criteria for Undertaking Water-Resource Developments," *American Economic Review* 50 (May 1960): 310–20.

[29]If it were determined that these land value changes were not simply capitalization of otherwise measured benefits and costs so that counting them would not be double counting, we would incorporate them into the benefit-cost analysis.

Elaborate accounting rules would have to be devised to keep analyses comparable. No similar ambiguity is present when using net benefits as long as the algebraic sign and the year in which benefits and costs accrue are known.

$N$ does not change if equal amounts are added to benefits and to costs. If benefits were $1600 and costs $1200, $R$ would be 1.33 and $N$ would be $400. If $800 is added both to benefits and to costs $R$ becomes 1.2 while $N$ remains unchanged. A larger investment is required. The second is an inferior opportunity unless investment funds are unlimited or there is no profitable way to invest that other $800. The ratio criterion rates the second opportunity inferior to the first, as any wise business-man would. The net benefit criterion is indifferent between them. That measure of desirability, without constraints, implies that capital is freely available. The net benefit criterion can be made more useful by stating the problem as: maximize net benefits subject to a constraint on costs and to the constraint that total benefits exceed total costs.[30] If the extra $800 required exceeds the constraint, that project will be infeasible.

### Optimal Scales Under Various Criteria

The benefit-cost ratio is very much like the reciprocal of an average cost figure. The latter has costs in the numerator and output in physical terms in the denominator, while the former has the value of output in the numerator, and costs in the denominator.[31] Now, the output level at which average cost is a minimum is not necessarily the output at which profit (revenue minus cost) is a maximum. Similarly, the scale of a project which maximizes the benefit-cost ratio is not necessarily the scale which maximizes net benefits.

We have followed Roy Radner's graphic illustration of the point in Figure 6.4.[32] Points under the curved line represent feasible cost-benefit pairs dictated by the technology. Starting from any point on the frontier, to achieve more benefits we must incur more costs. Along any ray, $A$, $G$, or $H$, the benefit-cost ratio is constant. $F$, $D$, and $E$ are parallel lines with slope of one. Along any one net benefits are constant. The highest $R$ shown is on ray $A$, the highest $N$ on line $F$. In the feasible set we can

---

[30] It may be that the maximum benefit minus cost position is where net benefits are negative. This point maximizes $N$, but we should not undertake that project because it results in a loss.

[31] The perfect analogue of average cost is the cost-effectiveness ratio; for example, $2,300 per dropout prevented.

[32] Roy Radner, *Notes on the Theory of Economic Planning* (Athens, Greece: Centre for Economic Research, 1963), pp. 74–82.

FIGURE 6.4. MAXIMIZING BENEFITS/COSTS IS NOT
EQUIVALENT TO MAXIMIZING BENEFITS MINUS COSTS

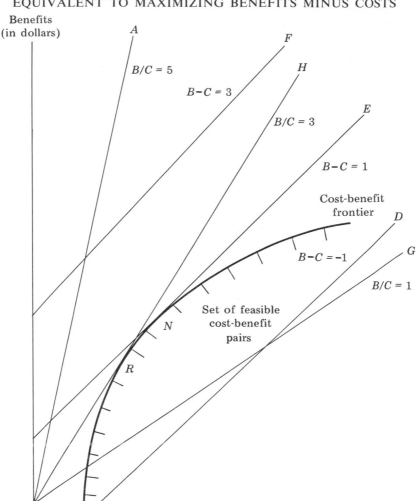

attain neither $A$ nor $F$. The best $\dfrac{B}{C}$ achievable in the feasible region is at
point $R$ on ray $H$. Highest net benefits come at point $N$ on line $E$. The
two criteria are not maximized at the same point: $R$ and $N$ are distinct.[33]

[33]The only case in which the two points coincide is the one in which the best benefit-
cost ratio attainable is unity.

## FIGURE 6.5. OPTIMAL PROJECT SCALES UNDER DIFFERENT CRITERIA

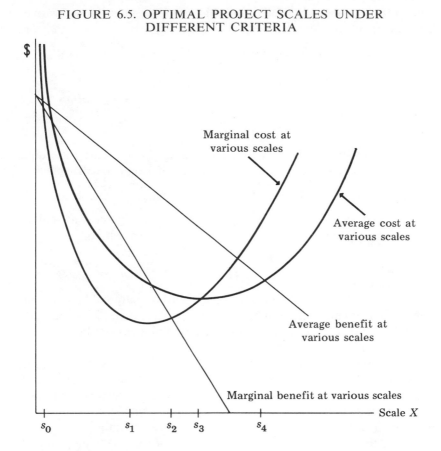

Note:
1: Optimal scale when criterion is max $R = B/C$ ($s_1$ is not necessarily directly below the minimum of the marginal cost curve)
2: Optimal scale when criterion is max $N - (B - C)$
3: Optimal scale when criterion is min $AC$
4: Optimal scale when criterion is $B \geqq C$ and agencies prefer large projects to small

Another way of seeing the difference between the net benefit and the benefit-cost ratio criteria is to think of an analogy to the theory of the firm. Figure 6.5 with quantity of output or scale, $x$, on the horizontal axis and dollars vertically, shows marginal benefit and cost curves.

If the criterion is to maximize the benefit-cost ratio,[34] $R = B(x)/C(x)$, $R$ will be maximized where $\dfrac{dR}{dx} = 0$; that is, where the derivative changes

---

[34]The notations $B(x)$ and $C(x)$ represent benefits and costs both given as functions of or dependent on the scale variable, $x$. For the moment we are ignoring discounting.

from positive to negative.[35] To find this point, we take the derivative of $R$ with respect to $x$ and set it equal to zero:

$$\frac{dR}{dx} = \frac{C \ dB/dx - B \ dC/dx}{C^2} \stackrel{\text{s}}{=} 0. \tag{5}$$

This implies

$$\frac{B}{C} = \frac{dB/dx}{dC/dx}. \tag{6}$$

In words, equation (6) states that the average benefit-cost ratio equals the marginal benefit-cost ratio or elasticity of benefits with respect to costs, $\dfrac{C}{B} \dfrac{dB}{dC}$, is one. In Figure 6.5, the ratio of marginal benefit to marginal cost is equal to the ratio of average benefit to average cost at scale 1.[36]

The maximum of $N \equiv B(x) - C(x)$ occurs only where

$$\frac{dN}{dx} = \frac{dB}{dx} - \frac{dC}{dx} = 0, \tag{7}$$

that is, where marginal net benefit equals zero or marginal benefit equals marginal cost. This condition holds at both scales 0 and 2 in Figure 6.5. Scale 2 maximizes net benefits, but scale 0 minimizes net benefits. Condition (7) is necessary for both situations.[37]

An agency might endeavor to produce a good or service at minimum average cost. In this case, the agency would choose scale or output 3 where average cost is at a minimum. Suppose agency heads want to maximize the size of their projects, but still fulfill their statutory directive that benefits exceed costs. Much of the literature on water resources suggests that the motive of cognizant bureaucracies is to develop "the full physical potential" of each site.[38] Then, they will push the scale of projects to just before scale 4, where benefits and costs are equal. They will overdevelop river basins, for example.

---

[35]The notation of the calculus is used here: $\dfrac{dR}{dx}$ refers to the instantaneous rate of change of $R$ with respect to $x$. The sufficient condition for this maximum in symbols is $\dfrac{d^2R}{dx^2} < 0$.

[36]In the example of Table 6.2 both ratios equal four only in alternative 1.

[37]The condition sufficient to insure a maximum of $N$ is that the slope of the net benefit function be decreasing (going from positive to negative) so that the point is at the top of a net benefit hill rather than at the bottom of a valley. In symbolic terms, the sufficient or "second-order" condition for a maximum is that $\dfrac{d^2N}{dx^2} < 0$, or $\dfrac{d^2B}{dx^2} < \dfrac{d^2C}{dx^2}$.

[38]See Fox and Herfindahl, "Attainment of Efficiency," pp. 201ff., and Leopold and Maddock, *The Flood Control Controversy*, p. 126.

TABLE 6.1. ALTERNATIVE USES OF A PARCEL OF URBAN LAND
(In millions of dollars, present value)

|  | | Costs | Benefits |
|---|---|---|---|
| 1. | No change | 2 | 8 |
| 2. | Park with swings, benches | 9 | 21 |
| 3. | Botanical garden and aquarium | 15 | 27 |
| 4. | University and cultural center | 24 | 31 |

Thus, all four objectives—(1) maximizing the benefit-cost ratio, (2) maximizing net benefits, (3) minimizing average costs, and (4) maximizing the size of the project subject to the constraint that costs do not exceed benefits—lead to different optimal scales.

### Mutually Exclusive Alternatives

So far we have been discussing project selection criteria. Frequently, a public agency will need to decide how to develop a particular resource. For example, an urban island may be available for one of several uses. All will be mutually exclusive, however, because only one can be pursued.[39]

First, we might leave it as it is and simply maintain it at an opportunity cost of $2 million[40] and allow people who could reach it by boat to enjoy it. This would yield $8 million in benefits. Second, we could develop a park with benches and swings and institute a public ferry service to the island. The costs (including opportunity cost) of doing so would be $9 million while benefits, let us suppose, would equal $21 million because the park would be more intensively used. Third, an elaborate botanical garden and aquarium could be created at a cost of $15 million. This would attract more visitors from a wider area because it would be a unique attraction in the region; its benefits would be $27 million. Fourth, the island could be developed as a university and cultural center including museums and an auditorium, with a bridge for easy access to the island. This elaborate plan would cost $24 million and yield benefits of $31 million.

The alternatives are summarized in Table 6.1 and Figure 6.6. In the figure, the lines connecting the several benefit levels and the several costs

[39]The problem of choosing the scale of a particular project is also a choice among mutually exclusive alternatives because a project can be pursued at only one scale.

[40]All costs and benefits are given as present values. The opportunity cost is the value in the best alternative use; for example, growing vegetables. If land is purchased, opportunity costs are usually measured as the purchase price of the land on the theory that the seller must be given this to induce him to forego the stream of benefits the land would yield if he held it.

FIGURE 6.6. ALTERNATIVE USES OF A PARCEL OF URBAN LAND

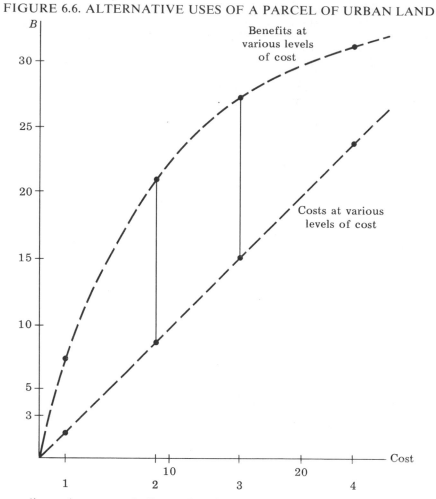

are discontinuous to indicate the discreteness of the four alternatives. Points in between the alternatives cannot be chosen. The curved line represents the benefit function and the straight line portrays the cost function. The cost function makes a 45-degree angle with the horizontal axis because its height at each point is equal to its distance along the cost axis.

The alternative with the highest benefit-cost ratio is 1. Alternatives 2 and 3 have the highest net benefits, and the city council would be indifferent between them if there were no budget constraints.[41]

---

[41]We defer discussion of constraints until a later section of this chapter. A budget constraint, for example, might require that no more than $10 million be spent by the city council on the development of the island.

TABLE 6.2. SUCCESS INDICATORS FOR FOUR HYPOTHETICAL
ALTERNATIVES
(In millions of dollars)

| Alternative | R = B/C | N = B-C | MB | MC | MB/MC |
|---|---|---|---|---|---|
| 1 | 4 | 6 | 8 | 2 | 4.00 |
| 2 | 2.33 | 12 | 13 | 7 | 1.86 |
| 3 | 1.80 | 12 | 6 | 6 | 1.00 |
| 4 | 1.29 | 7 | 4 | 9 | 0.44 |

Table 6.2 lists four alternatives in order of costs and shows the extra benefits and extra costs of each project compared to the one before. Assuming that there is no budget constraint, the council ought to prefer each successive scale to the previous one as long as extra benefits exceed extra costs. On this test, we would move from 1 to 2 and would be indifferent between 2 and 3. In considering alternative 4, the council would reject it over 3 because extra benefits are only $4 million while extra costs are $9 million. There would be a decrease in net benefits of $5 million in choosing the university over the botanical garden.

Suppose the city council did not consider alternatives 2 and 3. The incremental benefit of moving from 1 to 4 would be $23 million, and the incremental cost of choosing the university over the present state of the island would be only $22 million. Since incremental benefits exceed incremental costs, the council might decide to choose the university. Overlooked would be the superior alternatives of the park or botanical garden. This example shows the inferiority of the benefit-cost ratio to the net benefit criterion, the importance of examining the incremental benefit-cost ratio[42] and the necessity of examining all alternatives.

In Figure 6.6, the distance between the benefit and cost functions is greatest at a point part way between 2 and 3. It is here that the slope of the benefit function equals the slope of the cost function. This is another way of saying that marginal or incremental benefits equal marginal costs. But 2 and 3 are discrete alternatives so that points between them are not feasible. Of the discrete points, 2 and 3 have the greatest difference between benefits and costs. The net benefit criterion leaves us indifferent between two alternatives in this case. When we said that to maximize net benefits we invest as long as marginal benefits exceed marginal costs and until the two are equal,[43] we assumed no indivisibilities or continuously variable investment opportunities. This assumption does not hold in the present case. If other possible investments exist in addi-

[42]This is the ratio of the incremental benefits to incremental costs given in the last column of Table 6.2.

[43]Or, what is the same thing, until the incremental benefit-cost ratio is unity.

tion to these alternatives and funds can be used with marginal benefit-cost ratios greater than 1.0, then alternative 2 should be the use of the urban land.

The internal rate of return indicator falls down when there exist mutually exclusive projects, or different designs for a single project. Two mutually exclusive investment projects are depicted in Figure 6.7. On an internal rate of return criterion we should choose Project 1 because $r_1 > r_2$. However, at interest rates less than $r$, Project 2 has a present value of net benefits which is higher than that of Project 1.

## CONSTRAINTS

Benefit-cost analysis is usually done in a context of limited resources.[44] The upper bound on costs may not be known with precision (exist), but there is usually an implicit upper bound within which the government or agency must operate.[45]

The budget constraint may be on total expenditures: the sum of capital costs and operations, maintenance, and replacement (OMR) costs. More frequently, capital costs are constrained and OMR costs are expected to be kept "within reason." Examples of constraints are easy to find. The federal government may have an understood range for annual appropriations for civil works projects. A city library may have to operate on a capital account within bonding authority approved by the voters and on current account within a budget granted by the city council. A state may have a constitutional prohibition on deficit spending not approved in special ways, and the governor may have pledged not to increase taxes.

If resources are limited, a mechanism for allocating them must exist. All projects drawing on a single constrained budget—for example, in the Department of Agriculture—can be compared. Then one ought to test to see if the marginal benefit of $X in one use is as great as if $X

---

[44]Resources are limited to society; therefore, all projects are not pushed until marginal benefit vanishes, but only until marginal benefit equals marginal cost. Resources are limited to the agency so that a project will be undertaken only so long as marginal benefit exceeds or equals marginal cost plus a shadow price. See *infra*.

[45]The implication of imprecision in the budget constraint may be a weight on costs, which is a monotonically increasing function of costs. Cost overruns may be tolerable but at increasing costs. The necessary condition for an optimum is then that marginal benefit equal marginal cost multiplied by a certain factor. That factor is $\left[ W(C) + C \dfrac{dW}{dC} \right]$ where $W$ is the cost weight as a function of cost, $C$, and $\dfrac{dW}{dC}$ is the rate of increase of the weight with respect to $C$.

FIGURE 6.7. THE INCONSISTENCY OF THE PRESENT
VALUE OF NET BENEFITS AND INTERNAL RATE OF RETURN
CRITERIA FOR MUTUALLY EXCLUSIVE PROJECTS

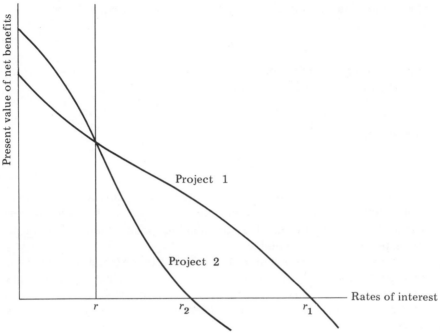

were spent outside the constrained budget, outside Agriculture; for example, in Health, Education and Welfare.[46]

When a budget is constrained, the concept of a "shadow price" for extra funds in that budget arises. Let us first examine an unconstrained situation and then a constrained situation to see how this shadow price arises.

Assume that we prefer larger values of net benefits over smaller and gross benefits, $B$, are a function of costs, $C$:

$$N = B(C) - C.$$

In order to find the optimal amount to spend, we maximize $N$. Under certain conditions,[47] we can locate the optimal value of $C$ by setting mar-

---

[46]This comparison is rarely made because of "incrementalism." This year's Agriculture budget is expected to approximate closely last year's. No test in Congress is made to ask if $X in Agriculture might profitably be redirected to HEW. In the Bureau of the Budget, this test is sometimes made.

[47]$N$ is twice differentiable with negative second derivative.

ginal net benefit, or the derivative of $N$ with respect to $C$, equal to zero:

$$\frac{dN}{dC} = \frac{dB}{dC} - 1 \overset{s}{=} 0.$$

This implies that the marginal benefit-cost ratio[48] be equal to one:

$$\frac{dB}{dC} = 1 \tag{8}$$

or that marginal benefits equal marginal costs.

When there is a constraint on total cost:

$$C \leq \overline{C},$$

a necessary condition for a maximum of $N$[49] is

$$\frac{dB}{dC} = 1 + \lambda. \tag{9}$$

Comparing (8) and (9), we see the effects of the constraint. The marginal benefit-cost ratio cut-off point must be larger by $\lambda$ under the constraint. The interpretation of $\lambda$, the shadow price, is the marginal net benefit per dollar of extra budget.

The situation is depicted graphically in Figure 6.8. If costs are unconstrained, they are incurred until marginal benefits equal marginal costs. If costs are constrained to be less than or equal to $\overline{C}$, costs are incurred only until the marginal benefit-cost ratio is equal to $1 + \lambda$, and not beyond.

The shadow price of money to a constrained budget is the extra national income to be obtained by shifting a dollar to this budget. If all the projects have positive net present values, then the shadow price will be greater than zero: national income could be increased by a shift of a dollar to this budget. This does not necessarily mean that the reallocation ought to be made. Each of the several constrained budgets may have a shadow price of funds greater than zero. Funds ought to be reallocated to the program with the highest shadow price until all shadow prices are equal, not necessarily at zero, and no further reallocation can achieve a higher level of national income.

When capital costs are constrained, but OMR costs are not, the value of an additional dollar spent on capital is greater than for one spent on OMR.

---

[48]The marginal benefit-cost ratio is defined to be $\frac{dB}{dC}$.

[49]Assuming all costs available are used, that the constraint is binding.

FIGURE 6.8. COMPARISON OF OPTIMAL SOLUTIONS WITH
AND WITHOUT A BUDGET CONSTRAINT

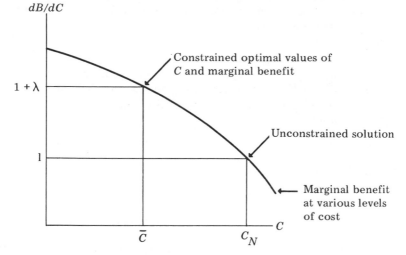

Let $K$ = capital costs, $M$ = OMR costs. The objective is to

$$\text{Maximize } N = B(M, K) - M - K$$
$$\text{Subject to } K \leq \overline{K}$$

where $B$, gross benefits, is a function of $M$ and $K$.

Necessary conditions for a maximum of $N$ are:

$$\frac{\partial B}{\partial M} = 1 \text{ while } \frac{\partial B}{\partial K} = 1 + \mu.$$

OMR costs can be incurred until their marginal benefit-cost ratio is one, but capital costs can be incurred only until the marginal benefit-cost ratio is $1 + \mu$.

When the capital constraint is not even nearly binding and when several projects are contemplated, some authors, notably Quirin,[50] argue for using a relative measure of desirability, the benefit-cost ratio, rather than the absolute measure, net benefits. This is appealing only when not all opportunities are known at the time the decision on one opportunity must be made. If $R$s usually fall in a range from 2 to 5, but costs vary widely, then 1.75 might be a cut-off $R$ to approve. Actual investment

---

[50]Quirin, *The Capital Expenditure Decision*, p. 55.

opportunities, however, may vary from an electric typewriter to a new fully-equipped plant.

It may be more realistic to look on the financial constraint not as a single quantity which is fixed, but as a succession of quantities in different time periods which are limited. Martin Weingartner[51] has suggested this approach in applying linear programming to the capital budgeting problem. The flood control budget is not fixed once and for all, but roughly $500 million is available each year to spend on flood control projects. Each project will require funds over several years.

The problem can then be set up formally as follows:

$$\text{Maximize } 35x_1 + 100x_2 + 80x_3 + 62x_4$$

subject to the constraints:

$$6x_1 + 20x_2 + 18x_3 + 11x_4 \leq 500$$
$$5x_1 + 25x_2 + 20x_3 + 13x_4 \leq 450$$
$$8x_1 + 18x_2 + 15x_3 + 9x_4 \leq 550 .$$

Four projects are being considered. Each is variable in scale, but the $x_i (i = 1, \ldots 4)$ can take on only integer values. The numbers $35, 100, 80,$ and $62$ represent the net benefits per unit of each project. In the first year $500 million are available. One year later a tight budget is contemplated in this agency because of the budgetary demands of other agencies, but after that the budget is a bit more permissive allowing $550 million.

The demands of each project operating at unit intensity are given in the matrix of coefficients of the three constraints. Project 1 at unit level requires $6 million in the first year, $5 million in the second and $8 million in the third. Project 2 requires $20 million in the first year; project 4 requires $13 million in the second year. This approach is particularly well suited to PPB. Multi-year costing will make the requirements of each project in the next several years known.

Mutual exclusivity can be introduced by requiring, for example,

$$x_1 + x_3 \leq 1$$

as a constraint. This says that either project 1 or 3 can be undertaken at unit level but not both.

The linear programming problem then seeks the optimal integer values of $x_1$ through $x_4$ subject to the constraints.[52] The solution of the dual problem will give the imputed value of an additional million dollars of funds in each year's budget.

[51]H. M. Weingartner, *Mathematical Programming and the Analysis of Capital Budgeting Problems* (Chicago: Markham, 1967).
[52]And the usual non-negativity constraint: $x_i \geq 0$ for all $i$.

In addition to financial constraints, physical, legal, and administrative constraints also exist. A decision the Chicago Public Library had to make was how to increase its storage capacity without using any more land than the present main building occupied. Alternatives considered were filling in the courtyard of the present building or demolishing the present building and building another on the same site. This building would be taller than the present one and might require use of the air rights over an adjoining alley.

Some existing constraints may preclude terminating projects that are shown to be unjustified by benefit-cost analysis. Employees cannot be laid off without creating problems—legal, moral, or morale. At times, tenured employees can be reassigned to other work, but even reassignments may create problems, especially with respect to older workers or professional employees (such as pharmacologists and social workers). Administrators often find it expedient to terminate the work of such employees gradually, as they retire or die. The implication is that failing the benefit-cost criterion does not imply that a project should be terminated.

Despite their limiting nature, constraints are often helpful to those who design projects; without them, project designers would have infinite freedom to choose possible projects, because there is always a multitude of things that might be done. The constraints bring the planners' imaginations back to reality—back to what is feasible. In the case of the Chicago Public Library, if the Board of Directors had had complete freedom to buy more land or locate elsewhere their decision problem would have been much greater.

## EXTERNALITIES

One justification for preferring government acitivity to private activity in certain realms is that the government's viewpoint can be more comprehensive than that of individuals. For example, a businessman is likely to base his decisions primarily on his own profit, with little or no regard for costs imposed on other firms or people. If a foundry operates next door to a laundry, it is not likely to take proper account of the impact of its soot on the laundry. The effect of the soot on the laundry's profits is *external* for the foundry. Costs or benefits imposed on others in the course of one's own activity, for which they receive or pay nothing, we call *external costs* and *external benefits* or, collectively, *externalities*. They have also been called *spillovers*, because brine created as a by-product of oil wells spills over into the underground water supply.

Externalities occur whenever someone makes uncompensated use of an environmental factor that he shares with others. External costs arise in polluting air or water. Externalities arise in river basins because what is done upstream has effects on downstream users.

Many communities on the Mississippi build their own levees to prevent flooding, but high upstream levees make floods more likely or more severe downstream. For this and other reasons, the phrase "one river— one problem" has come into use.

Externalities can be "internalized" by enlarging the decision-making unit. For example, federal involvement with the flood control problem on the Mississippi internalized formerly external costs and benefits. The broader the perspective of a decision unit, the broader its concept of costs and benefits is likely to be.

Two types of externalities have been identified: technological and pecuniary.[53] A technological externality involves *physical* effects on others. This would be the case, for example, if the foundry's soot increased the laundry's costs. A more general statement is that the marginal productivity of one producer's factor is affected by another producer's operation.[54] A pecuniary externality involves *financial* effects on others arising from changes in the supplies of the things they sell; an example would occur if the foundry's soot increased the demand for the laundry's services. If the action of one individual or firm bids up factor rates of hire, cuts down prices of substitute products, raises prices of complements to the good produced, or lowers the price of the good produced, a pecuniary externality can be said to exist. These are financial effects as distinct from physical effects.

A benefit-cost analysis that includes pecuniary externalities is *double counting*. For example, if a transportation improvement improves accessibility, time savings of commuters should be counted; to count the consequent increases in land values as well would be double counting. If a project lowers the price of electricity so that the total revenue of former sellers of electricity is reduced, would we say that society has not benefited from the additional electricity? No, because the effect of entry on the entrant's competitors is purely pecuniary and ought to be ignored.

In contrast, a benefit-cost analysis would be incomplete if technological externalities were ignored. If a dam is built for flood control, yet unintentionally provides recreational opportunities for picnickers and

---

[53] Tibor Scitovsky, "Two Concepts of External Economies," *Journal of Political Economy* (April 1954), pp. 149ff.; and Roland N. McKean, *Efficiency in Government Through Systems Analysis* (New York: Wiley, 1958), Chapter 8, "Spillover Effects."

[54] A technological externality can arise in consumption as well; for example, if foundry increased neighbors' needs for laundering.

boaters, then there has been a technological externality or spillover. More recreational services can now be provided with the same resources than before the dam was built. Willingness to pay for recreation should be calculated and included in the benefits of the flood control project. If local governments use salt to melt ice on roads in winter, they ought not to ignore the cost they impose on their citizens whose automobile bottoms corrode. A technological externality of the supersonic transport is likely to be a sonic boom heard wherever the plane flies. SSTs will consume silence, a dear commodity. These examples demonstrate the fact that the most frequent form of externality occurs when two products are produced simultaneously. Frequently, a good and a "bad" are produced jointly.

## APERCU

Quantitative evaluation produces three kinds of outputs. One consists of numerical estimates of the costs or benefits associated with various alternatives. Another output is the conclusion that one alternative is, by the benefit-cost or cost-effectiveness criterion, better than the others that were considered. The third result is qualitative by-products.

Benefit-cost or cost-effectiveness analysis may lead to better decisions. One way they can do this is by compelling a more deliberate and explicit evaluation of alternatives. Decision-makers who are provided with the results of a careful exploration and analysis of all the alternatives are more likely to perform their function wisely.

It is important, however, that qualitative elements that are not a by-product of the benefit-cost analysis and cannot be incorporated into the present value figures, such as income distribution and fairness, be considered also.

We have now situated benefit-cost analysis among its close relatives, inquired into the company it keeps, and examined its philosophical and analytic values. Let us look deeper into the dossier of this problematic adolescent. We shall see how he converts benefits and costs accruing in different periods into commensurable quantities. He has difficulty dealing with uncertainty. In his early youth he proved himself at several pursuits, mainly in the area of economic efficiency. Benefits have been attributed for the outputs of water, transportation and urban renewal projects; and human capital improvements through health and education. In doing so, this youngster has energetically estimated demand curves (sometimes even interpreting them properly) and calculated willingness to pay. He is less well practised at reckoning more subtle impacts on income distribution according to race, region, and age. Perhaps as he grows in wisdom he will learn to deal with other objectives.

Cost analysis has been one of his fortes, but he still has a long way to go before he can estimate costs accurately. Types of costs will be identified and the factors that govern them will be delineated, but there is still much error in the prediction of financial costs and social costs are rarely calculated. We shall assess the lad's achievement on an early apprentice effort, the evaluation of the California Water Plan; and more recently on the supersonic transport development program. We can ask whether his efforts really make any difference to ultimate decisions. Finally, we give a prospectus for his future: those areas in which he shows some promise and those in which he has no vocation at all.

# Seven

# TIME, INTEREST, AND UNCERTAINTY

Time is the quintessence of investment. Investments yield their benefits not only in the current period but in the future as well. Costs, too, are not accrued only in the present year, and the determination of which years are relevant is the first topic we treat in this chapter. Benefits and costs must be aggregated over time. How to aggregate them is our second topic. We will review theory in this context, but more valuable is the recounting of history to examine past behavior with its flaws and inconsistencies. Since the theory is not conclusive, how can practice be consistent? Finally, we broach that troublesome topic, perhaps the sixth essence of investment, uncertainty. That discussion is likely to leave us at sixes and sevens.

## WHAT YEARS ARE RELEVANT?

One might undertake to evaluate and then discount the costs and benefits of an alternative for literally any time span that can be specified. What span *should* one consider?

The major aspect of this time problem has been determination of what time horizon is *appropriate*. In practice, is it better to use a fifty-year or a one hundred-year time horizon? Some have said that the question is purely academic when a realistically high discount rate is employed. The present value of a dollar received fifty years hence, discounted at 8 percent is only two cents. But the problem is important when annual equivalents, especially annual cost equivalents, are calculated. These annual equivalents include interest plus amortization as do mortgage payments. In calculating the equal annual payment, it is important over how many years amortization takes place.

Unfortunately, we can give no infallible normative guidance on this problem. A *reasonable* time horizon is the economic or service life of the project's longest-lived fixed asset. A person's time horizon is his life expectancy; shorter horizons are appropriate for investments in the aged than for investment in children. Dams, on the other hand, probably last forever. Nevertheless, uncertainty should be considered. How long will the need for a particular good or service last?

Another aspect of the time problem is knowing when to start. This has been called the sequencing problem. Projects need not only be justified or rejected and ranked, but should be systematically placed in a queue. Normally, a starting date is chosen so as to maximize net benefits. The implication is usually to start as soon as possible if the project is worthwhile and benefits are functions of time since starting.[1] But for many projects, demand grows with population or calendar time. Many water projects would have better been postponed.

It may also be necessary to define when expenditures on a project are to stop. In justifying a single project it is not necessary to choose an optimal stopping date. That is because if any stopping date justifies the project, so will the optimal one. To reject a project, however, we must say that even with its best stopping date, costs exceed benefits. Only when we are choosing among several projects or several designs of a single project does the benefit-cost criterion become involved. The better of two alternatives is one that if started and stopped at its own best dates would have the larger difference (in present value) between benefits and costs between approval and infinity.

## AGGREGATION OVER TIME

### In Theory

The concept of present value must be understood before we discuss how to make benefits and costs commensurable when they accrue in many different years.

The present monetary value of the social costs or social benefits a project would produce between approval and infinity is the sum, over all relevant years, of the reduced value that each year's costs or benefits takes when its actual value is discounted back to a particular reference date at a particular annual rate of discount. The two questions that remain are: what reference date is appropriate and what discount rate is appropriate?

[1]S. A. Marglin, *Approach to Dynamic Investment Planning* (Amsterdam: North-Holland, 1963).

It is easy to specify an appropriate reference date. If the same rate of discount is used for every year and for both costs and benefits, any reference date will do. An alternative with a larger discounted value of benefits less costs at one reference date also will have a larger discounted value at any other reference date. However, for convenience in interpretation, and also to allow for varying discount rates, one particular reference date can be said to be best. That is the earliest date when the project is likely to receive final approval. The present value of cost or benefits will mean the at-approval value.

*The Many Functions of Interest Rates.* Establishing the appropriate discount rate is a far more complicated question. Interest rates serve many purposes: to represent the opportunity costs of capital, to indicate time preference, to stabilize economies, to attract foreign funds to a country's banks, to guide the choice of technique in production, and to regulate the size and rate of growth of the public sector. Only in an optimal and static world could the same interest rate be used to guide all these choices.

In order to allocate capital among many potential uses, rates of return are used as measures of desirability. Private enterpreneurs calculate internal rates of return on candidate projects and compare them with rates representing the cost of capital to their firm.[2] Market interest costs represent the cost of capital to the firm if it would raise capital by borrowing.[3] At the margin, in equilibrium, market interest costs represent the opportunity cost of capital. For the public sector, each new project undertaken should have an internal rate of return greater than the marginal social rate of return. The marginal social rate of return is the lowest internal rate of return on any project or separable part of a project that has been undertaken (social benefits and costs being correctly evaluated). Thus, interest rates ration capital.

Interest rates influence the choice of consumers in their spending and saving decisions. In static equilibrium they will consume until the marginal rate of substitution between present consumption and future consumption equals the rate of exchange or price ratio between present money and future money as observed in the market.

Interest rates are manipulated by central banking authorities to effect stabilization goals. Increase in interest rates is used to arrest excess eco-

---

[2]According to Joel Dean, in *Capital Budgeting* (New York: Columbia University Press, 1951), most businessmen calculate the period of time in which cash flow from investment will pay back their investment. This criterion has been criticized for many years. Perhaps the internal rate of return criterion is in use in larger business where more sophisticated analysis is done.

[3]Market interest rates may be adjusted for tax deductibility of interest paid by the firm and the effect of borrowing on earnings per share.

nomic activity and thereby combat inflation; a reduction in interest rates may induce borrowing and investment to combat a depression. Interest rates are also used to attract foreign funds to a country's banking system to serve balance-of-payments objectives. Frequently, stabilization and payments objectives are at odds and overtax interest rates as an instrument of economic policy.

Market interest rates may reflect expectations about inflation. The desired rate of return is a real rate. Inflation is a loading placed on top of the real rate of interest. In a context of 6 percent inflation, a bank is only getting a 3 percent real rate of return when it charges 9 percent. It was doing better when it was getting 6 percent and the rate of inflation was 2 percent. Inflation is irrelevant to social time preference (tastes) or opportunity costs (technology). Therefore, the government should not employ market interest rates that include inflation in making its capital expenditure decisions.[4]

What interest rate a firm or agency uses in its planning to indicate its cost of capital has great repercussions in its choice of methods of production. The higher the discount rate used, the dearer capital appears relative to labor. As a result, more labor-using methods of production will be chosen. Low discount rates favor school buildings over teachers (with the same amount spent on education); letter-sorting machines and optical character readers over clerks and mail handlers; dams over flood-plain zoning; and guided missiles, helicopters, and automatic weapons over soldiers.

Despite their importance for choice of technique, more emphasis has been placed on the implications of discount rates for the size of the government sector. Low interest rates are permissive to public investments that increase the size of the public sector, while higher rates restrain public investment by making projects more difficult to justify.

No single interest rate can serve all these masters. It is no wonder that planners ask which interest rate to use.

*The Social Rate of Discount and the Opportunity Costs of Investment.* We have been talking of observable interest rates. Some economists use discount rates for yet another purpose: to describe social as distinguished from private time preference. Everyone may be eager to consume early rather than defer consumption in the interest of growth. The society may decide that growth is important and justifies the sacrifice of present consumption. Few are willing to sacrifice their own consumption, even if compensated by the market interest rate, unless their fellow

[4]We shall argue below that the government should not ignore market interest rates entirely. The discount rate it uses should vary over the business cycle; for example, increase in times of inflation.

citizens do likewise. Making a particular investment requires sacrificing either consumption or another investment. To choose how much to invest we must balance the expected gains with either time preference or the opportunity cost of the displaced investment. Those opportunity costs depend in turn on whether the proceeds of the investment will be invested again or consumed.

The idea of a social rate of discount arose from Pigou's notion[5] that individuals tend to overdiscount the future. At one extreme, Marxists reject consumers' preferences entirely and use no discounting. They take the "egalitarian" view that a dollar of income to the next generation is as good as one to this generation. Baumol[6] and Eckstein[7] maintain that at least two time preferences exist: one for individuals acting on their own and one for individuals acting collectively. Both agree with Pigou that the benefits to future generations should be accorded more weight than the market gives them.

Marglin[8] has further developed and refined the idea of a social rate. He was troubled by high market rates of interest observed in underdeveloped countries. Despite this, most citizens of underdeveloped countries would vote for a rapid rate of economic growth. In the absence of huge foreign aid, such a high growth rate could be achieved only with a much lower discount rate and a greater willingness to invest for future returns by sacrificing present consumption.

Individual behavior differs from social behavior; in the latter one has reason to believe that his actions are being followed by others. People will agree to do (refrain from doing) certain things if they think it is good (bad) to do them *and* if they have some assurance that their fellows will follow. Stopping at intersections where there is little road traffic increases driving time and we would normally avoid it. We realize, however, that traffic laws decrease the likelihood of accidents. Because we are fairly confident that most people stop for red lights, we change our individualistic behavior and acquiesce in the social compact to obey traffic laws. When we give charity we often sign a statement which says, "In consideration of the gifts of others, I pledge. . . ." The *quid pro quo* is the assurance that other people are acting magnanimously also.

Similarly, life may be very precarious for an individual in a poor

[5]A. C. Pigou, *The Economics of Welfare* 4th ed. (London: Macmillan, 1949), p. 24. This book was first published in 1912.

[6]Baumol, *Welfare Economics and the Theory of the State* (Cambridge, Mass.: Harvard University Press, 1952), pp. 91–93.

[7]O. Eckstein, *Water Resource Development* (Cambridge, Mass.: Harvard University Press, 1958), pp. 99ff.

[8]S. A. Marglin, "The Social Rate of Discount and the Optimal Rate of Investment," *Quarterly Journal of Economics* 77 (February 1963): 95–111.

country. His individual welfare might best be served by a strategy of high consumption reflecting his high time preference, but his government may decide that if everyone acted that way there would be little growth and the country would remain poor. The government has a low rate of time preference to justify a high level of investment for economic growth. Although the citizen may not have decided this for himself, he does not revolt at the high rate of taxation and forced saving for social investment. He realizes that his children and grandchildren will benefit even if he will not, and he cares for their future welfare and for that of his nation enough that he will accede to the social policy. All market or observable interest rates, even the government bond rate, reflect *private* rather than *social* rates of discount, and must be accordingly adjusted for use in calculating present values.

Public spending, unless there is more than frictional unemployment, diverts resources from private use. The shift to public use is desirable only if the present value of net benefits of the use is higher in the public sector than in the private sector. Unless the rate of discount used in public investment planning reflects the benefits available in the private sector, shifts of resources may be made which lower the national income. If investing $1,000 in the public sector yields a present value (discounted at the social rate of time preference) of benefits of $1,500, it would appear a worthwhile investment. But if the $1,000 could yield a present value of benefits of $2,000 (also discounted at the social rate) in the private sector, then the opportunity cost of the public project is $2,000, not the apparent dollar cost of $1,000.

Two reasons exist for discounting public projects: to reflect a social preference for earlier over later benefits and to reflect the opportunity costs of public investment. Marglin has suggested that they be combined into "synthetic rate of discount" or social rate *cum* opportunity cost.[9] The following example will explain this concept.

Assume that a society decides on an optimal rate of growth that requires a rate of discount of 5 percent to sustain it. Investment opportunities in the public sector are such that under its constrained budget the marginal benefit-cost ratio is 1.5. In the private sector the internal rate of return on the marginal project is 20 percent. If $100 extra were invested in the private sector, it would yield $20 each year forever (or in addition to returning the original investment). Capitalized at the social rate of discount, this $20 has a present value of $400. Therefore, the marginal benefit-cost ratio in the private sector is 4.0. If we wish to maximize

[9] Hufschmidt, Krutilla, and Margolis, *Consultants' Report* (1963), pp. 13–14, footnote 6; and S. A. Marglin, *Public Investment Criteria* (Cambridge, Mass.: M.I.T. Press, 1967), pp. 47–69.

the present value of output of the economy, we should not undertake any project in the public sector that has a marginal benefit-cost ratio less than 4.0. If we did undertake projects with smaller ratios, the opportunity cost in the private sector would exceed benefits.

There is a way to take into account both reasons for discounting, impatience and other opportunities, by using a rate of discount that "synthesizes" the two. Let us assume that private sector opportunities yield at the margin $a$ in present value per dollar invested. In the previous paragraph $a = 4$. The marginal dollar yields $r$ each year in perpetuity, $r = 0.2$ above. The opportunity cost is present value per dollar invested,

$$a = \frac{r}{i} \tag{1}$$

where $i$ is the social rate of discount.[10]

Suppose that public projects yield $b$ per year for $n$ years. Public projects should be undertaken only so long as[11]

$$b \left[ \frac{1 - (1 + i)^{-n}}{i} \right] > a, \tag{2}$$

that is, the present value of benefit must exceed the present value of opportunity cost. Substituting (1) in (2), we have as a necessary and sufficient condition for a public investment to be efficient, that

$$b \geq \frac{r}{1 - (1 + i)^{-n}}. \tag{3}$$

Now we can define a discount rate synthesizing social time preference $i$ and the rate of return lost in the private sector by undertaking

---

[10]A perpetual stream is converted to a present value or "capitalized" by dividing the constant flow by the discount rate because the sum of the infinite geometric series

$$\frac{1}{1 + i}, \frac{1}{(1 + i)^2} \cdots$$

is given by

$$1/i.$$

Equation (1) is simplified in two respects. It assumes that public investments displace private investment dollar for dollar and all the benefits of public investment are consumed rather than reinvested.

[11]The sum of the finite series

$$\frac{1}{1 + i}, \frac{1}{(1 + i)^2} \cdots \frac{1}{(1 + i)^n}$$

is what appears in square brackets. The finite series represents discount factors for successive years in the future.

public activity $r$. Let us call this synthetic rate $s$. The identity which defines $s$ is

$$\frac{1 - (1 + s)^{-n}}{s} \equiv \frac{1 - (1 + i)^{-n}}{r} \, . \tag{4}$$

Notice that $s$ appears on one side and $r$ and $i$ appear on the other.

The condition for an efficient investment (2) becomes

$$b \frac{1 - (1 + s)^{-n}}{s} > 1. \tag{5}$$

Every dollar invested in the public sector, when discounted at the synthetic rate, must yield more than one dollar of benefits net of opportunity costs.

If a social rate of discount is used by the government, it should apply to private investment as well. Then all potential investments, public and private, that compete for the same funds will be on an equal footing with respect to time preference.

In reality, however, choices are never made between, for example, Bureau of Reclamation investment and IBM investment. Expenditure and taxation issues are considered separately in committee and in legislation.[12] Furthermore, private firms do not *use* the social rate of discount. Firms respond to market interest rates. The Federal Reserve System is unlikely to push market interest rates down to the social rate because of the functions market interest rates serve other than regulating the rate of investment.

We have been talking as if a social rate of discount existed and was unique, and as if there were consensus on what it is numerically. There is no such consensus. Furthermore, the concept of a social rate of discount is controversial. It is a concept which does not enter the minds of agents in private markets and does not have observable counterparts. Why, ask the skeptics, should government activity have these umbrellas to protect it from the cold rain that falls on the open market place? Does use of a social rate of discount imply overturning consumers' preferences or is it rather discovery of different *social* preferences; that is, preferences that would be observed if the individual had assurance that others would behave in a public-spirited way if he did?

Should the rate chosen vary over the business cycle? A rate that incorporates market information such as government or corporate bond rates will vary as economic conditions change, being higher during pros-

[12]Arthur Smithies lamented this fact in Committee for the Economic Development Research Study, *The Budgetary Process in the United States* (New York: McGraw-Hill, 1955), but the situation has changed little since he wrote.

perity than during depression. A rate that ignores market forces such as the social rate of time preference will not vary over the cycle. This is an argument against using a pure social rate of time preference. The synthetic rate reflects superior private opportunities available during prosperous times. If investments must be rationed in the private sector during an inflation, is there any reason the public sector should be exempt? Our answer is no. On the other hand, market interest rates are not perfect measures of opportunity costs. First of all, much private investment by firms is internally financed so that it does not necessarily have a marginal rate of return equal to the market interest rate. Secondly, market interest rates reflect the multiple functions of interest rates. When interest rates rose during 1966–70, private investments did not suddenly become more productive than they were before 1966. Rather, the Federal Reserve sold securities, raised the interest rate it charged banks for loans, and raised the percentage of deposits member banks must have on deposit at their Federal Reserve bank. In these ways, monetary policy was used for stabilization and market interest rates reflected the resulting tight money.

*The Size of the Public Sector.* In theory, the size of the public sector should be decided deliberately through the political process, and market interest rates should guide the choice of capital intensity or project design. In practice, discount rates are used more to regulate the growth and size of the public sector. They only exert a restraining effect. Encouraging effects are exogenous. The size of the public sector tends to grow over time. Wars and social upheavals tend to force public expenditures up through a "displacement effect." The resultant "examination process" creates felt needs for public activity and the relative size of the public sector never contracts all the way to the pre-shock level.[13] An interesting empirical question to examine is whether the mix between public spending on current account and public investment responds to market- and government-employed interest rates. Our guess would be that interest rates had no discernible impact on the choice between public spending on current or capital account. Legislation and appropriation for investment projects and spending for goods and services whose benefits accrue in the current period are independent. Public spending as a whole reacts more to the business cycle than to interest rates. When the opportunity cost of capital is low, that of labor is low also and public spending is urged to compensate for low activity levels in the private sector. Little differentiation is then made between current spending and

[13] Adolf Wagner, *Finanzwissenschaft* 2nd ed. (Leipzig: C. F. Winter, 1890): and Peacock and Wiseman, *The Growth of Public Expenditures in the United Kingdom.* National Bureau of Economic Research (Princeton, N.J.: Princeton University Press, 1961).

investment. When government expenditures are curtailed to compensate for inflation, little regard is paid to whether they are current or capital items.

The interest rate is not the only device for restraining public investment. Usually much more heavy-handed methods are used. Ideological issues sometimes prevail. President Eisenhower promulgated a "no new starts" policy for public works in 1953. This can be seen either as a cyclical response to the inflation of the Korean war or as an ideological option for a small public works program. It lasted three years. President Nixon promulgated a 75 percent "freeze" of construction funds during 1969.

Since there is not a consensus on the interest rate problem, the benefit-cost analyst does well to make parallel computations using several discount rates. In so doing, the sensitivity of his analysis to the discount rate is displayed. If the time profile of benefits and costs is known, it is not difficult to calculate the present value of both streams at various rates of discount. Typically, three rates—high, medium and low—are used. This effort is called *sensitivity analysis* or *parameterization* because one explores the sensitivity of the analysis to the variation of a parameter of the problem.

More discussion on this subject follows. First, let us see how some of these theoretical concepts have influenced recent use of discounting for public projects.

### In Practice

Public agencies have traditionally favored low discount rates in order to increase the quantity of work they are authorized to do. Beneficiaries of project outputs, especially those which are non-reimbursable such as flood control, have favored low rates to increase the chances of justification of projects in which they have direct interests. Democrats, to the extent that they favor growth of the public sector, have favored low rates because they allow more public projects to be justified. Often they have been unmindful of the implications for choice of project design. In business, managers who are more interested in expansion and growth of sales than in profitability may favor low discount rates for use in planning.

Thus, agencies, beneficiaries, Democrats, and managers favor low rates. Budget bureaus, taxpayers, Republicans, and stockholders conversely advocate higher rates in order to impede some expenditures.

*Discounting in Practice.* Not all agencies have even reached the level of sophistication indicated by using discounting. Elmer B. Staats, then Comptroller General of the United States, testified before the Joint Economic Committee in 1968 that thirteen agencies used no discounting in the analysis of Fiscal Year 1969 programs. The Interstate Commerce Commission, the Export-Import Bank of Washington, the Veterans Administration, the Treasury Department, and the Department of Commerce had no plans to use discounting in the future.[14]

As Table 7.1 indicates, various discount rates have been used both in benefit-cost analyses within different subdivisions of a single agency and within one year by different agencies. When the Corps of Engineers evaluated the proposed Champlain Waterway between the Hudson and St. Lawrence Rivers, they used $3\frac{1}{8}$ percent, but their counterparts on the International Joint Commission used a rate of $5\frac{3}{8}$ percent.[15] This practice is not conducive to optimal allocation of public investment funds. Almost all that can be said in its support is that it is preferable to the practice of using no discounting at all.

*Policy Statements on Discounting.* A number of federal agencies have studied the question of choosing an appropriate discount rate to use in benefit-cost analysis. Review of several of these reports—from the President's Water Resources Council, from the Secretary of the Treasury, from the Joint Economic Committee, and from the Bureau of the Budget—will also show the development of policy because they are discussed in chronological order.

In 1962, Senate Document 97 counseled using the average rate of interest paid by the Treasury on all U.S. obligations of 15 years' maturity or longer. The long-term cost of capital to the U.S. government was considered the appropriate rate. This fostered the use of the "coupon" or "nominal" rate of interest. Some of the outstanding bonds in 1962 had been issued at a time when Federal Reserve policy allowed the Treasury to borrow at artifically low rates of interest. The Fed would buy whatever bonds could not be sold to the public at low coupon rates. Unfettered interest rates could be considerably higher. If so, those bonds would have sold at a "discount"; that is, at a price lower than their redemption value. For example, a bond promising $1,000 at maturity and interest of $30 per year, but selling for $800, has a "yield to maturity" over 3.75 because it provides not only $30 per year but also a $200 capital gain.

[14]Statement of Hon. Elmer B. Staats, Comptroller General of the U.S. in Joint Economic Committee, Subcommittee on Economy in Government, *Interest Rate Guidelines for Federal Decision Making,* 90th Congress, 2nd Session (Washington, D.C.: U.S. Government Printing Office, 1968), p. 47.

[15]*Champlain Waterway Feasibility Report,* Report to the International Joint Commission, 1965.

TABLE 7.1. INTEREST RATES USED IN BENEFIT-COST
ANALYSES

| Source | Subject | Date | Rate in Percent |
|---|---|---|---|
| Dept. of Agriculture | "Benefit-Cost Analysis of Research on Live Poultry Handling" | c 1967 | 5.0 |
| Dept. of Agriculture | "Benefit-Cost Analysis of Research on Scab Resistant White Potato Varieties" | c 1967 | 5.0 |
| Dept. of Agriculture | "Benefit-Cost Analysis of Research on Southern White Pine Genetics" | c 1967 | 4.0 |
| | Rural electrification loans | 1969 | 4.875 |
| Defense: Corps of Engineers | *Salem Church Reservoir, Rappahanock River, Virginia* (Senate Document 37, 90th Congress, 1st Session) | 1967 | 4.625 |
| | Champlain Waterway (St. Lawrence Seaway) | 1965 1962 | 3.125 2.625 |
| Interior: Bureau of Reclamation | Oahe Unit, *Missouri River Basin Project,* South Dakota (House Document 163, 90th Congress, 1st Session) | 1967 | 3.125 |
| | Utility program        Low risk                Average risk | 1969 1969 | 6.0 12.0 |
| Transportation: Office of Planning and Program Review | Special analytic study: *Urban Commutation Alternatives* | 1968 | 10.0 |
| FAA | Radar components, en route automation | 1969 | 4.2 |
| Defense: Office of the Secretary | Shipyard, air base and similar analysis | 1968 | 10.0 |
| Tennessee Valley Authority | Hydroelectric power | 1969 | 4.5 to 5.5 |
| Office of Economic Opportunity | Job Corps Upward Bound Family planning program | 1969 1969 1969 | 3.0 and 5.0 3.0 and 5.0 5.0 |
| Agency for International Develop. | Bolivian highway | 1969 | 12.0 |
| Dept. of Health, Educ. and Welfare | Adult education, vocational, rehabilitation, work experience | 1969 | 0-8.0 |
| | Selected disease control programs | 1969 | 0-10.0 |
| | Cancer control | 1969 | 4.0 to 6.0 |
| Internation Jt. Commission | St. Lawrence Seaway | 1965 | 5.375 |

TABLE 7.1. *(Continued)*

| SOURCE | SUBJECT | DATE | RATE IN PERCENT |
|---|---|---|---|
| State of Calif. Dept. of Wtr. Resources | California Aqueduct | 1959 | 3.5 |
| Bechtel Corp. | California Water Plan | 1955 | 2.7 |
| Hirshleifer, De-Haven, Milliman | California Water Plan | 1960 | 10.0 |
| Margolis, Bain, Caves | California Water Plan | 1964 | 5.0 or 6.0 |

In 1965, the Secretary of the Treasury pointed out that coupon rates are misleading. While reporting that the average coupon rate on "long-term" bonds was $3\frac{1}{8}$ percent, Secretary Dillon expressed the correct opinion that the government's *current* borrowing costs were more relevant: $4\frac{1}{4}$ percent in 1964.[16] This meant the yields to maturity on long-term bonds rather than their coupon rates. One can argue that the government's "cost of capital" is not the correct rate of discount to use, but at least Secretary Dillon's suggestion moved in the right direction.

Clearly changes are needed over time. Senate Document 97 suggested recalculating the rate from time to time as borrowing costs changed. In fact, borrowing costs changed considerably between 1965 and 1970. The Water Resources Council, composed of all federal agencies with responsibility in the water field, seeks to coordinate policy among the several agencies involved. In 1965, they agreed to use the same discount rate in all their calculations.[17] The council also agreed in principle that the rate should be redetermined each year to reflect current borrowing costs with the provision that the rate could not increase more than $\frac{1}{4}$ percent each year. The rate to be used in fiscal year 1969 was $4\frac{5}{8}$ percent[18] and that in fiscal year 1970 is $4\frac{7}{8}$ percent. These rates are supposed to represent prevailing yields to maturity on treasury bonds.[19] Rates have been increasing in recent years, but they do not yet approach market rates. The council intends to increase the rate by $\frac{1}{4}$ percent each year

---

[16] Letter from the Hon. Douglas Dillon to the Hon. Stewart Udall, 17 November 1964, quoted in R. I., Banks and A. Kotz, "The Program Budget and the Interest Rate for Public Investment," *Public Administration Review* 26, no. 4 (December 1966): 283–92.

[17] *Federal Register* vol. 33, no. 145 (26 July 1965).

[18] *Federal Register* 33 (24 December 1968): 19170.

[19] *Federal Register* 33 (24 December 1968): 19170.

until it more nearly approximates the current costs of federal borrowing (about 7 percent in mid-1969).

In 1968, the Joint Economic Committee of Congress expressed itself on the interest rate problem: "The current minimum-risk interest rate which should be used for evaluating public investments is at least 5 percent."[20]

A memorandum to federal government agencies from the Bureau of the Budget indicated that the rate of $4\frac{7}{8}$ percent would be the minimum allowable to be used in fiscal year 1970. This rate was merely a minimum interest rate to be used. "The Bureau . . . will request specific higher rates for particular projects or program evaluation efforts."[21]

The Bureau's study of the opportunity costs of public investment concluded that they were 7.8 percent.[22] In the inflationary context of 1970, they ordered all agencies to use discount rates of 10 percent. The water agencies were successful in bargaining to retain the $4\frac{7}{8}$ percent rate for their projects, however.

This effort to value the present over the future and curtail certain public projects has had an ironic impact on some of the agencies. Purportedly, some tried to justify all the projects they could in that year, knowing that in the next year the interest rate would go up and it would be harder to justify projects. This has precisely the wrong effect in an inflationary context. Also, many agencies have taken an almost petulant attitude that if their discount rate must be raised, they would count "secondary benefits" in their analysis.[23]


## HANDLING UNCERTAIN OUTCOMES


Like all investments, public investments are fraught with uncertainty. In the 1820s a great "canal fever" swept the country. The early canals were successful, but by the time Indiana built the Wabash and Erie Canal the competition of the railroad, although unforeseen at the time, was

[20] U.S. Congress, Joint Economic Committee, *Economic Analysis of Public Investment Decision: Interest Rate Policy and Discounting Analysis* (Washington, D.C.: U.S. Government Printing Office, 1968), p. 16.

[21] Robert S. Mayo, Director, Bureau of the Budget, letter to Heads of Departments, 1 July 1969, accompanying Circular A-94.

[22] U.S. Bureau of the Budget, "A Conceptual Basis and Measurement Technique for Computation of a Social Discount Rate." See also Testimony of Jack W. Carlson in Joint Economic Committee, *Economic Analysis and the Efficiency of Government,* Part 3, 91st Congress, 1st Session (Washington, D.C.: U.S. Government Printing Office, 1970), p. 722.

[23] Gladwin Hill, "Conservationists See Conflict of Interest on U.S. Water Projects." *The New York Times* (11 August 1969): 31. See the section in the next chapter on secondary benefits.

destined to make the canal a failure. The St. Lawrence Seaway has not been as successful as was anticipated.

To evaluate costs or benefits, someone must predict the future. Although costs may appear to be easy to predict, they are not—if past experience is any guide. Similarly, predicting benefits when long-lived assets are involved may necessitate predicting future socioeconomic settings and tastes of people, a difficult task at best. Let us explore some different types of uncertainty, how they arise, and ways of dealing with them.

### Nature of Uncertainty

The converse of information is uncertainty. If we know everything there is to know about an event, there is no uncertainty about it. It used to be fashionable to distinguish between risk and uncertainty.[24] *Risk* was the name given to the situation in which a probability distribution of outcomes could be given. That is, all the possibilities could be enumerated (in cases with a finite number of possibilities) or described (in cases with an infinite number of possibilities) and a probability or likelihood of occurrence could be associated with each one or with any interval in a continuous range of outcomes given. The term *uncertainty* was reserved for the case in which, while the possible outcomes were known, there was no good way to estimate probabilities of occurrence, or, worse yet, the possible outcomes or states of nature could not even be enumerated. More recently, probability theorists[25] have not been using this distinction. The only type of lack-of-information problems that can be treated systematically are those of risk. In particular, the word uncertainty has come to be nearly synonymous with the variance, or second moment about the mean, of the probability distribution.

Variance, however, is an imperfect measure of risk. In particular, it is not correct to say that if the alternative with the smallest expectation of cost does not also have the smallest variance, then one cannot tell whether that alternative is best. To see why, suppose that one alternative has stochastically smaller costs, that is, suppose that the probability that the actual level of cost will exceed a selected level is less with one alternative than with any other, *for every level that one might select.* Then this alternative has the smallest expectation of cost, but it may not have the smallest variance. Nevertheless, this alternative is best even with respect to minimizing risk.

Several types of uncertainty can be distinguished. Every prediction must be made in a certain context or environment. Military planners

[24]Frank Knight, *Risk Uncertainty and Profit* (Boston: Houghton Mifflin, 1921).
[25]Most notably L. J. Savage, *The Foundations of Statistics* (New York: Wiley, 1954).

have borrowed the term *scenario* from the theater to describe the postulated military environment for which plans must be made. Several plans are made to fit several scenarios. For example, we are called upon to fight major wars in Asia and Europe and a minor war in South America. This leads to a set of military plans based on a scenario of two-and-a-half wars. Similarly, planning for civilian functions must assume a socioeconomic or technological environment of the future.[26] Since these assumptions may be in error, we have *scenario uncertainty*. In particular, almost all estimates of benefits are predicated on population estimates. Agencies were getting too optimistic in their expectations of population growth. This is a bromide for anyone short of benefits: water resource planners, highway planners, and the like. The Water Resources Council has sought to standardize these forecasts by making all agencies key their estimates to the Office of Business Economics—Economic Research Service (OBERS) projections forthcoming from the Departments of Commerce and Agriculture for nations, regions, and economic areas.[27] Planning for the St. Lawrence Seaway forecast user revenues that did not materialize. The scenario used for the forecasts did not include the existence of "supertankers," large ships that do not use the Seaway.

Another source of uncertainty is *sampling error*. When estimates are based on statistical analyses, the possibility exists of an error of prediction in the statistical or sampling sense. Sampling error occurs because of the conditional variability of the dependent variable given a value for the independent variables. Hence, two projects may have the same expected value of net benefits, but the possible outcomes of one may be more widely dispersed than the second. We say the first has greater *variance*. Sampling error is larger the smaller the amount of data from which the prediction is made.

### What to Do About Uncertainty

No project or design has a certain at-approval value of costs or benefits. It has, at best, a probability distribution over a set of possible at-approval values. The at-approval value of costs or benefits is not a number but a random variable.

In general, the relevant probability distributions will overlap. That is, the probability that one design will have a larger at-approval value of benefits less costs than another design will not be zero or one but in-

---

[26] A notable recent effort in scenario writing is available in Herman Kahn and Anthony J. Weiner, *The Year 2000* (New York: Macmillan, 1967).

[27] Water Resources Council, *Procedures for Evaluation of Water and Related Land Resource Projects* (June 1969), pp. 98, 104, 105 et passim.

termediate. For example, the at-approval value of project outlays could turn out to be smaller if vehicles were leased than if they were purchased, or it could turn out to be larger; the answer depends on what would happen with respect to contingencies such as repair bills and the salvage value of purchased vehicles at the end of the lease period. Similarly, the probability that the at-approval value of the costs of a project of given design will exceed the at-approval value of the benefits will not be zero or one but intermediate.

It is possible to develop measures of uncertainty associated with predictions of benefits and costs. We might do retrospective comparisons of prospectuses and actual project outcomes, as Summers has for cost estimates on major military hardware items.[28] Such a study could be done for benefits on areas of expenditure on which long series of analyses and historical results are available; for example, water resources. Results might be surprising. Planning agencies have not always been overly optimistic. In some cases whole classes of benefits that were ignored now yield the bulk of benefits.

The uncertainty of the future can be recognized by limiting the economic life of a project to be considered. Thus, one might limit to 50 or 100 years the allowable economic life of water projects—even though dams, once built, probably last forever.

The reason for the investment may have disappeared in 100 years. A natural catastrophe may have destroyed the project and thus caused its benefits to cease. Technology may have changed such that the average variable cost of output under the old technology may be greater than the average total cost under a new technology. Therefore the project is obsolete. With any sizable discount rate benefits accruing more than 50 years in the future are so severely discounted that we may as well ignore them.

Robert Haveman has made an interesting suggestion with regard to discounting. Noting the sanguine predictions of public agencies with regard to the benefits of the projects they advocate, he suggests discounting benefits more severely than costs in obtaining present values.[29] Even though engineers are notoriously poor at predicting costs, it appears that there is less uncertainty about costs than there is about benefits. Precedent exists for an asymmetrical treatment of some costs and benefits in the federal literature on standards and criteria. The "Green Book" of

[28]Robert Summers in Marschak, Glennan and Summers, *Strategy for R&D*. We discuss the results of this study in the chapter on costs.

[29]Robert H. Haveman, *Water Resource Investment and the Public Interests* (Nashville, Tenn.: Vanderbilt University Press, 1965), Appendix B.

TABLE 7.2. SST RATE OF RETURN SENSITIVITY

| | RATE OF RETURN | CHANGE |
|---|---|---|
| Basic assumptions | 23.8 | |
| SST price 10 percent lower | 26.3 | +2.5 |
| SST price 10 percent higher | 21.6 | −2.2 |
| Operating expenses 5 percent lower | 25.0 | +1.2 |
| Operating expenses 5 percent higher | 22.5 | −1.3 |
| Operating revenues 5 percent lower | 21.3 | −2.5 |
| Operating revenues 5 percent higher | 25.9 | +2.1 |
| Investment tax credit 0 percent instead of 7 percent | 21.8 | −2.0 |

Source: Lee R. Howard, "A Cost-Effectiveness Example: The Supersonic Transport," in J. Morley English, ed., *Cost-Effectiveness Analysis* (New York: Wiley, 1968), p. 207. Reprinted with permission.

1950[30] suggests that a $2\frac{1}{2}$ percent discount rate be used on government costs and at least a 4 percent rate to discount private costs and all benefits.

One useful way to handle scenario uncertainty is to perform parallel analyses for several constellations of assumed conditions. In the case of the supersonic transport (SST), it is not clear whether there will be a sonic boom restriction constraining it to fly mainly over water or constraining its speed over populated areas. Also variable is the price to be charged for the SST. The demand for SSTs can therefore be expressed as two matrices: one for no sonic boom restriction and another with a sonic boom restriction. Rows refer to various prices and columns refer to domestic and international demand in different years.[31]

While sensitivity analysis can add information, it does not in itself produce a ranking of alternatives. Of course, if one alternative has more favorable values of costs and benefits for every set of assumptions, then it is called *dominant* and it will be recommended.

A sensitivity analysis can also show the factors to which the worth of a particular alternative is sensitive. One has been done on the rate of return to airlines of operating the SST. Table 7.2 shows the airlines' rate of return to be relatively sensitive to changes in operating revenues and aircraft price. The other changes in variable factors are responsible for a 10 percent or lower change in rate of return.

[30] InterAgency Committee on Water Resources, Subcommittee on Evaluation Standards, *Proposed Practices for Economic Analysis of River Basin Projects* (Washington, D.C.: U.S. Government Printing Office, 1950, revised 1958).

[31] N. J. Asher, et al., *Demand Analysis for Air Travel by Supersonic Aircraft* (Arlington, Va.: Institute for Defense Analyses, 1966).

FIGURE 7.1. HYPOTHETICAL RANGES OF COSTS POSSIBLE
WITH ALTERNATIVE OUTCOMES FOR A GIVEN LEVEL OF
BENEFITS

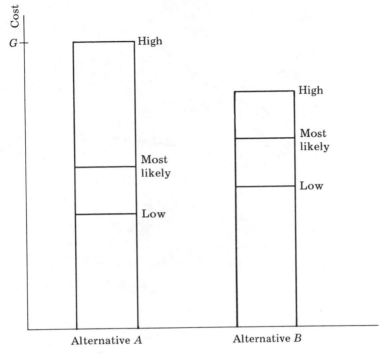

Consider two alternatives with the same effectiveness, such as two ways to move workers from their homes to the central business district of a city. Let A be an exclusive[32] bus lane and B a trolley. On the criterion of minimization of the most likely value of costs A would be chosen. But if there were an element of uncertainty related to the weather, such that costs of A could be very high if it were to snow frequently and the snow had to be cleared, the results might be different. Then Figure 7.1 might be useful. In the case of a winter of heavy snowfall the costs of A could be as high as G. If there were a severe budget limitation below G, the dedicated bus lane could not be chanced because its costs could conceivably exceed the budget. Alternative B, while likely to exceed A in cost, has less variability.

[32]An exclusive bus lane is reserved only for buses although it parallels and is adjacent to a road used by general vehicular traffic.

FIGURE 7.2. CONFIDENCE BAND FOR A COST ESTIMATING
RELATIONSHIP

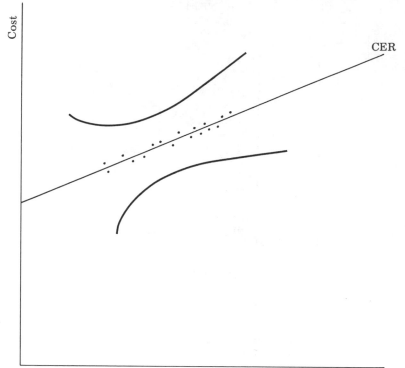

Uncertainty due to sampling error may be pictured as a confidence
band about the line showing point estimates for various values of the independent variable. If the cost of an airframe is predicted from its speed,
a cost estimating relationship (CER) such as the line CER in Figure 7.2
might be derived. The standard error of a prediction is smallest at the
mean of the independent variable. As speed of a contemplated new aircraft gets higher or lower we have less reliable information on it, and
a 90 percent confidence interval[33] gets wider. We have to take in more
possible costs if we want to keep the probability of incorrectly predicting

[33] A 90 percent confidence interval is a range of values such that there is only a 10
percent chance that a random variable will fall outside of it. In practice, it is found by taking an expected value and adding and subtracting from it a number. This yields the two ends
of the interval. The number will be larger the greater is the sampling error or the lower is
the precision of the prediction.

that cost will fall within the band down to 10 percent.[34] The standard error of the prediction depends on the estimated variance of the scatter of observations about the estimated line and also how far the speed to be predicted deviates from the mean of those speeds observed. In Figure 7.2, low speeds and high speeds differ considerably from the mean so that the confidence interval is wider at those speeds.

When benefits and costs are uncertain it is not possible to rank projects by the benefit-cost ratio, net benefits, or cost-effectiveness ratio and make choices on this criterion alone. There will be a positive probability that the project will have benefits that exceed costs and a positive probability that it will not. Some people have tried to transform probability distributions into a single number by using the "mean-variance" approach by which a project is ranked by a function of both:

$$W = E(N) - a\ \sigma_N$$

where $W$ is the measure of desirability, equal to the expected value of net benefits minus a constant $a$ times the standard deviation of net benefits. The variance of net benefits could be used as well.[35] This particular form implies that the rate of exchange between expected net benefits and its standard deviation is linear with expectation desired and deviation undesired with relative weight $a$.

In addition to discounting for time preference and opportunity costs, perhaps a discount for risk is appropriate. Private firms making investments discount for risk. They know there is variability in outcomes so they add a risk premium to their discount rate to allow for uncertainty. Ought the government to demand a risk premium also? Should public investments' costs and benefits be discounted by a risky rate or a riskless rate? On this question, some of the most eminent economists have locked horns.

Risk imposes a cost on private parties who bear it. Given two portfolios of investments with equal expected values, most people, except when gambling, would prefer the one with smaller variance. Investors try to bring into their portfolio investments which are either independent of one another (zero covariance) or tend to move in opposite directions (negative covariance). A "larger" portfolio, that is, one with more distinct investments, usually has a smaller variance. The variance of a sum

[34]Given a speed, the CER gives a point estimate of cost. Whatever its distribution, we know by Chebyshev's inequality that at least 75 percent of the probability lies in a band two standard deviations on either side of the mean. If cost is normally distributed then only 10 percent of the probability lies outside such a confidence band.

[35]Harry M. Markowitz, *Portfolio Selection* (New York: Wiley, 1957), Part IV; Jerome Rothenberg, *The Measurement of Social Welfare* (Englewood Cliffs, N.J.: Prentice-Hall, 1961), Chapter 10.

of random variables is the sum of their individual variances plus twice their covariances:

$$\text{Var}(X_1 + X_2 + X_3) = \text{Var}(X_1) + \text{Var}(X_2) + \text{Var}(X_3) + \\ 2\text{Cov}(X_1,X_2) + 2\text{Cov}(X_2,X_3) + 2\text{Cov}(X_1,X_3)$$

where $X_1$, $X_2$, $X_3$ are random variables. A "conglomerate" firm has less variability in its investments than an undiversified firm. The federal government has a very large portfolio. Therefore, its risk is lower than that of the typical firm. Does this mean it should use a riskless discount rate?

The bearer of risk demands a premium presumably because successive increments of income add less and less to his total utility. In other words, the rate of increase of a measure of his satisfaction with respect to income declines in the relevant range of income. We call this phenomenon diminishing marginal utility of income. It need not always obtain; in certain ranges of income additions may be of increasing worth. People gamble for small stakes[36] preferring a certain cost plus an uncertain prospect of larger gain to no loss with certainty. But for large changes diminishing marginal utility usually does obtain.[37] For this reason and because of the risk of disaster people buy insurance even though in actuarial terms it is a bad bet. The condition of diminishing marginal utility of money is also known as "risk avoidance."

Since the government pools so many investments, the law of large numbers assures that the actual value of its entire portfolio will be "very" close to its expectation. But the private business sector as a whole has a portfolio larger even than the government's. So if risk is not a social cost to the government, it should not be a social cost to business. Individal businesses tend to stop short of the optimum amount of investment because they must consider risk.

One can argue that since particular government agencies hold small undiversified (except geographically) portfolios they ought to reckon risk a cost and use a risky rate. Or one can argue that government ought to counterack the conservative individual firms by using a riskless rate of interest. Indeed, one of the functions of government spending is to

[36]The paradox that gambling and insurance coexist was noticed and lucidly explained by M. Friedman and L. J. Savage, "The Utility Analysis of Choices Involving Risk," *Journal of Political Economy*, vol. 56 (August 1948).

[37]The Friedman and Savage paper, a subsequent one by Harry Markowitz, "The Utility of Wealth," *Journal of Political Economy*, vol. 5, no. 60 (April 1952), and a recent one by Jack Hirshleifer, "Investment Decision Under Uncertainty: Applications of the State-Preference Approach," *Quarterly Journal of Economics*, vol. 80 (May 1966), all indicate that gambling is the exception. The rule is recognized in corporate finance and security markets as indicated by F. Modgliani and M. H. Miller, "The Cost of Capital, Corporation Finance and the Theory of Investment," *American Economic Review*, vol. 68 (June 1958).

undertake risks that private firms would not take. Finally, one can argue that the government should be neither a risk taker nor a risk avoider, but should maximize expected net benefits rather than the *utility*. It should have a constant marginal utility of money. Kenneth Arrow has taken this point of view in arguing that the government should use a risk-less discount rate.[38]

Jack Hirshleifer argues that the government should use a risky discount rate because this is consistent with the "present certainty equivalent value" rule.[39] A certainty equivalent is a risk-discounted expected value. All possible states of the world are enumerated. Contingent claims to goods have different prices under different states of the world. The probability that each state will obtain is estimated and the expected net benefits are calculated under each state.

The sum of probabilities times expected values each weighted by its price or utility is the certainty equivalent. The present certainty equivalent value is the analogue under uncertainty of the present value in a world of perfect certainty—it is what planners ought to maximize. Hirshleifer and Shapiro argue that a riskless rate of interest would be correct if

$$\frac{P_a}{P_b} = \frac{\pi_a}{\pi_b} \tag{6}$$

where $P_a$ and $P_b$ are the prices of goods under states of the world $a$ and $b$ and $\pi_a$ and $\pi_b$ are the probabilities that those two states of the world will obtain. Condition (6) does not hold because people tend to be risk averters and value goods more highly in times of low income. Therefore, the relative prices would not be strictly proportional to the relative probabilities. Income in the two states of the world is relevant to prices. Since (6) does not hold, Hirshleifer and Shapiro suggest using a discount rate including a risk premium for a risk class of comparable private projects.

There is a technical problem involved in incorporating uncertainty in the discount rate. Only if uncertainty compounds with time does this give the proper results. An acceptable alternative is to adjust each year's benefits minus costs for uncertainty and aggregate over time using a risk-free discount rate.

Thus, there is no consensus on what to do about uncertainty. Conservatism and skepticism has been suggested to overcome the uncer-

[38] Kenneth J. Arrow, "Discounting and Public Investment Criteria," in Kneese and Smith, eds., *Water Research* (Baltimore: Johns Hopkins University Press, 1966), p. 30.

[39] Jack Hirshleifer and David L. Shapiro, "The Treatment of Risk and Uncertainty," in Robert H. Haveman and Julius Margolis, eds., *Public Expenditures and Policy Analysis* (Chicago: Markham, 1970), pp. 291–313.

tainty due to the optimistic bias of the bureaucracy. Point estimates of expected benefits and costs could be rejected and interval estimates demanded instead. Because of the uncertainty of the distant future, benefit and cost streams can be truncated after 50 or 100 years. Any reasonable discount rate will do this for practical purposes anyway. A case has been made for asymmetrical treatment of benefits, discounting them more heavily than costs. When some parameters affecting costs and benefits are likely to vary by unknown amounts, sensitivity analysis of the benefit-cost problem can be done to gauge the impact of those changes on the success indicator. Sampling error can be treated by the well-known statistical means of confidence intervals.

Finally, in the debate between Arrow and Hirshleifer, Arrow counsels that governments should use riskless discount rates; Hirshleifer suggests using risky rates comparable to the risk class of similar enterprise in the private sector. If risk premiums are used they make discount factors smaller the farther in the future the costs or benefits accrue. As Eckstein observed, "The choice of interest rates must remain a value judgment."[40] We hope we have shown the relevant considerations in making this value judgment.

In this chapter we have discussed which years are relevant for calculating benefits and costs. We explained the theory of aggregation over time through discounting. The many functions for which market interest rates are used makes them of dubious value as guides in choosing between present and future and in choosing among project designs. Society may have a discount rate which differs from what its citizens display on markets. Public investments have opportunity costs, another reason to discount. Discount rates can be used as a rationing device for public investments to govern the growth of the public sector. We showed that the different federal agencies use different discount rates. Sometimes different rates are used by the same agency in one year. Some agencies use no discounting at all. All this leads to nonoptimal capital expenditure decisions. Finally, we surveyed the issues on possible public responses to the uncertainty of public investments.

Let us move now to a discussion of how benefits and costs are calculated. If costs and benefits are calculated inappropriately, how we discount them is of comparatively small importance.

---

[40] "A Survey of the Theory of Public Expenditure Criteria," in J. M. Buchanan, ed., *Public Finances: Needs, Sources and Utilization* (Princeton, N.J.: National Bureau of Economic Research, 1961), p. 460.

# Eight

# EFFICIENCY BENEFIT ATTRIBUTION

In this chapter we propose to define efficiency benefits, then to survey some of the current work done toward calculating them. First, we define efficiency and the concept of willingness to pay, and we advise calculating areas under income-compensated demand curves rather than ordinary demand curves when estimating gross benefits. We discuss the principles of collective demand curves for both private, "rival" goods and collective, "nonrival" goods. The received theory of demand is briefly reviewed, but its exclusive attention to relative prices of existing goods makes it unable to recognize substitutes adequately or to predict the demand for a new good. Indeed, one can question its applicability to an affluent economy in which characteristics of goods are as important as prices.

Next we move to several spending areas for which efficiency benefits have been estimated in the past: water resources, transportation, health, education, urban renewal, and technological developments. A brief review of the literature on water is presented, with a lengthy section on the treatment of recreation benefits, both for its own sake and as an exercise in evaluating the demand for a commodity that is not sold at market-clearing prices. This is frequently the case in government services. Calculation of benefits has met with more success in some fields than in others. Some public spending, such as that on resource development and transportation, is clearly intended to increase the efficiency of the economy. For health, education, and urban renewal this assumption grows increasingly dubious and methods of calculating benefits are increasingly arbitrary and fragmentary. Nevertheless, perhaps it is better to measure the rabbit and talk about the horse than to do all talking and no measuring. Measuring the rabbit may increase the level of the dialogue about the horse. We review studies, largely allowing authors to speak for themselves and the reader to judge whether their methods of accounting benefits are adequate. We hope we have been fair to the authors involved in this necessarily abbreviated treatment.

## THE EFFICIENCY OBJECTIVE

An economy is efficient if it is impossible to: (1) reallocate inputs among firms in such a way that the output of some products is increased and the outputs of others are not reduced, (2) reallocate products among consumers in such a way that some become better off and none become worse off, (3) increase the output of some products and reduce the output of others in such a way that some consumers become better off and none become worse off, or (4) alter the amount of leisure time or income that people consume and find that what they gain is worth more to them than what they lose. In other words, output and utility are maximized, the product mix maximizes utility and the optimal amount of leisure is consumed.

### National Income and Willingness to Pay

Maximizing output makes physical volume large; optimizing the output mix makes the value of national income large. So an efficient economy has the largest possible national income. Since the welfare of a society is presumed to be a monotonically increasing function of national income, national income is often suggested as the quantitative indicator of efficiency benefits.

A few problems are encountered, however, when using national income as a measure of welfare. Pecuniary spillovers and influences of all kinds are reflected in national income. They should be overlooked in order to discern "real" effects. National income measures the flow of goods and services in dollar units to aggregate diverse outputs. This excludes buyer and seller surpluses, which we discuss below. An increase in national income that is due to inflation is a pecuniary effect; it does not increase welfare. Therefore, we must remove inflationary effects to measure real national income. Increased leisure, which increases welfare if it is chosen freely, does not enter the national accounts to be included in the real national income. National income values government output at factor cost. It assumes the benefit-cost ratio is 1.0 and thus defines away the problem of evaluating government output.

While real national income itself may be an imperfect measure of welfare, it can be argued that changes in national income give reliable

indications of changes in welfare. If there are no important reverbera-
tions elsewhere in the economy—"general equilibrium" effects to be
included in a with-and-without analysis—then a measure of the change
in welfare is the value of incremental output minus its cost. The value
of incremental output should be measured by the *willingness to pay* of
beneficiaries of the output: not only that which might be collected in a
market, but buyer and seller surpluses as well.

Willingness to pay is sometimes identified with price. Prices represent minimum willingness to pay because they are actually paid. Prices
understate what those who received consumers' surplus may have been
willing to pay, however. Willingness to pay for an increment of a good,
in general, is the area under the (compensated) demand curve for a good
from the "before" quantity to the "after" quantity. (This concept is illustrated later in the chapter under the heading "Consumers' surplus
calculation.") If the quantity made available is larger relative to the pre-
existing availability, prices will be lowered by those responsible for marketing the larger increment. This situation is sometimes called an *in-
divisibility*[1] on the grounds that the large increment is made available
as a unit. When indivisibilities exist, price times quantity does not represent total willingness to pay. However, the area under the demand curve
represents it in both cases. If price does not decline appreciably on introduction of the new quantity of output, the area under the demand curve
is price times quantity. If the demand curve slopes downward, the area
under it includes consumers' surplus on inframarginal units.

### Measuring Willingness to Pay

Gross benefit for a single consumer is the largest amount of money
he would be willing to pay for the good or service he receives. Net benefit is gross benefit minus amount paid. Gross benefit is the area under
the "compensated" demand curve that we must define. Gross benefit
for a collection of consumers is the sum of their individual gross benefits
or the area under the *collective compensated demand curve*. If we use
ordinary instead of compensated demand curves, we must assume that
the marginal utility of money is a constant for every consumer.[2]

Estimating gross benefits by referring to the area beneath consumers'
collective ordinary demand curve, instead of to the area beneath their

[1] Abba P. Lerner, *The Economics of Control* (New York: Macmillan, 1944). Chapters 15 and 16.

[2] Or, more exactly, that the marginal rate of substitution between money and the commodity is independent of the amount of money a consumer has. This assumption allows
us to add together the willingness to pay of different individuals.

collective compensated demand curve, usually produces negligible over-statement. However, for goods with high income elasticity of demand; or for goods that form a sizable fraction of a budget, using the compensated demand curve may make a difference. The adjustment may be particularly important when the demand for broad classes of goods such as food, services, or housing is under study.

### Collective Ordinary Demand for Social Goods

Thus far we have discussed collective ordinary demand for *private wants;* that is, goods and services that are *rival* in consumption.[3] If one person consumes them they are not available to another person. There are other goods that are nonrival in consumption; once provided, they are available to all. Musgrave has called desires for these goods "social wants" and, more recently, "social goods."[4] They have been called "collective goods"[5] in a terminology which is perhaps more widely accepted. The major fact about such goods is that they are jointly supplied simultaneously to all who want them.

The collective demand for a social good is found not by summing horizontally, but by summing vertically. Instead of adding all the quantities demanded at a given price, as we do to get collective demand for a private good, the quantity is given and the consumers' willingness to pay are added together. The vertical summation shows, for each quantity, the sum over all users of the maximum price that each user would pay to have the quantity under consideration.

In the case of a good nonrival in consumption as shown in Figure 8.1, the total quantity consumed collectively, $Q_n$, is equal to the quantity consumed by each beneficiary:

$$Q_n = q_1 = q_2 = \ldots = q_i = \ldots = q_n = Q$$

where $n$ is the number of beneficiaries or consumers. This is sometimes called the condition of *fixed joint supply* because all consumers are sup-

---

[3]See Richard A. Musgrave, "Cost-Benefit Analysis and the Theory of Public Finance," *Journal of Economic Issues*, vol. 8, no. 3 (September 1969), and "Provision for Social Wants," in Julius Margolis and Henri Guitton, eds., *Public Economics* (New York: St. Martin's Press, 1969).

[4]Richard A. Musgrave, *The Theory of Public Finance* (New York: McGraw-Hill, 1959), pp. 9–12. Musgrave reserves the term "public goods" to those goods produced in the public sector. Collective goods need not be produced in the public sector. For example, a foundation dedicated to a particular idea may build a museum which is open to the public without charge. (See footnote 43 next chapter.)

[5]Paul Samuelson, "The Pure Theory of Public Expenditure," *Review of Economics and Statistics*, vol. 36 (November 1954).

# FIGURE 8.1. COLLECTIVE DEMAND OF TWO CONSUMERS FOR A NONRIVAL CONSUMPTION GOOD

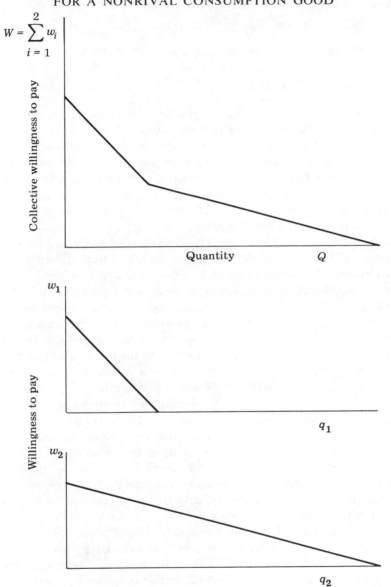

plied the same amount, for a pure collective good, at the same time. Willingness to pay is added vertically to get collective willingness to pay:

$$W(Q) = w_1(Q) + w_2(Q) + \ldots + w_n(Q).$$

All willingness-to-pay functions are evaluated at the same $Q$.

### Demand Curve Estimation

For many benefit estimation problems it is useful to estimate demand curves. This is true for project outputs that are sold and also for outputs for which there may be no charge, but that are rationed by means other than price. In the example below recreation at a particular lake may be provided free or the gate fee may be nominal. Other factors, travel costs in particular, determine how much a particular consuming unit will consume and thereby act as a proxy for price. They allow us to estimate an ordinary demand curve for recreation.

*The Traditional Approach.* The conventional procedure for estimating demand curves involves two steps. The first is to postulate that quantity demanded is equal to quantity consumed and is a fixed linear (or linearizable) function of the price charged (or a proxy for price) and a number of other variables that seem to be relevant. The second step is to estimate the parameters of the postulated function, usually by the method known as "least squares" or "regression analysis." The procedure involves a number of assumptions, and the estimate of demand that emerges is subject to considerable error even if perfect data are available. In addition, available data usually are quite imperfect.

The traditional theory of demand on which such analysis is based is deficient in several ways. In particular, it emphasizes relative prices as a way of accounting for the influence on behavior of potential substitutes. The traditional method is poor at taking account of the effect of substitutes, as we shall see in the example below. Finally, the received theory does not lead to predictions of the demand for a *new good*. Estimating demand for new goods is a case frequently encountered in market research for public or private goods.

The traditional theory of demand for single commodities comes in two varieties: demand by consumers and demand by producers. The consumer is assumed to maximize utility $U$ by choosing quantities of several goods $(X_1, X_2, X_3)$ to consume, but he is limited by a fixed budget; for example, his net worth $M$. The solution gives equilibrium values of $X_i$ as a function of net worth $M$ and the prices $p_1$, $p_2$, and $p_3$.

A producer may be assumed to maximize profit, $\pi = pY - p_1X_1 - p_2X_2$, subject to the production function, $Y = f(X_1, X_2)$, where $Y$ is output. Demand for inputs $X_1$ and $X_2$ are again functions of prices $p, p_1$, and

$p_2$, where $p$ is the output price. Demand for inputs can also be expressed as a function of relative prices $p_1/p$, and $p_2/p$. Alternatively producers may be assumed to minimize cost for a given output. The producer may not be able to determine his own output but may minimize cost for whatever output he produces. Now the problem is to minimize cost, $C = p_1X_1 + p_2X_2$, subject to $Y = \overline{Y}$ and the production function. Once again derived demands for inputs are functions of $\overline{Y}$, $p_1$, and $p_2$. Demands for "intermediate" goods are "derived" from the "final" demand for output $\overline{Y}$.

To summarize these cases, the ordinary demand for a good is a function of: (1) prices and net worth of consumers, (2) input prices and output price for a profit maximizing producer, and (3) prices and constrained output for a cost-minimizing producer. Notice that prices figure in all cases.

The influence of the existence of a substitute good or service on demand behavior is shown by the price of that substitute. The characteristics of that substitute and how consumers or producers view it are buried in the tastes or preference pattern of consumers and the production function of producers. If a good is not consumed or does not enter production under one technique it may be left out of the list of goods considered and its price may not enter the prices considered. For example, the demand for a particular mode of transport, say bus, between two cities may be a function of the price of bus transportation, the prices of alternative auto and railroad transportation, and other "gravity" type variables representing the two cities' attraction for each other. The price of a new mode, such as airplane service, which did not exist when the demand for bus service was estimated, would not figure in the analysis. The potential effect of the airplane on the demand for bus service cannot be estimated under the traditional model. The model we shall discuss below can say something meaningful about the demand for a new product.

Market research for the public sector can be criticized in that it is often too sanguine about prospects and does not recognize the interdependence of its own projects. For example, the Corps of Engineers estimates demand for services at several ports in connection with plans to dredge them in order to service larger ships. The Corps implicitly adds together all the demands. However, if one port is dredged it may detract from the volume of business done by another port. To obtain the net increase in navigation benefits one should subtract the lost trade at ports from which business has been diverted.[6]

[6]John Haldi, "Issues of Analysis in Cost-Effectiveness Studies for Civilian Agencies of the Federal Government," in David L. Cleland and William R. King, *Systems, Organizations, Analysis, Management: A Book of Readings* (New York: McGraw-Hill, 1969), pp. 273–75.

*New Approach to the Theory of Demand.* A new approach to demand theory, developed by Kelvin Lancaster,[7] emphasizes the attributes of commodities as well as their relative prices. Commodities are viewed as being consumed for their intrinsic physical and performance characteristics. The consumer is viewed as having preferences defined over a characteristic space. Goods are looked upon as production processes that produce characteristics in fixed proportions. Bread is consumed because it provides calories and bulk. A particular transport mode can be characterized by its speed, frequency of departure, and carrying capacity as well as its cost.

Quandt and Baumol estimated the demand between twenty California city pairs for air, rail, bus, and auto.[8] The effect of a competing mode on other modes is seen not only in relative price, but in relative frequency of leaving; that is, the mean waiting time to departure, and in relative speed. The impact of a change in either price or speed, for example, can be estimated. The impact of the introduction of a new mode could be estimated so long as its cost, speed, and frequency of leaving were known. Its technology need not be known, nor indeed completely worked out, to obtain an estimate of the demand for its services. The existence of other modes is explicitly recognized by a variable that equals the number of modes available on any particular link.

Similarly, the demand for all ports could be estimated simultaneously so that ports could be looked upon as a system. The demand for reservoir recreation in an area could be estimated as a system so the impact of substitutes could be shown. Then a new reservoir would generate visitors but also divert visitors from other reservoirs in the system.

Frequently price data are scarce or absent. The output to be evaluated may not be sold. More commonly, there is little variation in price over the period observed. Prices are sluggish and tend to remain for appreciable periods at a single level with only infrequent changes. Responses to varying prices cannot then be observed. One recourse is to "cross section" analysis in which prices vary over areas or groups. This recourse is particularly fruitful when a proxy for price is being used. Different consuming groups may have different associated cost[9] of exploiting the good or service to be evaluated as in the recreation case study

[7]Kelvin J. Lancaster, "A New Approach to Consumer Theory," *Journal of Political Economy* 14 (1966): 132–57. See also W. J. Baumol, "The Calculation of Optimal Product and Retailer Characteristics: The Abstract Product Approach," *Journal of Political Economy* 15 (1967): 674–85.

[8]Richard Quandt and William Baumol, "The Demand for Abstract Transport Modes," *Journal of Regional Science* 6, no. 2 (December 1966): 13–26.

[9]This term is defined in Chapter 10.

below. It may be that all segments of the consuming population face the same price. Then approaches other than the statistical estimation of demand curves must be tried.

## EFFICIENCY BENEFIT ATTRIBUTION FOR PARTICULAR OUTPUTS

### Water Resources

In the evaluation of water resource investments, analysts first used market prices to evaluate benefits. Hydroelectric power and community and industrial water supply were sold on markets. Navigation, flood control, and recreation were rarely sold.

*Navigation.* The estimation of navigation benefits can serve as a model for benefit estimation in other transportation projects. There are always two types of benefits: cost savings on present traffic and benefits on induced traffic.

When rivers are improved or canals are built, traffic is usually diverted from railroads. The Association of American Railroads, like the Sierra Club, is a natural enemy of the Corps of Engineers. Railroads are often the least costly alternative means of freight shipment. Bulk shipment by water is usually cheaper. A first approximation to benefits on existing traffic is the difference between costs of shipping by water and by the least costly alternative means.

Railroad rates are regulated by the Interstate Commerce Commission. They typically exceed incremental costs of freight shipment. Benefits, as cost savings, should be calculated as the difference in transportation costs rather than the difference in rates. To the extent that regulated railroad rates exceed incremental costs, the owners of the railroad collect a rent[10] from freight rates. Part of the lower cost to shippers by water is a transfer of income from railroad stockholders and therefore not a net social saving or benefit.

Sometimes, when canals are built, railroads reduce their charges. Because of these price concessions the expected traffic on the improved inland waterway may not materialize. Thus navigation benefits are frequently overestimated because of failure to foresee competition from other modes of transport.

Benefits may accrue to existing traffic not because of a change to a less costly mode but because of decreased costs on the water mode. Op-

[10]Economic rent is a return greater than that which would keep the owners in the railroad business.

eration and maintenance costs of a waterway or individual water carriers may be reduced by improvement of channels or locks, for example. The imputed costs of holding inventory as goods in transit must be counted as an associated cost of the water mode which is usually slower than rail.

The benefit creditable on induced traffic is the difference between the true value added by transportation and the cost of water transportation. The true value added by transportation is not simply the difference between the f.o.b. price at the origin and the c.i.f. price at the destination, but the maximum amount shippers would be willing to pay for moving the traffic; the area under the compensated demand curve between the least costly alternative mode of shipping and the lower cost of water shipping. The demand curve between these two points is assumed to be linear.[11]

*Flood Control.* Benefits of flood control include: (1) loss of life prevented, (2) damages prevented,[12] (3) income from more intensive use of land, and (4) savings in temporary costs of dealing with flood emergencies. Loss of life is difficult to evaluate in terms commensurable with other benefits. Perhaps lives saved should be listed as another dimension of the analysis. Some efforts to put a dollar value on the loss of human life are discussed below under the rubric of transportation.

U.S. Geological Survey data on hydrology or stream flow for a given river basin gives frequencies of floods of different magnitudes. The Corps of Engineers develops flood frequency tables that tell the probability of a flood of a given magnitude and the loss associated with each size of flood over a specified period of time such as 50 or 100 years. The difference in expected damage with and without the flood control measure is the benefit attributable for losses prevented. The "with-and-without principle" is one that comes up frequently in benefit-cost analysis.[13] It differs from the "before-and-after" principle, which measures changes over time that are not all necessarily attributable to the action being evaluated.

When stream flow data is available the behavior of a river can be simulated with its stochastic components by computer.[14] Then the be-

---

[11] U.S. Federal Inter-Agency River Basin Committee, Subcommittee on Evaluation Standards, *Proposed Practices for Economic Analyses of River Basin Projects* (May 1958), p. 41.

[12] How flood damages are defined is a controversial subject we do not have the space to discuss.

[13] M. M. Regan and E. G. Weitzel, "Economic Evaluation of Soil and Water Conservation Measures and Programs," *Journal of Farm Economics* 24, no. 4 (November 1947): 1275–94.

[14] Arthur Maass, et al., *Design of Water Resource Systems* (Cambridge, Mass.: Harvard University Press, 1962), Chapters 10, 11, and 12; and Myron Fiering, "Synthetic Hydrology," in Allen V. Kneese and S. C. Smith. *Water Research* (Baltimore: Johns Hopkins Press, 1966). pp. 331–42.

havior of a river basin under various flood-mitigation measures can be studied to observe the response in flood damages to different measures.

Damages from floods depend on flood stage, the number of feet by which a river exceeds its banks. Flood stage probability is computed by the Corps of Engineers at various sites where flooding might take place. The Corps estimates the damage done at each flood stage by conducting surveys of damages of past floods.

From a national income point of view reports of flood losses are often inflated. They include the loss of regional income during and immediately after a flood, but this income may have been diverted to another region of the country. Therefore the expectation of damages prevented may be correspondingly too high.

Floods in Northern California in 1964 prevented lumbering activity. California firms lost considerable revenues, but the lumber industry in other parts of the country thrived because of the removal of California competition.[15] To count California losses due to the flooding overstates losses because all were not net decreases in national income. Increases in income in the South and in New England offset some of California's losses.

In addition to preventing damages by reducing uncertainty due to flooding, flood control may induce increases in economic activity. These benefits can be taken as "the regional income under an optimal investment program with the project minus the regional income under an optimal investment program without the project,"[16] another example of the with-and-without principle. To obtain national income benefits, one would have to net out regional income diverted from elsewhere in the national economy.

Reduction in flood probability can change the optimal use of land.[17] Figure 8.2 shows the effect of a reduction in flood probability from $\gamma_a$ to $\gamma_b$. Note that in both cases, the present value of net benefits of a particular land use declines as the probability of a flood increases. This is because the expected value of damage increases. In Case I, because damages have been prevented the present value of net benefits in use Y is increased. In Case II, because the likelihood of flooding is diminished optimal land use is changed from Y to X. Any associated costs of increasing the return from property must be deducted to obtain the net

[15]C. Bart McGuire, *Economic Impact Study of December 1964 Floods in Northern California Coastal Streams* (San Francisco: U.S. Army Engineer District, 1967).

[16]McGuire, *Economic Impact Study,* pp. 127–28.

[17]The diagrams in Figure 8.2 are used by P. David Qualls, "The Russian River Project: A Case Study in the Economics of Water Resources Development," Ph.D. diss., University of California at Berkeley, 1968).

FIGURE 8.2. REDUCTION OF FLOOD PROBABILITY
FROM $\gamma_a$ TO $\gamma_b$

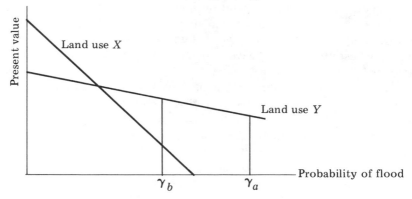

Case I.  Land use is unchanged but expected value of loss declines

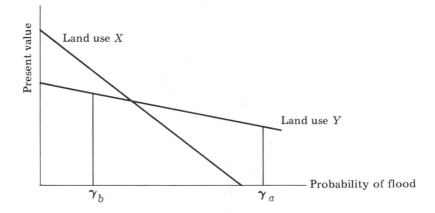

Case II.  Lower flood probability changes optimal purpose for which
land is used

increment from flood control. Such land enhancement may be capitalized
into land values.

Building dams is not the only way to provide flood control. Non-
structural alternatives such as flood-plain zoning, levees, and building
houses on stilts[18] should be considered as alternatives.[19] Unfortunately
the opportunity cost of putting such land into recreational or low-value

[18]These alternatives are "non-structural" in that the agency involved would not have
to build a structure to solve the problem.

[19]Robert W. Kates, *Hazard and Choice Perception in Flood Plain Management*
(University of Chicago, Department of Geography, 1962).

agricultural use is often higher than the cost of building a dam to protect the flood plain.

The Middle Fork, Eel River project[20] would protect against all floods save those with less than 1 percent chance of occurrence. Average annual damages would be reduced from $1,980,000 to $760,000. Therefore, average annual benefits from reduction in flood damages are $1,220,000. Because of the flood control protection afforded by the proposed reservoir, an estimated 4,500 acres of land could be converted to higher uses including low density residential, light industrial and commercial, and intensified agricultural developments at an annual value of $290,000.

*Irrigation.* The principles of estimating the benefits of irrigation of land are applicable to all means of enhancing land's agricultural productivity, including drainage and erosion control as well as irrigation. The general principle is to estimate the increase in annual net value of production from the affected land. This involves three steps: (1) forecasting additional agricultural output as a result of the irrigation, (2) evaluating this additional output, and (3) deducting the opportunity cost of inputs other than water.

The second step is particularly difficult because of farm price supports. Increases to national welfare are not measured very well if evaluated at supported prices. Perhaps a 20 percent average deduction in prices is appropriate for major commodities whose prices are elevated by federal support in order to estimate their true shadow value or increase to real GNP.

To produce extra output, other inputs besides irrigation water are needed. If farmers are kept in farming because of the program, their opportunity costs elsewhere ought to be deducted to obtain the net increase in production. The inputs used to make farm machinery also have opportunity costs; for example, what they could have produced if used to make trucks. If irrigation preempts water that might have been used for community water supply, then the opportunity cost of the scarce water must be reckoned as well, as we mention in Chapter 10. In some cases irrigation increases farm production in one part of the country at the expense of another region. George Tolley found that because of production of cotton on irrigated western lands 5 percent of southern farmers were forced into other occupations.[21] Such geographical redistribution of production implies no net national benefits unless the average cost of producing cotton is less in the West. Such redistribution may involve

[20]U.S. Army Engineer District, *Eel River Basin, California, Interim Report* (San Francisco (April 1968), p. 61.

[21]George S. Tolley, "Reclamation's Influence on the Rest of Agriculture," *Land Economics* (May 1959): 176–80.

net national costs in that social overhead capital becomes underutilized in one region and must be installed in another. In the recent past, some of the most powerful senators—Hayden, Kerr, and Mansfield[22]—have been from the midcontinent which contains most of the country's reclaimable land. Rhetoric has become more candid. Generation of regional income is now sometimes viewed as an explicit objective of public policy.[23] It has always been the covert objective of congressmen who sponsored expenditures in their own districts. Perhaps the misallocation of resources to reclamation is a small price to pay for a smoothly working democracy, but we should know what that price is.

Two types of secondary benefits have typically been discussed with regard to irrigation. "Stemming" benefits consist of income generated in processing the outputs due to irrigation water, such as sugar beets or cotton. "Induced" benefits consist of income generated in activities that sell to farmers. Since the criticisms leveled at the notorious Bureau of Reclamation handbook of 1952, "secondary benefits" has become a term of opprobrium. Since both types of benefits involve the generation of regional income they are now discussed under the rubric of "regional income benefits" to distinguish them from national income benefits.

Irrigation benefits were estimated to be in the area of $150 annually per acre-foot in the Southern California coastal plain and San Diego in the latter half of the twentieth century. Elsewhere, in Ventura County, they were calculated to be just over $100 per acre-foot.[24] Water is worth about $70 per acre-foot, but it costs $35 per acre-foot to transport it. After deducting the cost of transportation, the value of irrigation water is $35 per acre-foot.[25] Irrigation water is heavily subsidized. Irrigators pay only $2.80 per acre-foot for water from federal projects.[26] This gives a numerical example of the order of magnitude of such benefits.

*Hydroelectric Power.* Benefits from the production of hydroelectric power are usually evaluated at the beneficiaries' willingness to pay, but this is not allowed to exceed the costs of the least costly alternative source of power. If thermal power is available at a certain cost, willingness to pay for hydroelectric power cannot be greater than this alternative cost. Charges for private power are typically regulated to repay average variable costs of production plus a rate of return on capital acceptable to

[22]From Arizona, Oklahoma, and Montana, respectively.

[23]See President's Water Resources Council, *Procedures for Evaluation of Water and Related Land Resources Projects,* Washington, D.C. (June 1969).

[24]Jack Hirshleifer, J. C. DeHaven, and Jerome W. Milliman, *Water Supply* (Chicago: University of Chicago Press, 1960), p. 317, Table 42.

[25]Hirshleifer, De Haven, and Milliman, *Water Supply,* pp. 318–35.

[26]Charles Schultze, *The Politics and Economics of Public Spending* (Washington, D.C.: The Brookings Institution, 1968), p. 91.

## FIGURE 8.3. AVERAGE AND MARGINAL COSTS FOR A GOOD PRODUCED SUBJECT TO INCREASING RETURNS TO SCALE

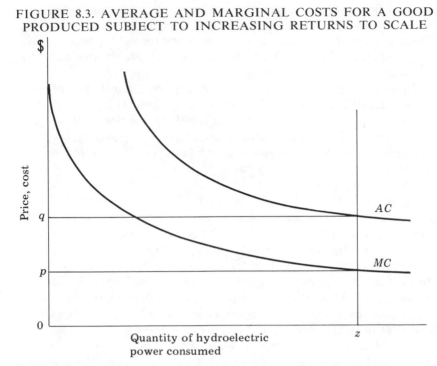

the regulatory commission. Sometimes regulatory commissions prevent price cuts intended to explore the elasticity of demand for power.[27] Private power companies usually have a monopoly in their area of distribution and one consumer of power cannot sell to another. Hence the power companies can segment their market into industrial and residential users and practice price discrimination, charging the residential consumers higher rates than their industrial customers. The industrial demand is more elastic because of the possibility that large firms would generate their own power. Such discrimination allows prices roughly equal to long-run marginal costs. If power is produced under increasing returns to scale or declining marginal costs with marginal cost below average cost, then a single price, such as $p$ in Figure 8.3, equal to marginal cost for that quantity $z$, would not recapture total costs. Prices equal to successive marginal cost (discrimination) can approximate the entire area under the marginal cost curve that is equal to total cost. That is, the area $q$ times $z$ is equal to the area under the $MC$ curve from 0 to $z$.

If a project promises to add an amount of hydroelectric power capacity which is large relative to that currently consumed in the area, the

[27]Joe S. Bain, *Industrial Organization* 2d ed. (New York: Wiley, 1968), pp. 642–43.

agency or firm which is responsible for marketing this power will need to consider lower prices in order to sell the large quantities forthcoming. Sometimes an average of the old power price and the new is used to evaluate the incremental power. This approach measures the area under the demand curve, by assuming the demand curve is linear.

When a new hydroelectric power station is to be installed, often as a by-product of a multipurpose river development, its benefits depend on the cost characteristics of the rest of the system of power production. When incremental power producing capacity is made available, it is most valuable if there is no slack power in the system or if its total costs are lower than alternative operating costs.

To the extent that incremental hydroelectric power is slack, its benefits are equal to the savings in operating costs of the thermal electric plant. Peak power increments obviate adding thermal capacity as well as operating it. The benefits of peak power are the incremental costs of constructing and operating a thermal plant yielding the same peak power.

Thermal plants wear out faster than hydroelectric ones do. Thus, even contributions to power supply in slack periods of the day or year will eventually obviate thermal replacement. Further, a growing demand for power tends to justify whatever electricity production capacity is added. But there is technological change in thermal power plants. Successive replacements are likely to be more efficient. Hydroelectric capacity retains the same technology for 100 years or more. When benefits are measured by alternative costs, it should be anticipated that alternative costs will steadily decrease.

*Recreation.* Until 1965 the Bureau of the Budget was skeptical about recreation benefits. No one doubted that recreation contributed to the welfare of consumers. The problem was to find an objective method which would not go overboard in claiming benefits. The land value approach was used by Jack Knetsch, who showed that TVA lakes increased the average value of a plot fronting directly on a reservoir by $65 more than nearby plots.[28] Thus, one way to approach the problem of valuing recreation is to assume that benefits are capitalized in land values.

If market prices were available for recreational services, and indivisibilities were not present, these prices could be used to evaluate benefits. But many sites charge no fee or only a nominal fee, and these prices are not market-clearing prices. Attendance is often rationed by the number of parking spaces available. Some method other than observing market prices must be found to determine willingness to pay.

[28]Jack L. Knetsch, "The Influence of Reservoir Projects on Land Values," *Journal of Farm Economics* 46 (February 1965): 231–43.

A few simple methods have been used to evaluate recreation benefits. For many years the Corps of Engineers used $1.60 per visitor-day
as the value. This figure, which originated in an old study of average recreational expenditures by participants, was revised once to reflect price
level changes, then was used uniformly regardless of relative scarcity
of recreational opportunity in the section of the country proposed for a
project. In 1964 the President's Water Resources Council established
new ranges of values for outdoor recreation.[29] "General" recreation
was worth $.50 to $1.50 per visitor-day while "special" recreation such
as horseback riding and fishing for certain rare fish was worth $2.00 to
$6.00 per visitor-day.

Another method of determining willingness to pay estimates benefits on the basis of observed behavior. The method was initially suggested
by Harold Hotelling in response to an inquiry from the National Park
Service.[30] Hotelling based his ideas on an 1844 publication of Jules
Dupuit relating to the concept of consumers' surplus.[31] Hotelling's method depends on observation of associated costs, particularly costs of
traveling to the site. People are assumed to know and respond to these
costs as they would to prices and to place no value on travel per se.
People living close to the park enjoy consumers' surplus. The amount
of their "surplus" can be estimated by assuming that some of them would
be willing to pay what travelers from the farthest zones paid in travel
cost. Their surplus then is their willingness to pay for the recreational
services of the site minus what they do pay. This method has several
steps:

1. Define areas from which visitors attended the reservoir.

2. Collect data on visitation, distance, time cost of travel, population, income, and other socioeconomic variables that might be relevant
on each area from which visitors arrive.

3. Estimate a demand function for a given site using travel costs
as a proxy for price. Assume that people would react to increases in
gate fee as they react to increases in travel costs. In the demand function, visits per year is a function of travel costs, socioeconomic variables,
and indices of alternative opportunities for recreation which exist for
any given county.

[29] U.S. Senate, Document No. 97, Supplement No. 1, "Evaluation Standards for
Primary Outdoor Recreation Benefits" (June 4, 1964).
    [30] U.S. Department of the Interior, National Park Service (Roy A. Prewitt), *The
Economics of Public Recreation* 1947, mimeographed.
    [31] Jules Dupuit, "On the Measurement of the Utility of Public Works" (1844), *In-
ternational Economic Papers,* translated from the French by R. H. Barback, No. 2 (1952),
pp. 83–110, reprinted under the title "Public Works and the Consumer" in Denys Munby,
*Transport* (Baltimore: Penguin, 1968), pp. 19–57.

4.   Use the demand function so estimated to predict visits to a site from each area.

5. Calculate the area under the demand curve in each county as an index of willingness to pay additional costs for the services of the site. These areas are bounded by the actual time, travel, and gate-fee costs of using the facility and a ceiling cost at which all attendance would be discouraged.

The following example is designed to illustrate three aspects of the problem: a way to treat recreation, a way to estimate demand functions generally, and a way to study demand when usuable prices are absent. The demand function for day use[32] on Lake Cachuma in Santa Barbara, California was estimated as follows:

$$\ln V_i = 2.63 - 2.2 \ \ln C_i + \ .63 \ln P_i + \ .13 \ D_i + E_i$$
$$\quad\quad (.4) \quad\quad\quad (.2) \quad\quad\quad (.06) \quad\quad\quad\quad\quad (1)$$

where ln stands for natural logarithm

$V_i$ = visitor-days of recreation per year by residents of area $i$
$C_i$ = total time, travel and disutility costs of getting to Cachuma from area $i$
$P_i$ = population of area $i$
$D_i$ = density of population in area $i$ per square mile, and
$E_i$ = natural logarithm of the error term for area $i$.

Estimated standard errors of the regression coefficients appear in parentheses beneath them. All coefficients are significantly different from zero at the .05 level.[33]

As travel costs increase, fewer people visit the site, given their area's population and density. The number $-2.2$ indicates that the price (travel cost) elasticity of demand for recreational services of Cachuma is roughly $-2$. Visits fall off with the square of travel costs, as in Newton's law of universal gravitation. The population elasticity of demand is .63 but is not significantly different from one.

We also tried to estimate an income elasticity of demand by estimating an equation in which the natural logarithm of median family income in the area was an independent variable. Such an estimated equation did not have a significant regression coefficient corresponding to

---

[32] As opposed to overnight use.

[33] This assumes: (a) that the model adequately represents demand for recreational services at Cachuma, and (b) that the errors, $E_i$, are normally and independently distributed with mean zero and finite variance.

income and was inferior to the estimated equation on criteria of good-ness of fit.

*Consumers' Surplus Calculation.* Given this demand curve and ignoring the $E_i$, we can find the consumers' surplus or extra willingness to pay collectible by a perfectly discriminating monopolist, that is, a supplier who charged each visitor the exact additional sum he would pay after traveling to the site. This can be done by finding the area under the demand curve from the actual cost in area $i$ to an infinite cost.

Figure 8.4 shows attendance as a function of cost. Area $i$ visitors experience cost $C_i$ in traveling to the site. Their willingness to pay for the site over and above their actual cost is given by the area under the curve from $C_i$ to infinity. The attendance curve does not hit the axis so the integral is improper. It is convergent, however, and can be evaluated.

FIGURE 8.4. ATTENDANCE AT A RECREATIONAL SITE AS A FUNCTION OF THE COST OF USING IT

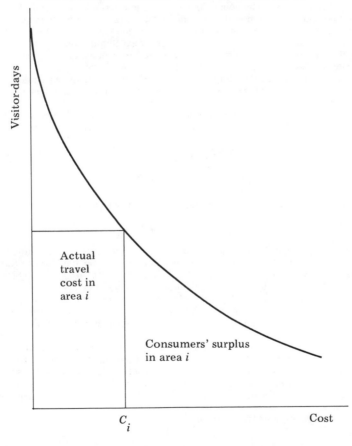

On the basis of 2,604 audited visits to Cachuma, a total consumers' surplus of \$3,873.85 was calculated, a mean consumer's surplus of \$1.49 per visitor-day.[34]

*Market Value Calculation.* Given the estimated demand function, we may also ask what single price, if charged visitors from all areal units, would maximize fee revenue to the state (or to a private owner).

We can visualize changing the current fee by an increment $f$ charged to visitors from all counties. Present gate fees are already included in data on $C$. Extrapolating from the pattern of reactions to observed costs, we can expect this extra fee to discourage some users who are not willing to pay this extra cost. They may go elsewhere or substitute another activity for boating or picnicking at Cachuma. For each area, visitors forthcoming will be:[35]

$$V_i = (C_i + f)^{-2.2} \, P_i^{.63} \, \exp\,(.13 \, D_i + 2.63).$$

[34] Let us inquire to what degree we overstate benefits by calculating the area under the ordinary demand curve. The point estimate of income elasticity was .504. Assume that the true compensating variation at the prevailing price, $C(p)$, is ten times the current total expenditure on reservoir recreation, an arbitrary assumption meant as an upper limit. Then a consumer would spend up to ten times his current expenditure on reservoir recreation without feeling worse than if denied completely the opportunity to visit reservoirs. For linear demand curves the exaggeration in compensating variation from using the ordinary rather than the compensated demand curve is proportional to the increase in quantity demanded at a given price going from one curve to another. For nonlinear demand functions this is nearly true.

The relative change in quantity equals the income elasticity of demand $N$ times the relative change in income.

$$\frac{\Delta q}{q_0} = N\left(\frac{\Delta Y}{Y_0}\right)$$

$$\frac{\Delta Y}{Y_0} = \frac{C(p_1)}{Y_0} = \frac{10(SY_0)}{Y_0} = 10(S)$$

where $S$ is the proportion of total expenditure spent on reservoir recreation.

$$\frac{\Delta q}{q_0} = N\,\frac{\Delta Y}{Y_0} = 10\,NS$$

These figures suggest that the maximum overstatement of the true compensating variation is likely to be less than 2.5 percent. This follows Gerald W. Dean and Norman R. Collins, "World Trade in Fresh Oranges," *Giannini Foundation Monograph* 18 (Davis, Cal.: University of California, Division of Agricultural Sciences, January 1967), pp. 35–40. In 1960 U.S. consumers spent \$1.6 billion on recreation at reservoirs. Personal consumption expenditures in that year were \$325.2 billion. Thus reservoir recreation represented 0.5 percent of personal consumption expenditures; the relative change in quantity due to the change in real income is limited by 10 (.5) (.005).

For most items that form modest fractions of consumers' budgets the overstatement of consumers' surplus from using the ordinary curve is not significant. In studying the demand for an entire class of goods or services such as all services, food, or housing, which form appreciable parts of consumers' budgets, the overstatement of consumers' surplus due to using the ordinary demand curve instead of the income-compensated demand curve may be significant.

[35] Substitute $C_i + f$ in equation (1) for $C_i$.

The revenue collected from each county would be price times quantity:

$$R_i = (f + .33)\,(C_i + f)^{-2.2}\,P_i^{.63}\,\exp\,(.13\,D_i + 2.63).$$

The figure $.33 represents the present charge of $1.00 per auto divided by the average of three persons arriving per car.

If the owner ignores the social cost of crowding, and if the marginal cost to him of a visitor-day is negligible, then he maximizes revenue in choosing the optimal fee increase $f$. In this case, a gate fee increase of $2.25 would maximize revenue collectible for day use at Lake Cachuma.[36]

*Critique.* This method has several disadvantages. It is retrospective, evaluating the benefits of an existing recreational site. A bank of studies of characteristic sites can be developed so that the prospectus for a new project can say it resembles project $x$ of which a study has been made.

An alternative is to pool data on several sites and estimate a demand function for recreation in general.[37] The arguments of the function would be distance (travel costs), characteristics of the areal units where recreationists originate and of the sites visited. Areal units might be described by income, population density, and ownership of consumer durables necessary for recreation. Sites might be characterized by square miles of recreational area, miles of developed shoreline for water sites, capital improvements, access roads, weather, and the like. The dependent variable would then become visits from area $i$ to site $j$, $V_{ij}$. If a new site were planned, its tributary area could be studied and attendance predicted based on characteristics of the area and planned characteristics of the new site. Also important, although rarely successfully measured, is the impact of competing sites on recreational attendance.

### Transportation

Benefit-cost analysis has been used extensively to evaluate transportation investments in highways, airports, and urban public transportation. Since transportation is often an intermediate good used in making something that can be valued, its contribution can often be measured in monetary terms. Many transportation improvements lead to cost savings, which can be used as measures of benefits.

*Urban Highways.* Urban highways lower the "price" and improve

---

[36]See Leonard Merewitz, *Estimation of Recreational Benefits at Some Selected Water Development Sites in California* (Berkeley: Planmetrics, 1968), pp. 43–44.

[37]This alternative is currently being pursued by the Center for Economic Studies, U.S. Army Corps of Engineers, and Craig T. Blake at the Institute of Business and Economic Research, Berkeley, California.

the quality of passenger vehicle-miles and lower the cost of freight movement. Some traffic will be diverted to a new highway from more direct but more costly and time-consuming routes. As highway use becomes less costly, it will be substituted by consumers for other means of transportation. Highway-using goods and services[38] will be substituted in consumption as they become less dear. They will also be substituted in production by using more highway-intensive methods.[39] Transportation improvements, like other investments, increase the productive capacity of the economy by releasing resources for other uses. These "national income" benefits are measured by benefits to diverted and generated traffic.

Highways often open up new areas to commercial and residential exploitation. As a result, land values increase considerably. Should such gains to landowners be counted as benefits of highway investments? Like "secondary benefits" of water projects, these benefits are accountable as *efficiency* benefits without double counting only if (1) the investment would not have been made in the absence of the highway improvement, (2) the resources utilized would have otherwise been unemployed, and (3) no similar economic activity is displaced elsewhere. *Distributional* benefits may be acknowledged even if these stringent conditions are not all fulfilled.

Consumers' surplus is the concept of benefits most often used to evaluate transportation benefits. In Figure 8.5 imagine that *OM* vehicle miles were consumed at price *OH* before a transportation improvement, and *ON* units were consumed later at the lower price *OK*. There are benefits to the users of *OM* vehicle-miles and to the users of the *MN* additional vehicle-miles. Benefits to existing users are measured by *HABK*, the number of units times the savings per unit. Additional willingness to pay (above what is actually paid) for the additional units of transportation generated by substituting lower-priced commodities is approximated by *ABC*, the area under the demand curve but above the price *K* between quantities *OM* and *ON*.[40]

Cost savings from transportation improvements come in the form of (1) wages of drivers saved, and (2) vehicle operating economies, includ-

---

[38]For example, shopping-center purchases (highway-using) will be substitutes for neighborhood-store purchases.

[39]A better transportation system will allow producers to exploit economies of scale more fully by having fewer, larger plants to serve a dispersed geographical clientele. Transportation is substituted for widely dispersed plants.

[40]Simplifying assumptions necessary to obtain this result are not too unrealistic: (1) the income elasticity of transportation is not very high and (2) transportation is not a large part of the average consumer's budget. Actually, as we explain above, the area under the ordinary demand curve is an upper limit on willingness to pay.

FIGURE 8.5. DEMAND CURVE AND CONSUMERS' SURPLUS
BENEFITS FOR A TRANSPORTATION IMPROVEMENT

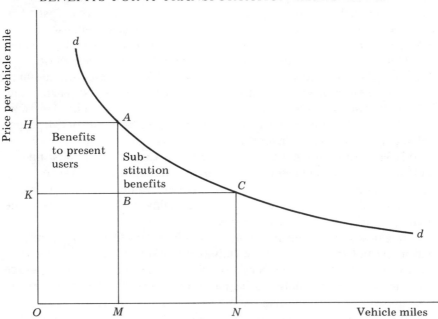

ing gasoline savings and accident reduction. One way of interpreting
Figure 8.5 is to include all these costs in the "price" on which demand
is supposed to depend. Perhaps accident costs could be segregated so
the worth of human life and injury could be evaluated separately.

Other people benefit from transportation improvements as well as
users of a new highway. Herbert Mohring has stressed the social costs
of crowding on highways: reduced average speed and increased time
costs of travel.[41] A new highway that diverts users from an existing road
reduces congestion costs on that road.

Crucial to evaluation of highway benefits is the value used for the
time of the drivers. Working drivers' time is sometimes evaluated at their
wage rate. The value of leisure time is more difficult to measure. Some
studies indicate that different income classes value their driving time at
their wage rate. Mohring infers the value of travel time from the "target
speed" chosen by the driver—the speed he would drive if the road were
not congested. This leads to a price of $2.80 per vehicle-hour for a mean

[41]The speed of 30 miles per hour minimizes operating costs. But higher speeds minimize total cost if time is imputed any substantial value. Total cost increases as average
speed is reduced from, say, 50 miles per hour.

driving speed of 48.5 miles per hour. If drivers drove more slowly than the mean, their operating and expected accident costs would be lower. To save time, however, they do not. If they minimize total cost, they must go faster than the minimum auto operating cost because time is worth something to them. Earlier, Mohring and Harwitz had estimated the value of time in a range between $.50 and $1.00 per person (in 1962 dollars). They arrived at this estimate by making some heroic assumptions and then observing increased land values on an island when a new bridge brought it within a much shorter drive of a city.[42] The American Association of State Highway Officials has used a figure of $1.55 per vehicle-hour in 1960.[43] Several comprehensive surveys of other studies of this valuation problem are available.[44] An English economist finds a wide discrepancy between the value of commuting time as inferred from behavior and the wage rate. Average workers value commuting time at one-third their wage rate whereas more highly paid commuters value their time at one-half their wage rate.[45]

*Highways—General Equilibrium Models.* The foregoing discussion was a "partial analysis," because only one market, that for highway services, was considered. A "general equilibrium analysis" makes allowance for ramifications not only in the particular market under study but in all markets in the economy.

Bos and Koyck,[46] following the work of Tinbergen,[47] have described a general equilibrium model for calculating the benefits of roads to an entire economy. They use a model of an economy with three geographical areas and four goods. The system of demand, supply, and other equations is solved for all prices, quantities, and the resultant national income. With new roads, the system is recalculated under the lower delivered prices. The net increase in national income is accounted as the transportation project's benefits. To count transportation cost savings

[42] Herbert Mohring and Mitchell Harwitz, *Highway Benefits* (Evanston, Ill.: Northwestern University Press, 1962), p. 179.

[43] American Association of State Highway Officials, "Passenger Cars in Rural Areas," in *Road User Benefit Analyses for Highway Improvement* (1960), p. 76. There are 1.8 persons in each vehicle, on the average.

[44] Dan G. Haney, *The Value of Travel Time for Passenger Cars* (prepared by Stanford Research Institute for the Bureau of Public Roads, 1963), and James R. Nelson, "The Value of Travel Time," in Samuel B. Chase, *Problems in Public Expenditure Analysis* (Washington, D.C.: The Brookings Institution, 1968).

[45] M. E. Beesley, "The Value of Time Spent in Travelling: Some New Evidence," *Economica* 32 (May 1965): 182.

[46] H. C. Bos and L. M. Koyck, "The Appraisal of Road Construction Projects: A Practical Example," *Review of Economics and Statistics* 43 (February 1961): 13–20.

[47] J. Tinbergen, "The Appraisal of Road Construction," *Review of Economics and Statistics* 39 (August 1957): 241–49.

alone, even if all are passed on in reduced transport costs, underestimates national efficiency benefits.

Friedlaender extends these Dutch arithmetic models to a still more general model. This model shows that one cannot say unequivocally whether transport cost savings underestimate or overestimate efficiency benefits. The answer "depends upon the elasticity of the various factor supplies, the nature of the factor substitutions, and the nature of the commodity substitutions."[48] Benefits to vehicles alone can be calculated, but calculating the *total* social benefit would require a knowledge of all supply and demand functions in the economy as well as a knowledge of the interindustry structure. Friedlaender does conjecture that her calculations of vehicular benefits are likely to understate total social benefits "if the supply of factors is elastic and if the transport cost reductions do not induce much commodity substitution."[49] Her conclusion on the U.S. Interstate Highway System is that vehicular benefits (a subset of total benefits) exceed costs so that total benefits exceed costs. If the markets are very unresponsive to price and factor cost changes, then the conclusion is in doubt because it is no longer clear that total benefits exceed vehicular benefits. Her sanguine results do not extend to the rural interstate system. She is not at all confident that total benefits exceed costs on that segment of the interstate highway system.

As in the case of navigation, the misleading prices of railroad freight transport enter the evaluation of benefits of highways. Trucks use highways. They would be used less if the Interstate Commerce Commission did not keep railroad rates above competitive levels. Thus, there would be a smaller total of vehicular benefits of highways if railroad rates approximated true social costs.

*Urban Mass Transit.* Foster and Beesley[50] estimated benefits of the Victoria Underground Line (V.L.) in London to include savings in travel time, savings in private vehicle operating costs, decreased congestion elsewhere, and the increased probability of getting a seat. Thus, beneficiaries included not only traffic diverted from elsewhere and traffic generated by the V.L., but traffic not diverted to the V.L. Cost savings accrue to riders of other underground lines in addition to benefits in the form of increased comfort and convenience because of a lower rate of utilization. Bus enterprises save costs by withdrawing some unprofitable runs and road users benefit in time and operating cost savings because

[48] Ann Fetter Freidlaender, *The Interstate Highway System* (Amsterdam: North-Holland, 1965), p. 20.

[49] Freidlaender, *The Interstate Highway System,* p. 23.

[50] C. D. Foster and M. E. Beesley, "Estimating the Social Benefit of Constructing an Underground Railway in London," *Journal of the Royal Statistical Society,* Part I, 126 (1963): 45–58. See also vol. 128 (1965): 67–88.

the V.L. reduces congestion on the roads. The single most important category of benefits is the time savings of vehicle-users from reduced congestion in London streets. *Thus the major beneficiaries of the V.L. are nonusers.*[51] Also notable in the Foster and Beesley study was the heroic attempt to quantify the benefits of comfort and convenience by studying the increased probability of getting a seat in the new system.

*Air Transportation.* Gary Fromm[52] has discussed how benefits ought to be estimated for these expenditures. Expenditures can be considered in two groups: (1) additional air-traffic control facilities at existing airports and (2) additional airports.

Additional facilities at existing airports are intended to reduce "ineffectiveness." Ineffectiveness is failure to minimize delays, diversions, cancellations, and accidents. Fromm estimates ineffectiveness costs in all categories for air carriers, general and military aviation. These represent total *potential* benefits if aviation were to operate without delays, diversions, cancellations, or accidents. This technique is worthy of note. To calculate the total potential benefits of removing a bad thing, calculate the bad thing's present cost to the economy. Potential benefits are all that could be gained by removing the bad thing. We shall see this technique used again below by Rashi Fein to evaluate potential benefits from removing mental illness and by Klarman to evaluate potential benefits from syphilis control. Benefits actually realized will be less than total potential benefits. For example, if half the airport ineffectiveness is removed, then perhaps half the potential benefits will be realized.

Accidents is the most costly category of ineffectiveness. The cost of accidents to air carriers in 1960 was $227 million and the cost to all aviation was $627 million.[53] Emphasis is properly placed on reducing or eliminating accidents. Delays, the next most costly item, amounted to $94 million for air carriers. Cancellations cost about half this amount, $48 million, and diversions $12 million per year.

Calculating these costs involves two ubiquitous valuation problems: human life and travel time. Both are endemic to transportation studies. Arbitrary assumptions are unavoidable. Fromm used a figure of $373,000 for the loss associated with one air fatality. This figure was based on the average decedent's value to himself, his family, his community, his em-

[51]This raises the finance or repayment issue of having users of one mode of transportation subsidize users of another mode; for example, bridge tolls on automobiles might subsidize mass transit.

[52]Fromm, "Civil Aviation Expenditures," in Robert Dorfman, ed., *Measuring Benefits of Government Investments* (Washington, D.C.: The Brookings Institution, 1965), pp. 172–226.

[53]Fromm, "Civil Aviation Expenditures," Table 2, p. 198. No accident costs were attributed to military aviation.

ployer, and the government, as well as the (noninsurance) cost to the airline. These values are measured as future earnings discounted to present value. A relatively high loss is attributed to a fatality in general aviation because general aviation passengers have higher mean incomes than passengers in commercial aviation. The value of delay time was approximated at the earning rate of the average air traveler. Most delays occur at peak hours of airport use.

Additional airports confer three kinds of benefits on passengers and operators in commercial and general aviation. First, when there is no airport close to a community, benefits can be evaluated by the alternative costs of making a typical trip. The time and cost saving of using air transport rather than a combination of other modes is the benefit of having an airport. This concept may overstate benefits for induced traffic which would not have made trips were the airport not available. Second, where airports already exist in a community but additional or relocated ones can save ground time, a different concept of benefits is used. The weighted sum of time and outlay costs of reaching the more conveniently located airport from the central business district is a measure of benefits. Each ground mode is weighted by the proportion its use represents in all ways of getting to airports. Third, the capacity of currently available airports may be saturated, as is now the case in the New York metropolitan area. Such airports are operating at average costs above the minimum. These additional costs appear in the form of ineffectiveness costs. The willingness to pay for reduced ineffectiveness—fewer delays, diversions, cancellations, and accidents—is then a measure of benefits.

Thus, we see that benefit estimation for transportation projects is firmly grounded and reasonable to the extent that transportation is an intermediate good that adds value to a commodity by changing its situation in space. When the transportation is a final or consumer's good, its benefits are more difficult to evaluate.

### Education

Many studies have been done on the benefits and costs of expenditures on education. A high point was a 1962 publication on investment in human capital.[54] In general, efficiency benefits have been measured by the higher income expected over a lifetime because of education.

In early studies the returns from education was estimated from cross-section data on mean annual incomes of individuals.[55] Census studies

---

[54]*Journal of Political Economy* 70, supplement (October 1962).

[55]W. Lee Hansen, "Total and Private Rates of Return to Investment in Schooling," *Journal of Political Economy* 71 (April 1963): 128–40.

were used and individuals were classified by age, sex, race, region, and education. Cross-sectional changes in income received were presumed to be due to education. The worth to society of an educated person's income is his private after-tax income plus his contribution to tax revenue. Education is an investment because it yields benefits in many future periods. Therefore its benefits must be capitalized or converted to a present value. Real growth should be counted but growth in income due to inflation should not be counted. Incomes should be projected in constant dollars.

Education confers benefits other than increased earning power. For example, earlier education is a prerequisite to more advanced education. The benefit of completing eighth grade is not simply the present expected value of eighth-grade graduates' income over that of graduates of seventh grade, but also some fraction of the gains from completing high school since completing eighth grade is prerequisite to being graduate from high school.

Besides census data on groups, data on individuals have been used when available. The impact of college expenditures on individual incomes was studied with data on individual ability, expenditure per pupil in the particular college, size of college, parents' education and type of occupation, and region of the United States in which the college graduate is employed.[56]

Many studies of college education have been biased in its favor. They have estimated internal rates of return on college education at about 15 percent and compared it with a long-term interest rate of 5 percent as a measure of the after-tax return to business capital. In 1960, Gary Becker attempted to make a fairer comparison. He concluded that when the total costs of education were considered (that is, not just what the student pays but also the part that is subsidized and the opportunity cost of not working while studying); when the fact that those who go to college are inherently more able on the average than those who do not; and when nonwhites, females, and rural persons were considered as well as the traditional urban male, the social rate of return was not materially different from that to business capital.[57] Social returns are measured before taxes but do not include external effects difficult to measure. Therefore, Becker concluded there was no compelling evidence of underinvestment in college education in 1960. Those who argued there was such evidence would have to rely heavily on external effects.[58]

[56]Shane J. Hunt, "Income Determinants for College Graduates and the Return to Educational Investment," *Yale Economic Essays* 3 (Fall 1963): 305–57.

[57]Gary Becker, "Underinvestment in College Education?" *American Economic Review* 50, no. 2 (May 1960): 346–54.

[58]In his article he estimated social rates of return at 9 percent. In his 1964 book (see footnote 59) the estimates of social rate of return were 10 to 13 percent.

## TABLE 8.1. EDUCATIONAL ATTAINMENT
## AND INCOME OF ECONOMISTS

| ACADEMIC DEGREE | MEDIAN SALARY ($1,000) |
| --- | --- |
| Less than bachelor | 16.5 |
| Bachelor | 14.7 |
| Master | 12.0 |
| Ph.D. | 13.5 |

Source: N. Arnold Tolles and Emanuel Melichar, "Studies of the Structure of Economists' Salaries and Income," *American Economic Review* 58, no. 5, part 2 (December, 1968): xxii.

The return to the private individual is a different story. Private costs do not include the roughly one-third of the costs that are subsidized. Returns are measured after taxes. Becker concluded that "the private real rate of return [to college education] has . . . been higher . . . than on physical capital."[59] On grounds of pure efficiency, then, society has little incentive to reallocate resources in favor of college education to the detriment of business fixed capital. Individuals, however, would be wiser to invest their savings in college education rather than in physical capital such as homes and businesses.

Criticisms of such benefit estimates for academic educational expenditures can be made. Surely income is too narrow a concept of the benefits of education. Also, there are dangers in using cross-section data to predict a change over time. Just because there was little difference in the earnings of nonwhite high school graduates and dropouts in 1949 does not mean that such educational differentials will not produce income differentials in 1969.

Education not only confers an ability to make money, but it confers an ability to choose a pleasant occupation. Table 8.1 shows a perverse relationship between 1966 median salary and educational attainment among economists. This demonstrates that simple comparisons of educational attainment and median salary can be misleading. The apparent perversity is explained by the longer experience of lower-degree economists and their tendency to be employed by industry rather than colleges and universities. Thus the relationship between education and earnings is not simple.

The study of nonacademic education has been even more successful. The goals of retraining for unemployed workers, vocational education, and dropout prevention are clearly economic. The same concept of benefits, the present value of increased lifetime income, is employed.

[59]Gary Becker, *Human Capital* (New York: Columbia University Press, 1964), p. 123.

Not surprisingly, the results have generally been positive. Scholars frequently set out to evaluate expenditures which they believe are worthwhile and to which they have some commitment. When evaluation is done within an agency, needless to say there is a bias in favor of the expenditures.[60]

Michael Borus[61] found the benefits of retraining unemployed workers in Connecticut exceeded the costs. The average annual gross income of workers who utilized retraining increased $500. Benefit-cost ratios, $R$, can be quoted for the worker receiving retraining for the government or for the entire society. Borus used a ten-year time horizon and an interest range of 5 to 15 per cent, (workers' lending and borrowing rates). For the worker $R$ was between 3 and 6. For the government it ranged between 15 and 20 and for the economy, $R$ was between 75 and 100.[62] Because of these larger benefits to government and society, Borus concludes that the government should continue to sponsor such programs. Similarly, David Page,[63] using a 10 percent rate of discount, but considering over a thirty-five-year remaining working life of trainees, found that net benefits of retraining 907 Massachusetts workers was about $3.3 million. Further income redistribution benefits occurred to the extent that subsistence benefits under the retraining program exceed unemployment compensation. Glen Cain[64] gave a range for the benefit-cost ratio for Job Corps expenditures. The region from 1.02 to 1.70 was likely to include the true ratio. Cain's study recognized that these ratios were lower bounds to comprehensive indicators because the only benefits considered were increased earnings.

In the context of all these positive results it is refreshing to find a negative study. Burton Weisbrod[65] studied expenditures on dropout prevention using a similar concept of benefits. Benefits were calculated as increased lifetime earnings based on retrospective census data for particular groups, 1949 mortality tables and a 5 percent discount rate. The weighted present value per dropout prevented was about $2,750 but the cost was about $6,500 in 1959 prices. Preventing dropouts may be a very laudable activity, valuable privately and socially to potential

[60] A U.S. Department of Agriculture Benefit-Cost Analysis of Research on Live Poultry Handling found a benefit-cost ratio of 1,164 to 1. U.S. Congress, Joint Economic Committee, *Analysis and Evaluation of Public Expenditures,* vol. 2, p. 766.

[61] Michael Borus, "A Benefit-Cost Analysis of the Economic Effectiveness of Retraining the Unemployed," *Yale Economic Essays* 4, no. 2 (1964): 370–429.

[62] Borus, "A Benefit-Cost Analysis," pp. 424–25. Ratios have been rounded.

[63] David A. Page, "Retraining under the Manpower Development Act: A Cost-Benefit Analysis," *Public Policy* 3 (1964): 257–67.

[64] Glen Cain, *Benefit-Cost Estimates for Job Corps* (Madison, Wis.: Institute for Research on Poverty, 1967).

[65] "Preventing High School Dropouts," in Dorfman, *Measuring Benefits,* pp. 117–71.

dropouts whose minds are changed. But since relatively few minds were changed by the program Weisbrod audited, perhaps it would be more advisable to spend similar monies on improving the school curriculum or counseling students at an earlier age.

## Health

Benefits of expenditures on health have traditionally been estimated on principles similar to education benefits. Health expenditures have been looked upon as maintenance expenditures, preventive or remedial, for human capital.[66] But most people would agree that we do not undertake health expenditures solely to prevent depletion of our human capital. We wish to reduce suffering and save lives for their own sake, not only for the sake of the net income they contribute.

Perhaps the traditional human capital approach is most appropriate in an underdeveloped country or a context of extreme scarcity and great health needs. In deciding priorities a public health agency might make a matrix of health problems: malaria, dysentery, tuberculosis, cholera, smallpox, malnutrition, cancer; and characteristics such as frequency of incidence, ages of victims, effects (disables, debilitates, or kills), seasonal incidence, and cost of treatment. In pure economic terms, the diseases to be treated first are those that affect adolescents about to enter the labor force, those that are very widespread throughout the population, and those whose cost of treatment is low.[67] Dorothy Rice did similar work for an international classification of diseases.[68] Benefits of preventing a death through health expenditures may be the loss of production avoided or the expected present value of what the cured or spared patient will earn over the rest of his life.[69]

Some problems that arise in evaluating this incremental production are: what level of unemployment to assume for the future, how to value the services of housewives, and whether to net out the amount a person consumes from society's gain from curing him.

Unemployment would deprive society of the productive services of the cured individual not because of illness but because unemployment prevented him from producing. That loss should be charged to unem-

[66]Selma J. Mushkin, "Health as an Investment," *Journal of Political Economy* 70, supplement (October 1962): 129–57.

[67]J. Cohen, "Routine Morbidity Statistics as a Tool for Defining Public Health Priorities," *Israel Journal of Medical Sciences* (May 1965): 457–60.

[68]Dorothy P. Rice, *Estimating the Cost of Illness* (Washington, D.C.: Public Health Service Publication 947-6, May 1966), and "Measurement and Application of Illness Cost," *Public Health Reports* (Febraury 1969): 95–101.

[69]The classic reference on this subject is Louis L. Dublin and Alfred J. Latka, *The Money Value of a Man* (New York: Ronald Press, 1930).

ployment—not to illness. Therefore, one should assume full employment in calculating expected future earnings of the cured.

Although housewives' services do not appear in the national accounts as income or output, they would appear if substitutes were hired to perform the same services. A loss occurs if housewives are unable to perform because of death, disability, or debility due to illness, but if health expenditures prevent this loss, benefits accrue. Housewives' services may be evaluated either at their opportunity costs (what they could earn in the marketplace), or at the alternative costs of housekeepers to perform housewives' duties.

If a person's life is prolonged, he not only produces more, but consumes more as well. Is the benefit only the net gain, as Burton Weisbrod[70] maintains, or is it the gross production? Prest and Turvey answered this question very convincingly.[71] If the person concerned is part of the society making the decision on the health spending, then his consumption counts as welfare that would be lost if he died. Therefore, they are in favor of including consumption, considering gross income as benefits without deducting consumption.

Poor health does not only result in death. It also leads to *debility,* in which a person can work but at a lower efficiency, and *disability,* in which a person cannot work. Using the expected-value-of-future-earnings concept of benefits implies that disability is equivalent to or worse than death. Disability is equivalent to death if consumption is valued for its own sake and not netted out of benefits. Disability is worse than death in the view that benefits include persons' net contribution to society; disability results in a negative net contribution because consumption continues while production stops. These implications contradict most peoples' views. In fairness, it should be said that a sympathetic interpretation would consider production as a lower bound to benefits—the other component being intangible. This demonstrates the tendency of benefit-cost analysis to emphasize the measurable at the risk of being preoccupied with it.

This traditional approach has been criticized by Thomas Schelling, who maintains that in an affluent society the productive loss due to disease is not as important as the loss of the individuals, their families, and society.[72] He distinguishes life from livelihood. One can insure one's livelihood with life insurance. One cannot insure one's life with a policy

[70]Burton Weisbrod, *Economics of Public Health: Measuring the Economic Impact of Diseases* (Philadelphia: University of Pennsylvania Press, 1961).

[71]A. R. Prest and Ralph Turvey, "Cost-Benefit Analysis: A Survey," *Economic Journal* 75 (1965): 723.

[72]Thomas C. Schelling, "The Life You Save May Be Your Own," in Chase, *Problems in Public Expenditure Analysis.*

that pays off in the currency with which one buys replacement. What we ought to measure as the benefit of a health program which reduces deaths is the value to the individuals and families themselves of reducing the statistical probability of death. For such a program Schelling would identify the individuals likely to pay to reduce the risk of death.

Estimation could be effected by using the price system and observing responses to different prices paid for increased safety. Alternatively, one could discern willingness to pay through interviews. The first technique is clouded by the fact that purchasing safety, for example, in a Cadillac, often involves purchasing other things like comfort, convenience, and prestige as well. The second is difficult because people do not like to think about death; small probabilities are not taken seriously. Although Schelling suggests a scaling technique to obviate the small probability problem, we are not convinced that one could elicit meaningful responses to hypothetical questions. Schelling's approach is further vulnerable in that it implies the government ought to incur greater expense to reduce the risk of wealthy peoples' dying than to reduce the risk of poor people, if wealthy people would be willing to pay more for such reduction of risk. Schelling's main contribution remains, however: One ought not to attempt the impossible task of valuing human life. Clearly, production is a poor measure. Health expenditures do not purchase saved lives. They purchase a reduction of mortality rates. Schelling seeks to determine the consumption value of a life rather than its value as a capital good.

Another study that sees health care as a consumer good as well as an investment good is Herbert Klarman's essay on measuring the benefits of syphilis control.[73] His work also calculates total costs as a measure of potential benefits of eradication. Total costs of the 119,600 syphilis cases newly incurred in 1962 were $117.5 million. This figure consists of (1) costs of medical care, (2) output loss due to treatment time or disability of the affected, (3) reduction in earnings because of the stigma of having syphilis, and (4) consumer benefit loss because of the discomfort of having the disease. If syphilis were eliminated, the control and surveillance mechanism would be obviated at an annual savings of $6 million. Counting all five costs of this nuisance, the gross present value of eradicating syphilis is $3.1 billion, if benefits are discounted at 4 percent. No costs of eradicating syphilis were ventured because an adequate epidemiological theory on the spread of the disease does not exist. In this case, potential benefits is a gross figure.

In Klarman's very careful study he is skeptical of reported figures,

[73]Herbert Klarman, "Syphilis Control Programs," in Dorfman, *Measuring Benefits*, pp. 367–414.

examining each and scrutinizing its accuracy, substituting his own when preferable. His innovations include a reasonable attempt to measure loss in earnings because employers know the affected individual's history of syphilis. He is not dogmatic about his calculations but his assumptions of 1 percent income loss when infectious or latent syphilis is reported, 0.5 percent when it is unreported, and 10 percent when late syphilis is discovered are reasonable. These illustrative figures result in 41.3 percent of the costs of syphilis due to this stigma category. Loss in consumer benefit accounts for 5.1 percent of the cost of syphilis. These are estimated by costs of treatment for psoriasis, a skin disease which entails no disability and can be ameliorated but not cured permanently. Expenditures on psoriasis treatment represent willingness to pay for alleviation of a skin disease over and above loss of productive ability.

Direct costs of syphilis in the form of the cost of treatment, surveillance, and control represents about 21 percent of its total costs. Loss of working time due to treatment or disability represents one-third of costs. Calculation of these figures requires assumptions as to labor force participation, normal unemployment (4 percent), and an imputation of the value of housewives' services. Klarman justifies these calculations very carefully.

Note should be taken of Klarman's use of discount rates. He accepts 4 percent as a discount rate intermediate among those used in 1963. He believes, correctly, that projections should be made in constant prices of the base year except where changes in specific prices greater than that of the general price level make it advisable to take them into account because they imply change in *relative* prices. He notes that physicians' fees were rising 1.25 percent faster than the Consumer Price Index and hospital costs were rising 4 percent faster. Productivity was rising 1.75 percent per year. He combined these effects as appropriate with time discounting in order to get the present value of future treatment expenses or the present value of future absenteeism prevented. Wage rates are expected to grow over time. Instead of inflating them for growth and then discounting them for futurity in two steps, he discounts them only mildly; for example, by a rate of 2.21 percent for absenteeism prevented.

It is possible to avoid quantifying dollar benefits of curing different diseases, if all lives are considered equivalent and decisions are made on cost criteria alone. In an excellent survey, Robert Grosse[74] reports on a series of studies in the Department of Health, Education and Wel-

[74] Robert Grosse, "Problems of Resource Allocation in Health," in Robert H. Haveman and Julius Margolis, eds., *Public Expenditures and Policy Analysis* (Chicago: Markham, 1970), pp. 518–48.

# FIGURE 8.6.

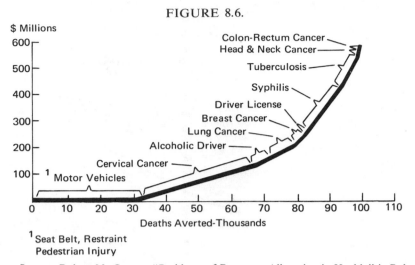

$^1$ Seat Belt, Restraint
Pedestrian Injury

Source: Robert N. Grosse, "Problems of Resource Allocation in Health," in Robert H. Haveman and Julius Margolis, eds., *Public Expenditure and Policy Analysis* (Chicago: Markham, 1970), p. 534.

fare[75] The comparative costs of saving lives by various methods were studied. A seatbelt education program was found to be the cheapest way to avert a death. Following that, in order, were programs to reduce deaths caused by cervical cancer, drunken drivers, and other hazards as shown in Figure 8.6. Sharply increasing costs were experienced in saving lives with programs in syphilis control, tuberculosis, and colon-rectum cancer. This represents the technology or cost side of saving lives.

Evaluation can exploit information on economic benefits of saving lives using a criterion of average discounted lifetime earnings. Control of syphilis then becomes more desirable than control of cervical cancer, presumably because of the differential age and sex of its victims. Prevention of arthritis, which does not kill but does debilitate, then becomes the second most advantageous way to spend money. The hierarchy for programs costing $600 million and yielding nearly $11 billion in savings is shown in Figure 8.7.

[75] U.S. Department of Health, Education and Welfare, Office of Program Coordination, Selected Disease Control Programs (September 1966), 38 pp., summarizing:
  (1) *Motor Vehicle Injury Prevention Program* (Program Analysis [PA] 1966-1), August 1966.
  (2) *Cancer* (PA 1966-3), October 1966.
  (3) *Arthritis* (PA 1966-4), September 1966.
  (4) *Maternal and Child Health Care Programs* (PA 1966-6), October 1966.

FIGURE 8.7.

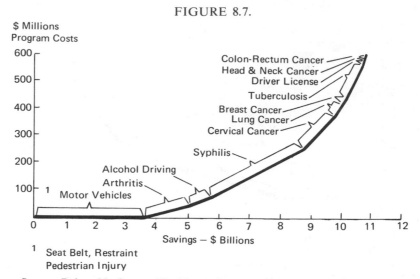

$ Millions
Program Costs

1  Seat Belt, Restraint
   Pedestrian Injury

Source: Robert N. Grosse, "Problems of Resource Allocation in Health" in Robert H. Haveman and Julius Margolis, eds., *Public Expenditure and Policy Analysis* (Chicago: Markham, 1970), p. 535.

Mental illness decreases national product; curing or alleviating its symptoms yields benefits. As in the cases of syphilis and airport ineffectiveness, potential benefits from curing mental illness can be estimated by the total costs to the national economy of the disease. An early study in 1958 by Rashi Fein estimated the direct costs of mental illness to the U.S. economy at $1.7 billion per year.[76] A more recent study suggests new concepts for measuring costs or potential benefits, and estimates them at over ten times Fein's estimates.[77]

### Urban Renewal

As Otto Davis and Andrew Whinston[78] have written, slums develop because maintaining one's property has externalities, also called "neighborhood effects." Looked at as a game, a property owner's best strategy is to fail to maintain his own property holding and have his neighbors maintain theirs. If all landlords opt for this strategy, the result will be that no property will be maintained. All landlords may prefer a situation

[76]Rashi Fein, *Economics of Mental Illness* (New York: Basic Books, 1958).
[77]R. Conley, M. Cromwell, and M. Arrill, "An Approach to Measuring the Cost of Mental Illness," *American Journal of Psychiatry* (December 1967), pp. 63–70.
[78]Otto A. Davis and Andrew B. Whinston, "Economics of Urban Renewal," *Law and Contemporary Problems* 26 (Winter, 1961).

in which all properties were maintained, yet there is no authority to insure that each one's efforts will be met by the efforts of others. In the absence of legislation the low-maintenance solution will prevail.[79] The situation is exacerbated by real estate tax laws that encourage an owner to allow his building to deteriorate and then to sell it to another who will in turn use it as a tax shelter for its depreciation value without maintaining it.

Substandard housing may not please urban planners, but residents, if they are poor, may prefer to have low-cost housing of the existing kind to having higher-cost, higher-quality housing. There is evidence to suggest that poor people live in central cities to economize on transportation costs in the journey to work.[80] In privately owned urban housing the phenomenon of "filtering" has been observed. Existing facilities are converted over time to successively lower quality levels of housing. This can transpire through "improvements" for more intensive use such as the conversion of a brownstone home to a rooming house accommodating many more people. Filtering can also take place through provision of fewer services such as maintenance. Filtering happens without coercion. People of modest income are willing to live close together to economize on housing expenditure in favor of other spending and in the center city where work is (or was) accessible. This makes provision of low-cost housing a potentially profitable enterprise.

Existing communities may support social relationships. Uprooting them may be painful and destructive. Jane Jacobs is a noted champion of old, established communities in which residential and commercial properties are integrated.[81] Harrison Salisbury and Martin Anderson, among others, have criticized urban renewal.[82] Urban renewal has not always provided the numbers of housing units nor the type of housing needed. No net loss of living units should transpire, but often after considerable time has elapsed fewer units have been replaced than have been destroyed. Thus urban renewal starts out with several strikes against it. Nevertheless, it has become a cliché that "we must do something about our cities."

[79]This type of situation arises in the discussion of the social rate of discount and is known in game theory literature as The Prisoner's Dilemma.

[80]A. H. Schaaf, "Public Policies in Urban Renewal: An Economic Analysis of Justifications and Effects," *Land Economics* 40, no. 1 (February 1964): 67–78; and John F. Kain, "The Journey to Work as a Determinant of Residential Location" (Ph.D. diss., Department of Economics, University of California at Berkeley, 1961).

[81]Jane Jacobs, *The Death and Life of Great American Cities* (New York: Random House, 1961).

[82]Harrison Evans Salisbury, *The Shook-Up Generation* (New York: Harper, 1958); and Martin Anderson, *The Federal Bulldozer: A Critical Analysis of Urban Renewal 1949–1962* (Cambridge, Mass.: M.I.T. Press, 1965).

Rothenberg[83] has contributed a good discussion of the effects of urban renewal expenditures. Renewal usually leads to less substandard and more standard housing. It increases the productivity of land in renewal, changes the composition of the housing stock and changes locational advantages that affect land prices. Renewal affects many different types of people: dispossessed property owners, evicted tenants, owners and tenants of adjacent property, owners and tenants of other areas, and potential developers and tenants of cleared areas. With all these effects listed, however, Rothenberg proceeds to measure the repercussions of very few of them.

Four types of efficiency benefits of redevelopment are: (1) internalization of externalities, which increases the productivity of land on the development site; (2) enhanced value of nearby property; (3) a decrease in the social costs of slum living; and (4) increased efficiency of public decision making. In addition, the important income-distribution effects of urban renewal are largely detrimental to the poor whose low-cost housing is removed in order to add to the stock of higher-cost housing.

The only type of benefit Rothenberg seems to be able to measure is the type which is due to an internalization of externalities. He does not believe this to be the major class of benefits. Governments are uniquely suited to achieving these benefits. Only they have the power of eminent domain: the power to condemn land in order to put together a large parcel of land to be used for complementary purposes. Once a large parcel is agglomerated, the owner or developer finds it worthwhile to improve or maintain part of it because he also owns the other parts which will benefit from the external effects of the improvement. In fact, the effects will no longer be external, but will have been internalized. Rothenberg assumes that these will be capitalized in the form of increased land values.

Land values may increase because of locational effects also. If renewal makes shopping easier in one area and harder in another, then land values may increase in the first area, but they will decrease in the second. The only change will be a redistribution with no increase in total land value because of locational advantages. There are some neighborhood effects on nearby property which genuinely enhance its quality. This represents a positive external effect, not just a relative change in locational advantage.

---

[83]Jerome Rothenberg, "Urban Renewal Programs," in Robert Dorfman, ed., *Measuring Benefits of Government Investments,* pp. 292–342; and *Economic Evaluation of Urban Renewal* (Washington, D.C.: The Brookings Institution, 1968).

The effects of renewal on the social costs of slum living are considerable. There is good evidence to show that renewal usually reduces fire hazards and may reduce health hazards, crime, personality disorders, and social adjustment difficulties. The case is not so one-sided, however. By disrupting supportive relationships among neighbors or family members, renewal may increase social adjustment costs. Rothenberg believes, nevertheless, that reductions in social costs of slums because of redevelopment are the major motivation for undertaking urban renewal. He does not attempt, however, to evaluate these benefits numerically. He believes that any such evaluations would be arbitrary and despairs of ever measuring such important values as the value of a human life or of interpersonal harmony.

Benefits can be limited by alternative costs. The mitigation or removal of the forces which contribute to the formation of slums may accomplish just as much as urban renewal. If poverty could be eliminated, then people would not opt to live in slums because of budget constraints. Therefore, we may limit the benefits of an urban renewal program by the costs of an educational, zoning, institutional, and income-maintenance program that would have an effect equivalent to the urban renewal program.

Changes in site land values alone accounted for 8, 5, and 37 percent, respectively, of the resource cost of three projects Rothenberg examined. Thus, without estimating the most important class of benefits, he can say that they would have to amount to at least 63 percent of project costs in order for the urban renewal projects to be economically feasible.

Unfortunately, Rothenberg's work is not very hopeful for the usefulness of benefit-cost analysis as applied to urban renewal.

## TECHNOLOGICAL DEVELOPMENTS

Recently, benefit-cost analysis has been used to organize evaluation of two technological development programs: large-scale desalting and nuclear breeder reactors. Paul MacAvoy directed both of these studies that are at the forefront of benefit-cost method.[84] In one he examined a 100 million gallon per day (MGD) distillation plant and found it ineffi-

[84]Paul W. MacAvoy and Dean F. Peterson, *Large-Scale Desalting: A Study in the Engineering-Economics of Regional Development* (New York: Praeger, 1969); and Paul W. MacAvoy, *Economic Strategy for Developing Nuclear Breeder Reactors* (Cambridge, Mass.: M.I.T. Press, 1969).

cient. The other suggests several desirable strategies for developing breeder reactors. MacAvoy's work is particularly sophisticated in dealing with uncertainty. Instead of point estimates of the present value of net benefits he gives frequency distributions based on the many uncertain events involved in these development programs.

The concept of benefits for water desalting is consumers' and producers' surplus. This encompasses: (1) the net value of agricultural production from the additional water, (2) the value of the distilled water as a dilutant that reduces salinity in existing ground water and surface reservoir systems, (3) the greater capability to provide "safe yield" in periods of extended drought, (4) the value of achieving the (Israeli) social goal of spreading the country's population to sparsely settled agricultural areas, and (5) worldwide gains from progress in the development of new desalting technology. The third type of benefit is, ironically, zero in Israel because of the large surface and ground-water storage available and the water supply mobility provided by the National Water Carrier. The fourth type of benefit is a "merit want," to use a term we present in the next chapter, something the government wants but the people would not freely choose. Desalted water was worth about 19 to 34 cents per thousand gallons in 1965 dollars, of which over half was the net value of additional agricultural production. MacAvoy concluded against desalting plants in the 100 MGD range for Israel and *a fortiori* for the rest of the world. Perhaps one in the 40 MGD range would be efficient, because its research value would be comparable but its costs much lower.

Benefits for breeder reactors were divided into three parts: (1) consumers' surplus on the increased demand for reactors (these "consumers" are producers of electricity), (2) producers' surplus on the same increased demand, and (3) producers' and consumers' surplus on an increased quantity of reactors demanded if their price declines as more firms produce them. Producers' surplus is the area above the marginal cost curve but below the price. The most economic single reactor project seems to be a gas cooled breeder reactor. Its present value of net benefits is $16.3 billion at a 10 percent discount rate. The probability is 50 percent that net benefits will be less than this. Similarly, the probability is 50 percent that net present value of a liquid metal fast breeder reactor program is less than $9.9 billion. These are expected values at a 10 percent discount rate but the whole frequency distribution of possible net benefits is given for both 10 and 15 percent discount rates. MacAvoy's most preferred alternative is a combination of parallel breeder reactor programs: one liquid metal and one gas cooled, whose mean value of expected benefits is $19 billion.

## RECAPITULATION AND CRITIQUE

Thus we have seen that for projects in diverse areas, efficiency benefits can be estimated where benefits have counterparts in market transactions or increased national income. The four most common ways of estimating efficiency benefits are: (1) willingness to pay of beneficiaries in the form of actual or imputed user charges; (2) increase in capital values; (3) cost savings, actual or potential; and (4) increase in national income due to the project.

A project may produce something which is sold or at least salable, for example, electricity, trash collection, or recreational opportunities. The monentary value of the social benefits might be measured by the largest amount of money the users would be willing to pay for what they receive between starting and stopping. This equals the amount of money that would be collected from users if the project's outputs were sold, not at uniform prices, but under perfect price discrimination. The required estimate of willingness to pay can come from the prevailing price, if that will not change, or from observing responses to different prices either over time or cross-sectionally. We demonstrated the estimation of a demand curve when differing prices were not observable but differing associated costs were. Willingness to pay is the area under a sequence of demand curves, between starting and stopping, that represent users' collective compensated demand for each output of the project. The area to be estimated lies between the price axis, the quantity axis, the curve and the line at the level of the quantity that users will choose at the price that will be charged. The income compensated demand curve differs from the ordinary demand curve when the income elasticity of demand is substantial or expenditure on the good forms a sizable fraction of the households' expenditures.

Even if the project produces salables, however, difficulties in estimating monetized benefits will result from four factors. First, the quantities that consumers would demand in any one year if confronted with each of various prices may depend on what decisions are made about other projects. That is, users' collective compensated (or ordinary) demand may depend on the existence and character of other governmental activities, both old and new. Interdependence of benefits may reflect complementarity or substitutability of outputs. For example, a park and a side road leading to it are complementary. If only one exists, demand and benefits for it are zero and for the other are those of an accessible park; if neither exists, each alone has zero demand and benefits. Interdependence of benefits also may reflect substitutability of outputs. For example, a park and a beach are likely to be substitutes for each other. Either one is likely to have smaller demand and benefits if the other is opened also. The Corps of Engineers has calculated potential benefits from deepening several harbors. Each study assumes the other ports remain as they are now. If all were deepened there would be competition among them and fewer than the total of all the predicted benefits would accrue. Because of such interdependence, the benefits of any one project are indeterminate until decisions have been specified for all interrelated projects.

Second, the quantities consumers would demand in any one year, if confronted with each of various prices, will be hard to estimate even if other governmental decisions are known. Future demand is unknowable. Even if one is willing to extrapolate from the past or present into the future, neither questionnaires nor historical data will provide an adequate basis for knowing the past or present. Questionnaires have doubtful reliability. People do not respond accurately to questionnaires when nothing is really at stake. A participant in a Brookings conference on benefit-cost analysis confided that he has found it useless to ask hypothetical questions.[85] Questionnaires also leave an analyst with the problem of generalizing to an unknown number of users. Historical data often contain no variation in prices and almost never contain the range of prices that is needed in order to estimate users' collective ordinary demand by statistical techniques. To use statistical techniques also requires making some arbitrary decisions concerning time period, shift variables, form of function, sampling errors, and the like. Anyone who has tried to estimate market demands will know what we mean.

Third, the maximum amount of money that users would pay for what they obtain depends on what they will obtain, and the latter depends on what prices and qualities will be in force. In order to obtain an answer, an analyst must specify these prices and qualities, and to do so may entail bold guesswork as to what project managers will decide.

It was once fashionable to say that there was a clear dichotomy between what should be done and how to pay for it—between design and repayment or financial policy. According to this viewpoint, willingness to pay would be calculated for all outputs and the project would be designed and its scale determined by maximizing net benefits. Assessing charges was irrelevant to the calculation of benefits and costs: it influenced income distribution only, not efficiency.[86]

[85]Chase, *Problems in Public Expenditure Analysis,* p. 19.

[86]This point of view was adopted in Maass, et al., *Design of Water Resource Systems* (Cambridge, Mass.: Harvard University Press, 1962), pp. 38–40; and John V. Krutilla, "Is Public Intervention in Water Resources Development Conducive to Efficiency?" *Natural Resources Journal* 6 (January 1966): 66ff.

More recently it has been recognized that the quantity of benefits that actually accrue depends vitally on repayment policy when prices are charged for salable outputs as part of the repayment scheme.[87] The price of project output determines the quantities beneficiaries will consume.

An example of the effect prices have on the amount of benefits forthcoming from a project is available in highway transport. The number of vehicles using a road will depend on the charge for using it. Some price is implicit in any prediction of quantity demanded. If the road's services are not intended to be priced, consumers' surplus is a measure of willingness to pay. But if financial policy later determines that a price is appropriate, less consumers' surplus will accrue than was predicted. Thus pricing policy is not irrelevant to the calculation of efficiency benefits.

Fourth, areas under users' collective demand curves represent only a money value to users of their own use. Because of external economies, other benefits will accrue. For example, when one's trash is collected, one's neighbors benefit too. If air pollution were ameliorated, certain producers and people with respiratory diseases would benefit discernibly. But the largest benefit would be the increased psychic income to the whole society from the amenity of clean air. Usually there is no satisfactory way to measure such intangible gains, so measurable benefits dominate the analysis.

The second type of transactional counterpart exists when a project changes capital values such as the future earning stream of individuals or land. For such projects, one might assume that the monetized benefits between approval and infinity equal the net increase in capitalized value of these future streams. The present value of future incremental earnings due to the health or education program is the typical measure of such benefits. Land value changes are estimated from actual or constructive market prices. Such changes have been used to estimate the benefits of urban renewal, recreational and transport expenditures. One school of thought, represented by Henry George and Charles Tiebout, claims that all benefits of local expenditures, for example, on education, parks, and sewers, are capitalized in land values.[88]

Three problems arise from this view. First, the increase in market value may depend on what decisions are made about other projects. For example, the increase in land value from redevelopment may depend on how the whole city is rezoned, what police services are provided,

[87]See John V. Krutilla, "Efficiency Goals, Market Failure and the Substitution of Public for Private Action," in U.S. Congress Joint Economic Committee, *Analysis and Evaluation of Public Expenditure*, Vol. I, pp. 284ff.

[88]Henry George, *Progress and Poverty* (New York: Robert Schalkenbach Foundation, 1929); and Charles M. Tiebout, "A Pure Theory of Local Expenditures," *Journal of Political Economy* 64 (October 1965): 416–24.

and where a new city hall is located. Second, the increase in market value for which the project deserves credit will be uncertain. For instance, one never really knows what prices would have occurred in the absence of the project. Third, increases in market value represent the money value that only the direct gainers might be expected to place on their gains. Because factor prices differ from values of marginal products, increases in factor values do not show how much improving factor quality raises national income. For instance, the extra earnings of men who have been retrained may be less than the growth in national income because of "monopolistic" pricing or because of multiplier effects, or may be greater than the growth in national income because of unemployment problems. Moreover, because various induced effects will occur, even the exact increase in national income that follows from improving factor quality does not represent the money value that all gainers would place on their benefits. Urban renewal for instance, as Mao and Rothenberg point out, affects not only land values but also disease, crime, schooling, living patterns, fires, labor supplies, and municipal tax revenues—among other things. These are formidable obstacles to measuring benefits.

The third type of transactional counterpart exists when a project reduces the expenditures made for certain purposes. For example, a new road may reduce motorists' expenditures for gasoline; an expanded sewer system may reduce builders' expenditures for septic tanks; a meat inspection program may reduce consumers' expenditures for medical care; a new office building may reduce agencies' expenditures for rent. In such cases one might assume that monetized benefits between approval and infinity equal the reduction in expenditures that the project produces between starting and stopping. Given this assumption, the task of estimating monetized benefits between approval and infinity reduces to the task of estimating the savings between starting and stopping.

Costs saved can be in the form of alternative costs or the total economic costs of a "bad" to be eliminated. Alternative costs are actual costs obviated. Total costs of a bad are potential benefits. Both are not strictly measures of benefit, but are rather upper bounds to benefits. Alternative costs are employed for hydroelectric power as an upper limit to willingness to pay. In studies of airport ineffectiveness, syphilis, and mental illness, total costs of the bad was used as an estimate of potential benefits. This concept could be used to value the eradication of any disease, the mitigation of air pollution, or the elimination of accidents of any type.[89]

[89]R. G. Ridker, *Economic Costs of Air Pollution* (New York: Praeger, 1967), p. 7 mentions air pollution costs of $11 billion annually. This is not his own, but rather a commonly quoted figure.

Here, too, three problems exist. First, the reduction in expenditures may depend on what is decided about other projects. For example, how much gasoline motorists will save from a new road may depend on which other roads are opened and what decisions are made about snow removal. Second, the reduction in expenditures for which the project deserves credit will be uncertain. For instance, estimates of motorists' aggregate savings on gasoline will be subject to error. Third, reductions in expenditures represent the money value that only the direct gainers might be expected to place on their gains. Because of unemployment, externalities, and varying ratios of prices to marginal costs, reductions in expenditures do not show how much national income increases when factors are freed for other uses. For instance, savings on gasoline do not necessarily raise national income by the same amount. Moreover, because of induced effects, even the exact increase in national income that follows from freeing factors does not represent the money value that all gainers would place on their benefits. For instance, a new road will save time as well as gasoline, and it will affect not only motorists and gasoline suppliers, but also merchants, property owners, and others.

Increases in national income have been used to estimate benefits of transportation improvements whose effects are pervasive throughout an economy. The same concept is employed when a mathematical programming model of an economy is used and the value of gross regional product can be increased by increasing the quantities of water available in several alternative uses. Such an analysis may be called a with-and-without analysis, calculating national income (or GNP or gross regional product) *with* the change minus national income *without* the change. This is also called a general equilibrium analysis connoting impact on several sectors of the economy. A producers' good, like transportation or water, is likely to have widespread impacts. A partial equilibrium analysis reserves attention to one market. A with-and-without analysis differs from a before-and-after analysis in that the former acknowledges that changes would have transpired over time in the absence of the project and is therefore preferable. A broader definition of national income than that employed in national income accounting is intended. For example, changes in consumers' surplus, the value of housewives' services, and the like are intended to be included in changes in national income as an index of welfare changes.

All of these concepts of efficiency benefits should overlap. They all seek to measure essentially the same thing: the gross welfare change due to an expenditure before its costs are subtracted. Regard them as alternative roads to the same end. As we hope to have shown, none is a royal road.

Because of the problems discussed above, a reliable estimate of monetized benefits should not be expected even when benefits have transactional counterparts. The only figure attainable even then is the money value that the direct gainers would place on their gains and estimates of this, too, will be subject to unknowable amounts of error. The most that an analyst will be able to claim for his estimate is that it is a plausible lower bound. We conclude that an objective estimate of monetized benefits is not obtainable.

# Nine

# NONEFFICIENCY OBJECTIVES

## BENEFITS AND OBJECTIVES

Benefit measurements are quantifications of the extent to which desirable effects occur. In order to know what is desirable we must know the objective of the policy maker. Therefore, benefits of a particular type exist only in the context of objectives, whether expressly stated or not.

Public expenditures are incurred in the service of many objectives, but benefit-cost analysis has concentrated on the efficiency objective exclusively. If it continues to do so, such analysis will be irrelevant to many of the real issues of public spending. In this chapter we discuss the objectives of public activity and we note their multiplicity. We discuss the question of how to deal with multiple objectives: whether to consider only one of the several objectives at a time or consider several simultaneously.

### Multiple Objectives

Governments are elected by people to serve many objectives. Among other things they seek to: (1) maximize "economic welfare," (2) achieve an "equitable" distribution of income, (3) provide for the national defense, (4) stabilize the economy, and (5) balance international payments over time. We might give names to these objectives and refer to (1) the *efficiency* objective, (2) the *equity* or *distribution* objective, (3) the *national defense* objective, (4) the *stabilization* objective, and (5) the *balance-of-payments* objective. Should the government have separate branches, each dedicated to the fulfillment of an objective, or should each branch try to serve several objectives? Should each agency seek a global optimum for social problems, or should there be a division of labor so that each agency can suboptimize on its own area, leaving the attainment of an *optimum optimorum* to the highest levels of government?

Under the influence of the "New Welfare Economics" in the 1930s only a single objective, efficiency, was officially considered. In fact, however, other objectives lay unarticulated "under the table." In spite of lip service to efficiency, congressmen might vote for a project because it benefits their district or the district of a fellow. More recently such objectives have been recognized more openly.

### Separation of Objectives

Richard Musgrave is a proponent of the idea that separate branches or divisions of government ought to devote themselves to the pursuit of single objectives.[1] He believes there ought to be an allocation branch to pursue the efficiency objective; a distribution branch to deal with the equity objective, and a stabilization branch responsible for keeping the economy in full employment without inflation. Each branch must assume the others are doing their jobs properly. Thus the allocation branch assumes full employment exists and the distribution of income is equitable. Each branch does not try to optimize with respect to all objectives simultaneously. Instead, it *suboptimizes,* or narrows its scope and seeks to optimize within it.

The allocation branch takes responsibility for seeing that resources are allocated such that economic welfare is maximized. In this branch might be an office of antitrust to see that industry is organized in forms conducive to the achievement of welfare, and an office of benefit-cost analysis to see that government spending yields the most welfare it can. This branch ought to see to the satisfaction of "social wants"; for example, clean air, which is consumed in roughly equal amounts by all and from the enjoyment of which no one can be excluded by failure to pay a price. Finally, according to Musgrave, the allocation branch should "correct individual choice"[2] and intervene to provide "merit wants" despite consumer preferences. An example of a merit want is integration of public schools which the judicial branch may deem a good thing even though citizens would not choose this solution themselves. The spending power is then used to "bus" children to achieve this merit want.

The allocation branch uses taxes and expenditures to achieve its goals. It assumes that the proper state of distribution has been achieved by the distribution branch and that full employment has been achieved by the stabilization branch.

[1] Richard Musgrave, *The Theory of Public Finance* (New York: McGraw-Hill, 1959), pp. 3–27.
[2] Musgrave, *Theory of Public Finance,* p. 9.

The distribution branch secures a predetermined distribution of income. Arguments for the optimality of perfectly competitive long-run equilibrium assume initial endowments to be given. A situation is Pareto optimal[3] without regard to income distribution. A different distribution of factor ownership or transfers yields a different competitive equilibrium, which also may be Pareto optimal. The distribution branch uses taxation and transfer payments, *not public expenditures,* to achieve its goals.

The stabilization branch is responsible for steering a course between depression and unemployment on the one hand and inflation on the other. Insofar as budget policy is used instead of monetary or debt policy, taxes and transfer payments ought to be the policy instruments of the stabilization branch. Spending ought not be done to cure an unemployment problem unless the spending is justified on a benefit-cost criterion that assumes full employment. Stabilization is outside the scope of the office of benefit-cost analysis, which should conduct its calculations on the assumption that the economy is at full employment.

Musgrave does not intend this normative identification of objectives and instruments of policy to be used as a blueprint for government. Obviously, many decisions will affect many objectives simultaneously. For example, imposition of a sales tax reduces efficiency, redistributes income from spenders to savers, and may reduce effective demand to allay inflation. Nevertheless, one policy maker does wear several hats—but only one at a time. The main burden of Musgrave's argument is that government spending power, with which we are primarily concerned, should not be used where it cannot help. A hierarchy of desirable projects must be identified, so that, when government funds are spent, only the most efficient projects will be undertaken. Building a bridge might be more efficient than raking leaves. The function of benefit-cost analysis is to rank projects and help decision-makers identify the most efficient ones.

### Simultaneous Attention to Multiple Objectives

The alternative view of this problem is upheld by Arthur Maass.[4] Maass and his school are not confident that further redistribution of income through the progressive income tax is likely. They are also skeptical about the large-scale use of transfer payments to redistribute income.

Maass' proposals correspond to practices developing within the federal government. A recent proposal submitted to the Water Resources Council suggested that the following objectives be pursued in water re-

[3]For a definition of this concept, see the section in Chapter 6, "The Pareto Criterion."
[4]Arthur Maass, "Benefit-Cost Analysis: Its Relevance for Public Investment Decisions," *Quarterly Journal of Economics* 80, no. 2 (1966): 208–26.

source development: (1) National Income, (2) Regional Development, (3) Preservation of the Environment and (4) Well-being of People.[5] The program structures of the Appendix to this book demonstrate that several objectives are served by each agency. Each serves the efficiency objective, but may serve some distributional and merit-want objectives as well.

Both Maass and David Major, an economist, show that regional income redistribution goals are evident in the legislative history of the interstate highway and Appalachia programs.[6] Income redistribution among classes was on the minds of legislators when discussing the Housing and Urban Development Act of 1965.

One way that attention could be paid to several objectives is by making benefits of the several types commensurable. Some trade-off or rate of exchange between efficiency benefits and equity benefits, for example, would meet this requirement. The rate of exchange between efficiency benefits and merit-want benefits must also be known. Then the goal would be to maximize a weighted sum of national efficiency benefits, regional income benefits (with income to different regions weighted differently), and class income-redistribution benefits. Maass hopes that by a careful study of the legislative history of a bill, the willingness of Congress to sacrifice one type of benefit for another will be discerned. Furthermore, if data on the likely consequences of alternative trade-offs are developed by planners and presented to the President and Congress as part of the Executive's legislative initiative, then there will be a greater propensity on the part of elected officers to consider and act on trade-offs. In principle, relative weights might be developed in the following way.

Churchman, Ackoff, and Arnoff[7] have described a method of assigning relative weights to several objectives by successive approximation. The method assumes that successive choices can be made between one objective and a combination of others. It also assumes additivity; that is, if $V_j$ and $V_k$ are values of objectives $j$ and $k$, then $V_j + V_k$ corresponds to the combined outcome or objective $O_j$ and $O_k$. This is not trivial. If $O_j$ and $O_k$ are mutually exclusive, then the combined objective $O_j$ and $O_k$ could not occur. Obviously, to talk of its value is meaningless.

For simplicity, let us examine the assignment of weights to only five

[5]Walter J. Hickel, et al., Special Task Force, *Procedures for Evaluation of Water and Related Land Resource Projects* (Washington, D.C.: Water Resources Council, June, 1969), mimeographed.

[6]David C. Major, "Decision Making for Public Investment in Water Resource Development in the United States" (Ph.D. diss., Department of Economics, Harvard University, 1965), Chap. 5.

[7]C. W. Churchman, R. L. Ackoff, and E. L. Arnoff, *Introduction to Operations Research* (New York: Wiley, 1957), pp. 136–54.

objectives. They would first be ranked in importance, the most important being given the tentative value of 1.0 and the others successively lower values [$v_i$] as we move down the hierarchy of objectives. Compare $O_1$ to the combined objective $O_2$-and-$O_3$-and-$O_4$-and-$O_5$. If $O_1$ is preferred to the combined objective, then the estimate of the value $v_1$ should be adjusted so that

$$v_1 > v_2 + v_3 + v_4 + v_5.$$

In other cases, $v_1$ could be either equal to or less than the right-hand side—the latter, if the first objective were less preferred than the combination. It is assumed that one's judgment on successive approximations is not totally influenced by one's initial judgment in assigning values. If the evaluator endeavors to maintain absolute consistency, he will never give any more information than was given in the first estimate of the values.

The next step is to compare $O_1$ to $O_2$-and-$O_3$-and-$O_4$ and adjust interim values to reflect preference between the alternatives. At such time as $O_1$ is preferred or equal to a combination, we can proceed to use $O_2$ as a standard of comparison. $O_2$ is compared to $O_3$-and-$O_4$-and-$O_5$ and then to $O_3$-and-$O_4$. Values are adjusted at each comparison to reflect choices. We move on to a new standard when $O_2$ is preferred to a combination or the evaluator is indifferent in a choice situation.

We continue making choices until we reach $O_3$ versus $O_4$-and-$O_5$. This is the final choice to be made because $O_4$ is preferred to $O_5$ by the original ranking. When each value is consistent with results of all comparisons, the weights are normalized by expressing each as a quotient: its last interim approximation divided by the sum of weights. The final normalized weights will add up to 1.0.

There are several problems with this method. If an objective is added or deleted the resultant relative weights will be different. The method is designed to rank either objectives or outcomes. Outcomes are easier to rank than objectives, however. Which is preferable, maximum economic efficiency or equitable income distribution and a stabilized economy and balance-of-payments equilibrium? Perhaps choices are more readily made when the degree of attainment of objectives is quantified and they become outcomes; for example, a $900 billion GNP versus a Gini coefficient[8] of 0.43 and 2 percent inflation per year, 4 percent unemployment, and a balance-of-payments deficit within $1 billion. The

[8]This is a measure of income-distribution inequality: the ratio of the area between the Lorenz curve and the diagonal to the total triangular area under the diagonal. See T. Paul Schultz, "Secular Trends and Cyclical Behavior of Income Distribution in the U.S. 1944–65," in Lee Soltow, ed., *Six Papers on the Size Distribution of Wealth and Income* (New York: National Bureau of Economic Research, 1969).

method is designed to reflect the subjective evaluation of an individual. The problem of group decisions, on the other hand, is called the problem of *amalgamation* of preferences and this is more formidable and less soluble.[9] Individual evaluations of weights can be made by members of a group in the manner suggested by Churchman, Ackoff, and Arnoff, and these weights can then be amalgamated by averaging them, but this is subject to problems noted by Arrow. If no rates of exchange are available, a "vector maximum" problem arises; one must then maximize several components of a vector simultaneously.

The vector maximum problem can be formulated as: maximize efficiency benefits subject to a constraint on income distribution. An example of such a constraint is seen in the 160-acre limitation on the size of farms that may receive federally assisted irrigation water.[10] Another way to formulate the vector maximum problem with the use of constraints is as follows: maximize benefits to a particular region subject to a constraint on efficiency benefits and perhaps a constraint on quality of the environment. This formulation closely approximates actual behavior with respect to public investment. There is a statutory constraint that aggregate efficiency benefits should exceed aggregate efficiency costs regardless of the incidence of benefits and costs.[11] Projects are often proposed and authorized mainly with attention to generating economic activity in a particular geographical jurisdiction. Requiring benefits to exceed costs does not insure that a project is among the set that maximizes the net present value of benefits, but it does screen out some projects that would be overtly wasteful.

It may sound ironic, but the existence of multiple objectives may enable large political bodies to come to decisions more easily than small ones do because of widespread ignorance of decisions and acceptance of majority rule. Further, agreement can often be achieved on concrete proposals whereas it will not be achieved on ends or objectives. A particular group may see victory in a concrete proposal while the entire assembly could not find a consensus on the point that the group sees achieved in the concrete proposal.[12] An example of this may be seen in

[9]See Kenneth J. Arrow, *Social Choice and Individual Values* (New York: Wiley, 1951).

[10]43 *U.S. Code* 431. A farm owned by a man and his wife can be up to 320 acres. Paul S. Taylor, "Excess Land Law: Execution of a Public Policy," *Yale Law Journal* 64 (February 1955): 477–514.

[11]"The benefits to whomsoever they may accrue must exceed the costs." Flood Control Act of 1936, *U.S. Statutes-at-Large* 1510 (1936).

[12]Julius Margolis, "Metropolitan Finance Problems: Territories, Functions and Growth," in National Bureau of Economic Research, *Public Finances: Needs, Sources and Utilization* (Princeton, N.J.: Princeton University Press, 1961), pp. 242ff.

## TABLE 9.1. ALTERNATIVE VIEWS OF THE MULTIPLE OBJECTIVES PROBLEM

|  | NEW WELFARE ECONOMICS | MUSGRAVE | MAASS |
|---|---|---|---|
| Objectives recognized | *Single* Economic Efficiency | *Multiple* 1. Efficiency 2. Equity 3. Stability 4. Merit wants | *Multiple* 1. Efficiency 2. Equity 3. Stability 4. Merit wants 5. Others |
| Legitimate instruments | *Multiple* Expenditures Taxes  Transfer payments | *Multiple* Expenditures Taxes  Transfer payments (Identified with particular objectives) | *Single* Expenditures (Others to a limited extent)  (Not identified with particular objectives) |

the Elementary and Secondary Education Act of 1965, which skirted the issue of aid to parochial schools by aiding all schools. Partisans of parochial schools saw something in it for them and the general population did not have its sensibilities on church and state matters aroused. A consensus on the philosophical question of whether parochial schools should be aided at all by the federal government might have been considerably more difficult to attain.

The debate over objectives is summarized in Table 9.1, which gives a synopsis of the views of the New Welfare Economics, Musgrave, and Maass. Maass' school may be viewed as a multiple-objective, single-instrument school. It holds that the use of transfers is ruled out by political constraints such as the Protestant ethic and that the taxation instrument is effectively tied to the stabilization objective.[13] In the Maass view expenditures are the instrument of government that must serve at least allocational and distributional objectives and perhaps others. Maass' formulation is a complete reversal of that of the New Welfare Economics, which was concerned almost exclusively with a single objective, efficiency, but considered several instruments legitimate.

[13] Perhaps we have overstated the Maass case. He is not so disenchanted with taxes and transfers but feels that we cannot rely on them exclusively to achieve objectives other than efficiency, so that these other objectives, like efficiency, should be sought through public expenditures.

## THE EQUITY OBJECTIVE

In the past, the efficiency objective has been considered the most important one. The statutory directive, "benefits *to whomsoever they may accrue* must exceed costs," was indifferent to incidence. Analysts have concentrated on efficiency because in many cases it is tractable. Nevertheless, attention should be paid to difficult problems as well as tractable ones. Distribution of income is a very important problem. In this section we shall explore what has been done and what can be done to discern the impact of public spending and taxation on income distribution.

Equity is, in a sense, a subset of economics but in another sense it competes with economics. Law has a similarly ambiguous relationship to equity. Someone may not have a right to something at law but may at equity. Principles of justice developed in England to make up for inadequacies of the common law had their root in the concept of equity. Eventually the two were amalgamated, but a connotational difference remains between what is legal and what is just, although not legal. Similarly, in economics there is a distinction between what is economical (efficient) and what is just, although efficiency and equity are both included in economics.

Income can be redistributed over many domains. It can be redistributed geographically—from one region to another, or socially—from one economic, sociological, or ethnic group to another. It may go to the young or to the old.

Most federal programs are originally authorized to serve either efficiency or merit wants or both, but details of actual appropriations are rarely given in the enabling legislation. For example, Article I, Section 8, Clause 7 of the Constitution gives Congress the power to establish post offices. Where and in what order they will be built is always at issue, because if a congressman can bring a new post office to his district, he will win the gratitude (and votes) of contractors, postal employees, and patrons. Procurement contracts are another, particularly desirable, prize. Senator Proxmire (D., Wisconsin) has commented that there are only two persuasive arguments for the SST: the senior senator from Washington and the junior senator from Washington.[14] Proxmire is not insensitive to the geographical distribution of spending; his foreword to a book on water resources was very critical of such spending.[15] Is it a

---

[14]The Boeing Company, a prime contender for the SST contract, has its headquarters and principal production facilities in Washington. Senate debate 17 December 1969 as quoted in *National Journal* 2, no. 18 (2 May 1970): 935.

[15]Robert H. Haveman, *Water Resource Investment and the Public Interest* (Nashville, Tenn.: Vanderbilt University Press, 1965).

TABLE 9.2. CONTRIBUTIONS OF DEFENSE INCOME
TO REGIONAL GROWTH, 1952–62
(Percentage of growth during period)

| Region | 1952–56 | 1956–62 | 1952–62 |
|---|---|---|---|
| New England | −15 | 24 | 13 |
| Middle Atlantic | −39 | 13 | − 3 |
| East north central | −73 | 10 | −21 |
| West north central | −17 | 10 | 8 |
| South Atlantic | − 7 | 19 | 13 |
| East south central | −21 | 15 | 9 |
| West south central | 1 | 13 | 11 |
| Mountain | 31 | 28 | 27 |
| Pacific | 2 | 28 | 21 |

Source: Roger E. Bolton, *Defense Purchases and Regional Growth* (Washington, D.C.: Brookings, 1966), p. 12.

coincidence that Wisconsin was lowest of all fifty states in per capita appropriation for water resource investment?[16] The situation is the same with regard to state expenditures. One of the success indicators of a legislator is the amount of economic activity he can bring into his district.

Some federal spending is done with the express intention of helping a lagging region. This was the purpose of the Appalachia program in the mid-1960s.[17]

In 1951 procurement officers were encouraged to increase routine procurement in regions where the unemployment rate was high. An earlier armed services policy of allowing contractors in labor surplus areas to meet low bids of others led to charges of unfair competition. Beginning in 1953 some defense procurement was set aside for contractors in labor surplus areas.[18] Thus intentional, articulated policy recognized income distribution as paramount.

Roger Bolton has attempted to discern the impact of defense spending on regional growth. He measures a state's dependence on defense spending as the ratio of defense spending to all exogenous income. In the period 1952 to 1962 defense spending contributed substantially to the growth of Kansas, Colorado, Utah, Arizona, New Mexico, and California. When state results are aggregated by region as shown in Table 9.2, a shift from east to west is discernible over the decade. Defense made a considerable contribution to growth in the mountain and Pacific

---

[16]Haveman, *Water Resource Investment*, pp. 53ff., Table 5. Wisconsin had a per capita appropriation of $1 in the 1946–62 period while North Dakota had $693.

[17]"Kennedy Plan for Aid to Depressed Areas," *Congressional Digest* (April 1961).

[18]Roger Bolton, *Defense Purchases and Regional Growth* (Washington, D.C.: The Brookings Institution, 1966), p. 143.

states while it made a negative contribution in the east north central region. Between 1952 and 1956 cutbacks after the Korean War were prevalent. Most regions grew despite declining defense spending. In the later period defense expenditures were increasing and contributed to growth in all regions of the country.

Geographical areas have endeavored to justify expenditures in their regions on the basis of "multiplier effects," which are demonstrable from a local point of view but may add up to zero over the nation. Multiplier effects in one region may mean equal effects lost in other regions. Because these effects do not involve the primary purpose for which the investment is undertaken they have been called secondary benefits.

### Secondary Benefits

The term "secondary benefits" has acquired a pejorative connotation because it was used especially by the Bureau of Reclamation to justify projects of dubious efficiency value.[19] Secondary benefits include those "induced by" or "stemming from" the original project. Stemming benefits include the profit of industries using the output of the project; for example, sugar beet processors who process beets grown with water made available by a reclamation project. Induced benefits, Keynesian multiplier effects, come from money spent on a project that is respent in the region. The effect is a total increase in income that is some multiple of the money spent on the project.

Secondary benefits have been discussed and criticized especially with regard to valuing irrigation water of reclamation projects. According to the Department of the Interior, the water benefited not only the farmer but the processor of his product, the wholesaler of the processed product, and the businesses that sold the farmer supplies and services.

From an economist's viewpoint, when federal money is being spent only the net national gains ought to be counted. If the region of a project benefits at the expense of other regions, these benefits are diversions and not net increases to national welfare.

Secondary benefits can be legitimately accountable as efficiency benefits only if some special conditions prevail: persistent unemployment, underutilized capital, or increasing returns to scale. If unemployment has existed for an extended period in region A but people are reluctant to move out, then a proposed project that employs people in A will add to national income. If A has lost population but still has "social

---

[19]U.S. Department of the Interior, Bureau of Reclamation, "Benefits and Costs," *Reclamation Manual,* vol. 13 (March 1952).

overhead capital"—roads, sewers, and schools—benefits will be account-able if this capital is more fully utilized when a project draws people back into A. Finally, if increasing returns to scale obtain in an industry in A, additional output can be produced in region A at lower average cost than in region B. In all these cases market prices differ from mar-ginal social benefits and costs.

Maass claims that no benefit is secondary; that is, such benefits are perfectly legitimate even though they are not efficiency benefits. Income redistribution, for example, is a primary, not a secondary benefit. Re-cently, secondary benefits have been renamed "regional development benefits."[20] How they should be weighted vis-a-vis national income or efficiency benefits is to be inferred from the legislative history of the particular program.[21]

### Income Distribution Effects

Burton Weisbrod has made Maass' suggestion somewhat opera-tional.[22] His method of inferring the rate of exchange between efficiency and income redistribution is highly imperfect, but perhaps it suggests some of the issues involved.

Suppose a legislature chooses a project with a much lower benefit-cost ratio than some others available. The benefit-cost ratio pertains only to efficiency. Weisbrod assumes the legislature had a reason for their choice, and offers the chosen project's desirable income distribu-tion properties to explain the legislature's choice.

Weisbrod assumes decision-makers endeavor to maximize "grand efficiency." Grand efficiency includes (narrow) efficiency and income distribution. He further assumes that no factors other than these two influence Congressional decisions. Dividing the population into four groups—white, nonwhite, under \$3,000 income, and over \$3,000 in-come—he implements his model for four projects, each in a different state, proposed to Congress about 1950. The model looks like this:

$$aB_{11} + bB_{12} + cB_{13} + dB_{14} = B_1$$
$$aB_{21} + bB_{22} + cB_{23} + dB_{24} = B_2 < B_1$$
$$aB_{31} + bB_{32} + cB_{33} + dB_{34} = B_3 < B_1$$
$$aB_{41} + bB_{42} + cB_{43} + dB_{44} = B_4 < B_1$$

[20] See Walter J. Hickel, et al., *Procedures for Evaluation.*

[21] See Maass, "Benefit-Cost Analysis."

[22] "Income-Redistribution Effects and Benefit-Cost Analysis of Government Ex-penditure Programs" in Samuel B. Chase, ed., *Problems in Public Expenditure Analysis* (Washington, D.C.: The Brookings Institution, 1968), pp. 177–208.

$B_1$ represents the benefits of project 1, $B_2$ of project 2, and so on. For simplicity, assume all projects have equal costs. (This assumption can be relaxed easily.) Let $B_{11}$ be the benefits of project 1 accruing to group 1, whites with income under \$3,000 per year; $B_{43}$ be the benefits of project 4 accruing to group 3.

We will see how Weisbrod measures the incidence of benefits, the $B_{ij}$. He makes the very simple-minded, probably contrafactual, but objective, assumption that benefits accrue to each group in proportion to the group's representation in the state population according to the 1960 census. The purpose of the model is to estimate $a$, $b$, $c$, and $d$, the implicit weights the legislature attaches to benefits or income accruing to each group.

Projects 2, 3, and 4 had less efficiency benefits than 1, yet were chosen first. Therefore, they must have had at least as much grand efficiency. Weisbrod sets the three last equations equal to $B_1$. With four projects and four groups, the equations can be solved for $a$, $b$, $c$, and $d$. If there are more than four projects, $a$, $b$, $c$, and $d$ could be estimated by least-squares with an error term posited in each equation.

Weisbrod inferred some interesting weights from actual Congressional behavior on four projects. In order to rationalize the choices made, weights on income distribution must have been 9.3 for nonwhites with income less than \$3,000; 2.2 for whites with income more than \$3,000; −1.3 for low-income whites; and −2.0 for high-income nonwhites. These results are reasonable: sacrifices in efficiency were made to help low-income nonwhites but not to help high-income nonwhites. Whites with income over \$3,000 were favored over those with low incomes.

Weisbrod's effort is positive, not normative. He does not tell us how to measure income redistribution benefits, but instead offers a concise way of recording history. It infers from Congressional behavior the implicit value accorded several groups' income if Congress' actions are consistent and if they maximize grand efficiency.

Unfortunately, a careful study of some actual Congressional behavior does not lend support to Weisbrod's assumptions. A. Myrick Freeman III looked retrospectively at six recent Bureau of Reclamation irrigation projects. He recalculated their efficiency benefits using proper procedures: charging projects the opportunity costs of water diverted to irrigation and of farm labor required to complement the irrigation water provided; eliminating secondary benefits; changing unrealistically low discount rates to 5 percent; and eliminating the effects of farm price supports. He emerges with a more believable measure of efficiency benefits. Income redistribution has generally been from higher incomes to lower incomes, but the average increase in farmers' incomes was only \$150 per year. The total number of farmers affected by these six projects was only 843. Given plausible social welfare criteria with which to weight increments to the incomes of particular farmers, none of the reclamation projects could be justified on redistribution grounds. Only one of the six projects examined had a welfare weighted benefit-cost ratio greater than one. Freeman finds, finally, that what does seem to influence decisions is a desire to be re-elected. "It is suggestive," he states, "that since 1950 Congressional authorizations in election years have exceeded those in odd-numbered years by a ratio of 7 to 1." [23]

Of course, many other factors beyond the two included in grand efficiency enter Congressional decisions. These might include favors to particular patrons, engineering considerations and ecological consequences. Because other factors enter, the stochastic model is probably slightly more credible than the simultaneous-equations model.

A consensus on how different groups' welfare should be valued has not been achieved. There are extreme solutions: complete leveling of income, "fix Whitey," "let them eat cake." Any particular numerical set of weights would be very controversial. It is unlikely that a government agency would survive the announcement of any specific weights. [24]

The desire and claimed ability to make equity benefits commensurable with efficiency benefits in an objective fashion may be frustrated. Surely, agreement on weights would be a heroic task in itself. Nevertheless, the counsel that we should display equity results of public spending programs is well taken. How different spending programs affect specific classes of people can be studied. Geographical studies are easy to make. Weisbrod's technique of assuming that benefits accrue in proportion to population in the absence of more information is defensible. Indeed, it was used in a recent study by the Department of Health, Education and Welfare. Ethnic studies of incidence can be made if we know whether benefits accrue in rural, urban, or suburban areas and if we know the preferences of different ethnic groups. For example, a mountain lake affects different people than an urban fishing pier does. Table 9.3 attempts an apportionment of benefits of expenditures for disease prevention and control to age, ethnic, income, and rural-urban groups. Particular programs affect the old more than the young. For example, the construction of 300 nursing homes yields benefits largely to citizens over fifty-five, only 7 percent of its benefits to those twenty-one to fifty-five, and no benefits to citizens under twenty-one.

Certainly it is candid and behaviorally accurate to observe that many

[23] A. Myrick Freeman III, "Six Federal Reclamation Projects and the Distribution of Income," *Water Resources Research* III (Second Quarter, 1967), p. 331.

[24] Note in Table 9.3 that HEW disclaims official responsibility for even calculating the distribution of benefits, not even weighting those benefits by some social-welfare-function type weights.

# TABLE 9.3. PRELIMINARY HEALTH OVERVIEW—DISEASE PREVENTION AND CONTROL

| Agency and expenditure purpose | Estimated expenses 1970 (millions) | Number of units fiscal year 1970 | Age -21 | Age 21 to 55 | Age 55+ | Race Negro | Race White | Race Other | Income -$4,000 | Income $4,000 to $9,999 | Income $10,000+ | Location cc≥250,000 | Location cc≤250,000 | Location Other urban | Location Rural | Benefits Subsidy value | Benefits B/C$_g$ |
|---|---|---|---|---|---|---|---|---|---|---|---|---|---|---|---|---|---|
| BIOMEDICAL RESEARCH | | | | | | | | | | | | | | | | | |
| HEW: | | | | | | | | | | | | | | | | | |
| Basic | $479.6 | (²) | 41 | 41 | 18 | 11 | 88 | 1 | 21 | 49 | 30 | 22 | 21 | 27 | 30 | 0 | |
| Targeted | 629.2 | (²) | 14 | 25 | 61 | 14 | 85 | 1 | 27 | 44 | 29 | 19 | 21 | 26 | 33 | 0 | |
| AEC: | | | | | | | | | | | | | | | | | |
| Basic | 83.9 | (²) | 41 | 41 | 18 | 11 | 88 | 1 | 21 | 49 | 30 | 22 | 21 | 27 | 30 | 0 | |
| Targeted | 16.4 | (²) | 6 | 17 | 78 | 11 | 88 | 1 | 39 | 43 | 17 | 18 | 0 | 0 | 0 | 0 | |
| NASA: | | | | | | | | | | | | | | | | | |
| Basic | 45.6 | (²) | 0 | 0 | 0 | 0 | 0 | 0 | 0 | 0 | 0 | 0 | 0 | 0 | 0 | 0 | |
| Targeted | 65.0 | (²) | 0 | 0 | 0 | 0 | 0 | 0 | 0 | 0 | 0 | 0 | 0 | 0 | 0 | 0 | |
| VA: | | | | | | | | | | | | | | | | | |
| Basic | 4.9 | (²) | 41 | 41 | 18 | 11 | 88 | 1 | 21 | 49 | 30 | 22 | 21 | 27 | 30 | 0 | |
| Targeted | 54.8 | (²) | 0 | 0 | 100 | 15 | 83 | 2 | 43 | 39 | 18 | 15 | 21 | 27 | 37 | 0 | |
| DOD: | | | | | | | | | | | | | | | | | |
| Basic | 48.9 | (²) | 41 | 41 | 18 | 11 | 88 | 1 | 21 | 49 | 30 | 22 | 21 | 27 | 30 | 0 | |
| Targeted | 55.4 | (²) | 18 | 34 | 48 | 15 | 83 | 2 | 25 | 46 | 29 | 21 | 21 | 26 | 32 | 0 | |
| Agriculture: | | | | | | | | | | | | | | | | | |
| Basic | 24.2 | (²) | 41 | 41 | 18 | 11 | 88 | 1 | 21 | 58 | 18 | 22 | 21 | 27 | 30 | 0 | |
| Targeted | 14.6 | (²) | 38 | 43 | 19 | 11 | 88 | 1 | 30 | 42 | 28 | 17 | 21 | 26 | 35 | 0 | |
| NSF: Basic | 24.4 | (²) | 41 | 41 | 18 | 11 | 88 | 1 | 21 | 58 | 18 | 22 | 21 | 27 | 30 | 0 | |
| BIOMEDICAL RESEARCH FACILITIES | | | | | | | | | | | | | | | | | |
| HEW: | | | | | | | | | | | | | | | | | |
| Direct | 15.1 | (²) | 41 | 41 | 18 | 11 | 88 | 1 | 21 | 49 | 30 | 22 | 21 | 27 | 30 | 0 | |
| Federal share | 96.3 | (²) | 41 | 41 | 18 | 11 | 88 | 1 | 21 | 49 | 30 | 22 | 21 | 27 | 30 | 0 | |
| Agriculture: Direct | 4.0 | (²) | 38 | 43 | 19 | 11 | 88 | 2 | 30 | 42 | 28 | 17 | 21 | 26 | 35 | 0 | |
| VA: Direct | 5.8 | (²) | 0 | 0 | 100 | 15 | 83 | 1 | 43 | 39 | 18 | 15 | 21 | 27 | 37 | 0 | |
| AEC: Direct | 3.6 | (²) | 41 | 41 | 18 | 11 | 88 | 1 | 21 | 49 | 30 | 22 | 21 | 27 | 30 | 0 | |
| BIOMEDICAL MANPOWER | | | | | | | | | | | | | | | | | |
| HEW: | | | | | | | | | | | | | | | | | |
| Student support | 118.4 | 15,000 studs | 11 | 25 | 64 | 16 | 83 | 1 | 28 | 44 | 29 | 19 | 21 | 26 | 34 | $4,813 | 1.00 |
| Institutional support | | 422 ed. inst. | | | | | | | | | | | | | | | |
| National distribution | | | 41 | 41 | 18 | 11 | 88 | 1 | 21 | 49 | 30 | 22 | 21 | 27 | ³0 | | |

| | | BEDS ADDED OR MODERNIZED: | | | | | | | | | | | | | | | |
|---|---|---|---|---|---|---|---|---|---|---|---|---|---|---|---|---|---|
| **HOSPITAL CONSTRUCTION** | | | | | | | | | | | | | | | | | |
| HEW: Direct | 5.2 | 0 | 39 | 44 | 17 | 6 | 34 | 57 | 48 | 43 | 9 | 40 | 0 | 9 | 51 | $14.50/pd | .50 |
| Federal share | 145.3 | 16,413 | 20 | 46 | 34 | 12 | 87 | 1 | 38 | 48 | 14 | 19 | 7 | 68 | 6 | $5.75/pd | .50 |
| VA: Direct | 77.7 | 476 | 0 | 29 | 71 | 14 | 84 | 2 | 35 | 60 | 5 | 15 | 17 | 22 | 46 | $14.50/pd | .50 |
| DOD: Direct | 58.1 | 600 | 38 | 47 | 15 | 17 | 82 | 1 | 37 | 44 | 19 | (*) | (*) | (*) | (*) | | |
| **NURSING HOMES CONSTRUCTION** | | | | | | | | | | | | | | | | | |
| HEW: Federal share | | 300 | 0 | 7 | 93 | 4 | 96 | 0 | 60 | 35 | 5 | 15 | 4 | 64 | 17 | $ 3.00/pd | 1.00 |
| VA: Direct | .9 | 0 | 0 | 7 | 93 | 4 | 94 | 2 | 60 | 35 | 5 | 15 | 17 | 22 | 46 | $ 7.00/pd | 1.00 |
| Federal share | 3.2 | 795 | 0 | 7 | 93 | 4 | 94 | 2 | 60 | 35 | 5 | 15 | 17 | 22 | 46 | $ 3.00/pd | 1.00 |
| **CLINICS** | | Fac. added: | | | | | | | | | | | | | | | |
| HEW: Direct | 2.7 | | 39 | 44 | 17 | 6 | 37 | 57 | 48 | 43 | 9 | 40 | 0 | 9 | 51 | $ 3.75/visit | 1.00 |
| Federal share | | 9,390 | 41 | 41 | 18 | 12 | 87 | 1 | 34 | 49 | 17 | 22 | 5 | 57 | 16 | $ 1.25/visit | 1.00 |
| DOD: Direct | .1 | | 38 | 47 | 15 | 17 | 82 | 1 | 37 | 44 | 19 | (*) | (*) | (*) | (*) | $ 3.75/visit | 1.00 |
| **PHYSICIAN MANPOWER** | | | | | | | | | | | | | | | | | |
| HEW: Student support | 116.9 | 1,586 grad | 35 | 42 | 23 | 8 | 91 | 1 | 23 | 50 | 27 | 24 | 23 | 27 | 26 | $265/stud | 1.9 |
| Construction | 80.7 | 439 spaces | 35 | 42 | 23 | 8 | 91 | 1 | 23 | 50 | 27 | 24 | 23 | 27 | 26 | $ 82/stud | 1.9 |
| DOD: Student support | 14.6 | 1,590 grad | 35 | 42 | 23 | 8 | 91 | 1 | 23 | 50 | 27 | 24 | 23 | 27 | 26 | $8,000 | 1.9 |
| **DENTAL MANPOWER** | | | | | | | | | | | | | | | | | |
| HEW: Student support | 30.8 | 1,743 grad | 37 | 48 | 15 | 6 | 93 | 1 | 15 | 56 | 29 | 25 | 24 | 29 | 22 | $265/stud | 1.1 |
| Construction | 18.6 | 180 spaces | 37 | 48 | 15 | 6 | 93 | 1 | 15 | 56 | 29 | 25 | 24 | 29 | 22 | $ 60/stud | |
| **NURSE MANPOWER** | | | | | | | | | | | | | | | | | |
| HEW: Student support | 52.6 | 14,369 grad | 40 | 42 | 18 | 11 | 88 | 1 | 21 | 49 | 30 | 26 | 26 | 26 | 22 | $100/stud | 1.6 |
| Construction | 16.8 | 570 spaces | 42 | 42 | 18 | 11 | 88 | 1 | 21 | 49 | 30 | 26 | 26 | 26 | 22 | 00/stud | 00 |
| DOD: Student support | 2.4 | 1,505 grad | 38 | 47 | 15 | 17 | 82 | 1 | 37 | 44 | 19 | (*) | (*) | (*) | (*) | $3,000/stud | 1.6 |
| **OTHER HEALTH PROF.** | | | | | | | | | | | | | | | | | |
| HEW: Student support | 74.3 | 5,862 grad | 41 | 41 | 18 | 11 | 88 | 1 | 21 | 49 | 30 | 22 | 21 | 27 | 30 | | |
| Construction | 3.7 | 149 spaces | | | | | | | | | | | | | | | |
| DOD: Student support | 3.6 | 993 grad | | | | | | | | | | | | | | | |
| AEC: Student support | .6 | 28 grad | | | | | | | | | | | | | | | |

## TABLE 9.3. (Continued)

| Agency and Expenditure Purpose | Estimated Expenses 1970 (Millions) | Number of Units Fiscal Year 1970 | Age | | | Race | | | Income | | | Location Outside | | | | Benefits | |
|---|---|---|---|---|---|---|---|---|---|---|---|---|---|---|---|---|---|
| | | | -21 | 21 to 55 | 55+ | Negro | White | Other | -$4,000 | $4,000 to $9,999 | $10,000+ | CC≥250,000 | CC<250,000 | Other Urban | Rural | Subsidy Value | $B/C_e$ |
| **OTHER HEALTH TRAINING** | | | | | | | | | | | | | | | | | |
| HEW: Student support | 130.8 | 31,020 train | | | | | | | | | | | | | | | |
| DOD: Student support | 103.4 | 2,444 train | | | | | | | | | | | | | | | |
| VA: Student support | 95.4 | ——— train | | | | | | | | | | | | | | | |
| Labor: Student support | 35.4 | 19,730 train | | | | | | | | | | | | | | | |
| **PROVISION OF HOSPITAL SERVICES** | | | | | | | | | | | | | | | | | |
| HEW: | | Patients: | | | | | | | | | | | | | | | |
| Direct | 93.4 | 130,604 | 39 | 44 | 17 | 6 | 37 | 57 | 48 | 43 | 9 | 40 | 0 | 9 | 51 | $335/pat. | 1.80 |
| Finance | 6,352.6 | 6,593,840 | 10 | 7 | 83 | 11 | 88 | 1 | 60 | 29 | 11 | 16 | 21 | 27 | 36 | $181/pat. | .66 |
| DOD: | | | | | | | | | | | | | | | | | |
| Direct | 791.9 | 1,354,105 | 31 | 69 | .4 | 17 | 82 | 1 | 74 | 22 | 4 | (²) | (²) | (²) | (²) | $442/pat | 2.60 |
| Finance | 183.4 | 270,829 | 38 | 47 | 15 | 17 | 82 | 1 | 74 | 22 | 4 | (²) | (²) | (²) | (²) | $348/pat | 1.90 |
| VA: | | | | | | | | | | | | | | | | | |
| Direct | 1,100.9 | 775,000 | 0 | 29 | 71 | 14 | 84 | 2 | 35 | 60 | 5 | 10 | 10 | 34 | 46 | $313/pat | .93 |
| Finance | 15.7 | 24,916 | 0 | 57 | 43 | 14 | 84 | 2 | 37 | 44 | 19 | 10 | 10 | 35 | 45 | $423/pat | 1.50 |
| **OTHER INPATIENT SERVICES** | | | | | | | | | | | | | | | | | |
| HEW: Finance | 936.4 | 20,107,584 | 10 | 7 | 83 | 11 | 88 | 1 | 60 | 29 | 11 | 16 | 21 | 27 | 36 | $181/pat. | .66 |
| DOD: Finance | .02 | 806,429 | 38 | 47 | 15 | 17 | 82 | 1 | 74 | 22 | 4 | (²) | (²) | (²) | (²) | $348/pat. | 1.90 |
| VA: | | | | | | | | | | | | | | | | | |
| Direct | 62.3 | 1,382,518 | 0 | 29 | 71 | 14 | 84 | 2 | 35 | 60 | 5 | 10 | 10 | 34 | 46 | $313/pat | .98 |
| Finance | 33.1 | | 0 | 57 | 43 | 14 | 84 | 2 | 37 | 44 | 19 | 10 | 10 | 35 | 45 | $423/pat | 1.50 |
| **OUTPATIENT SERVICES** | | | | | | | | | | | | | | | | | |
| HEW: | | Visits: | | | | | | | | | | | | | | | |
| Direct | 38.2 | 1,919,091 | 39 | 44 | 17 | 6 | 37 | 57 | 48 | 43 | 9 | 40 | 0 | 9 | 51 | $ 20/visit | 1.80 |
| Finance | 2,936.8 | 1,415,920 | 10 | 7 | 83 | 11 | 88 | 1 | 46 | 41 | 13 | 17 | 23 | 27 | 33 | do | .66 |
| DOD: | | | | | | | | | | | | | | | | | |
| Direct | 670.6 | 49,382,747 | 31 | 69 | .4 | 17 | 82 | 1 | 74 | 22 | 4 | (²) | (²) | (²) | (²) | do | 2.60 |
| Finance | 26.3 | 67,634 | 38 | 47 | 15 | 17 | 82 | 1 | 74 | 22 | 4 | (²) | (²) | (²) | (²) | do | 1.90 |
| VA: Direct | 177.4 | 6,277,328 | 2 | 70 | 28 | 14 | 84 | 2 | 24 | 58 | 18 | 10 | 10 | 35 | 45 | $ 25/visit | 1.90 |
| OEO: Direct | | | 60 | 23 | 17 | 65 | 20 | 15 | 95 | 5 | 0 | 45 | 15 | 20 | 20 | $ 20/visit | 1.43 |
| National distribution | | | 41 | 41 | 18 | 11 | 88 | 1 | 21 | 49 | 30 | 22 | 21 | 27 | 30 | | |

¹Percent distributions are approximate, not official agency estimates.  ²Not applicable.  ³Based on 1960 census data.

Source: U.S. Congress, Joint Economic Committee, *Economic Analysis and the Efficiency of Government*, Part 3, pp. 736–38, Hearings 25 (30 September, 6 October 1969), testimony of Jack W. Carlson.

spending projects are introduced primarily to effect goals of geographical income distribution or equity. Some projects are introduced in order to achieve income redistribution, but unfortunately they are not of the type that a majority of the nation would condone. For example, sometimes income is redistributed to the very wealthy. Under the title of "land enhancement benefits" many projects are justified because benefits greater than costs will accrue to someone—the beneficiaries are rarely identified. An elaboration entered the public record in 1950, but statements of this kind are not seen frequently.

> There are some 400 large landholders in the project area would would be likely to receive individual benefits averaging more than $500,000 apiece. . . . About 30,000 men, women, and children in the project area would stand to receive benefits of $50,000 each, all as a gift from the people of the other States. . . . If the . . . project is authorized . . . the idle land will immediately increase in value 6 to 10 times.[25]

This phenomenon argues against sole attention to efficiency benefits and argues for attention to the question of incidence of the benefits—who will receive them.

A study of California public higher education[26] by Hansen and Weisbrod found that university students were subsidized more than state college students who, in turn, were subsidized more than junior college students. Students who attend university tend to come from higher income families than those attending state colleges or junior colleges. The subsidy to a student who completed four years at the University of California was $7,140.[27] The average subsidy for those attending the university was $5,000; for state colleges, $3,000; and for junior colleges, $1,000. University of California students came from families with $12,000 average income. State college students' families had an average income of $10,000, and junior college families averaged $8,800.[28]

Therefore, "a small proportion—9 percent—receive rather large subsidies exceeding $5,000, more than half of California's young people receive under $750 [while] a substantial portion—41 percent—receive no subsidy at all."[29] Because the tax system does not alter the distribution of net benefits after taxes the authors concluded that public higher education in California heightened rather than narrowed inequalities in

---

[25] 95 *Congressional Record,* 10126ff.

[26] W. Lee Hansen and Burton A. Weisbrod, *Benefits, Costs and Finance of Public Higher Education* (Chicago: Markham, 1969).

[27] Hansen and Weisbrod, *Public Higher Education,* p. 63, Table IV-3.

[28] Hansen and Weisbrod, *Public Higher Education,* p. 69, Table IV-7.

[29] Hansen and Weisbrod, *Public Higher Education,* p. 68.

economic opportunities. The remedy, as they see it, is a more equitable pricing system or a broader offering of public subsidies to those who would opt for other ways of increasing their lifetime incomes, such as apprenticeship, on-the-job training, attending vocational school, or acquiring capital.

Much of the income redistribution impact of government spending programs has been regressive. James Bonnen has shown that cotton price support programs that are supposed to supplement low farm incomes actually result in proportionately larger benefits accruing to larger farms.[30] Subsidies of air transport are regressive because a majority of Americans have never flown, and those who do fly are in the higher income groups.[31] Because of this kind of incidence, some have observed that the purpose of the federal government is to take money from poor people and use it to benefit the rich, but authoritative knowledge of the subject presupposes awareness of the incidence of taxation, as well as the incidence of benefits.

Robert Haveman's studies of water resources are a bit more reassuring to those who believe in redistribution to ameliorate market-generated income distribution results. In his study of geographical distribution of Corps of Engineers appropriations for water resources projects, Haveman found that the South had experienced a net benefit of $1.3 billion between 1946 and 1962. The efficiency objective did not appear paramount. High benefit-cost ratios were frequently passed over, low-income areas were favored, and a strong tendency to equalize state per capita incomes through water-resource investment was found.[32] The coefficient of rank correlation between per capita water-resources appropriation and per capita income was $-.426$ indicating a significant negative association between the two.[33]

Certain states have done relatively well. Examples are Arkansas, presumably because of strong senators and congressmen; and West Virginia, presumably because of the decline of the soft coal mining industry. Table 9.4 shows how each state fared.

The net impact of federal taxation and spending has been discussed in several studies. Gillespie[34] has studied the subject both in Canada and

---

[30]James T. Bonnen, "The Distribution of Benefits from Cotton Price Supports," in Chase, *Problems in Public Expenditure Analysis,* pp. 223–44.

[31]Gary Fromm, "Civil Aviation Expenditures," in Robert Dorfman, ed., *Measuring Benefits of Government Investments* (Washington, D.C.: The Brookings Institution, 1965).

[32]Haveman, *Water Resource Investment,* p. 67.

[33]Haveman, *Water Resource Investment,* p. 57.

[34]W. Irwin Gillespie, "The Incidence of Taxes and Public Expenditures in the Canadian Economy" (Report No. 6.1, study prepared for the Royal Commission on Taxation, Ottawa: Queens Printer, 1965), pp. 1–25. "Effects of Public Expenditures on the Distribution of Income," in Musgrave (ed.), *Essays in Fiscal Federalism* (Washington, D.C.: The Brookings Institution, 1965), pp. 122–86.

TABLE 9.4. CORPS OF ENGINEERS—RIVERS AND HARBORS
*Total Appropriations, Per Capita Appropriations,*
*Per Capita Income, Rank in Per Capita Appropriations,*
*and Rank in Per Capita Income, by State, 1946 to 1962*

| STATE | TOTAL CONSTRUC-TION APPROPRIA-TION,[a] THOUSANDS OF DOLLARS | PER CAPITA APPROPRIA-TION,[b] DOLLARS | ANNUAL PER CAPITA INCOME,[c] DOLLARS | RANK IN PER CAPITA APPROPRIA-TION[d] | RANK IN PER CAPITA INCOME |
|---|---|---|---|---|---|
| North Dakota | 433,719 | 693 | 1496 | 1 | 35 |
| South Dakota | 427,033 | 640 | 1431 | 2 | 38.5 |
| Oregon | 603,971 | 367 | 1810 | 3 | 18 |
| Washington | 615,073 | 235 | 1922 | 4 | 12 |
| Arkansas | 404,232 | 219 | 1003 | 5 | 49 |
| Oklahoma | 326,471 | 143 | 1431 | 6 | 38.5 |
| Louisiana | 398,829 | 134 | 1313 | 7 | 42 |
| Kentucky | 372,802 | 125 | 1207 | 8 | 46 |
| Kansas | 251,562 | 123 | 1679 | 9 | 26 |
| Vermont | 40,744 | 106 | 1428 | 10 | 40 |
| Alaska | 17,693 | 99 | 2366 | 11 | 2 |
| Nebraska | 122,143 | 89 | 1724 | 12 | 23 |
| Idaho | 49,974 | 80 | 1501 | 13 | 33 |
| Tennessee | 271,363 | 79 | 1218 | 14 | 44 |
| West Virginia | 150,380 | 78 | 1336 | 15 | 41 |
| Mississippi | 161,065 | 74 | 900 | 16 | 50 |
| Montana | 36,373 | 57 | 1815 | 17 | 17 |
| Missouri | 229,214 | 55 | 1732 | 18 | 21 |
| New Mexico | 42,482 | 52 | 1456 | 19 | 36 |
| New Hampshire | 28,855 | 51 | 1600 | 20 | 28 |
| Florida | 187,141 | 49 | 1585 | 21 | 31 |
| Georgia | 178,380 | 48 | 1244 | 22 | 43 |
| Iowa | 128,896 | 48 | 1683 | 23 | 25 |
| California | 604,035 | 46 | 2171 | 24 | 7 |
| Texas | 395,360 | 46 | 1594 | 25 | 30 |
| South Carolina | 87,011 | 39 | 1064 | 26 | 48 |
| Alabama | 113,787 | 36 | 1111 | 27 | 47 |
| Virginia | 90,571 | 25 | 1485 | 28 | 34 |
| Ohio | 213,502 | 24 | 1910 | 29 | 13 |
| Michigan | 171,577 | 24 | 1925 | 30 | 11 |
| Hawaii | 12,863 | 23 | 1691 | 31 | 24 |
| Arizona | 22,759 | 22 | 1595 | 32 | 29 |
| Illinois | 198,027 | 21 | 2164 | 33 | 8 |
| Pennsylvania | 229,335 | 21 | 1854 | 34 | 15 |
| Delaware | 7,457 | 20 | 2505 | 35 | 1 |
| Indiana | 78,632 | 18 | 1764 | 36 | 19 |
| Connecticut | 40,380 | 17 | 2312 | 37 | 3 |
| Massachusetts | 79,798 | 16 | 1999 | 38 | 10 |
| Minnesota | 45,152 | 14 | 1670 | 39 | 27 |
| North Carolina | 58,465 | 14 | 1208 | 40 | 45 |
| Rhode Island | 10,313 | 12 | 1845 | 41 | 16 |
| Colorado | 19,100 | 12 | 1740 | 42 | 20 |
| New Jersey | 66,194 | 12 | 2144 | 43 | 9 |
| Maryland (including Washington, D.C.) | 33,906 | 10 | 2221 | 44 | 6 |
| Nevada | 2,146 | 10 | 2257 | 45 | 4 |

TABLE 9.4. *(continued)*

| STATE | TOTAL CONSTRUC- TION APPROPRIA- TION,[a] THOUSANDS OF DOLLARS | PER CAPITA APPROPRIA- TION,[b] DOLLARS | ANNUAL PER CAPITA INCOME,[c] DOLLARS | RANK IN PER CAPITA APPROPRIA- TION[d] | RANK IN PER CAPITA INCOME |
|---|---|---|---|---|---|
| New York | 144,012 | 9 | 2235 | 46 | 5 |
| Maine | 6,122 | 7 | 1448 | 47 | 37 |
| Utah | 2,497 | 3 | 1525 | 48 | 32 |
| Wyoming | 3,380 | 1 | 1858 | 49 | 14 |
| Wisconsin | 3,106 | 1 | 1730 | 50 | 22 |
| United States | 8,217,971 | 50 | | | |

[a]The data on total appropriations were computed from information in the House Reports on the Senate-House Conference on each of the annual Civil Functions Appropriation Bills as follows: 1946, *Congressional Record,* 79th Congress, 1st Session, p. 11049; 1947, *Congressional Record,* 79th Congress, 2nd Session, p. 3989; 1943, *Congressional Record,* 80th Congress, 1st Session, p. 10391; 1949, *Congressional Record,* 80th Congress, 2nd Session, p. 7897; 1950, *Congressional Record,* 81st Congress, 1st Session, p. 14051; 1951, *House Report 1797,* 81st Congress, 2nd Session; 1952, *House Report 1197,* 82nd Congress, 1st Session; 1953, *House Report 2497,* 82nd Congress, 2nd Session; 1954, *House Report 889,* 83rd Congress, 1st Session; 1955, *House Report 1892,* 83rd Congress, 2nd Session; 1956, *House Report 1085,* 84th Congress, 1st Session; 1957, *House Report 2413,* 84th Congress, 2nd Session; 1958, *House Report 1049,* 85th Congress, 1st Session; 1959, *House Report 2670,* 85th Congress, 2nd Session; 1960, *House Report 1152,* 86th Congress, 1st Session; 1961, *House Report 2181,* 86th Congress, 2nd Session; 1962, *House Report 1268,* 87th Congress, 1st Session; and from Conference Reports of the miscellaneous Supplemental or Deficiency Appropriation bills which contained Civil Functions appropriations. In each case the appropriation was allotted to the state in which the specific project was located. In the cases in which a project was physically in two or more states, the appropriation was divided equally among the states involved. In the cases in which the project was a comprehensive river basin project flowing through two or more states, the appropriation was allocated to the state in which the actual expenditures took place as determined from Chief of Engineers, U.S. Army, *Annual Report.* The Arkansas River project and the Mississippi River project are cases in which such an adjustment took place. Those items in the Mississippi River project, such as dredging and revetments whose location could not be so determined, were allocated to the states concerned in the proportion of their river bank mileage to total river bank mileage. The figures are adjusted slightly to eliminate some small transfers to other departments and some small allowance for slippages.

[b]The state population figures used for per capita appropriation estimates are averages of the 1950 and 1960 census figures for each state. They were secured from the *Statistical Abstract of the United States, 1961,* p. 10.

[c]The state per capita income figures are likewise averages of the 1950 and 1960 census figures for each state. They were secured from the *Statistical Abstract of the United States, 1962,* p. 319.

[d]The states are ranked from highest to lowest. The ranks are based on calculations to the nearest cent whereas the per capita data in the table is in terms of the nearest dollar. This allows states which have the same per capita appropriation in the table to possess different ranks.

Source: Robert H. Haveman, *Water Resource Investment and the Public Interest* (Nashville, Tenn.: Vanderbilt University Press, 1965), pp. 53ff.

in the U.S. Tucker[35] and Conrad[36] studied the U.S. in the mid-1950s. Particular states were studied by Brownlee[37] and Musgrave and Daicoff.[38]

Gillespie found federal expenditures difficult to allocate to individuals because of the preponderance of defense and foreign affairs. Such benefits can be assumed to accrue uniformly over families in proportion to income, to income from capital, or to disposable income. Gillespie chooses the second assumption (on the ground that the higher a family's income, the more it has to protect) as his standard case. Under this assumption the distribution of general expenditures is in proportion to income. State and local spending benefited the poor more than the rich. Tax incidence studies usually show a progressive federal and a regressive state and local tax structure. Combining the incidence of public expenditures and taxes, he finds that "the federal pattern of fiscal incidence generally favors low incomes, burdens high incomes, and is mainly neutral over a wide middle income range. The state and local pattern also favors low incomes, but it is essentially neutral over both the middle and upper income ranges."[39] Inclusion of expenditures reverses the role of the federal and state-local governments. Now state-local is more favorable to the poor than federal because of welfare spending, for example. The combined net burden of public finance—taxes and expenditures—is more favorable to lower incomes than the tax structure alone.

## MERIT-WANT OBJECTIVES

Certain goods are provided by government because they are meritorious. They are not justified on efficiency grounds; they do not raise national income. They do not necessarily redistribute income in desirable ways, although they may. *Merit wants,* as Musgrave terms this type of good,[40] are the second type of public want.[41] Unlike social goods, merit wants

[35]Rufus S. Tucker, "The Distribution of Government Burdens and Benefits," *American Economic Review, Papers and Proceedings* 43 (May 1953): 518–43.

[36]Alfred H. Conrad, "Redistribution Through Government Budgets in the United States," in Alan T. Peacock, ed., *Income Redistribution and Social Policy* (London: Cape, 1954), pp. 178–268.

[37]O. H. Brownlee, "Estimated Distribution of Minnesota Taxes and Public Expenditure Benefits," *Studies in Economics and Business,* no. 21 (University of Minnesota, 1960).

[38]Richard A. Musgrave and Darwin W. Daicoff, "The Incidence of Michigan Taxes," *Michigan Tax Studies: Staff Papers,* Michigan Secretary of Finances, 1958, pp. 131–84.

[39]Gillespie in Musgrave, *Essays in Fiscal Federalism,* p. 165.

[40]Musgrave, *The Theory of Public Finance,* pp. 13ff.

[41]Musgrave has changed his terminology. *The Theory of Public Finance* spoke of "social wants," emphasizing the utility function. More recently he opts for "social goods" to emphasize characteristics of the good rather than the utility function that wants it. "Provision for Social Goods," in Julius Margolis and Henri Guitton, *Public Economics* (New York: St. Martin's Press, 1969), p. 126.

are subject to the exclusion principle and they are rival in consumption.[42] Those who do not pay the price can be excluded from enjoying them. Each one's consumption detracts from the supply available for others. These goods could be supplied by a market but not "enough" people want them. Government leaders decide that more of merit wants *should* be wanted than would actually be demanded at a market price. Then, they either provide the goods free or induce more to be consumed by lowering the price through subsidy. In providing merit wants, leaders impose their preferences on the people.

Some merit wants that are sold at subsidized prices are desired by many, some are merely tolerated, and some involve blatant overruling of consumer preferences. Some serve government policy objectives to which people are largely indifferent; others serve the organic needs of the state or its leaders at the direct expense of the people.

If the government chooses to subsidize goods or services that are not social goods, that choice requires justification. If the subsized good is rival and excludable in consumption, then it must be a merit want. It may be desired by a majority of the people, bût not in quantities great enough or in the character government planners prefer. Second-class mail, for example consisting largely of reading matter, is the most heavily subsidized class of mail. If its price covered average costs, the large quantity deemed "desirable" would not be consumed (bought). The service is rival in the sense that the greater second-class burden a post office handles, the less resources it has available to handle other mail. This is an opportunity cost. It leads to dissemination of ideas and an informed citizenry, both beneficial externalities. So it has some aspects of a social good.

Low-cost housing is another example of a good that is subject to exclusion and rival in consumption. The government subsidizes it because people, in a market without zoning, would tend to economize on housing services in order to save money for other things. They would live more densely than planners believe is good for them. Public housing programs seek to provide housing with qualities planners believe are good, but for which not enough people would opt without government intervention.

Similarly, all transfer payments in kind are merit wants; governments seek to redistribute income without allowing consumer sovereignty to the recipients. Some merit wants are provided by public spend-

---

[42] A good is nonrival in consumption if it is jointly supplied to an entire group in a fixed amount available to all. This usage appears in "Provision for Social Goods" in Margolis and Guitton, *Public Economics*, and in "Cost-Benefit Analysis and the Theory of Public Finance," *Journal of Economic Issues* 7: no. 3. (September 1969): 797–806.

ing to educate the people and change their tastes in ways with which the people are retrospectively pleased. Library services, for example, are rival. Consumers are excludable. The justification for providing free public libraries is to educate people to their benefits. Busing to achieve integrated schools is another example of leaders' overruling consumer preferences. The majority of the people of all races in an area may be against busing. Perhaps leaders hope to change tastes over time.

Under an organic theory of the state, the state itself has some wants that do not represent needs of individual citizens. National prestige or national self-sufficiency[43] may be seen as things leaders want, but about which citizens may be indifferent. The leaders of a country may desire honor in international relations and a place in history, leading to the desire not to appear to "lose" an armed confrontation. The citizens may not feel threatened and may believe they have little to lose by backing down on the issues involved, but leaders are empowered to overrule citizens' collective preferences. Further, leaders may be concerned about conserving foreign exchange. This may explain federal spending on an elaborate system of telecommunications under Wisconsin to obviate a system of relay stations abroad. Yet citizens purchase French wines, indifferent to the impact of their purchases on the balance of payments. Leaders of the country may be eager for the national prestige that comes with leadership in commercial aviation, as we shall see in Chapter 11. Citizens however, may or may not value such ends.

Foreign aid may be seen as a merit want. Of all the federal spending programs investigated by Eva Mueller in 1961, foreign aid had the least support.[44] Only 7 percent of respondents advocated spending more to help other countries and only 2 percent would spend more if taxes had to be raised therefor. Compare this with the 70 percent who wanted to spend more on help for the aged and the 34 percent who would do so even though taxes would be raised. Nevertheless, the federal government persists in a program of foreign aid.

Mack and Myers[45] have claimed that recreation has some aspects of a merit want. They believe that recreation for some groups is more meritorious than for others. For example, they feel it is more beneficial to society when young people experience recreation than when older people do, and more beneficial when people who rarely get the opportunity for recreation have the experience. For them, high quality recrea-

[43]This has been stated as an objective by S. A. Marglin, *Public Investment Criteria* (Cambridge, Mass.: M.I.T. Press, 1967), pp. 22ff.

[44]Eva Mueller, "Public Attitudes Toward Fiscal Programs," in Fremont J. Lyden and Ernest G. Miller, eds., *Planning Programming Budgeting: A Systems Approach to Management* (Chicago: Markham, 1968), Table II, p. 68.

[45]"Outdoor Recreation," in Dorfman, *Measuring Benefits of Government Investments*, pp. 71–101.

tion entails a planned program that encourages use and teaches people how to enjoy recreation. These are things that Mack and Myers prefer and believe the government should support.

As in the above case, too often the rubric "merit wants" is a convenient label for justifying favorite projects and lobbying for particular goods and services. Even Marglin, a great apologist for multiple objectives, confesses that only on Mondays, Wednesdays, and Fridays does he really believe in merit wants, but on Tuesdays, Thursdays, and Saturdays he has his doubts[46] and is unwilling to condone blatant overruling of private preferences by planners.

Some people mistakenly classify as merit wants "good things" whose value is intangible. Thus in the objectives listed by the Water Resources Council, environmental enhancement and well-being of people might be classified as merit wants, but are actually social goods because no overruling of consumers' preferences is involved in providing them. Musgrave's definition is clear. "The satisfaction of merit wants, by its very nature, involves interfering with consumer preferences."[47] If everyone or even a majority agrees that children's recreation is a good thing and ought to be subsidized by public spending, then it is not a merit want, but a social good.

Most merit wants are simply private goods that have some beneficial spillovers and thus ought to be encouraged. This is true of second-class mail and library services. Other merit wants are requests for group redistribution in kind, such as low-cost housing. Learning-by-experience merit wants are exemplified by busing and library services. The other so-called merit wants are dubious and ought to be scrutinized.

Whatever one feels about the propriety of merit wants, there is no question that it is difficult to calculate their benefits. To do so requires the explicit statement of merit weights, such as Mack and Myers suggested for different types of recreation. In a real political situation, with many clienteles attacking any assigned weights, estimation of benefits is considerably more difficult.


## SUMMARY

Economics has a curious relationship to income distribution, which, although part of economics, has credentials less venerable than the purely economic concern of efficiency. A case has been made for considering

[46]Marglin, *Public Investment Criteria,* pp. 21ff.
[47]Musgrave, *Theory of Public Finance,* p. 13.

equity and merit-want effects in addition to efficiency benefits. Some would even argue that these effects should be quantified in the form of benefits serving the objectives, and then treated on a par with efficiency benefits. But we do not agree.

Educational benefits, as we pointed out, are often distributed to wealthy families, and public investment projects frequently benefit wealthy landholders in adjacent areas. We charted the geographical distribution of expenditures for defense, resource development, and agricultural price supports. In general, the progressive effects of expenditures make the state-local fiscal system progressive. The progressive income tax makes the federal system progressive if key assumptions are made about the distribution of defense benefits.

In order to estimate equity benefits one would need consensus on an equity goal such as the complete leveling of incomes or the specification of a social welfare function. This is not likely to be forthcoming. First, because goals are more difficult to agree on than concrete actions; second, because income distribution is a controversial question. Therefore the best we can do is to list income-distribution effects, as in the Preliminary Health Overview estimates of how health benefits were distributed over several spaces.

The worthiness of merit wants is hard to define. Merit wants that overrule consumers' preferences are difficult to condone. On the other hand, if they serve wants of the majority they are not properly called merit wants according to Musgrave's definition. Although everyone may not agree with our new examples of merit wants, they are likely to engender some interesting discussion.

# Ten

# COST ANALYSIS

Although benefits are not easily measurable, we shall see that costs are more tractable—more easily managed and accounted for. The theory of production is in a more developed and satisfactory state than the theory of demand. The cost side of benefit-cost analysis can be naive or sophisticated: apparent costs are obvious and often are readily calculable as out-of-pocket dollar cost; more subtle, however, are resource costs; most interesting and elusive of all are the real costs in lost opportunities to do other things.

Estimation and prediction of costs are usually on firmer ground than estimation and prediction of benefits. These endeavors are not without pitfalls, however, and journalists frequently discover that there have been "cost overruns" in military or civilian spending programs. The sophisticated cost analyst, who realizes he should expect these, will show his expertise in his ability to predict their extent and cause.

If one compares costs to benefits in order to determine whether a project is justified, he uses a different concept of costs from that which enables prediction of project outlays. The former, for example, does not include inflation and may include implicit costs, for which payment is never made, such as opportunity costs or external costs. The latter, on the other hand is a financial concept; it does take account of expected inflation. Typical cost projections blend two types of cost estimates. That is, while they may not include expectations of inflation, probably they do not include opportunity costs or costs external to the project. Nevertheless, they are used for both purposes—to determine economic feasibility and to predict total financial outlays—and we shall see that they serve neither purpose well. Economists are always recalculating benefits according to their canons while journalists are always viewing-with-alarm large cost overruns. In this chapter we review types of cost frequently discussed and try to distinguish the concepts.

Some of the problems of cost estimating are viewed here. Can social costs be properly evaluated? If not, can project outlays be predicted and with what precision? What effect does the passage of time have on costs? What should be done about inflation?

In estimating project outlays, the factors that determine costs will be encountered. Perhaps the best known of these factors are physical and performance characteristics: a Rolls-Royce costs more than a Chevrolet. Cost estimating relationships that predict costs of new or complicated systems, such as airframes or hospitals, will be discussed. The notion that average costs change with the rate of output is very familiar to economists. Less well disseminated, but well demonstrated, is the influence of cumulative output on cost per unit: the so-called "learning curve." Procurement contracting, a very important influence on costs of government activity, involves how the contractor is selected, who he is, and the type of contract let.

## TYPES OF COSTS

Most frequently, a cost analysis predicts the monetary or financial costs of a project. We call these *project outlays*. They may involve research and development costs, investment costs, and costs of operation, maintenance and replacement. If the program is one of spending on current account, some expenditures will be required by statute and others will be required for administration. Economists often look beyond these concepts of cost to *opportunity costs, associated costs,* and *social costs.* Finally, a cost of another color is *alternative costs,* more akin to benefits.

### Project Outlays

Investment costs are expenses incurred in order to obtain benefits in future periods. Investment results in the accumulation of a stock of capital. Operation, maintenance, and replacement (OMR) costs are expenses incurred that do not add to the stock of capital, but rather attempt to maintain, as far as possible, the value of the existing stock. Investment costs of a water resource project would be the planning and design, the purchase price of land inundated, and the costs of installing the dam. OMR costs, for example, are those of hiring skilled operators of the equipment and lubricating and replacing hydroelectric generators. Frequently, OMR savings can be bought by purchasing more sophisticated or expensive initial equipment, but they cannot be eliminated entirely and are often appreciable. Investment costs of an urban highway would include planning costs and the costs of procuring the right-of-way, including demolition of existing improvements, relocation costs of occupants, and purchase costs of the land. OMR costs include cleaning, policing, and repairing the road.

For current spending programs such as welfare or veterans' benefits, statutory costs will be the amount paid out according to formulas contained in the law regarding amounts of payment and eligibility. The number of cases requiring payment must be predicted by use of demographic data. Administrative expenses are more fixed in nature.

### Opportunity Costs

Opportunity costs are the value of lost chances to do things. Spending money one way preempts the opportunity to spend it another way. Public spending may preempt private investment, consumption, or other public spending. Which resources are impinged upon depends on how a project is financed. If the project is financed by creating debt that is sold to the public, opportunities are lost in the private sector. If the debt is sold to the central bank and money is created, prices may rise causing the real purchasing power of money to decline. Thus the opportunity cost is shared in the public and private sectors. If the public project is financed by taxation, those who pay taxes lose opportunities to consume or invest. If total public spending is predetermined one public project displaces another. Most narrowly, if the budget is fixed for an area of public spending such as work retraining, then a Job Corps project, for example, displaces a Neighborhood Youth Corps project.

On the assumption that federal expenditures are paid for by taxation, Eckstein and Krutilla estimated the opportunity cost of capital in the United States just prior to 1958 to be between 5 and 6 percent.[1] Reuber and Wonnacott have estimated the opportunity cost in Canada in 1960 of issuing debt to finance projects at about $5.6 \pm 0.5$ percent.[2]

Public projects may have opportunity costs not only because they preempt funds, but also because they directly preempt physical opportunities. An example is the development of public hydroelectric power which obviates a private development to achieve the same purpose. This was the situation in Hell's Canyon on the Snake River between Idaho and Oregon where a public power project was in competition with a private scheme to develop the same river basin. As a result of the preemption, private funds may be forced to exploit opportunities of lower

[1] John V. Krutilla and O. Ekstein, *Multiple Purpose River Development* (Baltimore: Johns Hopkins University Press, 1958).

[2] G. L. Reuber and R. J. Wonnacott, *The Cost of Capital in Canada, with Special Reference to Public Development of The Columbia River* (Washington, D.C.: Resources for the Future, Inc., 1961), p. 83.

yield. The difference between the net present value of the preempted private project and that of the marginal private project is the opportunity cost of the public power project in the private sector.

Peter Steiner has contributed a general model for taking account of opportunity costs in several sectors.[3] The public sector consists of:

$S1$:   the set of projects among which choice is to be made; for example, all public works projects.

$S3$:   the rest of the public sector (with known present value of the yield per dollar of investment, $a_3$).

The private sector consists of:

$S2$:   private projects alternative to $S1$.

$S4$:   marginal private investment opportunities (with known present value per dollar of investment, $a_4$).

The opportunity cost per dollar of funds transferred from the private sectors to the public sector, $a_2$, is assumed known. They the present value net of all costs from project $i$ for purpose $j$ will be

$$Y_{ij} = (G_{ij} - a_3 k_{ij}) - (G_j - a_4 l_j) - a_2 m_{ij}$$

where $G_{ij}$ is the present value of net benefits of public project $i$ for purpose $j$. The alternatives to be compared are the different ways of achieving purpose $j$. The cost of the project is $k_{ij}$.

$G_j$   is the net present value of achieving purpose $j$ as the private sector would exploit it and $l_j$ is the capital cost of the private project.

$m_{ij}$   is the number of dollars which must be transferred to the public sector to do project $ij$. Note that this is not the cost of the project, but the repayment demanded of the beneficiaries in the form of user charges or assessments.

Steiner's model recognizes explicitly the opportunity costs of scarce public funds ($a_3 k_{ij}$), of displacing a private project (only the project's supramarginality, $G_j - a_4 l_j$) and of funds transferred to the public sector ($a_2 m_{ij}$). Note that if a private alternative is displaced, not all its net benefits are lost, but only those which exceed the net benefits of the marginal private project that will be done instead. All the private net benefits might be seen as gross opportunity costs. Net opportunity costs are private net

[3] Peter Steiner, "Choosing among Alternative Investments in the Water Resource Field," *American Economic Review* 49, no. 5 (December 1959): 893–916.

benefits on the displaced project minus net benefits on the marginal private project.

It is curious that Steiner allows the government to consider several alternative facilities (values of $i$) to achieve a purpose $j$ while the private sector has but one choice. Nevertheless, Steiner's model makes explicit many possible cases. Fortunately, it simplifies in various situations. For example, if private alternatives do not exist, then $(G_j - a_4 l_j)$ vanishes. If there is considerable unemployment, then $a_4$ would become zero because there are no opportunity costs in transferring funds from the private to the public sector.

The coefficient $a_2$ has units different from that estimated by Eckstein and Krutilla or Reuber and Wonnacott. Theirs was in the form of a weighted average rate of return. If this rate of return accrued annually in perpetuity, it would be divided by a social rate of discount to yield an estimate of $a_2$, the present value of private opportunity cost of a dollar spent in the public sector. If a 6 percent rate of return could be earned in the private sector and the social rate of discount were 3 percent, then $a_2$ would be 2.

Opportunity costs should be studied anew periodically as changes occur in investment opportunities, tax incidence, government borrowing, and income distribution. A 1967 study of opportunity costs in the private sector indicated a weighted average rate of return of 13.5 percent.[4] A 1969 study for the Bureau of the Budget indicated an opportunity cost of 7.7 percent.

Steiner's model permits direct comparison of public projects of very different size. Whereas Krutilla and Eckstein assume that for any project not done there will be a tax cut, Steiner assumes other public projects will be pursued.

Opportunity costs exist for resources other than capital. Plans often allocated water to a particular use without counting opportunity costs of that water. Water diverted from streams to irrigation is treated as if it were freely available by the Bureau of Reclamation in calculating benefits of irrigation.[5] In fact, using water for irrigation may make the stream unusable for fishing, a benefit previously derived from the river. In calculating benefits of the Peripheral Canal unit of the California Water Plan, no deduction was made for the loss of flow of the Sacramento River into San Francisco Bay. This lower flow apparently means that the South

[4]J. A. Stockfisch, "The Interest Rate Applicable to Government Investment Projects," *The Planning-Programming-Budgeting System: Progress and Potentials,* Hearings before the Subcommittee on Economy in Government of the Joint Economic Committee, 1967, pp. 133–43.

[5]A. Myrick Freeman, "Six Federal Reclamation Projects and the Distribution of Income," *Water Resources Research* 3, no. 2 (1967): 319–31.

Bay will not receive the beneficial flushing action formerly enjoyed. Opportunity costs were not included in the analysis.

### Associated Costs

Associated costs are "any costs involved in utilizing project services in the process of converting them into a form suitable for use or sale at the stage benefits are evaluated."[6] Associated costs are incurred by beneficiaries. They are sometimes useful as an index of willingness to pay for project outputs. The beneficiary of educational opportunities forgoes income he could have been earning if he were not occupied in classes. Income forgone constitutes a cost. Associated costs of using a park are the incremental costs of travel, food, and lodging that would not otherwise have been incurred. Users of transportation must provide their own time or that of the goods they ship as an associated cost. Savings in associated costs of exploiting a new project are sometimes attributable as benefits to the new project. For example, if commuters save time because of a transportation project, the value of time saved is one measure of benefits. If an educational program formerly taking six months can be compressed to three months without loss of effectiveness, then savings in income forgone are additional benefits. If hospitals are located nearer their clientele, decreased travel costs in the form of morbidity and mortality in getting to the hospital will accrue as benefits.

### Social Costs

Social costs may be visualized as subsidies to every person who suffers from a project. Such subsidies would be sufficient to make them indifferent between (1) the project with these subsidies and (2) no project and no subsidies. They are "the value to those who forgo them of the goods and services forgone because resources are devoted to the project,"[7] and are to be distinguished from the taxes, borrowing, or printing used to finance a project.[8] The concept of social cost is more comprehensive than that of private, market, or monetized cost. Social costs include opportunity costs and external costs.

There are two ways to handle external costs.[9] They may be sub-

[6]Subcommittee on Evaluation Standards, Report to the Interagency Committee on Water Resources, *Proposed Practices for Economic Analysis of River Basin Projects,* Washington, D.C. (May 1958), "The Green Book," p. 9.

[7]Samuel B. Chase, *Problems in Public Expenditure Analysis* (Washington, D.C.: The Brookings Institution, 1966), p. 3.

[8]The burdens imposed by the method of financing are omitted both in order to focus on real effects and in order to avoid double counting.

[9]Ronald H. Coase, "The Problem of Social Cost," *Journal of Law and Economics* 3 (October 1960): 1–44.

tracted, as in the works of Pigou, from the market value of the output of a project to obtain net social value. Another approach, suggested by Ronald Coase, is to use opportunity costs. Suppose a project interferes with the welfare of people other than the beneficiaries. In order to test whether the project is justified, one could calculate the value of using the resources solely for the benefit of those affected by the externality. If the SST makes noise (uses silence) without compensating those giving up silence, we decide whether or not to allow it by estimating (1) the value of silence and no SST and (2) the value of the SST. Whichever yields the largest product is the proper use of the resource.

Coase's work is an apology for business enterprise that frequently creates external costs in the course of creating market benefits; that is, it is not always the perpetrator of an externality who should cease functioning. Sometimes the recipient of the external cost should yield in the competition for use of resources. The choice, in Coase's view, depends on the relative value of the two enterprises at conflict. For example, if a thermal power plant would raise the temperature of a stream, it may be better for it to yield to recreational use of the stream. But if this were done categorically, we would have little or no electricity; often recreation must yield to electricity production. We shall return to the question of social costs below when we ask whether costs, especially implicit costs can be properly evaluated.

### Alternative Costs

The alternative costs of a project are minimum costs of achieving the output of a project, by alternative means. Because alternative costs can be used as a maximum value for benefits of a project output, they are more relevant to benefits than to costs. For example, suppose a highway permits transportation of foodstuffs by truck, but for some reason the value added by transportation cannot be accurately calculated. Then the cost of transporting the same amount of food by rail (and, perhaps, truck) may be taken as an upper bound for the benefits of the road transportation. The alternative must provide exactly the same output as the project considered. That is why we add "and, perhaps, truck" to the above example. We must compare the costs of alternative transportation that would get the foodstuffs from the same origin to the same destination in the same time as it could be done by truck.

Steiner has argued that under some conditions, knowing alternative costs can obviate the measurement of benefits for a project.[10] If a viable alternative exists and will be executed in the absence of government

[10]Peter Steiner, "The Role of Alternative Cost in Project Design and Selection," *Quarterly Journal of Economics* 79 (August 1965): 417–30.

action, then the benefits of the government project may be seen as the obviated costs of the alternative which achieves the same results; for example, thermal power plants as alternatives to hydroelectric facilities.

Let us exemplify these usages by discussing costs of education. (1) Project outlays might include the investment costs of land and buildings, and the OMR costs of teachers' salaries, supplies, utilities, and maintenance. (2) Opportunity costs are student earnings that have to be forgone. (3) Alternative costs are the time, effort, and expense of an individual trying to teach himself what he can learn from professional teachers. (4) Associated costs are those for books, travel, and living costs insofar as they exceed the cost of living at home. Social costs include (1), (2), and (4). Private costs are the same as social costs except that (1) would be replaced by tuition and fees. Out-of-pocket costs would include (1) and (4), (2) being an implicit cost.

## GENERAL PROBLEMS OF COST ESTIMATING

In estimating costs for purposes of benefit-cost analysis, the ideal being approximated is social costs. Not all social costs can even be discussed, no less measured, in commensurable terms. Social justice, ideological values, silence, or clean air, for example, are *intangible* values, but they are very real. Therefore, project planners must attempt to measure the subset of social costs that can be subjected to the dollar yardstick for which transactional counterparts exist. Project outlays, the most often predicted, can overestimate monetized costs if, for example, labor is paid a wage higher than its opportunity cost. They can be underestimated if implicit costs are neglected.

Judging by experience, we are not even very adept at predicting project outlays. Overspending is rife in military hardware and in public works. Even so, estimation of project outlays will undoubtedly continue. In consideration of those who must do this work, we review pratical questions cost estimators must answer. What should we do about inflation? What effect does elapsed project time and calendar time have on costs and cost estimates?

### Evaluating Social Costs

A practical obstacle makes it difficult to obtain an objective estimate of the monetary value of the social costs of a given project or of each alternative project. It is no easy matter to identify, now or for any time in the future, those who, if fully informed, would be willing to sacrifice something in order to kill the project, even if it were to be financed by donations. Nor is it easy to learn how much money each such person, if fully informed, would require in the form of subsidies in order to make him indifferent to the project (see p. 135).

One method of approximation presents itself. Every design will involve purchased inputs, and the amounts of money that will be spent on the inputs in each year can be predicted.[11] One might assume that that these project outlays will be approximately equal to the monetary value of the project's social costs. If this assumption is made, the task of predicting social costs reduces to the task of predicting project outlays.

Two problems exist, however. First, future expenditures are hard to predict, for three reasons: the stream of outputs to be produced will be uncertain; the outlays needed to produce any given stream of outputs will be uncertain; and the outlays needed to produce any given stream of outputs will depend on what decisions are made about other projects.

The stream of outputs to be produced must be specified if future outlays depend on the quantity produced. This stream, however, depends on what users' demand will be and on what decisions project managers will make about quality and price. Both will be hard to anticipate.

Second, the outlays are also hard to anticipate. With respect to OMR, one must predict input bottlenecks, input prices, productivity gains, and contingencies such as repairs. With respect to capital outlays, one must predict lifetimes,[12] salvage values, and replacement costs. Each of these items can be estimated, but the estimates are subject to error—error of large and unknowable magnitude. We discuss below some retrospective studies of errors in cost estimation for military hardware items and for public works. Costs may be as difficult to predict as benefits. For research and development projects, Fedkiw and Hjort indicate that "some of our experience . . . suggests that the greater uncertainty may be associated with the total cost of achieving a successful research result [than with the benefits]."[13]

[11]With what degree of accuracy we discuss below.

[12]As Irving Fox and Orris Herfindahl have pointed out, "An increase in the nominal life of a project has a very sizable effect on the [benefit-cost] ratio if a low rate of discount is in use. An assumed 100-year project life decreases annual costs by 18 percent over a 50-year assumed life where capital costs are 80 percent of total [equivalent] annual costs, a 3 percent discount rate is applied, and the noncapital cost stream is level. With a benefit stream increasing at an absolute rate of 2 percent of the initial year's benefit, the combined effect is to improve the [benefit-cost] ratio by 35 percent. With an 8 percent discount rate, the combined effect is to improve the ratio by only 4 percent." "Attainment of Efficiency in Satisfying Demands for Water Resources," *American Economic Review* 54 (May 1964): 203.

[13]John Fedkiw and Howard W. Hjort, "The PPB Approach to Research Evaluation," *Journal of Farm Economics* 49 (December 1967): 1433.

One reason why outlays on any project will depend on what decisions are made about other projects is that inputs such as administrators and training programs often have excess capacity that could be used in other programs with no increase in outlays; any one new project might use, use up, or create such excess capacity. Another reason is that, for inputs such as office space, maintenance service, and financial control, economies of scale often cause the outlays needed to service a number of projects concurrently to be less than the sum of the outlays needed to service each project separately. Still another reason is that projects often use each other's outputs; for example, a given arrival time constraint can be met with fewer firehouses if a street project reduces travel time. Yet another reason is that retaining unfireable employees in a project will increase government expenditures, not by the amount spent for their salaries and benefits, but by the largest savings that could be realized by transferring them to another project. The amount of these savings will depend on what other projects are operating and what openings they have. Because of these interdependencies, outlays for any one project will depend on what is decided about various other projects. That is, future outlays are indeterminate until decisions have been specified about the existence and character of all interrelated projects, both old and new ones.[14]

How should interrelatedness be recognized? Prest and Turvey tell us, "Where the costs and/or benefits of two schemes are interdependent in the sense that the execution of one affects the costs or benefits of the other . . . they must be treated as constituting three mutually exclusive schemes, namely, A and B together, A alone and B alone."[15] The trouble with proceeding this way is that treating all projects whose costs are interdependent as a unit may produce a huge package—one for which it is impossible to predict either the stream of outputs or the outlays needed to produce any given stream of outputs.[16]

---

[14]It is not the use of future outlays as a proxy for monetized costs that undermines evaluation of costs for each project separately. Monetized costs (or benefits) themselves are indeterminate for any one project. In defining *monetized costs,* we pointed out that, to identify the hypothetical annual subsidies that, when summed, equal the annual monetary value of a project's social costs, one must suppose that someone knows what position everyone would be in without the project. These positions depend on what the government in question decides to do about other projects. Interdependence is a fundamental objection to a project-by-project approach.

[15]A. R. Prest and R. Turvey, "Cost-Benefit Analysis: A Survey," *Economic Journal* 75 (December 1965): 704.

[16]In practice, as a result, analysts seem to proceed quite differently than Prest and Turvey suggest. The analysts seem to take for granted that all existing projects will be continued, to consider as a unit proposed projects that seem to be "highly" complementary (such as a park and a side road), and to evaluate such units as if no other new projects were under consideration.

For these reasons, future expenditures are hard to predict. But this is only the first problem in trying to use project outlays as a proxy for monetized costs.

The second problem is that the outlays that will be made in a year do not in fact equal the monetary value of the project's social costs in that year. There are two factors that cause the two to be unequal—implicit costs and mispriced inputs.

First, future outlays reflect only explicit costs; they ignore implicit costs such as externalities or opportunity costs. These are costs that have no transactional counterparts. Implicit costs occur because activities impose burdens for which the law creates no liability, and because economic agents seldom pay compensation (or seldom are bought off by the victims) when the law does not require it. Requiring compensation solves the problem posed by Coase. For example, trash disposal programs do not pay compensation for making noise, polluting the air, or depriving junkmen of supplies. Unfortunately, there usually is no practical way to obtain an objective estimate of such implicit costs. For example, to find the money value that the people disturbed by noise would place on their losses, one would need to find and talk with all of them—at considerable length, judging by our experience with similar questions. In any event, because future outlays reflect only explicit costs, they do not show the money value that all losers, if fully informed, would place on their losses. The most that project outlays can show is the money value of the losses that will occur because the project will preempt inputs that could be used for other purposes.

Second, outlays reflect uncorrected input prices. When a program uses inputs, other output that the inputs could produce is sacrificed. The amount that this sacrifice adds to social costs is the amount of money that people would need to be given in order to make them as well off as they would be had the other output not been sacrificed. Under certain conditions, this amount of money would be equal to the market value of the forgone output, which in turn would be equal to the amount of money spent to acquire the project's inputs. In the real world, however, the required conditions are not met. Instead one finds price support programs, relative price changes over time, monopolies, externalities, ignorance, bottlenecks, and factor prices that differ from values of marginal products because of monopolistic labor markets, import barriers, and unemployment. Unfortunately, there is no objective way to adjust for these "imperfections."[17] Accordingly, future outlays do not show the money value that the persons who will lose from reallocation of resources

[17] As McKean puts it: "The cost of information . . . depends on the quality of the output. . . . Even for . . . Minuteman squadrons, it would cost little to provide some sort

would place on their losses. The most that project outlays can show is the extra taxes or user charges that the project will impose.

Market prices are inadequate measures of the real social costs of resources in a fully employed economy because they neglect consumers' surplus that would accrue in their alternate use. Consumers' surplus has been mentioned in benefit-cost literature with regard to benefits, but rarely with regard to costs. That consumers' surplus should be sought for benefit calculations but not for cost calculations perhaps shows the motivations of those involved in benefit-cost analysis: they are eager to raise estimates of benefits, but not costs.[18] There are losses of producer surplus in addition to monetized costs when factors are preempted for public projects. The usual justification for ignoring consumers' surplus on the cost side while counting it on the benefits side is that project costs impinge marginally on many markets while benefits are large, nonmarginal or indivisible changes in a single or few markets. If resource costs impinge on a particular market, then opportunity costs should include consumers' surplus. For example, if a highway building program uses resources specific to the contract construction industry—surveyors, contractors, concrete, earthmoving equipment, day laborers—then there is a case for counting consumers' surplus lost on the homebuilding displaced by the highway project.

Even extra taxes or user charges are not necessarily representative of monetized costs because peak outlays may be financed by borrow-

---

of shadow prices, yet it might be infinitely costly to prepare appropriate ones . . . what to do depends upon one's judgments about the cost and worth of the alternative results." Roland McKean, "The Use of Shadow Prices," in Chase, *Problems in Public Expenditure Analysis,* p. 47.

Concerning adjustments for mispriced materials, Prest and Turvey observe: "Small and remote divergences will cause biases . . . within [the] margin of error, while large divergences of an unknown sort . . . are necessarily irrelevant to action. Only those divergences which are immediate, palpable, and considerable thus deserve our attention. . . . The division of labor in administration . . . requires each part . . . to act as if the rest were doing its job properly. After all . . . it may be better if all . . . agencies value foreign exchange at a uniform but incorrect exchange rate than if they each have their own different shadow rates," Prest and Turvey, "Cost-Benefit Analysis: A Survey," p. 704.

Concerning adjustments for involuntary unemployment: "The arguments against correcting [labor] costs . . . and against including multiplier effects in benefits are largely practical: . . . (a) [E]quipment, fuel, materials, etc., . . . too . . . include in their costs some overpriced labour. . . . (b) Correcting future costs requires estimates of future unemployment. . . . (c) The effect of a project upon unemployment depends . . . upon the way it is financed. . . . These arguments suggest that in most cases it is best . . . for the agencies responsible for public works to confine their corrections . . . to divergences which are local or relate to some specialized factor. . . . National unemployment . . . should be no concern of the National Coal Board, but the . . . employment opportunities for miners in certain coal fields should," Prest and Turvey, "Cost-Benefit Analysis: A Survey," p. 694.

[18]R. M. Dunn, Jr., "A Problem of Bias in Benefit-Cost Analysis: Consumer Surplus Reconsidered," *Southern Economic Journal* 33, no. 3 (January 1967): 337–42.

ing. Borrowing (ordinarily by selling bonds) is especially likely when certain inputs are relatively expensive and durable. If peak outlays are financed by borrowing, the stream of taxes or user charges that the project entails will depend not only on future outlays but also on how the project is financed. The stream of taxes or user charges will reflect the rates of interest that the jurisdiction obtains and also whether, when, and how the principal of the loans is paid off. Accordingly, future outlays do not even show how much the project will increase taxes or user charges. All that future outlays represent is how much purchasing power the jurisdiction will use up on the project if it is approved, and, therefore, how much extra purchasing power the government will need to obtain.[19]

### Predicting Project Outlays

Robert Summers has done a retrospective study[20] of the quality of estimates of project outlays. He found what might be expected based on casual observation. Four-fifths of the 68 estimates examined were below actual costs. "Early cost estimates for major hardware articles in technologically-difficult, long-term development programs are likely to be too low by a factor of two to three." The earlier an estimate is made in a development program, the poorer it is likely to be. The greater the technological advance required, the poorer the cost estimate is likely to be. The longer the development period, the more uncertainty there is in forecasting the costs of the program.

Two gross adjustments that need to be made to any cost estimate are: 1) base the estimate of total costs on actual quantities rather than quantities originally projected, and 2) adjust for inflation. This will require an answer to the question of whether the cost estimate was made in current dollars or in constant dollars of some particular year.

For the first adjustment it would be desirable to have, instead of a

[19]This sentence applies only to a new project. For existing projects, an implicit outlay must be added if one wants to know the full amount that continuation of the activity will increase governmental demand for funds.

Existing projects usually have fixed assets, ranging from ashtrays to parks. A decision to continue a project with fixed assets will entitle the project to keep the assets. For it to do so will increase the funds required by the jurisdiction. The increase in funds is equal to the difference between the current salvage value of the assets and what their salvage value will be at the stopping date—or at the end of the assets' useful life, if that is sooner. (By *salvage value,* we mean the larger of two figures: first, the amount of money that would be realized by selling the assets and, second, the amount of money that the jurisdiction would save if the assets were assigned to other programs.) This difference is the value of the implicit outlay that must be added.

[20]"Cost Estimates as Predictors of Actual Weapon Costs: A Study of Major Hardware Articles," in Thomas Marschak, T. K. Glennan, Jr. and R. Summers, *Strategy for R & D: Studies in the Microeconomics of Development* (New York: Springer-Verlag, 1967).

single cost estimate, a cost-quantity schedule showing cost per unit as a function of quantity to be procured. Often a contract will be written on the assumption that a certain quantity will be procured. If fewer units are actually procured, the cost per unit is likely to be higher than anticipated. A complete cost-quantity schedule ought to anticipate reductions in average cost as more units are produced. Total cost can be the dependent variable as well, but here again, care must be taken to assure that numbers compared have the same meaning. The Bay Area Rapid Transit (BART) Composite Report[21] estimated the cost of 480 cars at $71.2 million. The BART District has decided it will start with 250 cars, but they will cost $69.1 million.[22]

Summers first considered the ratio of the actual cost of the military hardware article to its estimated cost. On the average, actual cost was 3.25 times estimated cost. This, however, is only a very rough measure of the accuracy of a cost estimate. When gross adjustments are made for quantity procured and inflation, an "adjusted $F$" is produced—a ratio of actual cost to the adjusted cost estimate, a preferable measure of the accuracy of a cost estimate. After these adjustments, actual costs were still an average of 1.79 times predicted costs. The equation which best explained the variation in $F$ (together with standard errors) was

$$\ln F = 2.479 + .097t - .032tA - .311A + .015A^2$$
$$\quad\quad\quad\; (.205) \quad (.019) \quad (.189) \quad (.007)$$

$$+ .008L - .075 \; (T-1940) + u \quad\quad\quad\quad\quad (1)$$
$$\;\; (.002) \quad (.020)$$

$$R^2 = .698$$

where

$t =$ the fraction of the development program which had elapsed when the estimate was made.

$A =$ a subjective measure, the degree of technological advance required by the development program. This is the composite judgment of a group of experts on a scale from 5 to 16.

$L =$ the length of the development period in months.

$T =$ the calendar year in which the estimate was made.

[21] Parsons Brinckerhoff-Tudor-Bechtel; Smith, Barney & Co.; Stone and Youngberg; Van Beuren Stanbery, *The Composite Report Bay Area Rapid Transit* (San Francisco: Bay Area Rapid Transit District, May 1962).

[22] Official Statement Relating to San Francisco BART District, Sales Tax Revenue Bonds, Series A (January 1970), p. 7.

$u$ = an error term representing extraneous factors not included in the equation, normally distributed with mean zero and variance $\sigma^2$.

Summers claimed that equation (1) can be used to "debias" a cost estimate. In fact, we can get an unbiased estimate only of the logarithm of the cost. Equation (1) can be written

$$\ln \left( \frac{\text{actual cost}}{\text{adjusted cost estimate}} \right) = f(t, A, L, T) + u. \qquad (2)$$

Whence

In actual cost $= f(t, A, L, T) + \ln$ adjusted cost estimate $+ u$.

or

actual cost $= [\exp(f(t, A, L, T)) \cdot$ adjusted cost estimate$] E(e^u)$. Since $E(e^u) = \sigma^2/2$, the antilogarithm is a biased estimate of cost.

The equation is difficult to use ex ante because the variable $t$ is hard to know. The variable $L$, the length of the development period, cannot be known before the development is complete. Nevertheless, Summers' research gives us an idea of the factors which influence the quality of cost estimates for weapon systems. Cost estimating technique seemed to be improving over the period studied, 1947–57, because cost divergence factors were declining as calendar year increased.

Equation (1) is consistent with a hypothesis that contractors consciously underbid as well as the possible explanation that there is a "change in configuration" of the product desired by the procuring service during the preprocurement phases of its life cycle.

If cost estimates exist for two vying systems, one should resist the temptation to compare them before adjusting for the stage in the development program of each and the degree of technological advance each requires. Only after such adjustments ought one dare say which is the lower-cost system. Furthermore, more consistent with knowledge of the uncertainty of the estimate, the sophisticated cost analyst gives a probability distribution of costs rather than a point estimate. A careful chemist, when asked how hot something is, will respond: "$XX$ degrees centigrade plus or minus $y$ degrees." The last clause gives you an idea of the *precision* of the estimate and usually takes in two standard errors on either side of the point estimate. It must be understood that cost is a random variable. The coefficient of variation of the price paid by the U.S. Post Office for a square foot of floorspace in 1966 was 25 percent.[23]

[23] Leonard Merewitz, *The Production Function in the Public Sector: Production of Postal Services in the U.S. Post Office* (Berkeley, California: Institute of Urban and Regional Development, 1971), pp. 52–55.

Summers then addresses the very vital question of the consequence on costs of guessing poorly. He does not fret about spiraling costs, but asks: Given the bias and uncertainty in cost estimating, do poor cost estimates lead to wrong decisions? In one of three studies examined carefully, the cost-effectiveness choice would have been different had the bias and variance of the cost estimate been taken into account. This was a case of missile systems for strategic bombardment. Another way of stating that question is: How much less do predicted costs for a preferred alternative have to be in order to be confident that actual costs will be less?

Summers' study is a landmark for military systems. A similar study ought to be done for civilian projects. Table 10.1 gives some idea of the quality of cost estimates for civilian projects. What factors make such estimates poor? Is it underbidding, unanticipated delays, changes in configuration, method of financing, or some other factor? What is sorely needed in this area is a sense of proportion or of history.

The Troy and Greenfield Railroad cost ten times its initial estimate. The Suez Canal cost 20 times its 1838 estimate and three times its 1887 estimate. Yet journalists are constantly railing at cost overruns. How bad these are must be judged in relation to other projects and to the special problems each encounters.

Thus, future outlays are hard to predict and do not in fact equal the monetary value of a project's social costs. Our shortcut has led us, not to an objective estimate of monetized social costs, but to a judgmental estimate of extra governmental demand for funds. An objective estimate of social costs, we conclude, is not obtainable.

TABLE 10.1. COMPARISON OF COST ESTIMATES AND ACTUAL COSTS FOR PUBLIC WORKS PROJECTS

| Project | Estimated cost (millions of dollars) | Year estimate made | Actual cost (millions of dollars) | Year completed |
|---|---|---|---|---|
| San Francisco-Oakland Bay Bridge | 62 | 1931 | 73 | 1936 |
| Richmond-San Rafael Bridge | 46 | 1951 | 56 | 1956 |
| Golden Gate Bridge | 33 | 1930 | 35 | 1937 |
| Chief Joseph (formerly Foster Creek) Dam | 141 | 1946 | 145 | 1962 |
| The Dalles Dam | 326 | 1950 | 247 | 1964 |
| Coyote Valley Dam and Reservoir | 18 | 1950 | 17 | 1959 |
| Bonneville Reservoir | 40 | 1934 | 84 | 1944 |
| Fort Randall Reservoir | 133 | 1946 | 183 | 1956 |
| Clark Hill Reservoir | 37 | 1945 | 78 | 1955 |
| Garrison Reservoir | 129 | 1945 | 287 | 1962 |
| John H. Kerr Reservoir | 40 | 1945 | 86 | 1957 |
| Wolf Creek Reservoir | 35 | 1941 | 78 | 1953 |
| McNary Lock & Dam | 131 | 1938 | 284 | 1958 |
| Holland Tunnel | 28 | 1919 | 49 | 1927 |
| Verrazano Narrows Bridge | 78 | 1948 | 300 | 1963 |

### Allowances for Time in Cost Estimates

Three questions must be considered in the following paragraphs. What happens to costs as calendar time elapses? How do costs behave as project time elapses? What happens to our ability to predict costs as project time elapses?

If experience of the past thirty years is a reliable guide, costs rise as calendar time passes. In the current institutional setting, inflation is the name of this game. Inflation—changes in the general price level— should be taken out of any estimate of social costs used for comparison with benefits. Changes in *relative* prices ought to be taken account of, however. Klarman, in his study of syphilis referred to in Chapter 8, observed hospital costs rising 3 percent faster than the general price level. Since this was a change in relative prices—hospital services becoming more expensive relative to other goods and services—these changes were taken into account. The logic of this step is that comparison of costs and benefits at present value ought to consider relative prices or values as they exist at one point in time. If prices change proportionately, only those goods or services that will become relatively more valuable in the future ought to get credit for increasing value. Klarman considered the present value of obviated hospital costs in the future. Since hospital costs were rising faster than the general price level, a saved patient-day twenty years from now will be relatively more valuable (in current, not present, value) than a saved patient-day in the present.

Planning agencies have been known to take the general rise in prices into account in their calculations. For the typical public investment, large costs are incurred at the outset, but benefits accrue in the future. General inflation, if it is counted, will inflate benefits more than it will inflate costs, and will be favorable to justification of the project.

One way to deal with the inflation problem is to predict not dollar outlays, but resource usage in physical units. Engineering hours, for example, for a development program, can be stated. The problem of applying a price factor to these resources can be left to others. This approach may be called *resource cost analysis* or simply *resource analysis*.

If budgetary demands need to be predicted for five-year financial plans or "full funding," dollar figures will be needed sooner or later.[24] For example, if a scientific research project, in the judgment of experts,

---

[24]These dollars are appropriated by the legislature although for the federal government, personnel-position maxima are also legislated. An agency frequently finds itself in the position of having plenty of money, but not enough positions to accomplish its mission. Full funding is discussed below and in U.S. Bureau of the Budget, *Budget of the U.S. Fiscal Year 1970, Special Analyses* (Washington, D.C.: U.S. Government Printing Office, 1969), p. 81.

FIGURE 10.1. SYSTEM COSTS TIME PHASING
(IDEALIZED CURVES)

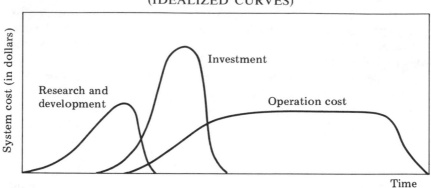

would require 24 man-months to complete, a valuable study would be similar to one by the RAND Corporation for the Air Force.[25] That study found that "between fiscal year 1954 and 1964, total costs per scientific man-month rose by 88 percent or by 6.5 percent per year." In other words, "The quantity of basic research effort that could be purchased for one million dollars in fiscal year 1954 cost nearly 1.9 million dollars in fiscal year 1964." In engineering sciences, costs increased 8.7 percent annually; the life sciences growth rate was 8.2 percent. The lowest rate of increase in costs, in chemical sciences, was 4.6 percent per year.

Changes in costs over time are recorded in price indices. One such index comes from McGraw-Hill's *Engineering News Record*. Their index of construction costs is based on the costs of a fixed collection of goods and services, using 1913 as the base year. Twenty city averages are available as well as index values for particular cities. Such indices are useful in explaining and summarizing cost increases due to inflation. The table shows that construction costs increased by one-third between 1965 and 1969.

ENGINEERING NEWS RECORD CONSTRUCTION COST INDEX

| *1949* | *1965* | *1966* | *1967* | *1968* | *1969* | |
|---|---|---|---|---|---|---|
| | | | | | *June* | *December* |
| 477 | 971 | 1021 | 1070 | 1154 | 1285 | 1306 |

As project time elapses, relative outlays on a project behave fairly predictably. The time profile of costs for a typical weapon system over its life cycle is shown in Figure 10.1. Research and development (R&D)

[25]E. D. Brunner, *The Cost of Basic Research Effort: Air Force Experience, 1954-1964*, RM-4250-PR (February 1965).

costs are skewed to the left because of considerable start-up costs in assembling a research and development team of personnel and setting up experiments. Once the mission is accomplished, however, R&D effort can be stopped in fairly short order. Investment costs may consist of the purchase of facilities, equipment, and spares, and the initial training of the first service personnel to use the new equipment. Investment costs reach the highest rate of the three categories of cost and are nearly normally distributed about their mean with no particularly notable start-up or phase-out costs. Operation costs are distributed nearly uniformly after an initial gradual buildup. Regular, planned replacement of equipment and facilities is usually considered part of operating costs as well as maintenance, pay, and allowances of the personnel identified with the weapon system; training costs; and fuels, lubricants, and propellants. When these three distributions are added together, total costs of all three types tend to be roughly normally distributed about a mean coinciding with the peak of the investment costs, but slightly skewed to the right, as shown in Figure 10.2. If the system is in operation for a long time, the right tail of the total system cost distribution may differ from the normal with OMR costs uniform for a period.

It is useful to know the life-cycle of costs for whatever is being procured to avoid the "foot-in-the-door problem." Relatively low R&D costs

## FIGURE 10.2. SYSTEM COSTS TIME PHASING (BY FISCAL YEARS)

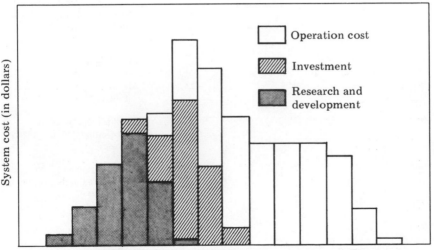

Source: J. D. McCullough, "Cost Analysis for Planning-Programming-Budgeting Cost-Benefit Studies" (RAND P-3479, November 1966), p. 18.

for a weapon system such as the Antiballistic Missile does not give any indication what the rate of spending will be at the peak of the investment phase, nor what the total cost or area under the curves will be. Congress has recently required "full funding," or disclosure of the full cost of a program before work actually begins. This measure, like multi-year costing, would give Congress greater awareness of the amount to which it is committing itself before it begins a program.

A partial case history for a project as yet incomplete is given in Table 10.2. The Bay Area Rapid Transit (BART) System has changed considerably in configuration since it was conceived in 1956. Its scope has contracted from five counties to three. It has been reduced from 123 miles to 75 miles. Nevertheless, its predicted costs have escalated from $873 million to $1,380 million, and it is not yet complete.

BART faced at least three obstacles: (1) a taxpayers' suit that held it up for over six months at a crucial time just after approval of the general obligation bonds, (2) the unanticipated Vietnam war inflation after 1966, and (3) another costly delay while the state legislature decided how to fund a $150 million deficit.

TABLE 10.2. BART COST ESTIMATES

| Report Date | No. of Counties Served | Mileage | Predicted Costs (millions of dollars) | Remarks |
|---|---|---|---|---|
| 1956 | 5+ | 123 | 873 | Plan presented by BARTC. Alameda, Contra Costra, Marin, San Francisco, and San Mateo Counties. |
| 1961 (June) | 5 | 120 | 1,287 | First BARTD plan. Almost the same as 1956 version. |
| 1961 (October) | 4 | 103 | 1,145 | Marin county leaves reluctantly. |
| 1962 | 3 | 75 | 990 | San Mateo county out. Three-county plan approved by voters. |
| 1966 | 3 | 75 | 1,180 (approx.) | Costs increased by delays and some embellishments. |
| 1970 | 3 | 75 | 1,316 | |
| 1970 (April) | 3 | 75 | 1,380 | |

Source: Robert L. Harrison, "An Economic Analysis of An Urban Transportation Investment: The San Francisco Bay Area Rapid Transit District" (unpublished paper, Berkeley, 1968) and later documents.

Thus, any estimate of outlays in the future will be uncertain. The farther into the future costs are predicted, the more uncertain the prediction will be. As project time elapses, the standard error of a cost prediction will decrease, and ability to predict total costs will improve with the approach of the end of the project.

## FACTORS GOVERNING COSTS

In estimating project outlays we encounter the factors that influence the cost of public programs. The first one is size and performance characteristics: big airplanes cost more than small ones; fast ones cost more than slow ones. Both the rate and the cumulative number of units procured influence average costs. In planning public facilities such as post offices, libraries, or hospitals an optimal (from the point of view of average cost) size or rate of output may be sought. Cost functions needed to answer such questions may also be used for annual budgetary predictions. Finally, project outlays are affected by the method of choosing contractors and the type of procurement contract employed.

### Physical and Performance Characteristics: Cost Estimating Relationships

As experience accumulates, cost analysts become able to predict costs of a new item on the basis of historical costs. Cost per item tends to be closely related to the characteristics of the item produced. The RAND Corporation was one of the first to become expert at developing *cost-estimating relationships* (CERs): mathematical expressions of functional relationships between cost and the characteristics of the item. CERs have been very helpful in estimating the costs of development and procurement of major items of military hardware. Costs of an item with desired characteristics can be predicted before its technology is developed. CERs are useful for long-range planning, but are not precise enough to be useful for short-run forecasting or contract monitoring. Had they been available, they might have been used, for example, in the 1950s to estimate costs of airplanes capable of flying at nearly twice the speed of sound. Costs might be predicted even though no aircraft had yet been designed that could actually attain this performance characteristic.

By observing twenty or thirty past aircraft development and procurement programs, statistical relationships can be estimated that relate a cost element, such as manufacturing labor hours, manufacturing material cost, or sustaining engineering, to (1) physical characteristics such as weight or length and (2) performance characteristics such as maximum speed, ferry range, combat radius, or maximum thrust. There is no reason why dams, roads, or schools cannot be studied similarly. Note that dollar costs are not predicted, but resource cost such as labor hours is the unit used wherever possible. This finesses the inflation problem.

Examples of CERs for materials and engineering costs are:[26]

$$C_{M,100} = -21 + 1100W^{-0.5} + 11S_a + 15T$$
$$C_E = 14 \ S_K^{0.54} \ W^{0.88}$$

where

$C_{M,100}$ = manufacturing materials cost per pound of airframe weight at unit 100
$C_E$ = nonrecurring airframe engineering cost
$W$ = airframe weight in pounds
$S_a$ = maximum speed in mach number
$S_K$ = maximum speed in knots
$T$ = log $(Y - 1944)$ where $Y$ = year of first delivery

An application to the field of medical care shows the influence of physical (size) and performance (capabilities) characteristics on hospital costs. The following equation was estimated from observations on 3,147 U.S. voluntary short-term general hospitals:[27]

$$ATC = -307,568 + .351 \times 10^{-4} \ PD^2 - .31 \ (S \times PD) + 23 \times 10^3 \ NS$$
$$(.029) \qquad\qquad (.07) \qquad\qquad (31.6)$$
$$+ 5,034 \ IR + 34.70 \ PD + 33.8 \times 10^3 \ S$$
$$(617) \qquad (1.19) \qquad (3.6)$$
$$+ 4.81 \ OPV - 1,805 \ N + 55.3 \times 10^3 \ IRP \qquad\qquad (3)$$
$$(.34) \qquad (295) \qquad (5.5)$$
$$+ 174.8 \times 10^3 \ MS$$
$$(43.7)$$

where

$ATC$ = adjusted total cost per year, adjusted to omit the geographical influence on wage rates
$PD$ = patient days per year, a measure of size or rate of output
$S$ = the number of services out of the first 28 listed by the American Hospital Association in its annual yearbook, *Hospitals*
$NS$ = a dummy variable that indicates the presence of a professional nursing school controlled by the hospital

---

[26] Harry P. Hatry, "The Use of Cost Estimates," in Thomas A. Goldman, ed., *Cost-Effectiveness Analysis* (New York: Praeger, 1967), p. 56.

[27] W. John Carr and Paul J. Feldstein, "The Relationship of Cost to Hospital Size," *Inquiry* 4, no. 2 (June 1967): 45–65.

$IR$ = number of interns and residents
$OPV$ = number of outpatient visits
$N$ = number of student nurses
$IRP$ = number of internship and residency programs offered
$MS$ = a dummy variable which indicates affiliation with a medical
      school

Total costs increased significantly with patient days and its square, the fifth and first variables, respectively. Costs increase significantly as the number of facilities and services available increase and if and to the extent that hospitals provide out-patient visits (sixth and seventh variables). Costs also increase with educational programs offered: number of internship and residency programs, number of interns and residents, and affiliation with a medical school. Having a nursing school apparently does not significantly increase costs. Each nurse actually decreases costs, perhaps because they contribute services in on-the-job training worth more than what they earn.

The significantly negative effect of the interaction of the number of services offered and the number of patient-days, $S \times PD$, the second variable, is problematic. When hospitals were stratified by service-capability group and regressions computed within groups, most $S \times PD$ coefficients were positive. The coefficient of multiple determination of equation (3) is .947.

That the rate of output, as roughly measured by $PD$, significantly affects cost is well known from the economics literature. This suggests the next influence of quantity on costs, the subject of scale economies and the optimal size of public facilities.

### Rate of Output: Cost Functions

There are many examples of the influence of rate of output on unit cost. Adam Smith lauded the "extraordinary advantage" to be gained by "a division of labour in [the] art"[28] of the pin-maker. Usually emphasis is placed on *economies of scale*, cost savings to be achieved by a large rate of output.

Figure 10.3, illustrates the phenomenon. The cost in shillings per ton of transporting crude oil declines uniformly as the size of tanker increases. Three ranges are evident: small ships could carry oil to Europe through the Suez Canal and return with ballast (water) in their holds via the same canal. Larger ships, when laden with oil, must travel around the Cape of Good Hope because the canal is not deep enough. Their cost

[28] Adam Smith, *The Wealth of Nations,* Great Books of the Western World (Chicago: Encyclopedia Britannica, 1952), p. 3.

FIGURE 10.3 COMPARATIVE COSTS OF TRANSPORTING
CRUDE OIL BY VARIOUS SIZES OF TANKER

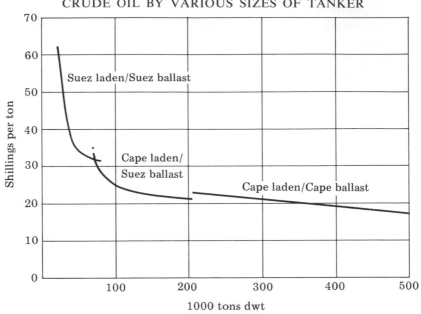

        Source: "The Challenge of Large Tankers" (Shell International Petroleum Co. Ltd.,
October, 1969).

per unit is approximately half that of ships with a smaller capacity. Finally, the super-tanker is so big that it must run around the cape even
with water in its hold. By economies of scale, however, it can cut seven
shillings off the average of twenty-five shillings per ton cost which characterizes the medium-size ship. Supertankers are about three times as
large as the medium-size vessels and about eight times the size of conventional ships.

    As a firm increases its rate of output without increasing its capital
stock or fixed costs, it achieves lower unit costs by spreading fixed costs
over more units of output. This might be called an *economy of density*
because the density of output per unit of capital is increasing. An economy of density, as opposed to an economy of scale is movement down
a short-run average cost curve. In the long run, the amount of fixed factor
used by a firm can change. The term economies of scale should be reserved for the long-run phenomenon. An example of this distinction
arises in transportation. An economy of density occurs when more trains
can be run over a given roadbed at lower cost per ton-mile of freight.
Economies of density cease when *capacity* is reached, where capacity
is defined as the minimum point on the short-run average cost curve.

Perhaps the most restrictive concept is *increasing returns to scale,* a type of economy of scale. When all inputs are multiplied by the same factor and physical output increases more than proportionately, increasing returns to scale obtains. This is stronger than declining average cost.

*Production Functions and Cost Functions.* Returns to scale can be studied by estimating either production functions or "cost functions." There is a duality between these two; once we have one, we can derive the other.[29] A production function is a mathematical relationship between inputs and output. For convenience let us use the following form:

$$Y = A K^{\alpha} L^{\beta} \qquad (4)$$

where $K$, $L$ are capital and labor and $A$, $\alpha$, $\beta$ parameters to be estimated. If we assume that output $\overline{Y}$ must be produced and that firms endeavor to minimize costs, given factor prices $r$ and $w$ for capital and labor respectively, the objective of the enterprise is to minimize cost

$$C = rK + wL.$$

The cost-minimizing values of $K$ and $L$, when substituted in the cost expression, yield the following cost function:[30]

$$C(\overline{Y},r,w) = D \ \overline{Y}^{1/\Sigma} \ r^{\alpha/\Sigma} \ w^{\beta/\Sigma} \qquad (5)$$

where $\Sigma = \alpha + \beta$, the degree of returns to scale of the production function and $D = A^{-1/\Sigma} \left[ \left(\dfrac{\alpha}{\beta}\right)^{\beta/\Sigma} + \left(\dfrac{\beta}{\alpha}\right)^{\alpha/\Sigma} \right]$.

In equation (5) total cost is a function of the constrained level of output, $\overline{Y}$, and the factor prices, $r$ and $w$. Total cost increases as $\overline{Y}$ increases because both $\alpha$ and $\beta$ are positive.

Average cost is $C/\overline{Y}$

$$\frac{C}{\overline{Y}} = \overline{Y}^{(1-\Sigma)/\Sigma} \ r^{\alpha/\Sigma} \ w^{\beta/\Sigma} \ D. \qquad (6)$$

If $\Sigma > 1$, $\overline{Y}$ has a negative exponent in (6) so that average cost decreases as $\overline{Y}$ increases. This is the case of "increasing returns to scale" because if both $K$ and $L$ are multiplied by $k$ in (4), $Y$ will be multiplied by $k^{\alpha+\beta}$ which is greater than $k$. Equation (5) shows that the elasticity[31] of cost

[29]The existence of this duality depends on some assumption as to optimization. The cost minimization assumption we use below is the most frequently used.

[30]From an econometric point of view, it is preferable to estimate (5) rather than (4) because (5) is a reduced form with only predetermined variables on the right-hand side, while (4) is subject to the "simultaneous equations" problem because K and L are jointly dependent variables. See J. Marschak and Andrews "Random Simultaneous Equations and the Theory of Production," *Econometrica* 12 (July-October 1944): 143–205.

[31]Elasticity of cost with respect to output is $\dfrac{\partial C}{\partial Y} \dfrac{Y}{C}$.

with respect to output is $1/\Sigma$. This is the inverse of the sum of the elasticities of output with respect to inputs. Hence, there is a reciprocal relationship between the (average) cost and the production function: increasing returns to scale implies decreasing costs; decreasing returns to scale implies increasing costs (assuming constant factor prices).

The "cost function" referred to above is a technical term whose arguments are factor prices and output. Cost expressions studied by Johnston,[32] for example, were simpler relations between cost and output. The relationship between cost and output was sought while factor prices remained constant. Account was taken of varying factor prices by "deflating" costs from different years or geographical areas by price indexes. Another way to hold variables constant to perceive the net effect of another variable is to enter the variables to be held constant in a regression equation. Marc Nerlove was the first to enter factor prices explicitly in the "cost function."[33]

*Cost Function for U.S. Post Offices.* To illustrate the use of cost functions, let us summarize a study of large U.S. post offices.[34]

Merewitz sought to determine optimal post office size, considering output that is fixed exogenously. Offices must handle as much mail as people put into the system, and try to minimize costs subject to constraints on five outputs. Cost functions were estimated for the entire sample of 156 offices and for three subsamples: small, medium, and large.

The overall cost function led to a conclusion of decreasing returns to scale in post offices. Breaking the sample into parts showed that to posit a single production or cost function holding throughout the range of size variation is an oversimplification.[35] The phenomenon of increasing returns to scale in small offices persisted in medium-sized offices, but decreasing returns to scale set in among the 52 largest offices. Therefore, Merewitz concluded that the optimal size of office is in the medium range, with about 1,400 employees. The New York city office (including many stations) had over 38,000 employees in 1966.

This finding, of decreasing returns to scale might suggest that all post offices among the largest 156 in the country were already too large. In fact, most offices of the 32,000 or so in the country are too small and ought to be amalgamated for efficiency. Only the largest fifty or so are too big.

[32]J. Johnston, *Statistical Cost Analysis* (New York: McGraw-Hill, 1960).

[33]Marc Nerlove, "Return to Scale in Electricity Supply," in C. Christ, ed., *Measurement in Economics* (Stanford, Cal.: Stanford University Press, 1963), pp. 167–98.

[34]Leonard Merewitz, "Cost and Returns to Scale in U.S. Post Offices," *Journal of the American Statistical Association* 66, no. 335 (September 1971).

[35]We can test formally for the statistical validity of the stratification by comparing the sum of squared errors in the stratified model (three cost functions) with that in the simpler model of a single cost function for the entire sample. An F-test shows that the three cost functions significantly reduce residual variation, thus justifying the stratification.

Further analysis on deviations from cost functions suggested a regional dummy variable: offices in the northeastern and far western sections tended to be more costly than others. Because of roughly constant national wages high-quality labor was more difficult to recruit and retain there. When that geographical adjustment was made, results were even more precise. The overall cost function as estimated, including the dummy variable, NEFW, equal to one if a post office is in the northeastern or far western part of the country was

$$c = -5.42 + .52\ x_1 + .40\ x_2 + .04\ x_3 + .11\ x_4 + .06\ x_5 - .01 v_6$$
$$\quad\ (.51)\ (.04)\quad (.05)\quad (.03)\quad (.03)\quad (.03)\quad (.01)\qquad (7)$$
$$+ 1.57\ w_7 + .12\ w_8 - .02\ SC + .08\ NEFW$$
$$\quad (.30)\qquad (.05)\qquad (.04)\qquad (.03)$$
$$R^2 = .981$$

This study considered the influence of several outputs on costs. To assert that output levels alone determine cost would be an oversimplification and a misspecification. Factor prices and regional variations significantly influenced cost as well.

When a cost function such as (7) has been estimated, it is useful not only for its implications as to economies of scale but because it can be used as a budgetary aid. It gives cost as a function of rate of output and factor prices under an assumption of cost minimization by the organization. Thus it allows one to predict the impact on an organization's budget of an increase in factor prices such as the wage rate or the cost of materials or floorspace. For example, if wage rates were to increase by 8 percent, and post offices were to reach a new cost-minimizing equilibrium, the impact of this increase on an office's costs could be estimated by the coefficient of the wage rate in the cost function. In this case it appears to be about 12.6 percent.

### Cumulative Outputs: The Learning Curve

In the production of airplanes at Wright-Patterson Air Force Base in 1925, a phenomenon was noticed that has come to be called the "learning curve" or "learning by doing."[36] It was observed again independently in private industry at the Buffalo plant of Curtiss-Wright.[37] It is based on the fact that the more frequently a manufacturing operation is performed, the less direct labor it requires. In airplane manufacturing, it

[36]Miguel Reguero, *An Economic Study of the Military Airframe Industry* (Dayton, Ohio: Wright-Patterson Air Force Base, Department of the Air Force, October 1957), p. 213. Another standard reference is Harold Asher, *Cost-Quantity Relationships in the Airframe Industry,* R-291 (Santa Monica: The RAND Corporation, July 1956).

[37]T. P. Wright, "Factors Affecting the Cost of Airplanes," *Journal of Aeronautical Science* 3 (February 1936): 122–28.

FIGURE 10.4. LEARNING CURVE ON LOGARITHMIC SCALES

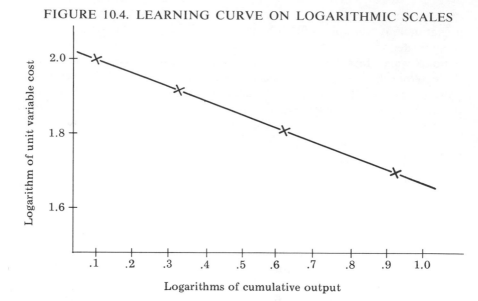

Logarithms of cumulative output

is frequently found that direct labor hours for the tenth airframe of a particular type manufactured are less than half those required for the first airframe.

Learning curves are often depicted as straight lines with negative slope where both axes are in logarithmic scales (See Figure 10.4) or as a curved line with negative slope on arithmetic scales (Figure 10.5). The basic point is that average cost declines as more cumulative output is produced and more learning is accomplished.

A learning curve can be expressed mathematically as

$$x_1 = ax_2^b$$

where $x_1$ is average direct labor input per unit and $x_2$ is the cumulative number of units produced. The constant $b$ is called the "slope" of the curve although it is really the elasticity of average labor costs with respect to cumulative output. It is sometimes called the "progress elasticity." If we transform to logarithms, as in Figure 10.4, it is the slope. The constant $a$ is the unit labor cost for the first unit.

Figures 10.4 and 10.5 depict the "80 percent learning curve": doubling output results in average unit costs 80 percent of former costs. The $b$ for such a curve is $-0.32$. The percentage decline in unit cost associated with a doubling of cumulative output is sometimes called the *progress ratio* which in this case is 20.[38]

[38]Werner Z. Hirsch, "Firm Progress Ratios," *Econometrica* 24 (1956): 136–43.

# FIGURE 10.5 DECLINING VARIABLE UNIT COST, 80 PERCENT LEARNING CURVE

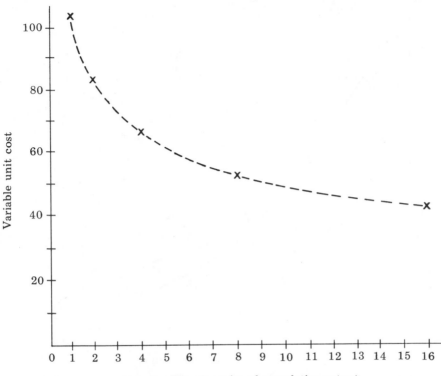

Length of run in units of cumulative output

There is much potential for learning where the job being performed is labor intensive. For example, airframe manufacture is about three-fourths assembly and one-fourth machine work. It often displays a learning curve of nearly 80 percent.[39] Human-paced operations are more susceptible to learning by doing than machine-paced operations.

The learning curve continues beyond what might be expected. Hirschmann claims it continues forever: no ceiling on learning exists.[40] Alchian claims, "There is evidence which seems to indicate that older, more experienced manufacturing facilities have a greater rate of decline than do new facilities."[41] Hirsch further substantiated this hypothesis,

[39] Winfred B. Hirschmann, "Profit from the Learning Curve," *Harvard Business Review* 42 (January-February 1964): 128.

[40] Hirschmann, "Profit from the Learning Curve," p. 138.

[41] Armen Alchian, "An Airframe Production Function," *Project RAND*, P-108 (1949), p. 12. See also "Reliability of Progress Curves in Airframe Production," *Econometrica* 21, no. 4 (October 1963): 679–93.

FIGURE 10.6. AVERAGE COST AND CUMULATIVE OUTPUT
FOR DIVISION OF DISBURSEMENT, TREASURY DEPARTMENT

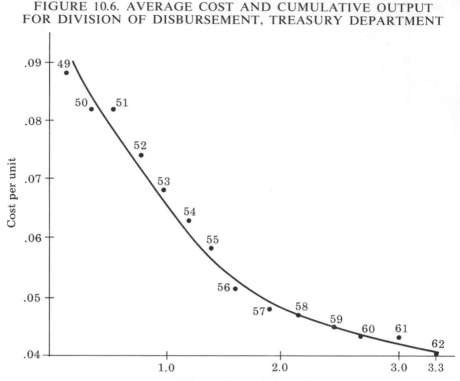

Millions of cumulative units

finding that "the progress ratio increases with experience: the more experience a manufacturer has, the greater the progress ratio promises
to be."[42]

The 80 percent learning curve is not found everywhere. Hirsch found
progress ratios averaging 24.6 percent in assembly of machine tools and
12.9 percent in machining those tools. Assembly is more labor intensive
and more limited by human factors than by machine factors. Hirschmann
displays a 76 percent learning curve for maintenance at a General Electric plant, and an 80 percent curve for construction of fluid catalytic
cracking units.

A learning curve for the Division of Disbursements, Department of
the Treasury[43] is given in Figures 10.6 and 10.7, on arithmetic and logarithmic scales respectively. The logarithmic data (Figure 10.7) may

[42] Hirsch, "Firm Progress Ratios," p. 143.

[43] U.S. Bureau of the Budget, *Measuring Productivity of Federal Government Organizations* (Washington, D.C.: U.S. Government Printing Office, 1964), p. 101, Table 20.

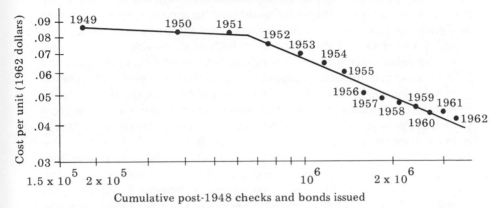

FIGURE 10.7. AVERAGE COST VERSUS CUMULATIVE OUTPUT
IN LOGARITHMS FOR DIVISION OF DISBURSEMENT,
TREASURY DEPARTMENT

Cumulative post-1948 checks and bonds issued

be summarized by breaking the curve into two periods, 1949–51, and
1952–62. During the first period the division was characterized by a
95 percent learning curve. The progress ratio was brought up to 26 percent in the second period, perhaps through the introduction of electronic
data processing methods of accounting and disbursal.

Preston and Keachie have examined the factors of rate of output
and cumulative output in a single study.[44] They concluded that both
factors, the one stressed by the economists (lot size) and the one stressed
by engineers (cumulative output) are significant in explaining costs. But
in all instances they studied, cumulative output was a more powerful
explanatory variable than lot size. Cumulative output was more important
in explaining changes in unit labor costs than changes in unit total (labor,
materials, and machine services) costs.

### Procurement Practices

The type of procurement contract used by the procuring agency
affects costs. During World War I so-called "cost plus percent of cost"
contracts were used for military procurement. These arrangements were
hasty and on the whole successful, but one can readily see that such
contracts not only gave the contracting firm no incentive to hold costs
down, but actually gave it an incentive to make costs high to increase
its earnings. Such blatant types of "blank-check" contracts were out-

[44]L. E. Preston and E. C. Keachie, "Cost Functions and Progress Functions: An
Integration," *American Economic Review* 54, no. 2, Part I (March 1964): 100–7.

lawed in the first War Powers Act of 1941.[45] Nevertheless, procurement of medical services, especially hospital services, were very similarly and hastily organized for Medicare recipients. "The inescapable question being raised is whether it is feasible for the government to guarantee any group or profession payment at any level the group may unilaterally elect."[46] The BART District's contract with its consulting engineers provided for reimbursement of 1.9 times salaries of all field employees and 2.25 times salaries of office employees, a generous cost-plus arrangement.

A distinction must be drawn between procurement involving development of new technology and that requiring production according to a known technology. The first is exemplified by procurement of advanced military systems; the second by "off-the-shelf" items such as uniforms. In the first case, much uncertainty is present and the scarce resources are time and technology, while cost is a relatively minor consideration. In the second case, cost is a major consideration because less uncertainty is involved. Procurement of medical services is in the second category.

It is not clear how relevant the experience in procuring advanced weapon systems is to the procurement of medical services or urban rapid transit systems, but some studies have been done of military contracting. The many forms of procurement contracts are discussed in the work of Peck and Scherer.[47] A spectrum of contract types is used, from very permissive cost reimbursement to the strict firm-fixed-price contract. No one type is best in every situation. Each has its justification in the uncertainty of the project and the amount of risk the contractor is asked to bear.

How a contractor is selected is also important because of its impact on final costs experienced. The federal government is required by law to conduct competitive bidding in certain circumstances. In other circumstances a design, prototype, or management competition is held to determine which contractor should receive the award. When conditions allow, the government endeavors to have more than one source for a particular item. Then it is assured continued access to the item should there be a work stoppage at a particular plant.

[45]55 *U.S. Statutes at Large,* 838f. Cost plus percentage was again outlawed by the Armed Services Procurement Act of 1948. 10 *U.S. Code* Section 2306 (a).

[46]The Brookings Institution, *The Future of Medicare and the American Hospital,* highlights of H. M. and A. R. Somers, *Medicare and the Hospitals: Issues and Prospects,* Brookings Research Report No. 72 (Washington, D.C.: The Brookings Institution, 1967), p. 5.

[47]M. J. Peck and Frederic M. Scherer, *The Weapons Acquisition Process* (Boston: Division of Research, Graduate School of Business Administration, Harvard University, 1962). Also, see Frederic M. Scherer, *The Weapons Acquisition Process: Economic Incentives* (Boston: Division of Research, Graduate School of Business Administration, Harvard University, 1964).

## CONCLUSION

This exploration of the cost side of benefit-cost analysis started with an explanation of the various types of costs relevant to public spending programs. We have seen that the best one can expect from an attempt to evaluate a project's social costs is a judgmental estimate of the project's effect on the government's demand for funds. Social costs are difficult if not impossible to measure. The difficulty of measuring project outlays has been recounted. Ways of dealing with inflation were discussed as well as the behavior of project outlays over time. We explored the factors that influence cost: physical and performance characteristics, rate of output, cumulative output, and procurement practices. Now that we have covered both the benefit and cost side of benefit-cost analysis let us see how these techniques have been employed in making decisions about the spending of public monies.

# Eleven

# BENEFIT-COST ANALYSIS IN PRACTICE

Benefit-cost analysis is most often used for planning large-scale public investments. Two such investments are the California Water Project (CWP) and the U.S. supersonic transport (SST) project.

In this chapter we review the records on the CWP and the SST to observe how benefit-cost analysis has been used in justifying and modifying each. We shall see that benefit-cost analysis has had only minimal impact on public policy in these two cases. Both projects have been evaluated several times from several points of view, but efficiency criteria have been largely ignored in the decisions to proceed.

## THE CALIFORNIA WATER PROJECT

The CWP has been discussed for two decades, and it has been controversial for many reasons. The source of water for the state is in the north. At first, northern California believed the southern section of the state was stealing water that rightfully belonged in the north. Some southern Californians (notably the Los Angeles Metropolitan Water District), feared the north would one day reclaim its water. Most economists who studied the project opposed it. The most recent attack has been on ecological grounds.

The CWP can be divided into three parts: the Feather River Project including the Oroville Reservoir, the California Aqueduct, and the Dos Rios project on the Eel River. The Feather River Project is intended to provide interseasonal transfer of water for irrigation and for domestic and industrial use, to create recreational lakes, to generate hydroelectric power, and to provide flood control. Water from the Feather River is to

TABLE 11.1. CALIFORNIA WATER PLAN
ESTIMATED CAPITAL EXPENDITURES 1952–85
(millions of dollars)

| | |
|---|---:|
| Upper Feather River Division | 27.3 |
| Oroville Division | 497.4 |
| North Bay Aqueduct | 16.5 |
| South Bay Aqueduct | 66.4 |
| California Aqueduct | 1,730.5 |
| Middle Fork Eel River Development | 162.9 |
| Delta Facilities | 148.8 |
| San Joaquin Drainage Facilities | 7.8 |
| Davis-Grunsky Loans & Grants (Recreation) | 130.0 |
| | 2,795.7 |

Source: State of California, Department of Water Resources, *The California Water Project in 1969*, Appendix C. Description and Status (Bulletin No. 132–69, June 1969).

be transferred via a peripheral canal[1] to the California Aqueduct whence it will be delivered to customers in the San Joaquin Valley and Southern California. The Eel River development is intended to reroute water south to San Francisco Bay from its normal flow northward into the Pacific Ocean near Eureka. Table 11.1 shows the principal features of the CWP and the cost of each to the state. The Eel River development cost does not appear large because the federal government's share would be another $245 million. The federal government is also involved in Oroville Reservoir, because of its importance in flood control.

Our reason for investigating the CWP is to study the impact of benefit-cost analysis on public decision-making. Benefit-cost analysis has not in fact had much impact on this project because the techniques were not applied to the project until major government commitments had already been made. Nevertheless, the project's history shows some ways benefit-cost analysis is apt to be abused. Costs have been grossly understated, benefits have been overstated, and poor or misguided economic analysis has been employed.

### Chronology and Studies

The California Water Plan was the brainchild of State Engineer A. D. Edmonston, who delivered a report to the legislature in May, 1951.[2]

[1] It is called "peripheral" because it is on the eastern and southern periphery of the delta formed by Sacramento, Stockton, and the intersection of the Sacramento and San Joaquin Rivers.

[2] A. D. Edmonston, *Report on the Feasibility of the Feather River Project and Sacramento-San Joaquin Delta Diversion Projects Proposed as Features of the California Water Plan*, Sacramento (1951).

A more serious proposal[3] made in 1955 motivated the legislature to seek a professional opinion on the engineering and economic feasibility of the plan. This report, by the Bechtel Corporation, has been cited as both an approval of and an unfavorable report on the plan.[4] The contradictions, unfortunately, are internal and inescapable. The report claimed that the project was feasible from an engineering and a financial point of view. But a financial analysis, quite different from an economic analysis, asks only if the beneficiaries would actually pay the costs of the project. The Bechtel *Report* did not even answer that question, but asked instead if somewhere the money for the project could be found. It answered affirmatively by including in the revenues of the project contributions from the State's General Fund, which are, of course, not revenues but a subsidy. Obviously, any project could be justified on such a test of financial feasibility. The Bechtel *Report* further favored the project by using the then current cost to the State of borrowed funds: 2.7 percent. In 1970, however, the state was not able to borrow funds at 5 percent; it sought and won the authority to pay 7 percent.

The next document to study the CWP was the first criticism.[5] Neuner, an economist, showed that cost allocations of the project did not generate enough revenue to pay for it. Although he objected to the use of the low interest rate, he continued to use it in his calculations. Later, a group of six ULCA graduate engineering students reported on the CWP in 1958.[6] This imaginative study incorporated a sensitivity analysis using four discount rates. The authors also considered reclaiming water from sewage as an alternative of importing water from northern California.

Perhaps the best known critics of the CWP are DeHaven and Hirshleifer, who published a critique[7] in 1957 in which they reckoned costs of water delivered (by two routes) to southern California at $48 and $83 per acre-foot (af). The 1955 *Program* of the Division of Water Resources had forecast a cost of only $45. The interest rate used in the 1957 critique was 5 percent.

[3] Division of Water Resources, *Program for Financing and Constructing the Feather River Project as the Initial Unit of the California Water Plan,* Sacramento (February 1955).

[4] Bechtel Corporation, *Report on the Engineering, Economic and Financial Aspects of the Feather River Project,* San Francisco (1955).

[5] E. Neuner, Jr., "Economics of the Proposed Feather River Project," *Proceedings of the 31st Annual Conference of the Western Economic Association, August 1956,* Salt Lake City (1957).

[6] H. Zeitzew, D. A. Meier, J. C. Monroe, E. H. Lynch, M. S. Mann, and F. J. Seufert, "An Economic Study of Water Supply for Southern California" (M. A. thesis, Department of Engineering, University of California at Los Angeles, 1958).

[7] J. C. DeHaven and Jack Hirshleifer, "Feather River Water for Southern California," *Land Economics* 33 (August 1957): 198–209.

A later study by Hirshleifer, DeHaven, and Milliman[8] found the Feather River Project (FRP) uneconomical at a 3.5 percent discount rate. At that rate FRP water cost $63 per af while small increments of water could be obtained from the Colorado River at $15 per af and a million af per year could be obtained at $50 per af. When a 6 percent interest rate was used, FRP water went up in cost to $105 per af.

By 1960 they believed 10 percent was the most appropriate discount rate. Using the lower-cost route, water at this discount rate would cost $221. By the higher-cost route, it would cost $287 per af.[9]

By 1957 the first legislative appropriations for the FRP had been made. The legislature and the Division of Water Resources were becoming committed to the project without adequate economic analyses.

Bulletin No. 78,[10] issued in February, 1959, described three alternative aqueduct routes. A publication of the bureaucracy, it was, of course, optomistic about the prospects of the plan, finding a benefit-cost ratio on the optimal route of 2.38. The prospectus used a 3.5 percent discount rate and a 105-year life. It estimated capital costs at $1.807 billion, not including the cost of Oroville, which eventually cost nearly $500 million.

In 1960 the Hirshleifer, DeHaven, and Milliman study predicted an ultimate cost for the CWP of $3 billion. In 1966 an estimate of $2.5 billion was made. In 1967 a task force appointed by Governor Reagan estimated costs at $2.825 billion—making prophets out of Hirshleifer, DeHaven, and Milliman. Latest state cost estimates at this writing are $2.796 billion.[11] The present value of gross benefits was estimated at $2 billion for irrigation and $5.6 billion for municipal and industrial water supply. A private report circulated among legislators before the bond election estimated the benefit-cost ratio at 1.3 using a 4 percent discount rate and an 80-year economic life.

Benefits were grossly overestimated in the state's *Bulletin No. 78*. This study valued urban water in desert areas at $150 per af. If transferred from irrigation canals, its cost would be $30 per af. Irrigation water, however, was not to be used, and the basis of the $150 value was an alternative cost calculation of sea water desalination. Nevertheless, demand forecasts were based on the unjustified low price of $32 per af.

[8] Jack Hirshleifer, J. C. DeHaven, and Jerome W. Milliman, *Water Supply* (Chicago: University of Chicago Press, 1960), p. 319, Table 44.

[9] Hirshleifer, DeHaven, and Milliman, *Water Supply,* pp. 341ff., Tables 48 and 49.

[10] California Department of Water Resources, *Investigation of Alternative Aqueduct Systems to Serve Southern California—Feather River and Delta Diversion Projects,* Bulletin No. 78, Sacramento (1959).

[11] California Department of Water Resources, *The California State Water Project in 1969,* Bulletin No. 132-69 (June 1969), Appendix C, p. 6.

These calculations are unrealistic and a sham. Both the state legislature and the Department of Water Resources had already declared that benefit-cost analysis does not furnish a proper guide to investment planning. The technique, they held, does not adequately reflect the public interest or political and economic considerations.[12]

Just before the bond authorization election in November, 1960, many tracts appeared. Hirshleifer and DeHaven wrote *Water Supply for Southern California: Rationalization or Expansion* in August. They held that more efficient pricing was a viable alternative to the FRP. Higher prices would induce people to recycle water where possible and, in general, treat it as the precious commodity it is in southern California. They recounted examples of water-saving behavior induced in other sections of the country. Under their leadership 50 professors of economics, business, and engineering at the Universities of Southern California, Stanford, and California (Berkeley and Los Angeles) signed a resolution condemning the bond proposal. The state legislature commissioned a feasibility report on the FRP by Charles T. Main, Inc.,[13] of Boston and a report on finance by Dillon, Read and Co.,[14] of New York. The financial report merely asked if the State could market the general obligation bonds. It was interesting to note how two different newspapers covered these reports: "Feather River Project Gets Sound Rating in Two Reports," and "State Water Plan Called Impossible." The first was the headline in the Los Angeles *Times,* which supported the project; the second was in the San Francisco *Chronicle,* which opposed it. Clearly, it was possible for both papers to read what they wanted into the two reports. Essentially, what did the reports say? They indicated that a $1.75 billion bond issue would be adequate to finance the aqueduct in the absence of much inflation, but they counseled deferring the construction of Oroville Dam for twenty years. Little wonder that there was a good deal of confusion among the voters on the issue.

The bond issue was finally approved by a margin of only 3 percent of those voting. The northern counties rejected the proposition; the southern counties, heavily in favor and with large voter turnouts, barely carried the day.

[12]See California State Water Resources Board, *The California Water Plan,* Bulletin No. 3, Sacramento (1957), pp. 223f; and California State Legislature, Assembly Water Committee, *Economic and Financial Policies for the State Water Project,* vol. 26, no. 1 (1960), pp. 11–16.

[13]Charles T. Main, Inc., *General Evaluation of the Proposed Program for Financing and Constructing the State Water Resources Development System of the State of California Department of Water Resources,* Final Report, Boston (1970).

[14]Dillon, Read and Co., Inc., *Interim Report of Financial Consultants to State of California Department of Water Resources on Financial Aspects of Program for State Water Resources Development System* (New York: Dillon, Read and Co., Inc., 1960).

A retrospective evaluation of the FRP in 1964 by Julius Margolis showed that it was "generally oversized or included large uneconomical segments."[15] At reasonable discount rates of 5 or 6 percent and economic lives of 50 to 80 years, benefit-cost ratios ranged from .69 to .90. Only at low rates of 3 and 4 percent did the benefit-cost ratio exceed unity; for example, 1.32 at a rate of 3 percent for an 80-year economic life.[16]

Revenue-cost ratios, in present values as of 1960, indicators of financial feasibility, are of the same orders of magnitude as benefit-cost ratios. The FRP is financially feasible only at a 3 percent rate of discount with an 80-year life. It will collect a larger fraction of its costs from its beneficiaries than will the Central Valley Project, built by the Bureau of Reclamation, or most other water resources projects. Thus, a lower fraction of the costs will accrue to the general taxpayer than is typical in such enterprises.

A benefit-cost analysis of the peripheral canal to take water from the Sacramento River to the California Aqueduct for shipment south was made by the Bureau of Reclamation,[17] which considered it part of the Central Valley Project. Like other parts of the CWP, it was to be a joint federal-state venture. Total construction costs would be $209 million, base power transfer would cost $5.1 million, and interest during construction would be $21.3 million. Total investment costs would be $235 million. Amortized over a 100-year economic life with interest calculated at 3.25 percent, annual equivalent capital costs were $7.7 million. OMR costs amounted to $1.5 million, for total annual costs of $9.2 million.

Benefits were expected in the recreation, fish and wildlife, irrigation, and municipal and industrial water supply areas. To estimate recreation benefits the Bureau enlisted the aid of the National Park Service, which estimated benefits in accordance with Senate Document 97, Supplement No. 1. One million vistor-days were expected in 1972 and valued at $1.16 each. In the year 2000, 2.5 million vistor-days were expected at a value of $1.36 per visitor-day, a higher value "due principally to the development of facilities to meet increased demand over time."[18] Recreation benefits (excluding fishing and hunting) thus would average $2.2 million per year. Fish and wildlife benefits, for example, were esti-

[15]Joe S. Bain, Richard Caves, and Julius Margolis, *Northern California's Water Industry* (Baltimore: John Hopkins Press, 1966), p. 571.

[16]Bain, Caves, and Margolis, *Northern California's Water Industry,* p. 569, Table 32.

[17]U.S. Department of the Interior, Bureau of Reclamation, Region 2, *Peripheral Canal Unit, Central Valley Project, California: A Report on the Feasibility of Water Supply Development*, Sacramento (September 1968).

[18]U.S. Department of the Interior, *Peripheral Canal Unit*, "Appended Material from National Park Service and Bureau of Outdoor Recreation," p. 20.

mated at $3.50 per man-day of fishing for striped bass, $6.00 per man-day for ocean sport or river sport, and $0.50 per nature study user-day. Fishing and hunting benefits totaled $3.6 million per year. Irrigation benefits, both direct and indirect, were attributed at $4 and $3 million per year respectively, and municipal water supply at $3.5 million per year. Total annual benefits were $16.5 million and the benefit-cost ratio was 1.8 on the joint project. The benefit-cost ratio was 1.5 if only direct benefits were counted.

In 1970 the Peripheral Canal was a controversial issue because of mass interest in ecology. This 43-mile canal deprives San Francisco Bay of a major part of the inflow from the Sacramento and Feather Rivers. Opponents of the canal claim that high inflows of fresh water from the Sacramento are necessary to abate salinity and water pollution from irrigation nitrates and industrial pollutants in San Fransisco Bay. This point of view was corroborated by a U.S. Geological Survey report, *San Franscisco Bay Urban Resources Study,* released in July, 1970. The California Department of Water Resources countered by claiming that tidal action is the principal mechanism by which pollutants are removed from the bay, far overwhelming the effects of river outflows from the delta. But the solution proposed to ameliorate the problem of the Peripheral Canal, the Dos Rios Dam, has problems of its own, and it is unlikely that the Peripheral Canal will be changed because it is the *sine qua non* of geographical water transfer from North to South.

The Dos Rios Dam in the Eel River is intended to replace the flushing water the San Francisco Bay loses to the Peripheral Canal. Water on its way downstream to Eureka and the ocean can be pumped back uphill and used in the bay. But conservationist interests are opposed because the Dos Rios will flood a valley, inundating agricultural land, the town of Covelo, and an Indian and deer habitat, and will destroy the salmon population of the Eel River. All these things have been done before, so theoretically, at least, compensation could be made to those directly hurt.

The Corps of Engineers subjected the Middle Fork Eel River Project to analysis in April 1968.[19] Investment costs were $438.5 million. With a 3.25 percent interest rate and a 100-year life, interest and amortization amounts to $14.9 million per year, OMR costs to $0.7 million per year. Flood control benefits were estimated at $1.27 million per year for flood damages prevented and $0.29 for higher land utilization. Water supply benefits were estimated two ways. By alternative costs of a substitute single-purpose reservoir they were $14.9 million. But "a truer

[19]U.S. Army Engineer District, *Eel River Basin California: Interim Report,* San Francisco (April 1968).

index of . . . water supply benefits, particularly for the Southern California area where a large part of the exported water is to be delivered, can be taken as the cost for desalinization of brackish or sea water."[20] The Corps thus values water at the higher alternative-cost value of $29 per acre-foot for an annual benefit of 26.1 million. Choosing the *higher* of two alternative costs as a measure of benefits is unjustified. In Chapter 10 we saw that the *least costly* alternative way of delivering the same amount of clean water might be used as a proxy for the *maximum possible* benefits.

Recreation was valued at $1.40 per day for $1.21 million in annual benefits, and hydroelectric power benefits were estimated at $0.21 million on the assumption of a 4,800 kw generator operating at full capacity. Additional benefits of $0.17 and $3.4 million respectively for the cost of floods to the nation and "Public-Works-and-Economic-Development" were not included in the benefit-cost ratio. They are a type of income distribution benefit calculated because Glenn, Trinity, and Mendocino Counties qualify for assistance under the Public Works and Economic Development Act of 1965.

Total annual benefits are thus $29 million—almost entirely for water supply. The claimed benefit-cost ratio was 1.9. At the interest rate the State has to pay in 1970, nearly 7 percent, the project is not economically feasible.[21]

In May 1969 Governor Reagan announced that he had directed the State Department of Water Resources to work with the Corps of Engineers to develop alternatives to constructing the Dos Rios Dam and to flooding Round Valley. The Department and the Corps have reported that no good alternatives are feasible. Nevertheless, experts believe that the Dos Rios project is defunct. We can only speculate on why it was stopped. It may be the inflationary situation, which argues against spending the money. It may be that the governor was very sensitive to the problems of the Indians whose land would have been inundated. It does not seem to be because of a low benefit-cost ratio (1.9 according to the analysis by the Corps[22]).

In any case, the Dos Rios project may yet be resurrected after the peripheral canal is built. There are hints of this in Department of Water Resources literature: "Eventually, increasing water use in the Sacra-

[20] U.S. Army Engineer District, *Eel River Basin,* pp. 61ff.

[21] Lowell D. Wood, "An Economic Evaluation of the Planning and Evaluation Procedures Employed by the U.S. Army Corps of Engineers with Particular Reference to the Proposed Dos Rios Project in Northern California" (Ph.D. diss., Department of Agricultural Economics, University of California at Berkeley, 1969).

[22] U.S. Army Engineer District, *Eel River Basin,* p. 64.

mento Valley will so deplete natural drainage to the [S.F. Bay] Delta that the Middle Fork Eel River Development [Dos Rios] will have to be added to the Project."[23]

Finally, the Dos Rios Dam is not the only way to reduce pollution in southern San Francisco Bay. Sewage treatment plants could be built that may be less costly than the Dos Rios Dam. The FRP is a *fait accompli* but other elements of the plan need not be. Perhaps there will be more quantitative evaluation of alternatives in the future. In particular, alternative ways of getting water for southern California could be explored such as exploitation of ground water, reclamation of waste water, desalination, and conversion of briny steam deposits.[24]

### Results of Studies

Did any of these studies have any discernible impact on the CWP? Many alternatives have been proposed over the two decades of discussion. Hirshleifer, DeHaven, and Milliman have urged pricing water higher for more economical use. They and many others have speculated on desalination of sea water as an alternative source. Joe Bain and others have criticized the forced growth of cities in the desert through the availability of subsidized water.[25] Charles Weber proposed a plan with barge canals and a fresh water barrier across San Francisco Bay.[26] Senator Richard Dolwig proposed a large reservoir in the midst of the Central Valley. Stephen Riess suggested wells in the Tehachapi and San Bernardino mountains. Postponing construction of Oroville Reservoir was suggested in the Bechtel *Report* of 1956 and by Main and by Dillon, Read in 1960. Soling and DeBeer offered to transport Feather River water to the south by gravity flow via the Owens Valley and the Mojave Desert.

There have been some revisions over the course of two decades, but these have come about because of budget constraints, not economic analysis. At first the $1.75 billion in bond proceeds and the revenues from state leases of tidelands oil rights seemed like a lot of money. When

[23]Department of Water Resources, *The California State Water Project in 1969*, Bulletin No. 132–69, Sacramento (June 1969), p. 2.

[24]David Seckler, *California Water: A strategy* (Sacramento: Planning Conservation League, 1970). Briny steam deposits are underground resources of salt water in the form of steam. The deposits can be mined and heat from the steam used to desalinate the water.

[25]Joe S. Bain, "Water Resource Development in California: The Comparative Efficiency of Local, State and Federal Agencies," in Allen Kneese and Stephen C. Smith, eds., *Water Research* (Baltimore: John Hopkins University Press, 1966).

[26]Charles M. Weber, *An Approach to a California Public Works Plan—Comprehensive Co-ordinated Public Works Planning: A Step-by-Step Water Plan for California* (Sacramento State Printing Office, 1960).

the Burns-Porter act authorized the tidelands oil revenues they were yielding $200 million. These were destined to grow to $500 million, although no one knew it at the time. But $130 million of the $1.75 billion were earmarked for recreational development of high Sierra lakes in order to placate Assemblywoman Pauline Davis. The oil revenues were earmarked for "second-stage works." Thus, a project which the engineers secretly "knew" would cost $2.5 billion had to be built with $1.62 billion.

The apparent $1.62 billion budget constraint for capital outlay over a decade led to scaling down in the following ways: The Balboa Terminus in San Fernando Valley was eliminated by sharing aqueduct capacity with the city of Los Angeles; the "right" to the Pacheco Pass Tunnel Aqueduct was ceded to the Bureau of Reclamation; and the Coastal Aqueduct to San Luis Obispo and Santa Barbara was "drastically shrunk" to a size which later turned out to be adequate for the water those two counties purchased. Thus, the influence that led engineers to consider alternatives was lack of funds, not a desire for economic efficiency.

The CWP shows again the supremacy of the distribution over the efficiency issue. As conceived in the 1950s it was a way around the 160-acre limitation of the Reclamation Law.[27] About 1950 the Bureau of Reclamation did a study of irrigable land in California. An area the size of Rhode Island, 750,000 acres, was owned by thirty-four owners. Southern Pacific alone owned 187 square miles. If the federal government would not subsidize them, the state would. These interests continue to fight the "excess land law." Senator George Murphy introduced in 1969 legislation that would repeal it. This embodied recommendations of Governor Reagan's Task Force to raise the 160-acre figure to 640 acres. The Task Force was headed by an attorney for Kern County Land Company, one of the largest landowners in the United States.[28] When the state was unable to market its bonds at the statutory maximal rate of 5 percent, it needed the permission of the voters to raise the interest rate it could pay. Whittaker and Baxter, the advertising firm that handled Nixon's presidential campaign, was retained to favor a proposition to allow the state to raise its interest rate. Opponents of the CWP took the opportunity to fight this proposition as a means of fighting the CWP. The challenge was ambiguous, however, because state bonds support other projects which would also suffer if the state could not sell its bonds. The battle for the CWP had been won a decade earlier and was not seriously challenged in 1970.

[27] 43 *U.S. Code* 431.
[28] Paul S. Taylor, "Statement on Water Policy," prepared for National Water Commission, Los Angeles hearing 27 October 1969.

Thus the California Water Plan has an interesting history. The Feather River Project seems to have survived unscathed. The Peripheral Canal will probably be built eventually. The one component that seems to have been permanently scuttled, the Dos Rios Reservoir, was eliminated for unknown reasons that probably involve conservation. Its benefit-cost ratio of 1.9 does not appear to have been influential in this decision. It may yet be resurrected when the Peripheral Canal is a reality and pollution in San Francisco Bay is an immediate problem.

## THE UNITED STATES' SUPERSONIC TRANSPORT PROJECT[29]

For the SST project, unlike the CWP, benefit-cost analysis has been recognized as an appropriate tool of evaluation. Until the defeat of federal subsidy for SST prototype development in March, 1971, it had appeared that benefit-cost analysis had little impact on decisions to fund the SST. Even after the defeat it is clear that benefit-cost analysis had little influence on the decisions of the intended client of the analysis: the Administration. The analysis may have brought certain issues into the open so that they could be used by legislative critics of the project.

The denial of the SST appropriation can be explained in at least five ways which are not mutually exclusive: (1) increased attention to efficiency in government spending, (2) increased concern with the physical environment, (3) decreased effectiveness of appeal to national prestige or technology alone as arguments for large commitments of resources, (4) ideological concern that private initiative would be stifled by sizable government intrusion in what could be a commercial venture were it to promise success, and (5) increasing concern with social problems, in this case the incidence of benefits from the SST among income groups and the opportunity costs of SST subsidy funds. Each legislator voted as he did for his own reasons which we may never know. The denial of funds may be a victory for the nation and a defeat for this subchapter which we completed before March, 1971. If so, we welcome it. Nevertheless, the Administration was committed to federal funding of SST prototype development despite most of the benefit-cost analyses we cite below.

A brief chronology of events in the program is followed by examination of the studies themselves—by research contractors, aircraft manufacturers, federal agencies, independent individuals, airlines, and the

---

[29] This section benefits throughout from the case on the SST in S. Prakash Sethi, *Up Against the Corporate Wall: Modern Corporations and Social Issues of the Seventies* (Englewood Cliffs, N.J.: Prentice-Hall, 1971).

*ad hoc* committee formed by President Nixon. Finally, we shall assess the impact of the studies on the decisions actually made.

### Chronology

In 1956 research began on an engine that would move airplanes at three times the speed of sound. Although they were intended for military applications, the Air Force commissioned a study to explore their commercial possibilities in 1959. The Federal Aviation Agency (FAA) sponsored a feasibility study in 1960.

Congress first appropriated funds for exploratory research in 1961. In 1963, after Pan American World Airways announced it was taking options on six Concordes, the supersonic airplane planned by England and France, President Kennedy committed the United States to develop a commercial SST in partnership with private industry. Kennedy and Robert McNamara believed, as did their advisors, in economic growth through significant technological advances, characterized by the SST and space programs. Successful development of an SST would enhance the national prestige of the United States. Besides, the USSR was developing a supersonic airplane, the TU-144.

The FAA was given the responsibility to design and develop a commercial SST that was safe, economically sound, and operationally superior. In Phase I, beginning in August 1963, it entertained initial proposals from the aircraft industry. Phase II, beginning in June 1964, marked the competition for procurement contracts. On December 31, 1966, the Administrator announced that Boeing had won the airframe contract over Lockheed and General Electric had won the engine contract over Pratt and Whitney. Construction of a prototype was Phase III, due to end in early 1972. Phase IV was to be flight testing and certification, and Phase V, production.

The decision to continue toward prototype construction was made in 1967 after the FAA analyzed the economic feasibility of the program. President Nixon reviewed the program on taking office and decided to continue it. In 1970 responsibility for the SST was taken out of the hands of FAA and was located elsewhere in the Department of Transportation.

In December, 1970, the appropriation bill of the Department of Transportation was challenged by a Senate amendment omitting $290 million for SST prototype development, but the house revived the project. Senator Proxmire filibustered, delaying decisive action until March, 1971. Then the House surprisingly turned down the SST appropriation 217 to 204 and the Senate followed by defeating it 51 to 46. Various

schemes for continuing the project without federal support were discussed, and one may succeed, but the federal government is out of the
SST business.

### The Studies

*Initial Feasibility Studies.* Before Congress ever appropriated any
funds for research on a commercial SST, the Air Force had commissioned
a study on the subject by Planning Research Corporation. Its final report was delivered in 1959.[30] In 1960 a study for the FAA by United
Research Inc. predicted that U.S. aircraft manufacturers would not develop an SST without government support. High initial costs, the risks
involved and the prospect of getting government support were the bases
for the prediction. The FAA commissioned studies by Stanford Research
Institute (SRI), which delivered its final report in August 1963,[31] but
the FAA synthesized some of the results itself[32] before the President
committed the nation to the project. SRI's report was negative: it found
"no economic justification for an SST program."[33]

*Studies by Aircraft Manufacturers.* The aspirant aircraft manufacturers did several studies on their own.[34] In 1965 the FAA set down
the ground rules.[35] The contractor studies culminated in the proposals
made to the FAA for its decision at the end of 1966.[36] Much of Boeing's
work and assumptions were made public in a speech by T. A. Wilson
in 1967.[37]

These studies involved the demand for SST aircraft, the present
and future air travel market, and the economics of the SST program as
it was constituted. The demand for aircraft was studied by a Lockheed

[30]Planning Research Corporation, *Economic Study of Supersonic Transports,* Summary Volume, Washington, D.C. (29 May 1969).

[31]Stanford Research Institute (SRI), *An Economic Analysis of the Supersonic Transport,* final report submitted to the Federal Aviation Agency (August 1963); see also *Interim Report,* ISU-4266 (December 1962).

[32]U.S. Federal Aviation Agency, Aviation Economics Staff, *Commercial Supersonic
Transport Aircraft and the Domestic Air Travel Market* (March 1962).

[33]SRI, *An Economic Analysis,* p. II-1.

[34]For example, Boeing Airplane Co., "Evaluation of the Boeing 707–320B as the
Subsonic Standard for SST/Subsonic Economic Comparison," Report S-449, Seattle
(September 1964); Lockheed-California Co., *Commercial Airplane Market Analysis by
Airline Simulation,* Report OEA/SST/188, Burbank (May 1966).

[35]U.S. FAA, *Supersonic Transport Economic Model Ground Rules,* Washington,
D.C. (1965). Mimeographed.

[36]Lockheed-California Company, *Supersonic Transport Development Program
Phase III Proposal* Vol. I; *Summary;* Vol. VII: *Economics,* Reports LR 19836 and 19851,
Burbank (September 1966).

[37]T. A. Wilson, "The Expanding Jet Age," *Vital Speeches* 34, no. 3 (15 November
1967): 88–92.

computer simulation that fit aircraft types to routes to optimize subject to several alternative sets of constraints.[38]

Revenue passenger-miles were forecast by socioeconomic group for business and personal travel. The passenger-to-population ratio in future years was extrapolated. Growth in GNP was correlated with growth in air travel and an income elasticity of demand of 1.7 was estimated for air travel.[39] The Institute for Defense Analyses (IDA), also studying demand, found growth in air travel better correlated with growth of discretionary income, yielding a discretionary income elasticity of 2.5.[40]

In February 1969 Boeing offered a document designed to sustain the SST through the inevitable reexamination by a new administration.[41] It argued that the SST was inevitable and therefore the United States ought to share in the benefits. If the SST were priced at $40 or $50 million, $20 or $25 billion in revenue would be forthcoming from sales of 270 to foreign and 230 to domestic airlines. Sales gained by a domestic producer of SSTs would mean a net increase in the aircraft account of the balance of payments of $28 billion between 1975 and 1990; the government would recoup its $1.2 billion investment through royalties if 300 aircraft were sold.

A later document argued that the SST would generate $5.4 billion in federal taxes and $1.3 billion in state and local taxes.[42] To arrive at these figures Boeing relied on secondary benefits of the Keynesian multiplier type. While it is legitimate to count increases in taxes as well as in other components of national income, it is not legitimate to include secondary benefits except in special circumstances given in Chapter 9.

*Studies by the Agencies.* The SST program has been constantly evaluated by the federal agencies since 1961. In that year Najeeb Halaby, Administrator of the FAA, established a Supersonic Transport Advisory Group. President Kennedy established a committee in 1962, and since then every President has had a committee reporting directly to him on supersonic transport. These committees consisted of the heads of federal agencies with responsibilities related to the SST. In 1964 the Department of Commerce reported favorably on the SST.[43]

[38]W. A. Gunn, "Airline System Simulation," *Operations Research,* vol. 12 (March-April 1964).

[39]Wilson, "The Expanding Jet Age," p. 39.

[40]N. J. Asher, et al., *Demand Analyses for Air Travel by Supersonic Transport* (Arlington, Va: Institute for Defense Analyses, December 1966), pp. 10ff. Discretionary income is family income in excess of $7,500 per year.

[41]The Boeing Company, *The SST Program and Related National Benefits* (Seattle: The Boeing Co., 13 February 1969).

[42]The Boeing Company, *Development of a National Asset—The American SST* (Seattle: The Boeing Co., October 1969).

[43]U.S. Department of Commerce, Office of the Secretary, *SST: An Economic Analysis,* Vol. I; and *Economic Study of the Supersonic Transport* rev. (Washington, D.C.: U.S. Government Printing Office, 18 June 1964).

In 1967 the FAA undertook to justify the SST with an *Economic Feasibility Report* (EFR).[44] To do so, it commissioned several "consultants" whose reports are discussed below. The EFR concluded that the SST was viable as a public investment. At least 500 airplanes, it predicted, would be bought at $40 million each. The government, having invested $1.3 billion through prototype construction and certification, would receive a return of 4.1 percent if 500 aircraft were procured and 10 percent if 1,200 aircraft were procured.

In July 1967 the House Committee on Interstate and Foreign Commerce requested a report on the SST from the Comptroller-General, head of the General Accounting Office. This report,[45] delivered in January 1968, reviewed several previous studies, especially the EFR and its component reports. Not all the consultants' ideas were included in the EFR and the General Accounting Office pointed out and summarized points of disagreement between the consultants and FAA. This makes the report a very valuable document and demonstrates how the General Accounting Office can serve Congress with the same kind of expertise that is available to the Executive Branch in the agencies.

*Studies by FAA Consultants.* Several contractors were selected to study particular aspects of the SST before the decision was made to build a prototype aircraft. The areas of responsibility of IDA, one of these groups, included passenger demand, consequent demand for aircraft, and balance-of-payments effects. IDA although commissioned by the FAA, was considerably more conservative on the prospects for the aircraft than either Boeing or the FAA. An example of this difference is in Table 11.2. Three predictions are listed of the demand for SSTs until 1990. A major determinant of this demand concerns possible restriction of SST flights over populated areas due to sonic booms.

The influence of discount rates is shown in Table 11.3. The net present value of the SST invesment at three interest rates is calculated under the IDA and FAA estimates of demand. At 5, 10, and 15 percent IDA calls the proposition economically inefficient, but it *is* feasible, according to the FAA, at 5 percent. By the IDA estimate, the project becomes feasible only at the ridiculously low 1.33 percent.

The IDA study risked disappointing the client, the FAA, who presumably would be favorably disposed to a project in its own program—

[44]U.S. Department of Transportation, Federal Aviation Administration, *Economic Feasibility Report: U.S. Supersonic Transport* (Washington, D.C.: U.S. Government Printing Office, April 1967).

[45]Comptroller-General of the U.S., *Review of Reports Relating to the Economic Feasibility of the Supersonic Commercial Transport* (Washington, D.C.: U.S. Government Printing Office, 15 January 1968) reprinted in Department of Transportation budget hearings (House) for fiscal year 1970, pp. 216–33.

## TABLE 11.2. DEMAND FOR SSTs TO 1990, ACCORDING TO FOUR DIFFERENT STUDIES

| | NUMBER OF AIRCRAFT | |
|---|---|---|
| PRICE PER AIRCRAFT | WITH RESTRICTION[a] | WITHOUT RESTRICTION |
| $30 million | | |
| Boeing | 650 | 1,100 |
| FAA | 500 | 1,200 |
| IDA | 454 | 1,062 |
| $40 million | | |
| FAA | 497 | 1,170 |
| IDA A1[a] | 366 | 847 |
| IDA A2[a] | 279 | 661 |
| $50 million | | |
| FAA | 333 | 841 |
| IDA A1[a] | 201 | 535 |
| IDA A2[a] | 155 | 422 |
| $60 million | | |
| FAA | 236 | 598 |
| IDA A1[a] | 128 | 347 |
| IDA A2[a] | 101 | 280 |

Sources: Glen Husack,"Supersonic Transport: An Evaluation of Demand and Its Implications" (December 1968), p. 13: Federal Aviation Administration, *Economic Feasibility Report: U.S. Supersonic Transport* (Washington, D.C.: U.S. Government Printing Office, April 1967); and N. J. Asher, et al., *Demand for Air Travel by Supersonic Aircraft* (Arlington, Va.: Institute for Defense Analyses, 1966).

[a] Assumption 1 was that subsonic fares would be based on an average of 707 and 747 fares. The FAA made this assumption. Assumption 2 was that subsonic fares vary for each type of aircraft according to operating cost.

## TABLE 11.3. NET PRESENT VALUE OF SST INVESTMENT
(in millions of 1969 dollars)

| | INTEREST RATE ASSUMED | | |
|---|---|---|---|
| ESTIMATOR | 5 PERCENT | 10 PERCENT | 15 PERCENT |
| IDA | −344 | −528 | −579 |
| FAA | 218 | −239 | −421 |

Source: Laurence Lynn, in Joint Economic Committee, *Economic Analysis of Public Investment Decisions: Interest Rate Policy and Discounting Analysis* (Washington, D.C.: U.S. Government Printing Office, 1968), p. 149.

according to the usual code of bureaucracy. We will examine the following questions: What were the major factors that led IDA to be less optimistic about SST prospects than previous students of the problem? What use was made of the IDA benefit-cost analysis? Does an unfavorable benefit-cost analysis have any impact on policy? Finally, what judgment can be made about FAA's treatment of IDA's conclusions?

IDA's study valued time savings at the earning rate, a valuation some would criticize as conservative. The FAA and the Bureau of Public Roads value travel time savings at rates higher than the earning rate, because this favors transport investments that speed up travel.

IDA calculated that the SST would have a negative impact on the balance-of-payments initially because it would induce more Americans to travel and spend abroad. After 1980 sales of the SST would swamp this factor and overtake the earlier Concorde. The balance-of-payments calculation is sensitive to the price of the SST and the sonic boom constraint. Table 11.4 shows the undiscounted cumulative gains to the balance-of-payments through 1990 due to the SST.

TABLE 11.4. CUMULATIVE SST CONTRIBUTION
TO U.S. BALANCE OF PAYMENTS THROUGH 1990
Undiscounted

| Price ($ MILLION) | No sonic boom restriction ($ BILLION) | Sonic boom restriction ($ BILLION) |
|---|---|---|
| 50 | 5.9 | −4.6 |
| 30 | 10.2 | |

Source: N. J. Asher, et al., *Demand for Air Travel by Supersonic Aircraft* (Arlington, Va.: Institute for Defense Analyses, 1966).

Since the time profile of benefits is negative at first and positive later as the SST increases its market share, discounting would cause the present value of benefits to decrease. Even without discounting there are negative payments contributions if SSTs cost $50 million each and can fly only over unpopulated areas. Under this scenario SSTs would be used principally over oceans, taking many Americans across the Atlantic to spend, and the lower-priced Concorde would increase its market share.

In taking the courageous position it did, IDA chose not to fulfill traditional research organization-client expectations. FAA countered this unexpected stand using consultants to scrutinize bothersome aspects. Among these consultants were Edmund Learned and John Meyer. They concluded that: (1) IDA had underestimated the rate of spending in the United States by foreign travelers; (2) IDA had failed to consider increased sales of U.S. products (apart from SSTs) due to an increase in American business travel and promotion abroad; (3) IDA's projection of a decline in the share of the United States in the supersonic market was mistaken.

FAA's calculations of balance-of-payments benefits yield a cumulative positive effect of $17.1 billion (undiscounted) by 1990 with a boom restriction and $32 billion with no sonic boom restriction. These more nearly approximate the airline point of view. The EFR differed considerably from IDA's conclusions although it purported to summarize contractor's studies. But since the FAA had already been given the mandate to develop the SST and initial feasibility studies were positive, what action could we expect on receipt of discouraging advice? Charles River Associates was commissioned to do a study of aircraft passenger demand. FAA, preferring this report to IDA's, integrated it into the feasibility report.

The major difference between IDA's and FAA's results were due to different assumptions about the value of travel time. IDA valued passengers' time at their earning rate while FAA valued time at 1.5 times the earning rate, as shown in the schedule of aircraft demand estimates to 1990, Table 11.2.

FAA also assumed subsonic fares would be based on the average of Boeing 707 and 747 fares while IDA assumed fares would be set according to the costs of the most economical aircraft on each route. This made IDA's assumed price for SST competition lower than FAA's. Thus according to IDA the SST would draw less trade from its competition than according to FAA.

Booz, Allen Applied Research (BAAR) studied development and production costs. A cost estimating relationship based on historical (military) data estimated development costs at $3.4 billion and production costs of $43.3 million per plane at a quantity of 500 planes. Again FAA demurred, preferring estimates supplied under subcontract to BAAR by Resource Management Corporation: $2.1 billion for development and $26.9 million per plane. As we have shown in Chapter 10, Summers' work shows cost estimating relationships to be biased downward. Nevertheless, the FAA preferred Resource Management's "engineering judgment" and called BAAR's method "statistically questionable" since it was developed from data on military supersonic aircraft which are lighter than commercial SSTs.

FAA accepted the estimates of the Research Analysis Corporation on operating costs and of the Planning Research Corporation on airport and enroute services costs. It did not object to Booz, Allen and Hamilton's findings on the prime contractors and airlines: their financing and their ability to procure SSTs when the aircraft become operational. Thus, FAA received a favorable report on the SST by selecting from among submitted reports only those that favored the aircraft's development.

*Independent Studies.* Stephen Enke was able to give a balanced view of the issues involved, without taking sides, at the 1966 annual meeting of the American Economic Association.[46] Enke stated the conditions that would have to prevail in order to justify the $2 billion he estimated the government would spend. He outlined problems concerning the public interest that would arise because of the government-created monopolies involved with the SST. He was troubled at the incidence of benefits because 85 percent of U.S. residents had never flown at that time, and because the SST was likely to affect only those flying among New York, Chicago, Los Angeles, San Francisco, Seattle, Washington D.C., and Miami. Regarding the distribution of ultimate benefits, he posed the question of repayment: How much of the government's contribution to the development of the SST ought it to recover? Enke sought a rate of return of 10 percent on all resources invested after 1966.[47] On balance, he was not yet sufficiently confident of overall efficiency to recommend construction of a prototype aircraft.

The opportunity for individuals to comment on the SST was given after the report of President Nixon's ad hoc committee, whose hearings during February and March 1969 were largely negative. The Department of Transportation kept the reports of the hearings secret until October 31, 1969, when James Beggs, Undersecretary of Transportation and chairman of the committee, prepared a summary report. Members of the committee claimed his report did not fairly represent their views. Hendrik Houthakker's comments were typical:

> The Draft Report . . . does not adequately reflect the views of the working panels and of the members of the Committee. It contains primarily the most favorable material, interspersed with editorial comments, and thus distorts the implications and tenor of the reports. . . . While the risks both economically and technically are great, the potential benefits are uncertain. With budget needs so great, I cannot see how this program can be justified at the present time and would recommend that no new funds be devoted to the project for at least fiscal year 1970.

Similar statements were made by Charles Johnson, Jr., Assistant Surgeon General; Arnold Weber, Assistant Secretary of Labor; and U. Alexis Johnson, Undersecretary of State.[48]

Elwood Quesada, FAA administrator from 1958 to 1961, changed his mind over the course of SST development. At first he supported the SST, but by 1969 he was lukewarm to the idea. His testimony was so

[46] S. Enke, "Government-Industry Development of a Commercial Supersonic Transport," *American Economic Review* 57 (May 1967): 71ff.
[47] This is close to CAB's target rate of return for airlines of 10.5 percent.
[48] Sethi, *Up Against the Corporate Wall.*

damaging that the Department of Transportation suppressed it until Congressman Reuss (D., Wis.) with difficulty extracted it from a safe in the office of the Secretary of Transportation.[49]

*Studies by Airlines.* Lee Howard of Pan American Airways contributed a detailed study from the point of view of the airlines.[50] He claimed that the investment tax credit and corporate income taxes affect income distribution but not efficiency. His result is a "discounted cash flow rate of return" of 23.8 percent.[51] Therefore, he concluded, the SST is a very good deal for the airlines. His study does not consider the foreign travel aspect at all, but only purchases of Concordes and SSTs. Howard calculates an (undiscounted) net benefit of $38.6 billion for the period until 1985.

Airlines have consistently maintained that the demand for air travel is price inelastic, since over 63 percent of passengers are on business trips for which others are paying. The CAB contests this, urging fare reductions to increase total revenue. IDA estimated a price elasticity of −1.7, which is considerable. The airlines' more recent estimates have been about −1.3. Therefore, premiums can be charged for SST over subsonic flight and most passengers will bear this cost. But if businesses do not fully reimburse employees for SST travel, supersonic flights may travel with lower load factors, resulting in less economical operation.

In 1969 the FAA solicited current opinions of the SST from the airlines. Optimism had waned. Airlines worried over SST fare premiums, its ability to meet airport noise criteria, sonic booms, the enormous risks of $50 million vehicles, and unsolved technical problems. Several expressed the opinion that the money being spent on SST development could more fruitfully be spent developing the country's airways and airports. The opportunity costs were higher than the benefits.

*Reevaluation.* When President Nixon took office a thorough review of the SST program was undertaken. An ad hoc committee including representatives from Defense, Commerce, HEW, State, Treasury and Justice Departments, the Council of Economic Advisors, NASA, and the Office of Science and Technology was chaired by James Beggs, Undersecretary of Transportation. The committee formed four panels on: balance-of-payments and international relations; economics; environmental and sociological impact; and technological spillover.

The payments issue, on balance, looked unfavorable. An American

---

[49] *Congressional Record,* 17 November 1969, H10947.

[50] "A Cost Effectiveness Example: A Hypothetical Supersonic Transport," in J. Morley English, *Cost−Effectiveness Analysis* (New York: Wiley, 1968), pp. 166−213 and Appendix C.

[51] "A Cost Effectiveness Example," p. 205.

SST would earn revenue on the aircraft account, but speed-induced travel would encourage more Americans than foreigners to travel and spend abroad.

The panel on economics recommended against any funds for construction of a prototype in fiscal 1970. It stressed the great uncertainty associated with predictions of the costs of an SST and the ability of the project to generate employment. It was uncertain that a safe, efficient aircraft could be built in the allotted time. It questioned FAA's prediction that 500 aircraft would be sold. The FAA assumed a 25 percent fare differential while the panel reasoned that this premium could easily climb to 36 percent, reducing sales of aircraft to 200. FAA had assumed that the SST and the Concorde would compete in different markets. The panel found this unlikely, given Concorde's five-year head start. The SST, although it will have lower operating costs, will not be able to set its fares below that of the Concorde (as FAA had reasoned) given the way that international air fares are set. The panel did not accept the FAA sales price of $40 million because Boeing retained the right to price the aircraft. Using an economic model, the panel calculated Boeing's profit-maximizing price at $48 million, whence the quantity demanded would be only 350. Finally, on finance, the panel observed that U.S. airlines' rate of return on investment had been falling since 1966. Thus their ability to finance SST purchases through either retained earnings or competitive borrowing was in doubt. The FAA predicted that the SST would generate 100,000 jobs. The panel discounted the importance of this factor, citing diversion from aerospace employment and the fact that most jobs generated would be in skills already in short supply. No employment benefits in low-skill levels were foreseen by the panel on economics.

The panel on environmental and sociological effects also recommended against prototype construction until some problems were solved. The problem of sonic booms and airport noise has been with the SST throughout its life and was a major reason for choosing Boeing's over Lockheed's original design. The ecological effects of water vapor released by the SST in the stratosphere are unknown, but possibly it will raise or lower the earth's mean temperature.

The panel on technological spillovers to the rest of the economy was positive in predicting technological advances in certain areas, but it said these were of minor importance; not of sufficient magnitude to affect the decision of whether or not to go ahead with the program.

Despite the reports of the four panels, a favorable report was presented to the President. This report, mentioned above, was written by James Beggs and kept secret until October, 1969.

TABLE 11.5. U.S. CIVIL SUPERSONIC TRANSPORT NEW OBLIGATIONAL AUTHORITY AND EXPENDITURES
(in millions of dollars)

| Fiscal year | 1963 | 1964 | 1965 | 1966 | 1967 | 1968 | 1969 | 1970 | 1971 |
|---|---|---|---|---|---|---|---|---|---|
| New obligational authority | 20.0 | 60.0 | - | 140.0 | 280.0 | 142.4 | - | 85.0 | 290.0[a] |
| Actual expenditures | 18.7 | 17.6 | 21.8 | 112.4 | 189.8 | 62.7 | 81 | 163 | - |

[a] Budget request.

*Source:* U.S. Executive Office of the President, Bureau of the Budget, *Budget of the U.S. Government* (Washington, D.C.: U.S. Government Printing Office, 1963 through 1971).

## The Results

The President and the Congress eventually acted to appropriate $85 million in fiscal 1970 to begin construction of a prototype. Although this was not a high appropriation (compared to $280 million in fiscal 1967 and $140 million in two other years), it did signify a willingness to go through with the project. Table 11.5 shows annual authorizations and expenditures for the SST.

Major decision points on the SST came in 1963, 1967, 1969, and 1971. In the first, President Kennedy decided to go ahead despite SRI's negative report, primarily in order to gain international prestige. Further, it was argued that business would not pursue a goal involving such uncertainty; therefore, government must. Both these motivations, prestige and uncertainty, are sufficiently nebulous that benefit-cost arguments are unlikely to be persuasive. In 1967 FAA's *Economic Feasibility Report,* typically supporting its own program, urged proceeding toward a prototype. The FAA chose, over the initial unenthusiastic reports, the newly-commissioned enthusiastic ones. In 1969 the Nixon Administration had to formulate a policy on what was up until that time a Democratic program. The report, which suggested continuing, suppressed the skeptical views of many experts. Expert testimony of one who had changed his mind was hidden in an Executive safe. In 1971 the federal government ended its subsidy of prototype development.

Each year is, in a sense, a decision point, as funds must be appropriated by Congress. It is hard to know whether such decisions depend on benefit-cost analysis. The analysis has been directed toward a client, usually in the Executive. Executive behavior is more closely associated with, although hardly very influenced by, such analysis. If the Senate refused funding in 1970, it probably responded to ad hoc considerations of quality of the environment. If the House-Senate Conference Committee reinstated some money to continue the program, it probably responded to unemployment in the aerospace industry and in Seattle. These are bona fide considerations. The point is that closely reasoned benefit-cost calculations that take all considerations systematically into account can hardly claim to be decisive in such political decisions. The reasons for the ultimate rejection are similarly ambiguous.

## WHAT DIFFERENCE DOES BENEFIT-COST ANALYSIS MAKE?

### The Consumer of the Analysis

In the two cases we have examined, benefit-cost analysis does not appear to have had much impact on the final decisions. Why then should governments bother with it? Part of the impact of a benefit-cost analysis depends on its consumer. The electorate may consume it. A strong and aggressive executive may consume it and ignore it in favor of his preconceived ideas. A weak and malleable executive may consume it and use it as a substitute for his own decision process. Frequently, there will be an intermediary between the authors and the consumer of the analysis. The intermediary will be called upon to summarize a lengthy document. His summary may have a great impact on the final decision.

In the case of the CWP decision the voters of the state had to decide whether or not to approve the bond issue. They had available to them several journalistic and academic interpretations. The Los Angeles *Times* was in favor of the plan, the San Francisco *Chronicle* was against it. The interpretations emerging from academic circles did not get the publicity that the journalistic opinions did. The resultant decision was, not surprisingly, in response to the newspapers. Voters in Southern California largely approved, those in Northern California disapproved. Because there were more voters in the South, the plan was approved. In this case, benefit-cost analysis in the engineering and financial consultants' reports were brought to the public through the intermediary of the newspapers. Each contradicted the other, and sound judgment was impeded.

The intermediary in one SST decision was James Beggs. He unfairly summarized the reports of the Ad Hoc Committee—either because he had an axe to grind or because he was (consciously or subconsciously) trying to please his superior. As McKean and Anshen note:

> Successive echelons of reviewers perceive that their superiors frown upon certain alternatives. It seems useless, perhaps even risky, to put the strongest case possible for the

unpopular alternatives. Gradually, the arguments against them are stressed or those alternatives are dropped from the study.[52]

## The Quality of the Analysis

Benefit-cost analysis is often ineffective because it may consider only a single alternative, it may not serve the needs of the client or it may be politically naive.

John Dewey usefully summarized the steps in problem solving: defining the problem, deciding on alternative actions, and deciding which alternative is best.[53] Herbert Simon has noted that businessmen spend the largest fraction of their time seeking to invent, design, and develop possible courses of action, a process he calls *design*.[54] A relatively small fraction of their time is spent choosing among alternatives. We believe that misplaced emphasis has been placed by public agencies on analyzing suggested projects, which Simon calls *choice*. Typically, one alternative is specified and an effort is made to show that it is "feasible." This is true of most river basin plans as analyzed by the Corps of Engineers or the Bureau of Reclamation. It was true of the California Water Plan and the Bay Area Rapid Transit proposal. It was less true of the SST, which was more fluid in design.

Most large decisions on public spending must be made politically, either by a legislature or by an electorate in a bond election. Collective decision-making, however, is very difficult because frequently the most one can ask the voters is "yes" or "no?" One proposal at a time is parliamentary; the simultaneous analysis of several alternatives is ministerial or appropriate to an executive branch of government. Although we do not necessarily agree with the conclusions, we refer the reader to two good examples of the latter case, in which means of dealing with transportation in cities are examined: Meyer, Kain and Wohl's, *The Urban Transportation Problem*[55] and a Department of Transportation Special Analytic Study, "Urban Commutation Alternatives.[56]

Some benefit-cost analyses may be theoretically correct but useless

---

[52] Roland N. McKean and Melvin Anshen, "Limitations, Risks, and Problems of the Program Budget," in Fremont J. Lyden and Ernest J. Miller, eds., *Planning Programming Budgeting: A Systems Approach to Management* (Chicago: Markham, 1968), p. 348.

[53] John Dewey, *How We Think* (New York: Heath, 1910), Chap. 8.

[54] Herbert A. Simon, *The New Science of Managerial Decision Making* (New York: Harper and Row, 1960).

[55] John R. Meyer, John F. Kain, and Martin Wohl, *The Urban Transportation Problem* (Cambridge, Mass.: Harvard University Press, 1965).

[56] Department of Transportation, Office of Planning and Program Review, "Urban Commutation Alternatives" (October 1968), reprinted in Joint Economic Committee, *The Analysis and Evaluation of Public Expenditures: The PPB System*, Vol. 2, pp. 698–733.

because the decision-maker does not accept the premises. Local governments, for example, are frequently more concerned with financial feasibility, that collectible-revenues exceed costs. The analyst may have been taught to analyze all projects from a national point of view, so that he might not agree with his client. Similarly, the analyst may have been taught to exclude "secondary benefits" unless persistent unemployment prevails, while a local government may be very interested in induced multiplier benefits. That a project displaces economic activity elsewhere may be of little consequence to a city government. Agreement on objectives between analyst and client ought to be achieved at the outset.

Frequently the analyst's work will be ignored because it is politically naive. Economics is not the only force that moves people. When a politician needs the support of others he incurs "exchange costs."[57] For their support he must promise favors later in the form of patronage, voting support for another politician's projects, or coercive measures such as vetoes or removing someone from office. If a politician opposed every measure that did not meet a benefit-cost test, he would antagonize some voters or colleagues and probably suffer retaliation. He must economize on negative votes to retain the support of his colleagues on issues important to him. He must approve some indefensible projects in order to survive. Benefit-cost studies may show that no projects are justified in a particular state. The economist may say, "Do nothing in state." But the politically-oriented man, who understands the lubrication of a smoothly functioning federal democracy, compromises. He accepts one or two projects from each state even though they are not justified on a criterion of maximizing total net benefits. "In return for sacrificing full adherence to the [benefit-cost] formula in a few instances, [he gets] enhanced support for it in many others."[58]

### The Value of Unreliable Rankings

Since benefit estimates are unreliable to an unmeasured degree and cost estimates are notoriously poor to a measured and depressing degree, why bother making these estimates? One reason is that benefit estimates, if made properly, are lower bounds on true benefits while cost estimates are usually lower bounds for actual costs. These two tendencies do not always counteract each other. If benefit estimates are made with unrealistic scenarios, especially buoyant expectations for population growth,

[57] Aaron Wildavsky, "The Political Economy of Efficiency: Cost-Benefit Analysis, Systems Analysis, and Program Budgeting," in Lyden and Miller, *Planning Programming Budgeting*, pp. 395ff.
[58] Wildavsky, "The Political Economy of Efficiency," p. 379.

they may be overestimates. We cannot rely on the two forecasts to be self-correcting. Benefit estimates may not be made properly and there may be a bias toward overstatement of benefits and understatement of costs.

High benefit-cost ratios may unrealistically suggest pushing ahead on a certain front. For example, a project in a field of research is unrealistic if highly skilled scientific personnel are not available. We would classify this error either as failure to specify one of the constraints of the problem—the limit on skilled personnel—or as counting average cost instead of incremental cost; that is, the incremental cost of a geneticist may be prohibitively high because all available are fully employed.

Benefit-cost analysis performs a function that is difficult to perceive. It does screen out projects that are even less appropriate than those currently authorized. One can argue that this is all Congress ever intended to achieve with benefit-cost analysis. Recall such analysis, as introduced by the Flood Control Acts of 1936 and 1944, never stated as its objective maximization of net benefits. That objective is subsequent marginal commentary due to later interpretations. Perhaps we should return to the original text for the original intent. While administrators tend to be economists and maximizers at heart, Congress is made up of politicians and "satisficers." That is, they set achievable goals and are content to achieve them, rather than seek the best possible goal, or maximize. All Congress ever expected benefit-cost analysis to be was a sieve to catch grossly uneconomic projects. They intended to slice the civil works pie with a "share-and-share-alike" philosophy.

There is reason to believe that better outcomes will emerge if legislatures refuse to authorize projects that fail a benefit-cost criterion—better in the sense that most of the legislators themselves would prefer the result. That legislators will prefer to let civil servants veto certain projects is a strange conclusion, but it has an analogy in the case of individual decision-making.

Depriving each member of a group of some of his freedom of choice can produce an outcome that most or even all members of the group prefer. For example, every resident of a region may feel that it is worth more to him to have others forbidden to pollute the atmosphere than to be free himself to pollute (and to sell his promise not to pollute). Still better would be to have everyone but oneself constrained, but this alternative seldom is available to anyone and never is available to everyone; the relevant alternatives are ordinarily to have no one constrained or everyone constrained. The latter will improve the outcome in the eyes of each person who feels that the advantages of having others constrained outweigh the disadvantages of his being constrained.

Similar possibilities exist with respect to group decision making. To rule out some alternatives in advance can produce a set of decisions that most or even all members of the group regard as better than the set that otherwise would have emerged, and also can reduce the costs of reaching decisions. To exclude certain alternatives will improve the outcome in the eyes of everyone who feels that killing the alternatives that he dislikes is more important than losing the alternatives that he favors. In addition, ruling out some alternatives can make it less likely that decisions will be reached in haste, can save a representative from pressure by constituents who would want some of the excluded alternatives,[59] and can reduce a legislator's need to barter his votes or to curry favor with powerful colleagues. Accordingly, most or all legislators might feel that the advantages of having civil servants prescreen certain types of projects outweigh the disadvantages.

For what kinds of projects will prescreening by civil servants produce an outcome that most or all legislators themselves prefer? Given a geographically apportioned legislature, the most likely cases are investment projects whose funding is national (or statewide) and whose benefits are predominantly regional (or local); for example, parks, roads, and water projects. Many such projects seem able to win approval even though they would be defeated on a secret ballot, the gainers could not compensate the losers, the proponents of the projects would become opponents if the tax burden were shifted to the region benefitted, the projects make the rich richer and the poor poorer, and the projects fail every other test that anyone would want to live with.

The explanation for this outcome seems to lie in several factors. First, the seniority system, together with the existence of appropriations subcommittees, enables some legislators almost to write their own tickets and enables others to buy favors. Second, votes are traded. Third, assembling regional projects in relatively small bundles reduces the opportunity to negotiate reciprocal cutbacks. Fourth, little effort is devoted to negotiating mutually agreeable cutbacks.

Whether or not these *are* the reasons, however, the effect seems clear. It is likely that a reduction in the number and scale of regional investment projects that win approval over a number of years could be arranged that would please every legislator, or at least every legislator not on the appropriations committee.

Since prescreening regional projects will serve to rule out some of

---

[59] As Wildavsky puts it, "The [benefit-cost] technique gives the responsible official a good reason for turning down projects with a public-interest explanation the Congressman can use with his constituents and the interest-group leader with his members." Wildavsky, "The Political Economy of Efficiency," p. 379.

the projects, prescreening seems likely to work in the "right" direction. However, whether prescreening actually will produce a set of projects and designs that most legislators, or we personally, would regard as an improvement, depends on the screening rule adopted and on the quality of its implementation. The benefit-cost criterion seems to be a good one for regional projects. Evidently, legislators find it acceptable. We would go farther, however, than benefit-cost analysis has gone in screening out undesirable projects; that we must go farther is indicated by the many undesirable projects that slip through the sieve and by the public needs that remain unattended—purportedly because of lack of funds.

Water resources benefit-cost analysis has gotten out of hand. Neither interagency committees nor the Bureau of the Budget have restrained the Corps of Engineers or the Bureau of Reclamation. Arthur Smithies, predicting this trend in 1955, declared, "Competition is likely to drive the agencies toward increasingly optimistic estimates and far from resolving organization difficulties, computation of benefit-cost ratios may in fact make them worse.[60] These agencies, venerable in public spending circles, have managed to avoid requirements applied to all other areas of spending. In 1969 all agencies were directed by the Bureau of the Budget to use at least an 8 percent discount rate and preferably 10 percent. The Water Resources Council successfully lobbied to retain its $4\frac{5}{8}$ percent rate. Multi-year costing of PPB required all agencies to display future implications of current programs. Under "full funding" the entire cost of a program is appropriated at the time it is started. Water resource appropriations are a notorious exception to this salubrious change.[61]

One cure for benefit-cost excesses would be an analytical arm responsible to Congress alone. Now, Congress funds analysis for all the Executive agencies and appropriates funds for a growing Executive Office of the President. It would be reasonable to establish an analytical function within Congress. The staff could be located in the General Accounting Office or in a newly created office. Fox and Herfindahl[62] have suggested an independent audit of agencies' work, but we would further recommend that the analysis itself be performed outside the agency.

[60]Arthur Smithies, *The Budgetary Process in the U.S.*, Committee for Economic Development Research Study (New York: McGraw-Hill, 1955), pp. 344ff.

[61]U.S. Executive Office of the President, Bureau of the Budget, *Budget of the U.S. Government* Fiscal Year 1970 *Special Analyses* (Washington, D.C.: U.S. Government Printing Office, 1969), p. 81; and Murray Weidenbaum, "Institutional Obstacles to Reallocating Government Expenditures" in Robert H. Haveman and Julius Margolis, *Public Expenditures and Policy Analysis* (Chicago: Markham, 1970), p. 245.

[62]Irving K. Fox and Orris C. Herfindahl, "Attainment of Efficiency in Satisfying Demands for Water Resources," *American Economic Review* 54 (May 1964): 205.

Otherwise, the agency can come to Congress with several notebooks of quantitive material and know that Congress will make little attempt at rebuttal. Congress, at present, does not care about efficiency, but concerns itself with geographical distribution only. Taxpayers cannot afford such a Congress.

Senator Proxmire made a start toward an analytic staff for Congress in strengthening the staff of the Joint Economic Committee. In addition, the appropriation subcommittees could be expanded to exercise more than passive oversight over Executive behavior.


## WHEN IS BENEFIT-COST ANALYSIS USEFUL?

The federal instructions for PPB suggested that a "Special Study" or benefit-cost analysis be made whenever a proposal for major new legislation is involved. Moreover, it instructs, "agencies should maintain a continuing program of Special Studies" to which the Bureau of the Budget may add in any new calendar year.[63] Perhaps this too, overstated the ideal frequency with which this activity should be pursued.

Benefit-cost analysis does not appear to be useful for big decisions. Despite the negative results of analyses of the economic feasibility of the CWP the voters of the State voted to proceed with it. In the case of the SST, early benefit-cost analyses were encouraging, and negative results reported later did not halt the momentum of the administration. Benefit-cost analyses seem poorly suited to decisions about whether to go ahead or not on a project but better suited to a comparison among alternatives. The former apparently have to be taken through the political process, either directly by the voters—as in the case of the CWP—or by their elected representatives. Cost constraints did enforce some modifications to the CWP. The hierarchy of components determining which were expendable was evidently not based on economic analysis.

One of the authors was a member of a citizen's committee reporting to the city council of Davis, California. The committee's task was to recommend action regarding a sewage treatment plant whose capacity at present was too small to accommodate the city's growing population. The decisions had already been made about (1) the quality of the ideal facilities (that is, a set of constraints) and (2) the objective—to obtain these facilities in the most economically possible way. The committee readily agreed to employ a consulting engineer to identify a number of alternative designs for the system, calculate his subjective expectation

[63] U.S. Bureau of the Budget, "Bulletin No. 68-2, July 18, 1967," in Lyden and Miller, *Planning Programming Budgeting*, p. 439.

of the present value of expenditures associated with each design (at the borrowing rate of 5 percent and also at 8 percent), and indicate the amount of money necessary to construct each design. This cost-effectiveness analysis cost about $10,000. It saved about fifty times that amount because the chosen alternative had an expected at-approval value of expenditures that was about $500,000 less than the alternative that probably would have been chosen if the study had not been made. There is obvious value in enumerating distinct alternatives and subjecting each to quantitative evaluation.

Another example of a benefit-cost analysis that had some impact is given by Charles Schultze.[64] In 1966 the Department of Health, Education and Welfare, interested in the problem of infant mortality, commissioned a study of alternative maternal and child health care methods. The study group examined the "production functions," or relationships between specific actions and the objectives of lowering infant mortality rates and incidence of physical handicaps. The incidence of these conditions was studied and it was found that one-fourth of the "excess" infant deaths (those over the tenth percentile rate) occurred in only 21 out of 3,130 U.S. counties. A specific program including early case findings, periodic medical treatment, and the screening of poor children was recommended in 1967. Despite the tightly constrained fiscal 1969 budget, substantial additional funds were awarded to this program because of its high scores on cost-effectiveness tests.

The list of successful benefit-cost analyses is populated with those that considered alternatives. Benefit-cost analysis does not appear to be well adapted to yes-or-no decisions, but is more effective as a ranking tool. "All California water projects thoroughly studied by the Bureau or the Corps and supported by local interests have ultimately received congressional approval and appropriations."[65] Benefit-cost analysis does not appear to be a very good sieve.

Furthermore, when intangibles are important, benefit-cost analysis may do more harm than good. If analysis is preoccupied with tangible, measurable benefits, it may divert attention from elements that cannot be quantified. To cite an illustration used by Dorfman, the rabbit in a horse-and-rabbit stew may be measured, but the horse dominates the flavor of the stew.[66] Schelling cites foreign affairs as an area in which many of the important decisions are nonbudgetary. He states, "Having more bombs than necessary is bad only because they cost money; using

[64]Charles Schultze, *The Politics and Economics of Public Spending* (Washington, D.C.: The Brookings Institution, 1968), pp. 59, 71ff.

[65]Bain, Caves, and Margolis, *Northern California's Water Industry*, p. 409.

[66]Robert Dorfman, ed., *Measuring Benefits of Government Investments* (Washington, D.C.: The Brookings Institution, 1965), pp. 2-3.

bombs or failing to use them can be bad irrespective of what the bombs cost."[67] Despite analytical criticism of the FRP it was consummated. The Dos Rios Dam was not, but in this case other considerations appear to have been more influential than benefit-cost analysis: it did not fail any formal benefit-cost test. Governor Reagan apparently responded to the political expression of local landowners, Indians, and conservationists.

Benefit-cost analysis is more useful in certain fields than in others. It is better adapted to the functions of government that are most like business: public utilities such as water, waste disposal, power production, and transportation projects in which the efficiency objective is parmount. In human resource fields it can be only a partial aid to decision-making.

Benefit-cost analysis is less useful where great uncertainties exist. This is true in choice among research and development projects. Results cannot be foreseen with much accuracy. Entirely new applications whose benefits could not conceivably have been foretold often result. Fisher reports, "In reality, most major long-range planning decisions must ultimately be resolved primarily on the basis of intuition and judgment. [T]he main role of the analyst should be to try to sharpen this . . . judgment."[68]

Quantitative evaluation is more appropriate for intraprogram choices than for interprogram choices. The total amount of spending in each field is a political decision. Developing priorities within a field is a more technical question, to which benefit-cost analysis can contribute. For example, if money is available to spend on health research, benefit-cost studies such as those mentioned in Chapter 8 can tell us the order in which to choose projects. The choice between better health and going to the moon is a value judgment that must be made by voters or their representatives.

To undertake quantitative evaluation before approving every project would be very wasteful, although it seems clearly worthwhile for some projects such as the Davis sewerage system. Benefit-cost analysis should be approved selectively, and probably should be requested or approved by the persons most likely to know if it would affect the decision. In particular, they are the persons most likely to know whether the project or the alternative designs would be judged at least in part on the basis of the analysts' figures for costs or benefits, not solely on the basis of nonmonetizable effects, distributional considerations, constraints, political consequences, instability, risk, or inflexibility. It would be up to

[67] Thomas C. Schelling, "PPBS and Foreign Affairs," Committee Print, Subcommittee on National Security and International Operations of the Committee on Government Operations, United States Senate, 90th Congress, 1st Session (Washington, D.C.: U.S. Government Printing Office, 1968), p. 2.

[68] Gene Fisher, "The Role of Cost-Utility Analysis in Program Budgeting," in Lyden and Miller, *Planning Programming Budgeting,* p. 186.

the users to predict whether quantitative evaluation would be valuable—and worth its cost.

Some preliminary discussion presumably would help the users to decide. It seems appropriate for the intended analysts to inform the intended users as to when in the past the benefits of their type of quantitative evaluation appear to have outweighed the costs. The analysts should (1) indicate which of the project's costs and benefits have, and which do not have, transactional counterparts and therefore which effects can, and which cannot, be evaluated in terms of money; (2) indicate which designs they would consider, what discount rates they would use, and what assumptions they would make about the existence and character of interrelated projects; (3) estimate an optimal amount of time and money to spend on the analysis; and (4) indicate how much less time and money a purely qualitative analysis would involve. Then it would be up to the persons who must approve the project itself to decide whether the quantitative evaluation would be worthwhile.

This selective approach will not appeal to people who want public funds to be allocated scientifically. If quantitative evaluation is undertaken only when the decision-makers request it, many projects will be approved and many designs will be chosen without benefit-cost or cost-effectiveness analysis. Furthermore, even when quantitative evaluation has been performed, officials will be free to disregard the results. Spending decisions, therefore, will continue to be governed by officials' personal impressions.

Unfortunately, there is no better alternative. It is some comfort to recall that subjective judgment also governs spending decisions in the private sector.

# Twelve

# SUMMARY

PPB, introduced in 1961, had become epidemic by 1968. It had spread from the Department of Defense to the whole of the federal government and also to a number of state and local governments.

PPB has five distinguishing features: program accounting, multi-year costing, detailed description of activities, zero-base budgeting, and quantitative evaluation of alternatives or benefit-cost analysis.

Program accounting involves classifying expenditures—past, permitted, proposed, or predicted expenditures—in terms of objectives or outputs. Two steps are involved: first, define a hierarchy of programs, each program representing activities with a common purpose; second, ascertain for each program in the hierarchy the sum of all kinds of expenditures. Because adoption of performance budgeting, as recommended by the Hoover Commission, was incomplete, program accounting more often supersedes the conventional method of government accounting. By the conventional method expenditures are classified by object of expenditure and by agency. They are not classified by purpose unless agencies are organized according to purpose, but both classifications are useful. Because the advocates of PPB do not recommend reorganizing agencies, nor expect that conventional accounting will soon be abandoned, their demand for program accounting amounts to a demand for moving from a two-way to a three-way classification of expenditures—by object of expenditure, by agency, and by program.

Program accounting supposedly will produce better decisions by enabling decision-makers to see how much money is being spent for each purpose and by enabling high-level officials to exercise greater control in budget formation. However, the information being generated has limited value: it reflects arbitrary cost allocations, and it tells little about how much money a partial or even a total cutback in a program would save. As to enhancing central control, no one knows how much centralization is desirable.

Costs are certain to occur in program accounting, which entails struggles with program delineation, confusion over joint costs, difficulties in instructing personnel, an additional set of ledgers, an additional process of reconciliation, and periodic revision of the whole supplementary set of accounts. It is very doubtful that adding the third classification of expenditures is worth the cost. Reorganizing agencies according to function is an alternative way to obtain both output-oriented cost information and greater centralization. Reorganization would be less costly in the long run than requiring program accounting across agencies each year.

Multi-year costing consists of tabulating expenditures for years beyond the budget year. What assumptions should underlie the predictions have not been clearly specified, and there is so much room for judgment that decision-makers will not know what the figures really mean.

Multi-year costing supposedly will lead to more frequent rejection of programs that are not worth their cost. There is reason to undertake multi-year costing only in special cases. It should be undertaken only when the present decision would create a commitment to make expenditures in future years or when benefits do not accrue unless future expenditures are also undertaken. It would be irrational to reject worthwhile current expenditures on the grounds that future expenditures are excessive when the future expenditures can be cancelled later on. In this case multi-year costing is not useful.

Multi-year costing is costly. It consumes time and paper, and it is likely to reduce flexibility because officials will be inclined to hold both their subordinates and themselves to what has been recorded.

Detailed description of activities involves six features: objectives, targets, choices made, alternatives considered, outputs, and effectiveness. Requiring a statement of objectives in all cases is dangerous. In some cases, state aid to parochial schools, for example, ideological issues are involved, and requiring a statement of objectives may lead to an impasse. In other cases, such as urban renewal, failure to agree on objectives at the outset may result in participants' working at cross purposes. It is difficult to discriminate *ex ante* between these two types of situations. When resources are scarce, agreement on objectives is more vital. When resources are relatively plentiful, all parties can be satisfied without raising delicate issues of principle.

Describing the other five features may alter decisions in the direction preferred by high-level officials, primarily because access to the five kinds of information may (1) help them understand what their subordinates are seeking and (2) encourage them to decide that the costs are too high. Whether this effect is worth the cost is hard to say, since no information about the cost is available.

Zero-base budgeting consists of defending a budget request without making reference to the size of previous appropriations. The purpose is to discourage agency heads from taking program perpetuation for granted and to encourage them to reallocate funds as they think appropriate.

Zero-base budgeting is not a promising way to encourage reallocation. Whether an expenditure is worthwhile is not something that can be demonstrated but is rather a matter of judgment; zero-base budgeting does not produce the kind of information that will help agency heads to judge whether the allocation of funds among programs could be improved. Furthermore, excluding reference to previous years' appropriations excludes some very useful information. Zero-base budgeting in the U.S. Department of Agriculture appeared to have no significant effect on decisions. That experiment was, however, quite costly. It consumed over 180,000 administrative man-hours, and it would also have had political costs if legislative policies really had been challenged.

There is an alternative way to encourage officials to reallocate funds. Each administrator in the budget-making hierarchy can be instructed to inform his superior what would be gained or lost if his agency's appropriation were expanded or contracted by selected amounts. This alternative appears to be both more promising and less costly than zero-base budgeting.

Quantitative evaluation of alternatives involves either cost-effectiveness or benefit-cost analysis. A cost-effectiveness analysis seeks to indicate which is the best of a number of alternative ways to produce a given level of output, while a benefit-cost analysis seeks to evaluate spending proposals either for ranking or for yes-or-no choice.

The initial federal instructions for PPB were overstated. Multi-year costing was required for all spending. The impression was given that zero-base budgeting should be used every year for every program. It seemed that an up-to-date benefit-cost analysis was to be available on every spending program. Looking back now, perhaps we can excuse these demands. To get results out of a bureaucracy one must ask for more than one expects to get. There will always be excuses and unfulfilled attempts in every group of efforts. For difficult chores like PPB, the impression must be given that compliance is mandatory or few results will be forthcoming. Charles Schultze admits that PPB gave too little consideration to selectivity. More recently the enforcers in the Bureau of the Budget have become more selective in application.[1]

---

[1]Charles Schultze, *The Politics and Economics of Public Spending* (Washington, D.C.: The Brookings Institution, 1968), p. 80.

But benefit-cost analysis has long had difficulties of its own. Agencies often perform benefit-cost analyses on projects they themselves will execute if they can demonstrate feasibility. In other cases, consulting engineers perform feasibility analyses on projects in which they have a future interest. Such situations lead to possible conflicts of interest. Perhaps a centralized Congressional analytical facility similar to the U.S. Bureau of the Budget or the California Legislative Analyst would be a healthier environment in which to consider fiscal demands.

We examined the welfare economics that underlies benefit-cost analysis. The criterion most frequently used, the Hicks-Kaldor criterion, pays exclusive attention to economic efficiency, but it is not so easy to agree on an alternative criterion. A look at analytical measures of effectiveness disclosed problems in each: net benefits *ought* to be maximized, but that indicator alone does not measure relative worth of projects of different sizes. Other criteria in use, such as the internal rate of return and the benefit-cost ratio, were mentioned and their problems examined. Looking at the public enterprise from the viewpoint of the theory of the firm, we saw what scales are implied by several alternative objectives: maximum benefit-cost ratio or net present value, minimum cost or maximum scale subject to an efficiency constraint. Ironically, constraints can facilitate solving problems of choice. Technological externalities should influence evaluation but pecuniary externalities ought to be ignored.

Our example of alternative uses of a parcel of urban land in Chapter 6 was intended to show the importance of discovering several alternative uses for specific resources rather than investigating one use thoroughly. Federal law requires the latter in project justification, but we believe more effort should be expended on the former. Choosing among alternatives is easy: generating imaginative ones is more important. In the example, all alternatives had benefit-cost ratios greater than one. Failure to consider some alternatives would lead to inferior decisions.

Benefits and costs must be made commensurable even though they accrue in greatly separated years. The way to do that is to reduce them all to present values at a reference date. When to start and when to stop counting benefits and costs is sometimes a problem. While discount rates are necessary to obtain present values, it is not an easy matter to choose one; the many functions of market interest rates make observing the market misleading. The two basic reasons for discounting are: (1) individuals prefer present gratification to an equal amount of future gratification and (2) capital can be used in many ways to increase welfare over time. Committing it to one use sacrifices welfare in another area. Social rates of discount may differ from market rates; usually they are lower. Partisans of low discount rates like to see rapid economic growth led by public investment. Those who prefer to see the private sector allocate capital resources prefer the opportunity cost approach. One compromise synthesizes the social rate of discount and opportunity costs in the private sector.

We offer the spotty record of the use of discounting in government. Understanding of this technique is spreading and policy is becoming increasingly sophisticated financially, but the present situation is hardly optimal. In addition, there is a debate as to whether the government should employ a risky or a riskless rate. This introduces the problem of uncertainty, which, with spreading over time, is characteristic of all investments.

Present benefit-cost analysis does not give enough attention to uncertainty. Sensitivity analysis displays responses to changes in assumed parameters. Retrospective studies of estimated and actual outlays have been done. These give some idea of the uncertainty of cost estimates. More work has to be done, especially on public works projects.

In many cases, agencies overestimate benefits; in others, they do not foresee entire classes of benefits. Some case studies on the retrospective evaluation of benefits have been done but more is needed on individual projects. A statistical study of a sample of thirty or forty projects could yield some idea of the uncertainty of benefit prediction.

Chapter 8 outlined the principles of efficiency benefit estimation. Central is the willingness to pay of beneficiaries. There are several ways to measure them. One is the additional area under the collective income-compensated demand curve measured from the quantity available without the project to the quantity available with the project. These demand curves must be estimated for many of the goods provided by public projects in order to evaluate them. Received demand theory is deficient both because it is preoccupied with relative prices and because it cannot predict the demand for a new good. Lancaster has provided the theoretical foundation for changes researchers had groped for and stumbled on before. Quantity demanded is a function of prices, but it is also a function of physical and performance characteristics of goods and services.

Benefits have been estimated in the transportation area of public investment since 1844. A century later this tradition was revived for highways and river basin projects. Education and health care can be looked upon as capital augmenting services, but they are not undertaken exclusively for economic efficiency reasons as are transportation and water projects. Benefit estimation by inference from human capital changes is therefore more tenuous. Urban renewal benefits are extremely difficult to calculate, by admission of the foremost practitioner of that art, Jerome Rothenberg. The next probable application for estimating benefits will be pollution abatement. We can proceed by first estimating the total costs of the nuisance. These are total potential benefits. Any scheme that would remove an estimated fraction of the nuisance is worth that fraction of total nuisance costs. Concepts of benefits such as alternative costs and changes in capital value were also explored.

Objectives other than efficiency are sought through public spending. Income-distribution effects, for example: should they simply be described and measured or should they be made commensurable with efficiency effects? Although we urge display of income distribution results of public projects, we doubt they can be measured in terms commensurable with other benefits. Maass and Weisbrod claim that income-distribution weights can be discerned from the political process, but Freeman showed that when Congressional choices are examined and agency calculations corrected, the income-distribution impacts of some projects are insufficient to rationalize their choice. This controverts Weisbrod's assumption that Congressional choices can be rationalized by income-distribution effects. Commentators differ in the degree to which they would allow public spending to be used to effect income redistribution goals. Musgrave's norms do not allow it; Maass' observations encourage it. Other objectives that public spending serves—national prestige, balance of payments, "decent" housing—can be grouped under the rubric of merit wants.

Several types of costs were defined. Project outlays are the type usually predicted. Frequently overlooked in agency practice are opportunity costs of real resources and of capital. Associated costs of beneficiaries must be deducted from willingness to pay. Observing the response of quantity demanded to changes in associated costs is one way to estimate a demand curve when market-clearing prices are absent. Social costs are the real concern, but they are terribly elusive. Only part of them have transactional counterparts and can be monetized. Monetized costs differ from project outlays. The former is a theoretical concept, the latter an easily measurable, if not predictable, quantity. Like nuisance costs, which can be used as a measure of potential benefit, alternative costs can be used as a limit to benefits, if a purpose can be achieved in another way.

Social costs are difficult to measure because of implicit costs and externalities. Even project outlays are hard to predict. Many believe that agencies, especially *ad hoc* agencies formed for a single project, underestimate costs in order to increase the chances of approval of projects they advocate. If this is true, of what use is a cost estimate? Can formulas based on past experience be derived to "debias" them?

Costs grow over time, especially construction costs. In such a context delay is very expensive. Several factors influence costs: characteristics of what is procured; rate of output, often highly correlated with size of facility; cumulative output; contractor selection; and contract form. We proposed a new use for cost functions as aids in budget projection with an example from U.S. post offices.

Two large government projects were recounted: one federal and one state sponsored. Both were criticized by disinterested analysts. Both were supported by cognizant agencies. One was subject to a popular bond election; the other to periodic Congressional review. One has been pursued despite some unfavorable benefit-cost analyses. The other was recently arrested, but not clearly because of benefit-cost analysis. On the other hand, lower-level decisions, especially choices among alternatives such as sewage treatment plants or maternal and child health care programs, have been facilitated through benefit-cost analysis.

Thus we concluded that quantitative analysis was more effective in choosing among projects than in deciding whether or not to do them. Routine project justifications required by law are almost worthless. They have served the purposes only of the agencies doing them despite the efforts of the Bureau of the Budget. In the 1930's Congress sought to assure that the agencies would put forth an efficient set of projects among which Congress could choose. This responsibility cannot be so delegated. Congress must do its own analysis if it cares about efficiency. To do this it needs an analytical arm which will apply uniform national economic criteria to all spending.

The recommendations above originate from economists so we can offer no assurance that they will be politically acceptable. One virtue of the status quo is that it is politically viable.

# APPENDIX

### DEPARTMENT OF COMMERCE
### (October 1968)

I. Business development
  A. International business development
    1. Advancement and protection of U.S. commercial interests
    2. International commercial information
  B. Promotion of travel to the United States
  C. Business assistance
    1. Industry analysis
    2. Domestic business policy
    3. Technical business services
  D. Defense production and industrial readiness
    1. Priorities and allocations
    2. Industrial readiness planning
  E. Export control
    1. Policy planning
    2. Licensing and operations
    3. Enforcement
  F. U.S. expositions
    1. HemisFair
    2. Inter-American Cultural and Trade Center
  G. Foreign direct investment control
II. Area and regional development
  A. Areas
    1. Industrial and commercial development
    2. Infrastructure and environmental improvement
    3. Human resources
    4. Planning, information dissemination and research
  B. Districts
    1. Industrial and commercial development
    2. Infrastructure and environmental improvement
    3. Human resources
    4. Planning, information dissemination and research
  C. Urban area

        1. Industrial and commercial development
        2. Infrastructure and environmental improvement
        3. Human resources
        4. Planning, information dissemination and research
    D. Special problem areas
        1. Industrial and commercial development
        2. Infrastructure and environmental improvement
        3. Human resources
        4. Planning, information dissemination and research
    E. Indian areas
        1. Industrial and commercial development
        2. Infrastructure and environmental improvement
        3. Human resources
        4. Planning, information dissemination and research
    F. Regional development
    G. General administration
III.  General purpose data production, analysis, and statistical services
    A. Data production
        1. Manufacturing and mineral industries
        2. Trade, services and construction
        3. Transportation
        4. Foreign trade
        5. Agriculture
        6. State and local government data
        7. Population and housing
        8. Composite data
    B. Construction and analysis of national economic accounts
        1. National income and product accounts
        2. Input and output accounts
        3. Balance of payments accounts
        4. Regional accounts
        5. Analysis and projection of accounts
    C. Statistical assistance and services
        1. Age and citizenship searches
        2. Foreign statistical training
        3. Other assistance and services
    D. Data processing equipment and systems development
IV.  Physical environment
    A. Weather and marine forecasts and warning services
        1. Public weather and warning
        2. Special weather
        3. Basic weather
        4. Marine environmental predictions
    B. River and flood prediction and warning services
    C. Earth description, mapping and charting services
        1. Geophysical
        2. Aeronautical charting
    D. Marine description, mapping and charting services
    E. Telecommunications and space services
        1. Telecommunications

      2. Space "weather" forecasting
   F. Environmental satellite services
   G. Environmental data services
   H. Research
      1. Earth sciences
      2. Oceanography
      3. Meteorology
      4. Aeronomy
   I. Retirement pay commissioned officers
V. Physical measurements and standards
   A. Basic measurements and standards
      1. Development of the basic core of the measurement system
      2. Dissemination services
      3. General research, consultation and facilities
   B. Materials measurements and standards
      1. Standard reference materials
      2. Standard reference data
      3. Research materials
      4. Data on properties of matter and materials
      5. Scientific and technical services
   C. Technological measurements and standards
      1. Building technology
      2. Automatic data processing
      3. Electronic technology
      4. Systems analysis
      5. Motor vehicle safety
      6. Engineering materials
      7. Industrial and consumer products
      8. Fire programs
VI. Marine transportation
   A. Active foreign trade capability
      1. Operating differential subsidy
      2. Construction aids
      3. Manpower training aids
   B. Research and development
      1. Advanced shipping system
      2. Joint surface effect ship program
      3. Technological development program
      4. Technology support
   C. Reserve capability for emergency needs
      1. Emergency shipping resources
      2. National defense features on construction differential subsidy ships
   D. Capacity for interchange of waterborne cargo and passengers
      1. Ports and port facilities
      2. Coordination of through-put systems
   E. Services to other government agencies
   F. General support
VII. Technology
   A. Protection of intellectual property

      1. Patents
      2. Trademarks
    B. State technical services
      1. Industrial extension service
      2. Special projects
    C. Information dissemination
      1. Collection and announcement
      2. Central reference and referral
      3. Distribution
    D. Innovation policy and encouragement
      1. Policy
      2. Inventor assistance
      3. Innovation education

VIII. General administration
    A. Executive direction of the department
    B. Departmental staff services
    C. Other services
    D. Gifts and bequests
    E. Special statistical work

# DEPARTMENT OF HEALTH, EDUCATION AND WELFARE
## (February 1968)

I. Education
    A. Development of basic skills
      1. Improving the education of the general population
      2. Improving the education of the economically and socially disadvantaged
      3. Improving the education of the physically and mentally handicapped
      4. Improving international education
    B. Development of vocational and occupational skills
      (Same as 1–4 above.)
    C. Development of advanced academic and professional skills
      (Same as 1–4 above.)
    D. Library and community development
      (Same as 1–4 above.)
    E. General research
      (Same as 1–4 above.)
    F. General support
      (Same as 1–4 above.)

II. Health
    A. Development of health resources
      1. Increasing knowledge
      2. Providing facilities and equipment
      3. Increasing and improving the health manpower pool
      4. Improving the organization and delivery of health services
    B. Prevention and control of health problems

      1. Disease prevention and control
      2. Physical environment control
      3. Consumer protection
      4. Social factors affecting health
   C. Provision of health services
      1. Health services for the aged
      2. Health services for the poor
      3. Health services for Indians
      4. Health services for children and mothers
      5. Other health services
   D. General support
      1. Scientific and health information
      2. Program direction and management

III. Social and rehabilitation services
   A. Improving individual capability for self-support
      1. Work incentive activities
      2. Work experience and training program for unemployed
      3. Vocational rehabilitation program for physically, mentally and socially handicapped
      4. Provision of social services for the improvement of individual capability for self-support
      5. Service to Cuban refugees
      6. Foster grandparent program
   B. Improving the social functioning of individuals and families
      1. Maintaining and strengthening family life
      2. Promoting the welfare of children
      3. Meeting other family and individual needs for social services
   C. General development of social and rehabilitation resources
      1. Increasing knowledge (general research)
      2. Increasing the social and rehabilitation manpower pool
   D. General support
      1. State and local administration
      2. Federal administration
      3. Non-profit and other organizations

IV. Income maintenance
   A. Aged assistance
      1. Old-age assistance
      2. Old-age insurance
   B. Disability assistance
      1. Aid-to-the blind
      2. Aid-to-the permanently and totally disabled
      3. Disability insurance
   C. Other individual and family support
      1. Aid to families with dependent children (with persons in training)
      2. Aid to families with dependent children (with unemployed fathers)
      3. Survivors insurance
      4. Cuban refugees
      5. Aid to repatriates
      6. Migrant families
      7. Emergency assistance

D. Increasing knowledge (general research)
E. General support
    1. Public assistance eligibility determination
    2. General support (other)

# DEPARTMENT OF HOUSING AND URBAN DEVELOPMENT
## (November 1968)

I. Assuring decent housing for all Americans
    A. Assuring an adequate supply of low- and moderate-income housing
        1. Low-rent public housing—newly constructed
        2. Low-rent public housing—acquisition and rehabilitation—existing construction
        3. Low-rent public housing continuing program
        4. Low-rent public housing—leasing
        5. Assistance to nonprofit sponsors of low- and moderate-income housing
        6. Counseling services
        7. Private rental housing
        8. Home ownership assistance
        9. Housing for the elderly or handicapped—direct below-market interest rate loans
      10. College housing—housing and related facilities for students, faculty, nurses and interns
      11. Rehabilitation loans at below-market interest rates
      12. Rehabilitation grants for low-income families
      13. Alaska housing
      14. Special assistance support for mortgages on assisted housing
    B. Promoting the efficient functioning of private housing markets
        1. Federal Housing Administration
        2. Government National Mortgage Association
        3. Federal Insurance Administration
        4. Interstate Land Sales Full Disclosure
II. Assuring adequate and efficient local public and private facilities and services
    A. Improving public facilities and services
        1. Public works planning advances
        2. Public facility development loans
        3. Basic water and sewer facility grants
        4. Neighborhood facility grants
        5. Advance acquisition of land for public purposes
    B. Improving private facilities and services
        1. Mortgage insurance for nonprofit hospitals
        2. Mortgage insurance for group medical practice
        3. Mortgage insurance for nursing homes
        4. Mortgage insurance for commercial facilities in rental housing projects
III. Improving the physical environment of urban communities

A. Improving the quality of urban development
1. Urban renewal
2. Open space land for parks, recreation, etc.
3. Urban beautification and improvement programs
4. Historic preservation
5. Area wide development incentive grants
6. Land development—insured financing for new towns, residential subdivisions and related activities (Title X)
7. New communities

IV. Improving the social environment of urban communities
A. Creating model neighborhoods in demonstration cities
1. Model cities program
B. Easing the impact of relocation on families and business displaced urban development
1. Relocation payments for moving and loss of property
2. Small business displacement payments
3. Relocation adjustment payments
4. Replacement housing payments
C. Assuring equal opportunity in access to housing and other facilities
1. Fair housing enforcement program
2. Enforcing nondiscrimination in HUD assisted programs
3. Enforcing nondiscrimination in employment in HUD assisted programs

V. Improving management of community development activities
A. Improving governmental planning and executive management of community development
1. Grants for comprehensive planning
2. Grants to metropolitan councils of governments
3. Workable programs for community improvement
B. Improving urban information and technical assistance support to state and local governments
1. Urban information and technical assistance program
2. Urban clearinghouse service
C. Additional education and training for efficient urban development and management
1. Community development training programs—grants
2. Fellowships for city planning and urban studies—grants

VI. Improving management of departmental programs and resources
A. Research and demonstrations in urban technology
1. Urban research and technology
2. Low-income housing demonstrations
3. Comprehensive urban planning research
4. Demonstration grants for urban renewal techniques
5. Public works planning surveys
6. Open space land, urban beautification and historic preservation demonstrations
7. Urban mass transportation
8. Technical studies in construction, building materials and land development (FHA)
B. Liquidate assets of terminated and other programs

    1. Community disposal operations
    2. Liquidation of assets of certain war and emergency housing and community facility programs
    3. FNMA management and liquidation function (except FHA sales housing)
    4. FNMA pool participation sales
  C. Provide technical services for other federal agencies
  D. Provide executive direction and general support

# DEPARTMENT OF LABOR
## (May 1968)

I. Manpower development assistance
  A. Training
    1. On-the-job
    2. Institutional (classroom)
    3. Communication and employment skills
    4. Apprenticeship
  B. Special manpower programs
    1. Experimental and demonstration projects
    2. Mobility assistance
    3. Bonding assistance
    4. Experimental social laboratories
  C. Work programs
    1. Neighborhood youth corps
    2. Community employment
    3. Work incentive program (WIN)
  D. Research
    1. Internal
    2. External
  E. Policy, planning and evaluation
    1. Policy determination
    2. Planning
    3. Evaluation
  F. Administration
II. Employment assistance
  A. Employment market information
    1. Area skill surveys
    2. Classification of labor areas
  B. Job development and placement services
    1. Assistance to jobseekers and employers
    2. Agricultural employment
    3. Employment assistance for veterans
  C. Employability assistance
    1. Specialized services
    2. Services to smaller communities
    3. Occupational testing
  D. Civil rights compliance

       1. State and federal agencies
       2. Contractors
       3. Voluntary compliance
    E. Administration
III. Income maintenance
    A. Unemployment insurance
       1. State-federal administration
       2. Benefits
    B. Workmen's compensation
       1. Federal employees compensation administration
       2. Longshore and harbor workers
       3. District of Columbia compensation
    C. Pension and retirement
    D. Research
       1. Problems of income maintenance for unemployed and injured
       2. Operating tools, technical manuals and procedures produced
    E. Administration
IV. Wage and labor standards
    A. Wages and working conditions
       1. Regulations and interpretations
       2. Special wage standards
       3. Enforcement
       4. Information and education
       5. Labor standards improvement
    B. Occupational safety
       1. Maritime industry
       2. Assistance to states, private groups
       3. Federal employee safety promotion activities
       4. Compliance with Federal contract safety and health regulations
    C. Utilization of women workers
    D. Research and development
       1. Impact of fair labor standards
       2. Development of occupational safety and health standards and materials
       3. Research on other wages and working conditions
       4. Development of federal legislative proposals
    E. Administration
 V. Labor-management relations
    A. Administration of the Labor-management Reporting and Disclosure Act and the Welfare Pension Plans Reporting and Disclosure Act
    B. Veterans reemployment rights
    C. Labor-management relations assistance
    D. Research and policy development
    E. Administration
VI. Data collection, analysis and dissemination
    A. Manpower and employment statistics
       1. Employment and unemployment analysis
       2. Urban employment statistics
       3. Labor force studies
       4. Job opportunities

     5. Industry employment statistics
     6. Occupational employment statistics
     7. Manpower and occupational outlook
     8. Injury statistics
  B. Prices and living conditions
     1. Consumer prices and price indexes
     2. Revision of the consumer price index
     3. Industrial prices and price indexes
     4. Price and index number research
     5. Consumer expenditure surveys
     6. Family budget studies
  C. Wages and industrial relations
     1. Compensation and labor cost studies
     2. Wage economics studies
     3. Occupational wage surveys
     4. Industrial and labor relations
  D. Productivity, technology and growth
     1. Sector productivity measurement
     2. Industry productivity measurement
     3. Economic growth and labor requirements studies
     4. Technological studies
  E. Foreign labor and trade
     1. Foreign labor conditions
     2. International labor comparisons
     3. Foreign trade and U.S. employment
     4. International technical cooperation
  F. Field services
     1. Public services
     2. Regional analysis
  G. Administration
     1. Staff and administrative services
     2. Data collection and survey operations
     3. Data processing
VII. General support
  A. Executive direction and management
     1. Staff direction
     2. Policy planning and research
     3. Legislative liaison
     4. Management support services
  B. Legal services
     1. Litigation
     2. Interpretations and opinions
     3. Legislation
     4. Labor-management laws
     5. Field legal services
     6. Administration
  C. International labor activities
     1. International labor policy and program development
     2. International technical assistance
     3. International trade policy, development and negotiation

4. Participation in intergovernmental organizations
5. Participation in administration of the Foreign Service
6. Cultural and information programs
7. Research
8. Administration

## DEPARTMENT OF TRANSPORTATION
### (April 1969)

I. Urban transportation
 A. Highways
   1. Interstate
   2. Other primary
   3. Secondary system
   4. Urban extensions
   5. Topics
   6. Parking
   7. Advance acquisition of rights-of-way
   8. Special safety programs
   9. Highway beautification
   10. Relocation assistance
   11. Metropolitan area planning
 B. Mass transit
   1. Capital investments
   2. Research, development and demonstration
   3. Training
   4. Planning and technical studies
   5. Administration
II. Inter-urban transportation
 A. Highways
   1. Interstate system
   2. Other primary
   3. Secondary system
   4. Urban extensions
   5. Topics
   6. Advance acquisition of rights-of-way
   7. Special safety programs
   8. Motor carrier safety
   9. Highway beautification
   10. Relocation assistance
 B. Rail
   1. The Alaska Railroad
   2. Railroad safety
   3. High speed ground R & D
   4. High speed ground demonstrations
 C. Air
   1. Airport development
   2. Air navigation services

      3. Air traffic and other airspace activities
      4. Regulation
      5. Noise abatement
      6. National capital airports
  D. Water
      1. Short-range aids to navigation
      2. Alteration of obstructive bridges
      3. Domestic icebreaking
  E. Inter-administration: Northeast Corridor program
III. International transportation
  A. Highways: inter-American highway
  B. Air: development of civil supersonic transport
  C. Water
      1. St. Lawrence Seaway Development Corporation
      2. Long-range aids to navigation (Loran A)
      3. Ocean stations
IV. General transportation safety and other national interests
  A. National security boundaries and treaties
      1. Military operations
      2. Coast Guard military preparedness
      3. Coast Guard reserve forces
      4. Aid to navigation (Loran C)
      5. Polar operations
      6. Enforcement of maritime laws and treaties
  B. Support of science
      1. Oceanographic activities
      2. Polar operations
  C. General transportation safety
      1. Highways: National Highway Safety Bureau
      2. Water
      3. Intermodal: National Transportation Safety Board
  D. Maritime pollution control
  E. Other highway programs
      1. Natural disaster repair
      2. Access to federal lands
      3. Alaska highway
      4. Chamizal Memorial Highway program
V. General support
  A. Research, development and general planning
      1. Departmental
      2. Federal Railroad Administration
      3. Federal Highway Administration research
      4. General highway planning
  B. Administration
      1. Departmental
      2. Federal Highway Administration
      3. Federal Aviation Administration
      4. Coast Guard
      5. Federal Railroad Administration
  C. Coast Guard retired pay

## STATE OF CALIFORNIA

I. Legislative
  A. Legislature
  B. Legislative Counsel Bureau
  C. Law Revision Commission
  D. Commission on Uniform State Laws
  E. Contributions to Legislators' Retirement Fund
II. Judicial
  A. Supreme Court
  B. Judicial Council
  C. Commission on Judicial Qualifications
  D. District Courts of Appeal
  E. Contributions to Judges' Retirement Fund for Justices of the Supreme and Appellate Courts
  F. Salaries of Superior Court Judges
  G. Contributions to Judges' Retirement Fund
III. Executive
  A. Governor's Office
    1. Governor
    2. Secretary for Business and Transportation
    3. Secretary for Human Relations
    4. Secretary for Resources
    5. Secretary for Agriculture and Services
    6. Youth and Adult Corrections Agency
    7. Disaster Office
    8. Council on Intergovernmental Relations
  B. Lieutenant Governor
IV. General administration
  A. Public Employees' Retirement System
  B. Department of General Services
  C. Office of Management Services
  D. Intergovernmental Board on Electronic Data Processing
  E. Advisory Commission on Marine and Coastal Resources
  F. State Exposition and Fair Executive Committee
  G. State Fair and Exposition
  H. Capitol Building and Planning Commission
  I. Commission on California State Government Organization and Economy
  J. Commission on Interstate Cooperation
  K. Personnel Board
  L. Secretary of State
  M. Heritage Preservation Commission
V. Agriculture
  A. Department of Agriculture
    1. District Agricultural Associations
    2. Assistance to County Agricultural Fairs and Citrus Fruit Fairs
    3. Salaries of County Agricultural Commissioners
    4. Assistance to Cities and Counties for Land Under Contract
  B. Poultry Improvement Commission

VI. Commerce
    A. Department of Commerce
    B. Office of Consumer Counsel
VII. Corrections
    A. Department of Corrections
    B. Department of the Youth Authority
VIII. Education
    A. Department of Education
    B. State Teachers' Retirement System
    C. Debt Service on Public School Building Bonds
    D. School Building Construction Bonds
    E. Coordinating Council for Higher Education
    F. University of California
    G. Hastings College of the Law
    H. Trustees of the California State Colleges
    I. Board of Governors of the Community Colleges
    J. State Scholarship and Loan Commission
IX. Fiscal affairs
    A. Board of Control
    B. State Controller
    C. Board of Equalization
    D. Department of Finance
    E. Franchise Tax Board
    F. Department of Housing and Community Development
    G. State Treasurer
X. Health and welfare
    A. Human Relations Special Services
    B. Medical Fee and Related Services Cost Increases
    C. Department of Health Care Services
    D. Department of Human Resources Development
        1. Commission on Aging
        2. Department of Employment
        3. Office of Economic Opportunity
        4. College Work Study Program
        5. Service Center Program
    E. Advisory Commission on Indian Affairs
    F. Job Development Corporation Law Executive Board
    G. Job Training and Placement Council
    H. Department of Mental Hygiene
    I. Department of Public Health
    J. Department of Rehabilitation
    K. Department of Social Welfare
XI. Industrial relations
    A. Department of Industrial Relations
    B. State Fire Marshal
    C. Workmen's Compensation Insurance
        1. Compensation Insurance Fund
        2. Workmen's Compensation Benefits for Subsequent Injuries
XII. Justice
    A. Department of Justice

            E. Department of Motor Vehicles
            F. Department of Public Works
                1. Southern California Rapid Transit District
                2. Folsom Lake Bridge Authority
  XVII. Veterans affairs
            A. Department of Veterans Affairs
            B. United Spanish War Veterans Commission
 XVIII. Miscellaneous
            A. Advisory Commission on Status of Women
            B. Arts Commission
            C. Bicentennial Celebration Commission
            D. Chile-California Project
            E. Commission of the Californias
            F. Colorado River Boundary Commission
            G. Earthquake damage repair
            H. Los Angeles Riot Commission
            I. Personal services not elsewhere reported
            J. Refunds of taxes, licenses, and other fees
            K. Storm and flood damage repair


# CITY OF NEW YORK
## (April 1969)

    I. Human resources
        A. Income support
        B. Early childhood
        C. Community development
        D. Individual and family services
            1. Youth services
            2. Dependent and neglected children
            3. Family services
            4. Other
        E. Manpower and career development
        F. Drug addiction: prevention and rehabilitation
        G. Support
   II. Elementary and secondary education
        A. Instruction
            1. Primary
            2. Intermediate
            3. Career preparatory
            4. Special education
            5. ESEA, Title I and urban education
        B. Community and recreational activities
        C. Curriculum development, research and evaluation
        D. Headquarters Administration
        E. District Administration
        F. General support
        G. Debt service

      H. Transfers to other departments
      I. Emergency savings
  III. Higher education
      A. Senior colleges
         1. Day session
         2. Evening and extension
         3. Summer
         4. Special programs
      B. Community colleges
         1. Day session
         2. Evening and extension
         3. Summer
         4. Special programs
      C. Support
         1. Administration
         2. Library
         3. Student services
         4. Buildings and grounds
  IV. Administration of justice
      A. Crime prevention and control
      B. Investigation and apprehension
      C. Emergency services
      D. Adjudication
         1. Prosecution and appeals
         2. Judicial
      E. Rehabilitation and custody
         1. Probation services
         2. Institutional detention
         3. Institutional sentence
         4. Institutional rehabilitation
      F. Support services
   V. Health services
      A. Public health
      B. Municipal hospital care
      C. Payments to voluntary hospitals for inpatient care of Medicaid
         eligibles
      D. Payments for eligible services provided Medicaid eligibles by private
         practitioners and institutions
      E. Mental health
      F. Chief medical examiner
      G. Support
  VI. Fire prevention and protection
      A. Extinguishment
      B. Prevention
      C. Support
 VII. Protection of the environment
      A. Refuse removal
         1. Street cleaning
         2. Refuse collection
      B. Refuse disposal

    C. Snow removal
    D. Air resources
    E. Water resources
       1. Pollution control
       2. Supply
       3. Fee collection
    F. Support services
VIII. Parks, recreation and cultural affairs
    A. Recreation
       1. Playgrounds
       2. Recreation centers
       3. Pools
       4. Beaches
       5. Sports facilities
    B. Cultural enrichment
       1. Museums and cultural institutions
       2. Library services
       3. Cultural programs
       4. Cultural assistance
    C. Environmental preservation and enhancement
       1. Parks
       2. Zoos
       3. Natural science societies and gardens
IX. Economic development
    A. Commercial and industrial development
    B. Waterfront development and management
    C. Markets development and management
    D. Consumer protection
    E. Support
X. Finance
    A. Tax collection
    B. Funds management
    C. Assessment
    D. City Register
    E. Support services
XI. Municipal services
    A. Central management
    B. Construction of public buildings
    C. Services provided municipal agencies
    D. Services provided the public
XII. Housing and development
    A. Executive management
    B. Rehabilitation financing
    C. Community development
    D. Housing and facilities production
    E. Housing sponsorship
    F. Special improvement programs
    G. Code enforcement
    H. Rent control
    I. Relocation services

# AUTHORS' NOTE

In June 1971, after the manuscript of this book had been completed, the U.S. government quietly abandoned its compulsive version of PPB.

The retreat occurred with respect to budget proposals for fiscal 1973, due in the Office of Management and Budget (OMB) in September 1971. In a message addressed to the heads of all federal departments and establishments, George P. Shultz, director of OMB, declared:

> Agencies are no longer required to submit with their budget submissions the multi-year program and financing plans, program memoranda and special analytical studies as formally specified in Bulletin No. 68-9; or the schedules (previously required under Circular No. A-11) that reconcile information classified according to their program and appropriation structures.[1]

In other words, the agencies need not send any more PFPs, PMs, or SSs, nor any more crosswalks! Shultz explained that the simplified requirements are an attempt to lessen the workload and time pressures on the agencies.

Where does this leave PPB? The PFPs, PMs, and SSs are the documents that embody PPB (see page 2), and the crosswalks translate PPB's program accounting into the agency and input format on which Congress acts (see page 28). It would appear the federal government has abandoned PPB. This conclusion, however, is too strong. There are two reasons.

---

[1]U.S. Office of Management and Budget, "Circular No. A-11, Revised, Transmittal Memorandum No. 38," June 21, 1971, p. 2.

First, OMB's new instructions refer to what is required, not what is permitted. Some federal agencies may continue to prepare—and even transmit—PFPs, PMs, and SSs. In fact, we have been told that the Defense, Agriculture, and Treasury Departments have decided to continue to prepare at least the PFPs.

Second, other parts of Director Shultz's memorandum indicate that OMB itself will occasionally require multi-year costing and benefit-cost analysis. The memorandum continues:

> However, the substance of multi-year program planning, analysis, and evaluation will continue to be stressed. Agencies should be prepared to furnish future year estimates when requested, and should provide memoranda and analyses in support of program proposals and related issues.

And before both of the passages quoted, the memorandum states:

> [A]gencies are required to submit future year projections . . . for ongoing activities for which authorizing legislation is required, as well as for new programs under proposed legislation.

In other words, multi-year costing is required whenever acts of Congress are needed (and OMB may demand it at other times too), and benefit-cost analysis is required whenever something novel or different is advanced.

What has really happened, then, is that OMB, rather than abandoning PPB, has discarded three of its five components and adopted a selective approach to the other two. OMB has discarded program accounting, detailed description of activities, and zero-base budgeting, and it has restricted multi-year costing and benefit-cost analysis to expenditures that would represent new policy decisions.

We regard OMB's new instructions as a great improvement. We doubt that either program accounting or, in the form chosen, detailed description of activities was worth the cost (see pages 31 and 58). Indeed, we understand that OMB found them worthless. As to zero-base budgeting, we regard it as simply foolish (see page 65). We regret, however, that no attempt is being made to obtain the asserted benefits of both detailed description and zero-base budgeting by the alternative budget approach (see pages 55 and 70).

OMB's selective approach to multi-year costing and benefit-cost analysis is not the same as the selective approach we advocate (see pages 39 and 271), but in practice the difference may be slight. This will be true if the set of expenditures that require "authorizing legislation" is approximately the same as the set of expenditures that introduce a multi-year commitment or a multi-year investment, and if "program proposals and related issues" are similar to regional investments and other cases in which decision-makers have indicated they will utilize the results of a benefit-cost analysis if it is made. In short, we are pleased with OMB's new requirements.

There remains, however, apart from the uses of PPB, a long list of other naked emperors for our youth to expose.

# AUTHOR INDEX

Ackoff, R. L., 182–83
Alchian, A., 233
Anderson, Martin, 169
Andrews, W. H., 229
Anshen, Melvin, 1, 5, 16, 19, 23, 24,
    25, 28, 29, 37, 40, 54, 262, 263
Arnoff, R. L., 182, 183
Arrill, M., 168
Arrow, Kenneth, 131, 132, 184
Asher, Harold, 231
Asher, Norman J., 253, 255, 256

Bain, Joe S., 92, 121, 147, 245,
    248, 269
Banks, R. L., 121
Barback, R. H., 149
Baumol, William J., 113, 140
Becker, Gary, 160–1
Beesley, M. E., 156, 157–58
Beggs, James, 258, 259, 260, 262
Bell, David E., 59
Blake, Craig T., 153
Bolton, Roger, 187
Bonner, James T., 196
Borus, Michael, 162
Bos, H. C., 156
Boulding, Kenneth, 8, 86
Brown, Donaldson, 7
Brown, Edmund G., 4
Brownley, O. H., 199
Brunner, E. D., 222
Buchanan, J. H., 132

Cain, Glen, 162
Carlson, Jack W., 122
Carr, W. John, 226
Caves, Richard, 121, 245, 269
Chamberlain, Neil, 6
Chase, Samuel B., 54, 156, 174, 189,
    210, 216
Christenson, Charles, 8
Churchman, C. W., 182, 183
Cleland, David L., 139
Coase, Ronald, 210, 211, 215
Cohen, J., 163
Collins, Norman R., 152
Comte, August, 80
Conley, R., 168
Conrad, Alfred H., 199
Cromwell, M., 168

Daicoff, Darwin W., 199
Davis, Otto A., 71, 168
Davis, Pauline, 249
Dean, Gerald W., 152
Dean, Joel, 8, 111
DeHaven, J. C., 11, 121, 146, 242,
    243, 244, 248
Dempster, M. A. H., 71
Dewey, John, 263
Dillon, Douglas, 121
Dolwig, Richard, 248
Dorfman, Robert, 11, 158, 162, 165,
    170, 196, 201, 269
Dublin, Louis L., 163

# SUBJECT INDEX

**309**